Handbook of the Turf

A Treasury of Information for Horsemen – Information about Horses, Tracks and Horse Racing

by Samuel L. Boardman

with an introduction by Jackson Chambers

Self Reliance Books

Get more historic titles on animal and stock breeding, gardening and old fashioned skills by visiting us at:

Introduction

I am pleased to present another title in the "Horse" series.

The work is in the Public Domain and is re-printed here in accordance with Federal Laws.

As with all reprinted books of this age that are intended to perfectly reproduce the original edition, considerable pains and effort had to be undertaken to correct fading and sometimes outright damage to existing proofs of this title. At times, this task is quite monumental, requiring an almost total "rebuilding" of some pages from digital proofs of multiple copies. Despite this, imperfections still sometimes exist in the final proof and may detract from the visual appearance of the text.

I hope you enjoy reading this book as much as I enjoyed making it available to readers again.

Jackson Chambers

1

COB.

1. Арабская Л. 2. Англо-норманская Л. 3. Першеронъ.

4. Бельгійская Л. 5. Шведскіе пони. 6. Венгерская Л. 7. Шотландскіе пони. 8. Іоркширская Л.

9. Ольденбургская Л. 10. Трансенонская Л. 11. Англійская чистокровная Л.

INTRODUCTION

THE general plan of the present work was conceived by the author some four years ago, and the task of compilation begun. Other engagements, however, soon demanded attention and prevented completion of the work, which the past year has given an opportunity of bringing to a close. Within its pages he has attempted the compression of what is believed to be the greatest body of information about the horse in his relation to drivers, sulkys, tracks, riding, trotting, racing, and the laws pertaining thereto, that has ever appeared in a single volume in this country. In doing this his aim has been to produce a book of reference, the usefulness of which will render its possession material to every intelligent individual who breeds, trains, rides, cares for or loves a horse. It is the author's hope that the execution of the work will, in some measure at least, equal what he believes to have been the merit of its conception.

Within the past twenty years a complete revolution has taken place in the breeding and management of horses, government of tracks, appliances used on the turf, and the rules of racing. During the last half of this period the most profound scientists in England, France, and this country, have made careful and long continued studies on the anatomy, conformation, and external points of the horse; while years have also been devoted to an analysis of the laws of motion, the study of speed inheritance, the physical basis of the several gaits, and the laws of breeding. Moreover, all the progress and extreme development in these lines during the period named, has really been crystallized within the past two years into the most wonderful form, as evinced by the use of the pneumatic sulky and the accomplishment of phenomenal speed on the American turf. Yet with these great changes no useful handbook,

INTRODUCTION.

coming within reach of the everyday horseman at a modest price, and embodying what science has taught as authoritative upon these subjects, has been published. A few elaborate treatises, beyond the range of the practical horseman in scope of information, and quite beyond his reach in price, have appeared, of the benefits of which he has been unable to avail himself, because by far too scientific for his use, or too expensive for his purse.

The present volume is believed to do for this class of readers what no other single book on the horse and racing, has ever attempted to accomplish. Its range of information embraces terms relating to the horse; his exterior conformation and uses as an animal for riding and driving; to the track or race course; the sulky and track vehicles; the harness; the driver and rider; to equestrianism; the trotting and racing turf; the racing and trotting rules; laws of the States in their relation to horses, tracks, and racing; the phrases and catchwords of great drivers and riders; terms used in the veterinary art so far as they relate to the locomotory organs of the horse, and to general soundness, vices, and faults; with the folk-lore of horses, old sayings, and useful general knowledge of an historical and practical character. While numerous books are ready at hand to aid the student and practical craftsman in the arts, sciences, literature, the special processes of mechanics, printing, botany, gardening, and the textile arts—the vast body of intelligent horsemen has been, heretofore, without any single book, presenting in a comprehensive way, the historical, scientific, legal, and practical features of their business. In short, this book attempts to do for them, and for the gigantic industry which they represent—the horse-breeding, racing, and trotting business of the United States—what the numerous readers' handbooks, dictionaries of phrase and fable, dates, general allusions, common things, scientific handbooks and trade glossaries do for students of art and literature, and skilled workers in the arts and industries. The sources of information have embraced the entire range of horse literature as represented in the incomparable collection in possession of the Boston Public Library; files of sporting and turf journals and magazines of this country and England; an extended correspondence with well known turf authorities in the United States, and wide personal acquaintance among practical horsemen, breeders, and trainers.

It is interesting to note to what an extent the horse industry and turf business of the country has invented its own language — a language expressive, unique, and peculiar; one which until now has existed beyond the realm of literature, because it has had lodgment only in the general practice and rugged brains of trainers, drivers, stablemen, and others who have had to do with horses all their lives. So far as the author is aware, the present volume is the first attempt to embody in collected form the technical vocabulary of the track and its equipments, the fraternity of drivers and riders, and the large body of intelligent gentlemen practically interested in horses, driving, racing, and trotting. Hence the book has been compiled from original information obtained on the turf and in the stable, as well as from the horse literature of two centuries.

The author wishes to say further, that the book is not an English dictionary, a book on stable management, a cyclopædia about horses, a treatise on breeding, a trotting register or yearbook, a work on veterinary practice, or on the training and driving of horses—and yet there is something in it under each of these different headings. In memoirs of horses, it includes only the five or six representative or foundation animals in England and America; and no one family or individual is given prominence in preference to another. It contains no expression of opinion that can by any possible construction provoke controversy or lessen the value of the facts presented; nor does it discuss theories of breeding, training, or management. It floats no advertisement of breeder, track or vehicle. The terms pertaining to equestrianism are not generally those of the schools devoted to fancy riding, but those of practical horsemanship. Many terms pertaining to the English turf are included, because our own turf history is founded upon that of the mother country, and because the intelligent driver or equestrian wishes to be well informed upon all matters relating to turf history and practices, whether in his own country or abroad. In consulting the book the reader will generally understand in what cases the subject matter refers to the trotting or racing turf, without a repetition of explanation, or a particular statement that such fact pertains to the one or the other. The veterinary terms have been limited mainly to those which relate to the organs of locomotion, to age and soundness, with such as pertain to common ailments, or those most closely related to the horse as a track and riding animal. In law, the general statutes and special acts of States relating to horses, tracks, and racing are given, down to the close of the year 1893. The incidents and facts of turf history; accounts of remarkable horses, races, and events; interesting anecdotes illustrating curious facts; biographical notices of distinguished persons, and the copious references to trotting and racing performances of a noteworthy character, have all been carefully compiled from trustworthy sources. In brief, the book makes plain to the non-professional reader, groom, driver, rider, and horseman, the accurate meaning of scientific terms relating to the horse, usually given in technical books only, in the language of science, thus educating them in a practical but thoroughly correct manner, in the sciences upon which so much of a true understanding of their business and its successful prosecution is founded. Few duplications or cross references have been used. Where a choice has existed the preferable term alone has been defined, or that which a person consulting the book would be most likely to first refer to; while cross references not only take up space to no purpose, but are usually very unsatisfactory to whosoever wishes to consult such a book. Owing to its alphabetical arrangement, the book is its own index; hence, as the title indicates, it is a handbook of reference for facts under special headings, rather than a work to be read for the purpose of obtaining a general view of the subjects which it embraces.

Especially is the work useful as a compendium of the turf rules of the United States, because the widest publicity that can be given these rules not only enlightens horsemen and members of associations and societies, but also the spectators who attend fairs and patronize the races. Such persons are much better satisfied when they see a decision made or penalty imposed, if they know the rule and reason for it. They can see there is fair play and no choice between stoga boots and patent leather when they understand the rules and see them enforced without fear or favor, and when they can so understand them, they enjoy the races better. The national rules have elevated the trotting sport of America to a high standard, and fostered a breeding interest which is represented by millions. Every penalty imposed on man or horse for fraud or misdemeanor of any kind, by one member or association, is equally recognized by each and every other member. Thus the power to enforce rectitude and good behavior upon the turf all over the country is absolute.

It is evident that a work of this kind, which is believed to be unique, and which must be compiled without having the advantage of any similar work upon which it might be based, and from which materials might be drawn, must of necessity be more or less incomplete. The field covered has been indefinitely large, and the aim has constantly been to keep the book within reasonable size, consistent with adequate treatment of subjects. To this end, while it is hoped no important omissions will be found, insignificant terms, those of obvious meaning and simple facts known by practical horsemen, have generally been excluded. For the purpose of making future editions more complete, the author will be thankful to any one for facts, information, phrases and words which will contribute to this end.

The author desires to express his gratitude to the many friends and correspondents who have aided him in the preparation of this work. Thanks are especially due to M. M. Morse, Secretary of the National Trotting Association, Hartford, Conn.; J. H. Steiner, Secretary of the American Trotting Association, and of the American Trotting Register Association, Chicago, Ill.; E. C. Hopper, Secretary of the American Turf Congress, Covington, Ky.; I. B. Nall, Secretary of the National Saddle Horse Breeders' Association, Louisville, Ky.; Sanders D. Bruce, editor of the *Turf, Field, and Farm*, New York; Simon W. Parlin, and J. W. Thompson, editors of the *American Horse Breeder*, Boston, Mass.; W. B. Fasig, New York; Charles

INTRODUCTION.

E. Walker, South Framingham, Mass.; C. W. Williams, Independence, Iowa; Dr. George H. Bailey, V. S., Deering, Maine; C. B. Tillinghast, State Librarian, Boston, Mass.; Arthur M. Knapp, keeper of Bates Hall, Boston Public Library, Boston, Mass.; L. D. Carver, State Librarian, Augusta, Maine; and the editors of the *Spirit of The Times*, New York, and *Wallace's Monthly*, and *The Horseman*, Chicago, Ill. Acknowledgements are also due to the publishers of copyrignted books, quoted in the work, for permission to make extracts from the same.

HANDBOOK OF THE TURF

EXPLANATIONS

The abbreviations used in the following pages are: ENG. for terms relating to the English turf ; EQ. for those pertaining to equestrianism; LAW. for legal terms and information.

A

Abdallah. One of the foundation sires of the American trotter. He was bred by John Treadwell, Salisbury Place, L. I., N. Y., and foaled in 1823; by Mambrino, by imported Messenger, dam Amazonia. Imported Messenger was foaled in 1780, by Mambrino, dam by Turf, and tracing back through the Byerly Turk to a natural Barb mare. The dam of Mambrino was by imported Sour Crout, second dam by imported Whirligig, third dam old Slammerkin, a race mare by imported Wildair. Wildair's get was so highly esteemed in England that those interested in racing stock in that country sent over here, bought him and took him back to England again. He was by Cade, by the Godolphin Arabian. Of Abdallah's dam but little is definitely known. It is supposed that her sire was a descendent of imported Messenger. Indeed, it is stated by Mr. J. H. Wallace, (American Trotting Register, I, 60), that she was purchased near Philadelphia by Mr. B. T. Kissam, a dry goods jobber of New York, when on a trip to that city, and she was represented to him to be by a son of imported Messenger. She is described as a chestnut in color, 15.3 hands high, and rather coarse in quality and ill in shape. Abdallah has been best described, probably, by the late Mr. B. T. Kissam, who knew the horse well. His description, which applies to him in his four years old form, is: "He had a long, clean head; ear long and tapering; eyes lively, and of medium size; neck light, and set low on the withers; up carriage, and when in action head carried perpendicularly; shoulders upright; deep in girth; full chested; fore legs very wide apart, causing him to stand with his toes in; light bone, especially below the knees and hocks; knees a little forward, flat-ribbed and short in flank; roached back; hips and loins

11

medium breadth; peaked from hips to setting on of the tail, which was very thin-haired; long from hip to hock; rather thin quarters and short fetlocks." Mr. Kissam omits to say, however, that his color was blood bay, and that he had a star in forehead, with left hind-foot white above the ankle. He stood 15.3 hands high. He was never broken to harness, being ridden under the saddle. He was kept at the farm of his breeder in 1828 and 1829; at Flatbush and Gravesend, N. Y., 1830; near Jamaica, N. Y., 1831; at different places on Long Island and in New Jersey till 1839; at Lexington, Ky., 1840; at Union Course, L. I., 1841 and 1842; at Goshen, N. Y., 1843; at Freehold, N. J., 1844 and 1845; at Chester, N. Y., 1846-48; at the Bull's Head, N. Y., 1849; at Union Course, N. Y., 1850; and at Patchogue, L. I., 1851. He died of neglect and starvation upon a sandy beach on Long Island, in November, 1854. Abdallah got more fast trotters than any horse of his time. The records show that at least twenty-two of his sons and daughters started in races, and twenty of the number were race winners. Three of his get are found in the 2:30 list, viz.: Sir Walter, 2:27; O'Blennis, 2:30; Frank Forrester, 2:30. He seems to have transmitted the tendency to trot with much greater uniformity through his daughters than through his sons. His daughters are credited with producing eight trotters that are found in the 2:30 list, including Goldsmith Maid, 2:14; and the records show that thirty-two stallions out of daughters of Abdallah have got 2:30 performers.

Abdomen. The cavity which occupies the rear part of the trunk or body of the horse; the exterior part of which is known as the flank.

Abductor. One of the great locomotive muscles of the horse, the function of which is to draw away a limb from the axis of the body; to extend.

Abingdon Mile. A famous old English race-course, the length of which was seven furlongs, 211 yards.

Abrasion. An abraded spot or place; applied chiefly to a fretting or rubbing of the skin, by which the underlying tissues are exposed. Even though slight, and requiring but little care, abrasions are, until perfectly healed, an unsoundness.

Action. The manner of moving; an exertion of power or force; the real relation of a cause to its effect. Action takes its direction from the hips, and power is invariably resident when a horse has a long and somewhat oblique, rather than horizontal quarter. The stifle should never be lower than the elbows, as contributors to leverage and power in the hock.

Action-controlling Power. That quality of instinct in the horse which governs the movements in a balanced form, without loss of muscular exertion.

Added Money. Money added to a regular purse or stake as an extra inducement for entries. It is given by the track or association in a larger or smaller sum; as in a sweepstakes, the horses put in $25 each, and the track adds $100.

Adductor. The function of drawing towards; the name of several muscles of locomotion which draw certain parts to, or toward, one common center or median line; the opposite of abductor.

Against Time. A performance against the watch; a trial of speed. All performances against time are required to be made at a regular meeting of a track, society or association in membership with the National or American trotting association, in strict accord with the rules of the trotting turf, and under the conduct of judges and timers regularly appointed. No animal can start in such race pending a heat or trial by another animal, nor until the result of such heat or trial has been announced. There shall be three judges and three timers, and no performance shall take place earlier than 10 o'clock A. M. If a performance against time takes place at a postponed or continued meeting, such postponement must have been made in accordance with the rules of the trotting turf. The horse starting must start to equal or exceed a specified time, and a losing performance shall not constitute a record or bar. All entries for such performance must be duly made with the official secretary, appear in the printed program of the day, or posted legibly at the judges stand. A regular meeting means a meeting advertised in at least one newspaper not less than one week before the commencement of the race, at which time no less than two regular events, (purse or stake), are advertised for each day, one of which must take place. A match race is not considered a regular event. No "matches against time" are allowed by the trotting rules.

Age of the Horse. Modern science has divided the age of the horse as determined by the dentition into five general periods. They are: 1, the eruption of the incisors of the first dentition, or from birth to about eight to ten months old; 2, the leveling, progressive use and falling out of the incisors of the first dentition, or from about one year to about two years old; 3, the eruption of the permanent or adult teeth, or from the age of two, or two and a half years, to between five and six years old; 4, the leveling of the permanent incisors, or

from about six to about eight years old; 5, the wearing away
of the crowns, or from about nine to after nineteen years old.
In order to ascertain the age of the horse, it is necessary to
observe some structural part of the animal, which is liable to
little change and may be easily examined; hence the teeth are
the only organs that can furnish a guide to age, and they can
generally be trusted with a considerable degree of certainty.
The incisors of the lower jaw are the ones examined for the
age of the animal, as it is seldom that much importance is
attached to the appearance of the tushes. The pincher teeth
or middle incisors, generally appear when the foal is from six
to eight days old, the upper teeth appearing first. At four
months there are four teeth in the upper and four in the lower
jaw, and at about eight to ten months old the corner incisors
and intermediate teeth are entirely through the gums. At
about two and a half years of age, the dental arch is complete.
The central nippers of the lower jaw are the first permanent
teeth, the middle and corner nippers being temporary, the former, or permanent teeth, being much larger than the latter.
At about three and a half years of age, the middle nippers give
place to a permanent pair, and from a year later to five years
of age the corner nippers are replaced by permanent ones. At
this age the horse has what is termed a "full mouth;" or in
other words all the permanent nippers are in place. From
this age up, the spots or marks in the center of the teeth, the
dentine, must be the chief guide in determining the age. At
five years of age the central nippers are somewhat worn, leaving a small black spot in the center, but their shape, which is
oval, has not yet changed. The marks of the middle nippers
are not so large as formerly. At six years of age the central
nippers have but a very small spot of dentine in their center,
the middle pair have lost much of theirs, and the corner pair,
while showing less than two years previous, are yet quite full.
In the male the tushes are fully up, but are showing no appearance of wear. At from six to seven years of age the teeth
show more wear, although they have changed but little; the
center marks being less distinct, and the corner nipper smaller.
At eight years of age the teeth are quite oval in form, their
character, however, is not much changed. After this age they
begin to become triangular in form, particularly that of the
central incisors, or nippers. At nine years of age the central
marks have nearly disappeared, only a small black speck
remaining; the central incisors are slightly triangular in form,
and the tusks are more rounded at the points. The wear of
the corner nippers is much indicated. At ten years of age the

central pair of nippers is markedly triangular in shape; the marks in the center are nearly obliterated, the teeth are longer and project forward more than in the case of younger horses. At eleven years of age all the teeth become more triangular in form, they increase in length, project forward, and the tusks are greatly rounded at the points. These characteristics have increased at twelve years of age, and the front corner nippers are worn away even with the middle pair—the wear being less on the back portion. From thirteen to nineteen years of age the same general characteristics appear, the shape of the teeth becomes more triangular, the nippers are longer and project forward in an increased degree, and the tushes are round at the points.

If a horse's mouth presents exactly the characters which indicate a certain number of years of growth, we say that it "*is* — years;" if it has not quite attained the age, it is described as "rising — years;" if it has passed the period and has not yet attained the markings of another year, it is counted as "— years off."—Age of the Domestic Animals, Rush S. Huidkoper, M. D.

By the teeth, only, in my judgment, can the age be known *certainly*, and by them, *certainly*, only until the ninth year.—Horse and Horsemanship of the United States, Henry William Herbert.

Age of the Horse. Buffon says that the duration of the life of the horse is, as in all other species of domestic animals, proportionate to the duration of their period of growth or increase. The period of increase of the horse continues throughout four years, and he can live six or seven times as long; that is to say twenty-five or thirty years. The life of mares is ordinarily longer than that of horses. At ten years of age, if a horse is sound and free from objectionable habits, he is a safer purchase than one five years of age. The older horse is less liable to sudden or acute attacks of disease such as colic, etc., and if properly cared for, is good for many years of reasonable service.

Albertus Magnus mentions that in his time, 1193–1280, there was an instance of a charger proving serviceable at the advanced age of sixty; and Augustus Nephus says there was a horse in the stable of Ferdinand the First, 1503–1564, that had attained the extraordinary age of seventy years. This is the oldest horse which I have ever heard of, and, in all probability, the only one on record which had reached that age.—Authentic Anecdotes and Sketches of Horses, Capt. Thomas Brown, London, 1830.

Age of Trotters. Records show that the trotter and pacer are longer on the turf than the thoroughbred race-horse. Forty-one horses have trotted in 2:30 or better at fifteen years of age; eleven at sixteen years of age; sixteen at seventeen years of age; seven at eighteen years of age; one at nineteen years of age, and one at twenty-one years of age. At seventeen years of age Goldsmith Maid trotted a mile in 2:14.

Age, Rule of. The National, American and Racing rules provide that the age of a horse shall be reckoned from the first day of January of the year of foaling.

Aged. In trotting and running parlance, any horse over six years of age.

Agistor, Agister. An officer of the royal forests of England having the care of horses and cattle agistered, and of collecting the money for the same; one who receives and pastures horses and cattle for hire; a law term used in describing a lien on horses.

Aids in Riding. [Eq.] The hand and the heel are denominated aids of the rider.

Air Pump. An apparatus for the compression or transmission of air. In the common form the air is given motion by means of a cylinder and piston. With the use of the pneumatic sulky the air pump has become a necessity with every driver for inflating the rubber tires of the sulky.

Alfalfa. The Spanish name of lucerne, *Medicago sativa.* It is largely used in California as a forage for horses, and while it does very well for brood mares and youngsters, it is regarded as a washy grass and affects the kidneys of horses in training most unfavorably.

Alix. Bay mare, 15.3 hands high, white in the face and one white hind ankle. Bred by Daniel Hayes, Muscatine, Iowa, and foaled in 1888. By Patronage, 4143, by Pancoast, 1439; dam, Atlanta, by Attorney, 1005, second dam Flint, by General Hatch, 139, third dam Dolly by a son of imported Gleucoe. Holding the World's records to the close of 1893, for one mile by a mare in a race, Washington Park, Chicago, September 14, 1893, 2:07¾; for one mile by a four year old filly, Nashville, Tenn., November 5, 1892, 2:10; for fastest first heat in a race, Chicago, Ill., September 14, 1893, 2:07¾; fastest fifth heat in a race, Columbus, Ohio, August 25, 1893, 2:09¾, and fastest ninth heat in a race, Chicago, Ill., September 16, 1893, 2:09¾.

All Abroad. When a horse jumps cross-legged at the start, or is in some other way out of form, especially in a running race, so that he is a long time in recovering, and it is evident the heat is lost to him at the start, he is said to be "all abroad."

Allowance. A favor granted a horse, by the rules, on account of age, sex, or other condition. While penalties are obligatory, allowances are optional; but if claimed, the claim should be stated when the entry is made. In all heat races of the Turf Congress, an allowance of five pounds is made from the scale of weights; and in all races excepting handicaps and those in which the conditions are absolute, fillies and geldings two years old are allowed three pounds, and mares and geldings three years old and upward are allowed five pounds before the first of September of each year, and three pounds after that date. In a race exclusively for three-year-olds, for instance, the weight to be carried is 122 pounds. Now, if a horse was entered that had won two races, he would carry 127 pounds; or, in other words, carry a five pound penalty; but if another horse should enter that had not won a race, it would carry 115 pounds only, or receive an allowance of seven pounds.

Amble. The pace; said to be the first natural gait of young colts. In ambling, the horse moves two legs on the same side at the same time, and both feet strike as one; then the limbs on the other side advance and strike as one, the strokes—one, two—completing the revolution. In England, in the time of Edward II, (1307-1327), horses were taught to amble or pace by the use of trammels made of strong listing, or irons, which were attached like chains and fetters, to control the gait.

Some horses are amblers first, and afterwards learn to trot, and travel equally well in both paces; indeed, considering the small proportion of horses that fall into this pace, and the record made by them on the turf, it may be thought to have no disadvantage over the regular trot. It would seem to give great advantage to a short-bodied horse, as there is no danger of overreaching.—The Horse in Motion, J. D. B. Stillman.

American Derby. Names of several events in the United States, which have been maintained with greater or less regularity for the past thirty years. The first Derby ever run in this country was at Patterson, N. J., in 1861. In 1863 the Kentucky Derby was established at Lexington, Ky., but it was not run till 1864, the event taking place at Louisville. The following is the list of American Derbys: American, Chicago, Ill.; Arkansas, Little Rock, Ark.; Brooklyn, Brooklyn, N. Y.; Cony Island, Sheepshead Bay, N. Y.; Kentucky, Louisville, Ky.; Latimer, Covington, Ky.; Twin City, St. Paul, Minn.; Tennessee, Memphis, Tenn. But one American Derby was run in 1893—that at Washington Park, Chicago, Ill.

American Eclipse. A famous horse in the stud and upon the turf. Bred by Gen. Nathaniel Coles, Dosoris, L. I., N. Y. Foaled May 25, 1814. Chestnut; 15¼ hands high, with star in forehead, near hind foot white; heavy-set, and full of bone and muscle. By Duroc, by imported Diomed; dam, Miller's Damsel, by imported Messenger, by Mambrino, out of an imported mare by Pot-8-os, son of the famous English Eclipse. He was trained at three years old. Winner of the great sectional match between the North and South,

2

against Henry, run over the Union Course, Long Island, N. Y., May 27, 1823, for $20,000 a side. The first heat (four mile race) was won by Henry in 7:37½; the second and third heats were won by Eclipse in 7:49 and 8:24 respectively. Henry carried 108 pounds, Eclipse 126 pounds. The measurements of Eclipse were: Head 23¾ inches; neck 25 in.; from point of shoulder to point of buttocks 65¾ in.; girth 74 in.; around the arm 21½ in.; below the knee 7¾ in.; around the tibia 18¾ in.: the hock 16¾ in.; from hip to point of hock 37½ in.; same around the flank as the girth 74 in.; same height at hip as at the withers 61 in. He died in Shelby County, Ky., August, 1847, in the 34th year of his age.

American Newmarket. Monmouth, N. J., has been called the American Newmarket.

American Phenomenon. An American bred horse was so called, although his name was Tom Thumb. After defeating all comers at home he was taken to England, and it is recorded that on February 2, 1829, on Sudbury Common, he trotted one hundred miles in ten hours and seven minutes. This performance was to a match-cart, or gig, built at Albany, N. Y., by a Mr. Gould, and was probably the first sulky built in this country. It weighed 160 pounds, and was regarded too frail for safety.

American Stud Book, (Bruce's). The first volume of the American Stud Book, edited by Mr. Sanders D. Bruce, New York, was published in 1873, and the second the same year; Vol. III in 1878; Vol. IV in 1884; Vol. V in 1888; Vol. VI in 1894. "I have not attempted," says Mr. Bruce, "to fix any definite standard of what constitutes a thoroughbred. It is the custom to call those thoroughbred having five uncontaminated crosses to a thoroughbred; but none are, strictly speaking, thoroughbred that do not trace, without contaminating blood, to Oriental origin. Many animals are registered in the sixth volume which connot be traced the requisite number of (five) crosses, but public form and producing excellence justifies their registration." The pedigrees of the animals are arranged alphabetically, the produce of mares are indexed, and there is also an index to sires, the mares appearing under their sires. More than thirty thousand animals, young and old, are recorded.

American Trotting Association. The American Trotting Association was organized at Detroit, Mich., March 2, 1887, and duly incorporated according to the laws of that State, March 9, 1887, its object being "to improve the breed of horses by promoting the interests of the American trotting turf." It is managed by a board of five directors, (the president and secretary being *ex officio* members); and holds biennial meetings or congresses on the first Tuesday in May. It has a board of review, board of appeals, has authority to impose fines and penalties, announce decisions and administer oaths. In 1893 it had eight hundred and six members—a member being a track, society or association.

American Trotting Register, (Wallace's). Mr. John H. Wallace published the first volume of his American Stud Book, (devoted to running pedigrees), in 1867; and the first volume of the the American Trotting Register in 1872. With the publication of Vol. IV, in 1882, the pedigrees of stallions first began to be numbered consecutively, and, to the end of Vol. XII, (1893), they had reached No. 23,499. Standard bred mares and geldings are registered alphabetically, and non-standard animals are also included, (registered alphabetically). Pedigrees of pacers were first included in Vol. X, for 1892, and the work now embraces trotters and pacers. The twelve volumes published register more than one hundred thousand pedigrees. Published at Chicago, Ill., by the American Trotting Register Association.

American Turf Congress is composed of the nine jockey clubs in the United States, and the Americo-Mexican Blood Horse Association of the city of Mexico, S. A.; and has for its object "the improvement of the breed, and the development of horses through the promotion of the interests of the American running turf; the prevention, detection and punishment of fraud thereon, and the adoption of regulations and rules, to be known as the American Racing Rules, for the uniform government of racing."

American Year of the English Derby. The year 1881. The year in which the Derby and the St. Leger were won by the American horse Iroquois; the same year in which the French Derby—the Grand Prix of Paris—was won by the American horse Foxhall. See IROQUOIS and FOXHALL.

Ankle-cutter. A horse that from faulty conformation, strikes his ankles, or inside of the fetlock joint, when in motion, inflicting a wound, is called an "ankle-cutter."

Anterior. Situated to the front; the head; opposite of posterior. Thus the term anterior extremity means the foreleg. The head is anterior to the neck, and the neck in turn is anterior to the back.

Appeals. Rules of the American Trotting Association

allow appeals to be taken in cases of suspension imposed by the judges of a race or an officer acting for the member; and all decisions and rulings of the judges of any race, and of the members and proprietors of the Association, may be appealed to the Board of Review or Board of Appeals, and become subject to review upon the facts and questions involving the proper application and interpretation of the rules of the Association.

Appeals. Under the by-laws of the American Trotting Association, appeals from the decision of the judges, members or officers of members, lie to the Board of Review for that State, unless the appellant shall in his notice of appeal signify his desire for it to go to the Board of Appeals, in which case it shall go direct to such Board; or unless all parties reside west of the continental divide, in which event the case shall go to the Board of Review unless the parties otherwise agree. All appeals must be taken within ten days from the date of the decision appealed from, or if from a decision made at a meeting of a member, must be taken before the close of the meeting. Appeals must be filed with the secretary of the Association, accompanied with a fee of $5, and also all written evidence in the case, at least ten days prior to the meeting of the Board to which the case goes. A fine of $100 is imposed provided all the terms and rules pertaining to appeals are not complied with.

Appeals, Board of. The Board of Appeals of the National Trotting Association consists of fifteen members, three from each of the official districts of the Association, viz.: Eastern—comprising the New England States and foreign countries; Atlantic—comprising the States of New York, Pennsylvania, Delaware, Virginia, New Jersey, Maryland, and the District of Columbia; Central — comprising the States of Ohio, Indiana, West Virginia, Kentucky, Missouri, Arkansas, Louisiana, and all States south of the southern border of Virginia and Kentucky; Western—comprising the States of Illinois, Wisconsin, Minnesota, Michigan, Iowa, and Texas, and all the Western States and Territories not included by name in other districts; Pacific — California, Oregon, Nevada, Washington, Montana, Colorado, and Idaho. Upon this Board is "conferred the management, direction, and control of all the business and affairs of the Association." It has "power to settle all disputes between members, to hear all complaints, to determine with whom its corporators shall do business, review and regulate the manner of reviewing all decisions of the individual corporators, or of the judges of a race on the track or course of any corporators, enforce the rules and by-laws and exercise all the power of the Association." In the American Trotting Association the Board of Directors constitutes the Board of Appeals. It has jurisdiction of all appeals as well as original jurisdiction to prevent and punish all frauds, abuses and violations of the by-laws, rules, and regulations of the Association in any manner relating to the course, by fine, suspension, or expulsion of the offender, but no fine shall exceed $1,000. It has also the power to relieve horses from erroneous records and correct the same, and generally has "the power to do justice and prevent injustice in all cases not specially provided for.

Apple Tree. The quarter-pole or half-mile pole is called the apple tree by drivers. To "go out round the apple tree," is to spin the horse round the course; to give him an exercise.

Arabian. The Arabian is one of the three great classes of Oriental horses, the two others being the Turkish and Barb. The true Arabian is now bred in great purity by the Sultan of Turkey, and while he is found in various degrees of excellence in the region from Damascus to the Euphrates, rather than on the isthmus of Arabia, he is an animal which few Europeans have ever seen. A sub-race, somewhat larger than the Arabian, known as the Turk or Turkish horse, is found in Asia Minor and in portions of European Turkey. In Northern Africa is found the third branch of the family, and from his home in the Barbary States is known as the Barb. For several centuries, and indeed still, it has been found in the greatest perfection among the Moors. Pure Arabians range from fourteen to fifteen hands high, and they very rarely exceed this standard, being rather small, compact, possessed of great powers of endurance, and capable of going long journeys and continuing longer without food or water than the more artificially reared horses of more civilized nations. They are docile, spirited, sagacious, attached to their masters, active, intelligent, noble.

Arab of the Cloak. In the district of the Nejd on the border of the desert in Central Arabia, is a family of horses of great renown descended from a mare of which this tradition exists: Her owner was once flying from the enemy, and, being nearly overtaken, he cast off his cloak in order to relieve his mare of that unnecessary burden. But when, having distanced his pursuers, he halted and looked around, what was his surprise to find that his cloak had lodged on the mare's outstretched tail and still hung there. Ever since, the heroine of this incident has figured in the unwritten pedigrees of the desert, as "the Arab of the cloak." All Arabian horses carry their tails high, and, next to the head and its adjustment, the tail is the feature which the Arabs consider of highest importance in selecting a horse.

Arm. The humerus or true arm consists of a single bone situated between the scapula or shoulder-joint and the bone of the forearm or elbow joint, in an oblique direction downward and backwards.

Arm-cutting. An injury to the forearm which frequently takes place in consequence of excessive knee action, upright pasterns, and a lofty carriage of the head, especially in cases where the horse has sufficient speed to trot quarters in thirty-five seconds.

Arrears. That which is behind in payment. By the rules of the American Turf Congress, arrears include all sums due for entrance money, subscriptions, stakes, forfeits, fines, purchase money in races with selling conditions, and any default incident to the rules. A horse cannot become a starter in any race until all arrears of whatever nature have been duly paid.

Articulation. A word meaning the act of putting together so as to form a joint or joints; the junction of bones. A term much used in veterinary language for a union of two bones; a joint.

Artificial Gaits. The acquired gaits of the horse, as distinguished from the natural gaits. They are: the amble or pace, broken amble, running walk or fox-trot, racing gallop, and their various modifications.

Artist of the Pigskin. A jockey.

Ascot Heath. Seat of the Ascot races, Winkfield, Berks, England, six miles from Winsor, which were begun by the Duke of Cumberland, uncle to George III., about 1727.

It was here that the first recorded bonus of £1000 was added to a stake, to wit, the Alexandra Plate, a race of three miles for four-year-olds and upwards, which was inaugurated by the success of the celebrated mare Fille de l'Air, the property of Count de Lagrange. Since that time the wealth and the liberality of the Royal meeting have increased *pari passu*, till in these days so great is the value of the prizes, so great the prestige which attaches. to the winning thereof, that all which is most excellent in horseflesh, most ambitious in ownership, is annually attracted to that favored spot. The Badminton Library: Racing, The Earl of Suffolk and Berkshire.

Assistant Starter. Under the American racing rules the starter, with the approval of the officers of the course, may appoint assistant starters, but should they strike a horse at the post, or use ungentlemanly language towards the jockeys, the judges have power to impose a fine.

Asterisk. (*) The asterisk or star, in the American Trotting Register, denotes that the performances were made against time, to distinguish them from race records. In Chester's Trotting and Pacing Record it denotes that the time made was over a short track, and is a bar, not a record.

Asthma. Is closely allied to heaves or broken wind, but is less continuous and more paroxysmal. It is generally believed to be due to spasm of the small circular muscles that surround the bronchial tubes, and its continued existence leads to a paralysis of them. It is legal unsoundness.

Assumed Names. The American racing rules allow persons to subscribe or enter under an assumed name, but their real and full names must be registered with the clerk of the course, and such persons cannot enter or subscribe in any other, until they resume their own names or register another assumed name. The real or assumed name of any person who runs, or, within twenty years, has run horses in the United States, shall not be registered.

Atavism. Taking back. The return to an early or original type by its modified descendants; reversion, through the influence of heredity, to ancestral characters; resemblance to some remote ancestor, exhibited by an animal or individual.

Attention. Station; the attitude of a horse when awaiting command. In this position he has his head and neck raised; ears pricked forward; the profile of his face at an angle of about 45 deg. to the ground, and at about a right angle to the upper line of the neck—the crest; the weight proportionately distributed on all four limbs; and, as a rule, the fore foot of one side not so far advanced as its fellow, and its hind foot more to the front than the other hind foot.

Aubin. [Eng.] A moderate gallop or canter.

Average Time. If the timers of a race catch the time of a heat which is found to vary in comparison, the average time taken is that which is usually hung out.

Axle. The arm or spindle on which a wheel revolves, or which forms the axis of the wheel and revolves with it. The axle of a sulky, carriage or wagon wheel, is the round arm of the axle-bar or axletree which is inserted in the nave or hub of the wheel, but the name is frequently applied to the complete axletree. Burgess, in his work on Coach Building, says the commonest kind of an oil axle is called the mail, because the peculiar mode of fastening was first used in the mail coaches. *Axle-bar*—The bar of an axletree. *Axle-box*—The box which contains the bearings for the arm of an axle; the bushing or metal lining of the hub which forms the rotatory bearing of the axle of a sulky or carriage. *Axle-socket.*—A section of seamless steel tubing in the ends of which are fitted brass bushings made of interior dimensions of different sizes to fit any make or size of axle, and to which is attached the upper ends of the wheel-forks used in changing an axle of the high wheel sulky to a sulky receiving the pneumatic wheel. *Axletree*—A bar or beam fixed crosswise under the body of a vehicle, having rounded axles at the ends for a pair of wheels to revolve upon.

B

Baby. A pet term used in describing a young colt. Train and educate the colts early—to halter, to bit, to harness; handle them, teach them, let them become accustomed to your presence. *Baby trotter*—A term applied to a colt under two years old accustomed to the training track.

Back. That portion of the spinal column to which the ribs are attached. Bounded in front by the withers; behind by the loins; on each side by the ribs.

Back. The walk extended backwards.

Back End. [Eng.] The last two months of the racing season. A "back ender" is a horse which appears on the race course at the end of the season.

Backing. Gibbing. A disagreeable form of restiveness, and when so fixed as to have become a habit is a serious vice.

Back Sinews. The flexor tendons or cords which form the posterior line of the limb between the knee and the fetlock of the fore leg, and between the hock and the fetlock of the hind leg.

Back Strap. The back band of a harness extending from the saddle to the crupper. With the surcingle and bridle, it is used in giving the colt his first lessons in education.

Back Stretch. That part of a race track which is opposite to the home stretch; the back side of an oval course; the place where patrol judges are stationed during a heat or race.

Badminton. The seat of the Duke of Beaufort, K. G., at Cheltenham, Wiltshire, England; and name given to the volumes of the Library of Sports and Pastimes, including Racing, Riding, Driving, edited by him.

Baked; Burnt; Grain Burnt. A horse that does not sweat-out easily and freely after sufficient exercise, is said to be "baked" or "burnt." It is very rarely a constitutional defect, and is generally due to having been overfed with grain.

Balance; Balanced Action. The harmonious action of the front and hind limbs of the horse; to go smooth. It seems to be one of the mechanical peculiarities of rapid trotting action, that the hind stroke should overreach the front stride. This is the prolific cause of the manifold interferences between the hind and front pairs of limbs and feet. It is plain, however, that if the body is balanced and the action equally balanced, then no interference can take place. But it is a difficult matter to accomplish, because the individuality of each animal is so unlike. Some horses are long, low striders; some are high, short striders; some require heavy, some light shoes; some require bar, some open shoes; some, shoes that are concave on the ground surface; some, flat shoes; some, rolling-motion shoes to quicken the action in front; some need toe-weight shoes to lengthen the stride; some long toes, others short ones. These are peculiarities which must be determined by the owner and driver. By balancing the hoofs is not meant to make them of precisely the same size, as very often, especially in case of the front feet, one, usually the off one, is the larger. But the foot is balanced when, taking the center of the cleft of the frog as the base line, the outer margin of the wall, at points equidistant from the leveled heels, measures precisely alike on both sides.

Balk; Balking; Balky. A check or defeat; to stop short and obstinately refuse to move; a vice.

Ball. A horse or nag, originally white-faced; used appellatively like dun, bayard.

Ball. A dose of medicine; a form in which certain kinds of medicines are administered. They are cylindrical in shape, two inches in length and about three-fourths of an inch in diameter, and are generally wrapped in tissue paper when administered. It is the best form in which to administer medicine when it is extremely disagreeable, when the dose is not too large, when the horse is hard to drench, and when the medicine is intended to act slowly.

Ball Bearings. Practically perfect spheres, rolled-forged from tool steel, hardened and burnished for the axle-bearings of sulkies. The sizes chiefly used are 4-16, 5-16 and 3-8 of an inch. From twenty to twenty-four are placed in the cone of each hub.

It is the ball bearing itself that is most instrumental in reducing the friction, and, consequently, the power required to propel the vehicle; but the pneumatic tire also contributes very materially to the general result, inasmuch as, to a great extent, it makes a rough road smooth by equalizing small obstructions with much less concussion than the ordinary wheel. The tires and non-friction bearings have brought a great revolution in the sulky and in speed.

Balling-up. The filling of the shoe with snow, damp earth or mud.

Bandages. Strips of linen, cotton or flannel used to swathe the legs of the horse. They should be from three to four inches wide, and of sufficient length to wrap the leg round from the lower part of the fetlock to the under part of the knee or hock, the folds overlapping, and be provided with two strings sewn on to one end, by which the folds may be tied and secured in their places. It is quite an art to put on bandages properly, especially where a horse has to take his work in them. First have the bandage rolled up smoothly, and commence a little below the knee, or hock, winding it carefully so that there are no creases, till you reach the coronet; then go back with another fold, till you come back above the place where you commence, and tie with the same care, keeping the strings flat as they cross over each other, and fasten. It is a good plan to have oiled silk or rubber material for wrapping outside the bandages used for applying liniment, to prevent them from drying up. The purposes served by bandages are: To support the legs, their tendons, blood vessels and synovial vessels; to dry and keep the legs warm; to protect them from injury, and by means of which to apply lotions and hot and cold water.

Bar. An obstruction; to exclude. Time taken on any track is a bar, whether made on a short track or one full measurement, or whether on a free or an association track. Time made under the saddle, or on snow or ice, is a bar for races of the same character only; but time made to wagon is a bar or record, as the case may be, in races of every character. If it should appear, upon investigation, that any record was fraudulently obtained, it is not a record, but a bar. If a race takes place upon a track where no purses or prizes are contested for, and where no admission is taken at the gate, time made is a bar, provided judges are appointed and time made is announced. If there are no judges and no time announced, time made is not a record. In making entries, time previously made is a bar to admission in a class slower than the one in which the horse is to be entered.

Bar. Except. The word bar is used instead of the common compound form, "debar." When a bookmaker says "ten to one *bar* one," he means that he will lay ten to one against any horse, *bar* (that is, except) one.

Bar Bit. The plain, straight mouth-piece of a bridle, connecting the checks. Used with straight or curved bars on the Liverpool slide principle, and operated on the jointless Pelham plan, but differs in construction. It is said that the bar, where the guards pass through the end of it, slips up and down, having a play of about half an inch, which eases the mouth when the reins are slackened, by letting the bit slip down from the pressure on the corners of the mouth.

Bars of the Hoof. The portions of the wall of the hoof which are turned inward at the heels, and run more or less parallel to the sides of the frog, along the inner border of the sole.

Bars of the Mouth. The continuations of the two bones of the lower jaw, on each side, between the back, or corner teeth, and the tushes. It is on these that the bit rests.

Bars of the Tree. The narrow front portions or side-pieces connecting the pomel and cantle of a saddle.

Bar Plate. While the American racing rules do not allow a horse to start in a race in ordinary or training shoes, and while they give the judges authority to rule off a horse if started in shoes, they do allow bar plates to be used, with the consent of the judges.

Bar Shoes. [Law]. If bar shoes are required to enable a horse to do his ordinary work, it is regarded as an unsoundness.

Barb. The horse of the Barbary States—Tunis, Tripoli, Fez, Algiers and Morocco, all lying on the northern coast of Africa to the west of Egypt. The Barb is not as tall as the Arabian, seldom standing more than 14.2 hands high; but in other respects is acknowledged to be superior to the Arabian in all points of external conformation. The barb blood brought into Spain during the Moorish wars so improved the Spanish horses that for several centuries they were considered the best riding horses of Europe.

Barrel. The body of the horse; the space between the back and the stomach. A large, barrel-shaped body is evidence of a horse's possession of good health and high powers of endurance; it is, therefore, a sign that he is sound.

I would regard roundness of barrel behind the girths; depth of body, (as compared to length of body), in the center of the back, and being well ribbed up, as the great signs, in conformation, of a horse having good breathing power.—The Points of the Horse, M. Horace Hayes, M. R. C. V. S.

Bay. The best, most desirable and most fashionable color of the horse. Such a color indicates the best blood, the highest breeding. Bay, black from the knees and hocks to the feet, no white markings, is almost invariably the first choice of the purchaser. The color is so called from its resemblance to that of dried bay leaves.

Bearing Rein. The check-rein; the rein by which the head of the horse is held in place, and by which it is partially controlled.

Beaten. To lose in a race. "When you are beaten, stop riding," says Sidney in the Book of the Horse; "don't punish your horse to win second or third place."

One of John Turner's strong points is that when he is beaten and he knows it, he stops punishing his horse right there, and instead of wearing him out trying to do something impossible, saves him for another day.—Life with the Trotters, John Splan.

Beauty. Gracefulness, pleasing proportions; an outline which delights the eye.

Beauty of form is never lost sight of in the construction of the horse; and even great sacrifices of mechanical power are made to maintain graceful lines, and that general contour of form that gave to him his matchless beauty — beauty so great that to the eye of a superficial observer it is difficult to decide whether it is subordinate to strength or conversely. Both are developed in a perfect horse to such a degree that he has been a favorite theme of poets and painters since æsthetic culture has had a place in the history of our race. —The Horse in Motion, J. D. B. Stillman.

Bedding. Litter: the material of which a bed is made for a horse, in his stall or box. Wheat and rye straw are the best materials for bedding. They are better than oat straw, because stronger, tougher, and more easily spread. From eight to ten pounds of straw per day furnishes a good bed. Sawdust answers very well for a bedding in summer, but in winter should only be used when covered on top with a layer of straw. Sawdust is also used in cases where horses have the bad habit of eating the straw used as bedding. In town stables peat-moss, or moss-litter is largely used. It is a powerful deodorizer and absorbent, makes a soft, elastic bed, and is not eaten, as a rule, even by the most inveterate bedding-eating horse. Its use keeps the feet soft, and it is said that horses bedded with it never require to have their feet "stopped." It is found abundantly in countries on the European continent, whence it is imported to England and this country.

Bell. The trotting rules require that the bell from the judges' stand shall be rung ten minutes previous to the time announced for the race or heat to take place. If the word is not given, all the horses in a heat shall immediately turn at the tap of the bell, when scoring, and jog back for a fresh start.

Bell. In the time of James I., of England, 1603–1625, the race courses were called bell courses, the prize being a silver bell. The winner was said to bear or carry the bell. The first bells awarded as prizes for goodness in horses in Britain were wooden, trimmed with flowers, and were given to the winners in the train-scents, so called from the body of some animal which had previously been drawn across hedge and ditch. The scent being certain and strong, the hounds would run upon it with terrible speed, and the matched horses followed them. These wooden bells were replaced by silver ones, and were given "to him who should run the best and fleetest on horseback on Shrove Tuesday." Hence the phrase "bearing away the bell." In 1607 this silver bell was replaced by a small, golden bell. In 1552 there was an arrangement for an annual horse race at Haddington, Scotland, the prize being a silver bell. These silver bells were subsequently replaced by plates, called king's plates, donated by the king, of the value of one hundred guineas.

Belly. The abdomen; the large cavity which contains the stomach, liver, spleen, intestines, kidneys, bladder, etc., of the horse; the underneath portion of the body which is not covered by bone.

Bellies of the Tree. The broad boards of the saddle on which the rider sits.

Bent Before. When the fore legs of the horse are bent forward at the knee, he is said to be "bent before." This may proceed from overwork or from pain in the feet, resulting from contraction, inflammation, etc., but it more frequently proceeds from flat feet. In such cases the animal is unsound. When the profile of the fore legs has a deviation of anything more than the very slightest, it is a blemish.

Bet. To pledge as a forfeit to another who makes a similar pledge in return, on a future contingency; a stake; a wager.

Betting Round. Laying fairly and equally against nearly all the horses in a race so that no great risk can be taken.

Bezoar Stones. Calculi concretions; hair-balls. Foreign bodies or substances found in the stomach and bowels of the horse and other domestic animals. They are sometimes round, solid concretions, the size of a turkey's egg, of a limestone nature, composed of a number of concentric coats or laminæ, each adhering, but, when broken, peeling off in distinct pieces. Their outsides are generally polished and perfectly smooth. They originate from some matter taken into the stomach which the animal has not been able to digest. What are known as triple-phosphate calculi are very common in horses, especially if they are fed much on shorts. Dr. Noah Cressy of Connecticut took a mixed calculi from a horse in Vermont, which caused its death, that weighed thirteen ounces, measured four inches in diameter, and was so large that it could not pass the bowels.

B. h. These letters, in a summary of a race, following or preceding the name of the animal, denote "bay horse."

Big-gaited. A term used to describe a long-striding horse, one which has a sweeping gait, going wide apart behind, and moving strong but easy with every step.

Bike. Used, for short, to distinguish the pneumatic sulky from the high wheel sulky; contraction for bicycle.

Billets. The ends of the reins or of the check-pieces of the bridle, which buckle on to the bit.

Bishoping. The method employed by gyps and unprincipled dealers to change the appearance of the incisors of the lower jaw, to make the horse seem younger than it really is—a method which can only deceive buyers who are ignorant of the horse's mouth. The art consists in giving to the tables or surface of the teeth an artificial cup of a dark color. The teeth are first filed even, and a new cup is made by the aid of a graving instrument, which is blackened by the point of a white-hot iron or the use of nitrate of silver. The trick is seldom effected in a natural manner, for the mark is of a brownish hue rather than black, and, moreover, a ring of a lighter color encircles it, occasioned by the heat of the instrument employed. The tushes are generally filed down to point them and make them appear fresh and small, like those of a horse five years of age, as this is the age "bishopers" all try to imitate — but the work may be detected by the unnatural shape and roughened surface.

A cant term made use of by farriers' jockies, by which they mean the unfair practices which are made use of to conceal the age of an old horse or the ill properties of a bad one.—A Dictionary of Farriery, J. Hunter, London, 1796.

This name is derived from the name of an English body-snatching miscreant, Bishop, who used to sell the teeth of his murdered or exhumed corpses to dentists for the refitting up old mouths.—Tricks and Traps of Horse Dealers, Henry William Herbert.

Bit. The metal part of a bridle which is inserted in the mouth of a horse, with the appendages, rings, side-pieces, etc., to which the reins are fastened. The bit rests against the bars of the lower jaw, those parts of the jaw where there are no teeth—that is, between the corner incisors and the tusks. They are used for controlling the horse according to his own peculiar disposition and the service required of him. As a general rule, horses requiring bits of extraordinary severity or power are either naturally vicious, or were spoiled when being educated to the bit. Bits may be described under two classes: Standard, or those for general use; and special, or those for particular horses and purposes. The former embrace those for road, driving, coach and park uses; and the latter those used in handling, training or driving trotting and racing horses. The first class is much the smaller, comprising those standard bits which have been used unchanged for more than a quarter of a century, and are still so well adapted to their purposes as to be incapable of improvement. The second class is characterized by great variety. As has been said, doubtless with much truth, that nearly every horse on the course or turf requires a different bit, it will readily be seen how the various forms and peculiarities of bit now in use, have an excuse for their being. A great driver uses a bit of some novel form for a great horse, and it at once becomes adopted by other drivers, and upon horses of supposed similar peculiarities of mouth or disposition. This is one reason for the increase in the number of bits of diverse patterns. Again, different bits are required for hard or tender mouths, for tongue lollers, for side pullers, for horses having peculiar dispositions or odd ways of going special to their own individuality, and this calls for bits of different form or bearing, designed for the particular service the horse is performing. Under these two classes, only the leading bits, those best known and most popular among the great trainers, drivers and riders, are named, with a brief description of their characteristics. I. *Bar.* Straight bar with guards; Bridoon or watering, a plain jointed bar with small side rings; Bridoon, with half guards; Bridoon, with double joint and half guards; Carriage, with bar for curb and bearing rein; Carriage bit and bridoon, with arched bar for the play of the tongue; Cavalry or military, a powerful, severe bit, has an arched bar and single rein; Cavalry (U. S. Army) bit and bridoon, has two bits, a curb, two reins; Common snaffle, straight bar and single jointed; Double-jointed snaffle for hard pullers; Double-barred snaffle, similar in action to the double pantograph; Expansion snaffle, opening in the center of the bar; Liverpool with straight or curved bar and sliding attachment; Mexican ring, a severe, cruel bit, the ring hard and unyielding, pressing on the roof of the mouth, the bar having two or three tags similar to a mouthing bit; Mouthing, a jointed bar having three tags, and also a straight bar with from six to ten pendants or tags; Plain snaffle, stiff or jointed bar with guards or half guards; Plain jointed snaffle, with crest strap; Pelham, a plain or jointed bar, the joint more of a hinge than a loop; Pantograph snaffle, a double barred bit, the joints unequal, making a double converging action; Shifting, the bar having a shifting motion across the mouth from side to side, as one or the other rein is drawn, and acting like a gag; Wire snaffle, of twisted wire, thin, sharp and rough. II.

1: *Driving*—Allerton, a steel jointed snaffle, rubber covered; Allie Wilkes, rawhide covered with pork rind, for a tender mouth; Adjustable curb, curb overdraw; Axtel, rawhide, covered with leather; Baldwin, a straight bar with half guards for pullers and side pullers; Britt, bar bit for pullers; Case's easy check, with chin rest; Cribbing bit; Cribbing and wind sucking, for preventing wind sucking and cribbing; Crit Davis, overcheck, with loop bar to prevent lugging; Colby, leather, with adjustable nose band; Colt mouthing; Chain, a plain chain mouth-bit with rings; Dexter, jointed bar, or stiff, plain ring with no cheek-piece; Double-bar, overcheck, to prevent lugging; Dan Mace snaffle; Ellis' all-leather, overcheck; Fairbanks check, leather covered; Four-ring; Furlong, for pullers; Flexible, rubber track, a wrought chain, rubber covered; Golden, plain bar, half guards; Hanscom, flexible mouth-bit, leather covered; Henry check, plain bar; Hercules rubber, a double jointed snaffle, rubber covered, with half guards; Imperial, for tongue lolling; J. I. C., with double bar, half guards; Leather, leather covering a wrought chain; Lever overcheck, to prevent pulling; Lindsey humane, with chain rest and overdraw check attachment; Magic safety, adjustable bar with rings; Miles' sensible controlling, for tongue lollers; Merriam's pulley; Ne Plus Ultra, a double arched bar; Nodine, rubber covered, with half guards; Perfection, jointed snaffle and double bar, for pullers and tongue lollers; Plain overcheck, plain or jointed, with rings; Racine, double bar; Rockwell; Rowley Spring, rubber covered; Prof. Sanborn's controlling, jointed bar, with ball, and inside rings for nose band; Squires' Hercules, a double-jointed snaffle; Springsteen, a hinge-bar, with extra rings for overcheck, the hinge not allowing the check-pieces to come close together; Sloat's automatic curb; Squires' humane driving; Stalkers' breaking; Tongue lolling, a stiff bar with center pad, rubber covered; Victor, jointed snaffle for side pullers; W., mouth bit for pullers; Wilson, four-ring, with plain joint, or middle joint; Woodmansee, for pullers. 2: *Riding*—Burgess' combination, a double jointed bit with half guards; Dan Mace, hand forged steel, plain bar; Daniels' English steel port; English riding bridoon; Frost's rubber covered; Kentucky racking, curved cheek; Norton bit; Pelham, jointed bar; Rockwell, jointed snaffle; Whitman riding; Wilson, single or double joint, buckle overchecks, and cheeks with small rings. 3: *Coach bits*—Balloon check, sliding mouth; Buxton, sliding mouth, loose cheek; Duke's bend; Hanoverian, both stiff and loose check, wrought bar, two loops; Liverpool, sliding mouth; Pul-

ley bridoon. 4: *Gig bit*—Squirrel-tail style, stationary cheek.
5:    *Miscellaneous*—Burton's drenching bit for administering
medicines; Green's operating bit, having an adjustable double-
bar, with sliding side-pieces fastened by set-screws, to hold the
jaws open while performing operations.

> The bit has a wide field in both its general use and in its individual
> operations, which, in the saddle horse's mouth, is or should be.
> magical. Every horse we see employed, has a bit in his mouth;
> every race is lost and won with the bit, and under its management
> millions of dollars a year change hands. It plays its part in all the
> equine feats, interests and operations in every land, whether
> civilized or barbaric, in both peace and war, and in the truck, cart,
> car and agricultural interests it plays its most humble, yet impor-
> tant part. While in war, a nation might as well lay down its arms
> as to relinquish the bit.—The Bridle Bits, Col. J. C. Battersby.

Bit and Bridoon. A double bridle. The bridle has
two distinct bits—the curb bit and the bridoon bit. If one bit
or rein should break there is one of each left. Each bit has a
separate headstall, and to each bit there is a separate rein. A
martingale is used with this bridle, and so looped on the overlapping girth that both girths shall fit tight to the horse. A
perfect bit for pleasure riding. The bridoon rein on which the
martingale hangs is less than an inch wide, but its strength
corresponds with the power used with it in holding the horse
up while riding in ordinary, lifting him at the leap, or in bearing the strain of the martingale if necessarily short. Col.
Battersby says of it that "for use on the road or in the park, it
is the embodiment of perfection, and can never be improved
upon or surpassed."

Bitting Rig. The bitting rig for gentling and educating young colts consists of bridle, saddle or surcingle, and
crupper. The bit should be the plain, jointed snaffle, and the
bridle will have the ordinary side check.

Bitting, Good. The characteristics of good bitting are
lightness, accuracy, easy motion and a total absence of stiffness, constraint or painful action. If these be attained as the
result of careful handling and correct education, ready obedience to the rider's hand and heel will be the result.

Blanket. See CLOTHING.

Blaze. A white spot on the face of a horse of dark
color.

Blemish. A defect; any mark or imperfection which
impairs beauty or diminishes value. Among the blemishes in
the exterior of the horse are: Enlargements upon the limbs
which do not impede the horse in his work, like curby hocks;
roach back; scars from wounds or sores; bald places on the
skin, and the profile of the fore legs when they have a deviation forward of anything more than the very slightest.

Blind. A hood so constructed that it will cover the eyes of a horse if he attempts to run; a piece of horse clothing.

Blind Bridle. A bridle having blinders or side-pieces to protect the horse's eyes.

Blinkers. Blinders, blinds, blinkers, winkers; the leather flaps placed at the sides of a horse's head, and attached to the bridle or headstall, to prevent him from seeing sidewise or backward.

For the buggy, cart, car, stage, wagon, truck and general business horse they are unnecessary. In the carriage or park horse, wanted for show or fashion, they may be used, as they admit of crest or ornament, and set off the horse and harness in fine style.—The Bridle Bits, Col. J. C. Battersby.

Blindness in a horse constitutes an unsoundness.

Bl'k. c., bl'k h., or bl'k m., in a summary of a race, preceding the name of the horse, indicate black colt, black horse and black mare, respectively.

Blood. The use of this word, or term, signifies more or less of pure descent from animals of the English stud-book, or from high-cast Arabs, or the great sires of the American bred trotting and running horse.

Blood and Bog Spavins usually produce lameness, and both constitute unsoundness.

Blood Lines. Explained by the quotation :

The brood mares at the Browne farm are standard under the highest rule that has yet been formulated. They are either the possessors of records of 2:30 or better themselves, have produced a 2:30 trotter, or are out of mares to which the same distinction attaches; and when it is said that every one of them—100 per cent.—comes under this head, the high standard of the form in regard to blood lines is seen.—Life with the Trotters, John Splan.

Blow; Blow Out. Labored breathing; to let a horse get his wind after a heat. Occasionally a horse will do it in five minutes, they are good ones; others will be from a half to three-quarters of an hour. Some horses, those of strong, perfect wind, show no labored respiration after a heat. Charles Marvin says of one he drove: "She cooled out to please me and did not blow in the least."

Blue Bull. The great pacing sire of trotters; the phenomenon of trotting-horse history. He was bred by Elijah Stone, Stone's Crossing, Johnson County, Indiana. Foaled in Switzerland County, Ind., in 1854. By Pruden's Blue Bull, by Merring's Blue Bull; dam Queen, by Young Selim, second dam unknown. "A plebeian of the plebeians." He was chestnut in color, and stood a trifle over 15 hands high. He died, the property of James Wilson, Rushville, Ind., July 11, 1880. He was wonderfully fast at the pacing gait, and even after having been crippled, could show great flights of speed—pacing quarters in 30 seconds. He stands second only to the greatest of trotting sires, although it is not known that he could trot a step, nor that he inherited a drop of trotting blood. For many years he figured as the sire of more trotters than any horse that ever lived, and it was only during 1887, three years before his death, that he yielded the honor to George Wilkes.

Blue Grass. The *Poa pratensis* of botanists, otherwise known as June grass, green meadow grass, common spear grass, smooth-stalked meadow grass. It accommodates itself to a wide range of climate, soil and other conditions, and is found in Great Britain, Asia and Australia. Prof. W. J. Beal, of the Michigan Agricultural College, says, in his " Grasses of North America," that " frequent experiments and careful study by botanists, prove that the Kentucky blue grass and June grass of the Northern States are identical—one and the same. It stands at the head of the list of cultivated grasses, and repeated analyses show it to be nearly twice as nutritious, weight for weight, as timothy; but it attains its highest luxuriance and perfection as a pasture grass. It requires about three years to become well established, but makes a firm sod and bears close and heavy grazing."

Blue Grass Region; Blue Grass Trotters. Applied to the State of Kentucky, and to Kentucky horses.

Blue Ribbon of the Turf. The English Derby. The highest honor within the bestowal of the Crown of England is the Knighthood of the Garter, and the insignia of the Garter is a blue ribbon. Noblemen and wealthy or influential commoners have striven their utmost to obtain this crowning honor; but none of them have used more energy, skill or daring than has been applied during the last thirty years to the winning of the greatest honors of the turf. Admiral Rous, who was president of the Jockey Club from 1848 to 1860, is credited with applying the name " blue ribbon " to the winner of the Derby, and the name was accepted. Mr. Louis Henry Curzon's history of the Derby, published in London in 1890, under the title, " The Blue Ribbon of the Turf," was printed with blue ink.

After the Derby Day, in 1848, which was won by Surplice, formerly owned by Lord Charles Bentinck, Lord Beaconsfield—Mr. Benjamin D'Israeli—made celebrated the "superb groan" that escaped the lips of Lord Charles on hearing of the victory of this colt—which he had formerly owned and then so ruefully regretted having parted with, so long had he been eager to win the Derby, which honor he never obtained. Beaconsfield was endeavoring to sympathize with Lord Bentinck on his sorrow, in the library of the

House of Commons, and the latter moaned out: "You do not know what the Derby is." "Yes I do," replied Beaconsfield, "it is the blue ribbon of the turf."—The Blue Ribbon of the Turf, Louis Henry Curzon.

Body-wash. A preparation used as a body-bath for the trotter after he has been given work. The formula generally used is: Compound soap liniment, sixteen ounces; liquid ammonia, two ounces; tincture cantharides, two ounces; tincture opium, two ounces; mix and add about two ounces of this preparation to one pint of water and one pint of Pond's Extract of Witch-hazel. After the horse has come in from work, scrape quickly, wash as above, rub the loins and muscles of the shoulders, and put on his clothing according to the weather.

Bolt. To swallow hurriedly without chewing. Where horses are addicted to this habit, Dr. James Law recommends that they be given a little hay, to appease hunger, before being fed grain.

Bolt. To spring aside or away, suddenly. A horse that bores to one side, or out of the line the rider wishes to take, is called a bolter. By the racing rules, if a horse bolts or leaves the course, he must turn back and run the course from the point at which he left it. When bolting results from defective vision, or a rush of blood to the head, it renders the horse unsound.

Bones. The total number of bones entering into the skeleton of the horse is 189, viz.: In the vertebral column, 44; head, 28; thorax, 37. In the following parts of the skeleton, which are called the double regions, the bones are the same in number on each side, and in the enumeration the total number is given, viz.: Shoulder, 2; arm, 2; forearm, 4; fore foot, 32; pelvis, 2; thigh, 2; leg, 6.

Bone Spavin in the hock is unsoundness, and a breach of warranty, though not producing lameness at the time, or even for years after.

Book-maker. One who makes a book on a race, or other contingent event. In betting, there are two parties— one called "layers," as the book-makers are termed, and the others called "bookers," or "bookies," in which class may be included owners of horses, as well as the public. The backer takes the odds which the book-maker lays against a horse, the former speculating upon the success of the animal, the latter upon its defeat. Taking the case of Cremorne, for the Derby of 1872, just before the race, the book-maker would have laid three to one, or, perhaps, $5,000 to $1,500 against him, by which transaction, if the horse won, as he did, the backer would win $5,000 for risking $1,500, and the book-maker lose the $5,000 which he risked to win the smaller sum.

> Past Epsom's spring, again we try
> Our luck with bookies and with horses
> On yet another field, where lie
> The mysteries of the Guineas' courses.
> —Bird 'o Freedom.

Boots. Protective coverings for the hoof and leg of the horse, designed to guard them against injury from cutting, overreaching, or interfering when in motion. From the plain, simple quarter boot or scalper of 1870, to the more than two hundred patterns of artistically made and ingeniously contrived combination boots of the present day, the evolution has been rapid, varied, and remarkable; and the universality of their use may be inferred from the fact that one single house in Boston alone, sells more than $10,000 worth annually of the various patterns. Boots are used on both the racing and trotting turf, and no stable is complete without an outfit sufficient for every horse and for all emergencies. Among the leading types are: Ankle; ankle and shin; ankle and speedy cut; ankle with heel extension; arm; arm and knee; calking; coronet; double shin; double shin and ankle; elbow; elastic compress; elastic knuckler; heel; hinged knee, shin, and ankle; hock; hoof and speedy cut; knee; knee, shin, and ankle; knee and arm; loaded, or weighted; passing; pastern; quarter; ring; running; scalping; shin; shin, ankle, and speedy cut; soaking; swivel; toe; toe and speedy cut. Under each of these leading forms are numerous ingenious combinations adapted for horses of peculiar conformation or erratic gait which cannot be well described. They are made of French calfskin, felt, Kersey, cording, elastic shirring, and buckskin, according to the different purposes for which they are used. Boots are very necessary for colts when they are being gaited, and when the gait is established they may for a time be left off with safety; although very few trotters are able to dispense with them entirely, while many of them could not be used on the turf at all except for these appliances.

No horse or colt will fail to hitching and hobbling if he is properly protected with boots, unless he is sore or over-hurried. Because we boot a colt is no reason for supposing that we know he will strike himself. They are used as a safeguard—as a precaution against possible accidents and injuries that may come to the truest-gaited and most honest of horses; and it gives the horse confidence to strike out fearlessly. No judicious or experienced trainer will ever attempt to work colts without first properly booting them.—Training the Trotting Horse, Charles Marvin.

A horse may go for a month or a year and never hit himself, and then some day he may step in a hole or some other accident befall him, and for the want of a boot in the proper place ruin him as a race horse. No horse should ever be driven without shin boots on the hind legs. Very few, if any, horses can go without scalpers. I think it absolutely necessary that a horse should have quarter boots. Some horses wear knee and arm boots, a few wear elbow boots, and still others have to wear what is called a brisket pad; and if a horse shows a disposition to hit himself in any place the first thing to do is to have him properly booted. After a horse has hurt himself a few times he gets timid and won't try to extend himself.—Life with the Trotters, John Splan.

Boots are absolutely necessary with horses that habitually interfere, and with colts whose peculiarities in this respect are unknown, and with all horses doing strong work. They should be worn up to the time they start for a race. It may also be sometimes necessary to put them on in the stable in case of horses that are restive when being groomed, apt to throw their legs about, paw, and otherwise incur the risk of accident. They must fit the leg, and the buckles must not be drawn too tightly so as to impede the circulation or fray the skin. They should be always kept clean and dry.—How to Train the Racehorse, Col. R. Warburton.

Boring. A habit with some horses of carrying the head too low, or too far out to one side, at the same time boring on the bit as though they would drive the fore feet into the ground. It is inveterate with some horses. To overcome the habit, hold both curb-reins and the left snaffle-rein in the left hand, in the proper position; then with the right snaffle-rein only in the right hand, draw it upward so as to press the snaffle against the corner of the mouth on one side. This has an effect that an upward pressure on both snaffle-reins entirely fails to produce, and is said to be effectual in overcoming this bad habit; which habit occasionally leads to the disqualification of a horse for the course.

Boston. A famous American race horse. Bred by John Wickham of Richmond, Va. Foaled in Henrico County, Va., in 1833. He was chestnut in color, stood 15.2 hands high; was short-limbed, with a flat barrel, his neck and head were unsightly, and his hips ragged. By Timoleon, by Sir Archy, by English Diomed; dam by Florizel, by English Diomed; second dam by imported Alderman. Between 1836 and 1841 he started forty-five times; won forty, lost five; total winnings $51,200. Defeated by the chestnut mare, Fashion, at Union Course, Long Island, N. Y., May 10, 1842, in four-mile heats for $20,000 a side; time 7:32½; 7:45.

Botfly; Gadfly. (*Gastrophilus equi*). A dipterous insect. The fly deposits its eggs on the shoulder, base of the neck and inner parts of the fore legs, especially about the knees, as in these situations the horse will have no difficulty in reaching the ova with its tongue. In a little less than three weeks from the time of the deposition of the eggs the larvæ have made their escape, having been hatched by the warmth and moisture of the tongue. As maggots they are transferred to the mouth and ultimately to the stomach along with food and drink where they firmly adhere to the cuticular portion of the stomach by means of two large cephalic hooks. After the bots have attained perfect growth, they voluntarily yield their hold and allow themselves to be carried along the alimentary canal until they escape with the fæces. They sooner or later fall to the ground and bury themselves under the surface to undergo transformation into the pupa state, where, after a period of six or seven weeks they emerge from their pupal cocoons as perfect insects. Bots usually pass about eight months of their lifetime in the digestive organs of the horse.

Bottom. Native strength; stamina; courage; power of endurance. Of a horse possessing great courage and staying quality, it is said that he has " great bottom;" " good bottom."

Bow Legged. A defective conformation, usually noticeable in the hind legs, whereby the feet are so shaped that the greater strain comes upon the outside, the hocks bowing outwardly.

Box; Box-stall; Loose Stall. A room into which a horse is turned loose. The average size is 14 by 16 feet, although 14 by 18 is preferred by some. They are generally without any manger or feed rack for the hay, with an iron feed box fastened to one corner. Many, however, prefer that the feed box should be entirely detached from the stall, and be removed as soon as the horse is done eating. The hay is placed on the floor in one corner of the room, and thus there are no projections, boxes, mangers, racks, or sharp angles upon which a spirited horse may injure himself. In such a room the horse is not confined by halter, has perfect liberty of movement, and the liability of injury is reduced to a minimum.

Boxes. Metal tubes fitted to the arms of the axletree, fixed firm in the hub or nave of a sulky or carriage wheel to contain oil.

Brace. The iron part supporting and connecting the axle of a bicycle sulky to the shaft or thill, where the same has been changed over from the high wheel sulky.

Bran Mash. Given as a conditioner, periodically, and according to the best judgment of the trainer regarding the characteristics of his horses, bran or shorts, made in mashes with boiling water poured upon it and allowed to cool, is the best laxative. Thus prepared, it is not without nutritive qualities. By the action of the boiling water a mucilage is formed which cannot be created in the stomach of the animal. Its laxative action is caused by the mechanical friction of the grains on the mucous membrane. It should not be given dry or mixed with oats, or moistened with cold water. It is hardly necessary to state that it should be fresh and sweet.

Break. To change from one gait to another; to disunite the diagonal beats. In doing this the horse endeavors to accelerate his speed by longer strides without passing into the gallop, which he would do if not held back or if the urging by whip or voice were continued. Also, a common but wrong word used to designate the early training or education of the colt; to break a colt is to accustom it to the harness and vehicle; to subdue, to train, to educate.

Breaking. The act of changing gaits at speed. In breaking, a horse usually gives some sign to the driver, either by a wobble, jerk or instantaneous change, that he is to break, and by understanding this peculiarity of the horse, the driver can generally save the break, provided the horse is under good control. In the early days, before the wholesome discipline of the trotting rules came into force, horses were taught to break in order to gain, but now such a manner of training is obsolete —it is the square, steady trotter that wins and always has the protection of the track and judges. The National and American rules provide that a horse in breaking must be immediately pulled to his gait, and if this is not done, the driver is liable to lose the heat even though he come out ahead, and the next best horse given the heat. Repeated breaks, running or going in a mixed gait, while another horse is trotting, is liable to result in punishment to such horse. A horse breaking four times in one heat is regarded as "repeatedly breaking." If a driver, in the opinion of the judges, allows his horse to make repeated breaks for the purpose of frandulently losing a heat, he is liable to severe penalty. The judges must call out by colors, letters or numbers, and the clerk or assistant shall record the breaks made by each horse in each heat.

I for one believe that the time will come when no horse will be entitled to a heat if he makes a break in it, and I would vote for that now.— Life with the Trotters, John Splan.

Break-and-Catch. The art of driving in a way to make the horse catch quickly after a break, is one of supreme importance to the driver. The methods, however, will vary with horses of different dispositions, and the driver should find out by careful study, the best way in which a horse can be brought to his gait. In whatever manner it is done, after ascertaining that which is best, do it exactly the same every time, using the same rein, the same pull or catch of bit, and the same word. There are many good reasons why the horse should be taught to catch on the inside rein, or near side.

Break Away. A horse that gets control of his driver, and jumps and runs at the score or when getting the word, is said to "break away."

Break Down. A strain of the suspensory ligament; the severest form of injury which this sinew can endure. The structure lies between the shank-bone and the back tendons and extends from the back of the lower part of the knee to the sesamoids, or small bones which form the pulley for the tendons behind the fetlock. The seat of the sprain or break may be at any part, but is usually in the lower third of the shank, where it divides into an inner and an outer branch. The sprain may cause but a slight swelling, or the ligament may be completely torn across, the fetlock descending to the ground and the toe turning up. In the case of severe injuries of this nature the limb is spoiled for life, and no art can ever replace the structures which have been disorganized.

Breastplate. The wide strap of the harness which goes round the breast of the horse, to which the tug or trace is buckled, and by which the sulky or carriage is drawn.

Breeching. That part of the harness which goes round the hind legs or breech, from one side to the other, to prevent the carriage or sulky from pressing against the horse, and to back it when required.

Breeching Straps. Straps attached to the breeching at that point on each side where the hip straps are connected with it, extending to the hold-back irons of the shafts.

Breed. A race or progeny from the same line of ancestry having an alliance by some distinguishing qualities in common, which are transmitted by heredity.

Breeder. According to turf rulings the breeder is the man who owns or controls the mare when she is bred to the horse; not the person who owns the dam when the colt is foaled.

Breeders' Certificate. A writing given by a breeder to the purchaser of a horse, containing a copy of his pedigree as given in the stud book or trotting register, certifying that the horse is the one described; or containing a pedigree and certificate that such horse is eligible to registry.

Breeders' Record. A term formerly much used to describe the results of a private trial of speed. It has no meaning, or significance, or value. There is no such thing recognized as a breeders' record.

Breeding. The rearing of live stock of any class, particularly by combining or crossing one strain of a species or variety with another, with the object of improving the breed. Scientific breeding consists in throwing the strength of all the inherited tendencies into one channel, concentrating all the ruling forces on one objective point, and thus reaching a certain result. In breeding for the turf, we should couple a sire and dam of trotting inheritance and that are trotters themselves; or those combining purity of blood and the racing lineage, with the true conformation for speed. These are the requisite qualities, and we should be able to judge of the merits of the prospective offspring, according to the trotting or racing merits of the sire and dam, the grandsire and grandam, and so on backward, the chances of success being in proportion to the strength and unity of the inheritance. Offspring from such unions will be colts that trot naturally, that can be developed rapidly with little help from artificial aids; and also those that make the highest winners on the racing turf.

Br. g. An abbreviation for "brown gelding," when used before or after the name of a horse in a list of entries or in the summary of a race. Also used with a *c, m,* or *h,* to denote a colt, mare or horse of the same color.

Bridle. That part of the harness which is fitted to the horse's head, and by which it is controlled. Its pieces are: Crownpiece, which passes over the horse's poll; cheek-pieces, which connect the crownpiece with the bit; throat-latch, a part of the crownpiece which serves to prevent the bridle from slipping over the horse's head, by passing under the throat; forehead band, browband or front, which goes across the horse's forehead; headstall, the name given to the foregoing leather work, when in a collected form, and to which is attached the snaffle, the bit and bridoon, the Chifney bit, (an English bit very severe in its action,) or the Pelham; lipstrap, which serves to keep the curbchain in its place; reins, connected to the rings of the curb or snaffle; billets, the ends of the reins or of the cheek-pieces of the bridle, which buckle on the bit; loops or keepers, which serve, when buckles are used, to retain the ends of the billets; stops, used with reins which have buckles, to prevent the martingale rings catching on the buckles; bridoon head, the headstall of the snaffle or double bridle—it has neither throat latch nor forehead band.

Bridle Hand. The left hand is called the bridle hand in contradistinction to the right hand, which is termed the whip hand.

Bridoon; Bradoon. A light snaffle or bit of a bridle used in addition to the principal bit, and with a separate rein.

Bring Home. Riders and drivers carrying weights during a heat must bring home with them the weights which have been approved or announced correct.

Brisket. The lower part of the horse's chest.

Broken-back. Horses that are broken-backed, or "chinked in the chine," are unsound.

Broken Wind. Heaves. An unsoundness.

Bronchitis. Inflammation of the large air tubes within the lungs. An unsoundness.

Brush. A fast spurt of speed; a fast clip; an effort of extreme movement; a short work—usually half a mile; to go a short distance at a high rate of speed.

It is not well to brush the horse always over the same ground, for he will then learn to stop at certain places on the track.—Training the Trotting Horse, Charles Marvin.

At the end of every mile I would brush him a hundred yards or so, as fast as he could go.—Life with the Trotters, John Splan.

Brushy Horse. A brushy horse is one capable of a high rate of speed for a short distance only; a quarter horse.

Arab and J. Q. were two very brushy horses.—Life with the Trotters, John Splan.

Buck and Fly. [Eq.] The bucking leap is similar to that of a deer, and obtaining its name from thence. The fore legs and hind quarters are gathered in under the body, and the horse springs from all four legs at the same moment. The fore legs are tucked close under the body, while the hind limbs are thrown out as far behind as possible. In the flying leap the chief object of the rider is to maintain firm hold with his legs and thighs, and to lean sufficiently backward the instant the spring is felt, remaining in that position until the horse has firmly landed with his hind feet.

Bucking; Buck-jumping. [Eq.] A bucking horse, with the quickness of thought, throws his head down between his fore legs, arches his back at the same instant, bounds in the air with all four feet together, either forward, to one side, or even backward, till he dislodges his rider, breaks the girths, gets through the saddle, or tires himself out. Buckers are generally quiet to mount, but the moment they feel the weight of the rider in the saddle will do their best to throw him. The instant the rider feels the horse arching his back, preparatory to bucking, he should pull him quickly round to one side or the other; or put into the horse's mouth, in addition to the riding bit, a racing snaffle, having a strong rein knotted close to his neck, the slack end to be held in hand. This will not annoy the horse unless he tries to get his head down, when it will generally be effectual in stopping it.

Buckle. A metallic clasp, with one or more movable tongues within the clasp, for the purpose of holding together two straps, or belts, or the ends of the same piece of leather, upon a harness.

Buck Knees. Knees inclining towards each other.

Buggy. [Eng.] A light, one-horse, two-wheeled vehicle, without a top or hood. In the United States the word is applied to a light, one-horse, four-wheeled carriage, with one seat, and either with or without a top.

Buttock, Point of. The bony prominence which is the rearmost point of the pelvis. It is a few inches below the root of the tail.

Buttresses. The points of the wall of the hoof, on each side near the heel, where it suddenly bends inward and forward.

C

Cade. To bring up, or nourish by hand, or with tenderness; domesticated. The name of a great stallion by the Godolphin Arabian, out of Roxana; foaled in 1734. He was so called from the fact that he was brought up on cow's milk, his dam dying when he was ten days old. Roxana was by Devonshire Childers, owned by Lord Godolphin.

Cadence. That motion of the gallop in which the fore feet and hind feet strike the ground with equal force, the neck and tail being perfectly supple.

Cadger. A knavish horse-dealer.

Calk; Calkin. A spur projecting downward from the horseshoe, serving to prevent slipping. See SHOEING.

Calks are detrimental under any circumstances, and should always be avoided if possible.—Prof. D. D. Slade, Harvard University.

Campaigning. Taking horses through a circuit, or from one place to another, and entering them for purses at the various races.

Canker. A stubborn inflammation of the frog, by some attributed to a parasitic fungus. It is an unsoundness.

Canon Bone. One of the complete metacarpal, or metatarsal bones in the legs of the horse. The former, in the fore leg, extends from the carpus, or so-called knee, to the fetlock joint; and the latter in the hind leg from the tarsus, or so-called hock, to the fetlock joint. A line dividing the canon from the fetlock is one drawn across the leg immediately above the prominence caused by the fetlock joint.

Canter. A gait of transition which the trotter assumes temporarily, and in which he gallops on one of his legs, fore or hind, while he continues to trot on the others.

Canterbury Gallop. The hand-gallop of an ambling horse, commonly called a canter. Said to be derived from the monks riding to Canterbury on easy ambling horses.

Cantle. The hind part of the saddle.

Capped Hock. A serious distention of the synovial cavities, or bursæ, which are placed between the skin and the bone of the hock, to aid the gliding of the one over the other; the sprain of the tendon on the point of the hock. Arising from either cause it is an unsoundness.

Car. The large increase in the business of campaigning during the past ten years, at once created a great demand for suitable cars in which to safely and comfortably transport valuable horses long distances. This demand railroad companies were unable to meet, hence several private corporations began the building of special cars for campaigning purposes, the first of which were constructed about 1883. The business has so increased that there are now a number of companies building and operating palace horse cars, independent of railroad companies, which are equipped for service in either freight or passenger trains, and are handled by all railroad and express companies on mileage rates. These cars are, as a rule, forty-four feet long, not including the platforms. While they differ somewhat in interior arrangement, it may be said that they are fitted for twelve, sixteen or eighteen horses. In some there are four sections, of three stalls each; in others four sections, of four stalls each—the stalls extending lengthwise or crosswise of the car, or in a diagonal crosswise manner, according to the different pattern of car. In most cars the stall partitions are adjustable, and can be changed to accommodate large or smaller horses—be made in narrow stalls (twenty-six inches wide), or a room, as desired. The cars are well lighted and thoroughly ventilated, the windows being fitted with outside screens and inside shutters. They are provided with water tanks, mangers, provender and hay compartments, storage boxes for carrying dunnage of all kinds, apartments for attendants, and other conveniences. They are so thoroughly built, equipped with so many of the best appliances in car construction, and ride so easily, that they may be well called palace cars. Most companies rent these cars for a fixed rate per mile on runs of three hundred to two thousand miles, or lease them at a fixed rate per month for a shorter or longer time.

Carpus. The so-called knee of the horse, corresponding to the wrist joint in man. Below the carpal and tarsal bones, (the knee and hock), the fore and hind limbs of the horse are almost an exact duplicate of each other.

Carriage. The general style, action and bearing of a horse when in motion; as a horse of fine carriage; he has a proud carriage; an elegant way of going; graceful movement.

Carriage Bit-and-Bridoon. A double bit of varying degrees of power in itself. The degree of severity of the curb is regulated to suit the particular mouth, by buckling the reins to the upper or lower slot in the guards, as the need may be.

When the bridoon is used with this bit the check-rein is put on the bridoon, and thus the bit is relieved of contrary action. This bridoon bit is used on the carriage horse with a check-rein only, and is not used in any way in guiding the horse; its chief use being to give the horse a stylish carriage and handsome appearance.—The Bridle Bits, Col. J. C. Battersby.

Cart; Break-cart; Track-cart. A vehicle especially adapted for educating the colt to the use of the shafts and a carriage. Its peculiar features are: Wide seat, rear foot-platform, shafts of extra length, (usually three feet longer than the shafts of the standard sulky), and heavier construction—their weight being usually 160 pounds. They vary somewhat in design and make from different houses. A track cart is a combined speed and road cart, weighing generally about 85 pounds.

Cartilage. A non-vascular animal tissue; gristle. When these tissues become ossified, which indicates a conversion into a hardened structure of the cartilages naturally developed upon the rings of the coffinbone, it constitutes unsoundness.

Catch. To catch a horse after a break; to bring him to his gait. Almost every driver has a different way of bringing a horse to his trot after a break, according to the disposition of the horse and the way he has been trained; but all agree that a dead pull on both reins will not do it. Almost invariably the horse will jump to his gait when a twist or sudden pull is made on one rein. Sometimes it is done with the off rein, sometimes with the near one. A particular word or sound should also be used when this pull is given the rein, that the horse may know what it means.

Always try to teach a horse to catch on the inside rein, for if you are going round the turn in the lead and someone trailing, and he should break, obliging you to pull your horse on the outside rein, your opponent might slip through between you and the fence and beat you the heat, where he would not be able to go round you and do it. Then too, if you are head-and-head with a man he might, when your horse broke, crowd you in so close that you would be unable to pull him to the outside without running into him, whereas, if he caught on the left rein you would have no trouble.—Life with the Trotters, John Splan.

Catch Driver. A driver put up at random, when from any cause, the judges take out a driver, and put another in his place.

Catch Weights is where the driver or rider is not obliged to weigh out or weigh in. Generally, in a race or heat at catch weights there is no distance except for foul driving.

Cauterizing. The act of searing or burning some part of the horse's body by the application of the firing iron. See FIRING IRON.

HAST thou given spirit to the horse? Hast thou clothed his neck with a mane? Canst thou make him bound as a locust? The majesty of his snorting is terrible. He panteth in the valleys and exulteth; he goeth on to meet the armed men. He mocketh at fear, and trembleth; nor turneth he back from the sword. Against him rattleth the quiver, the glittering spear and shield. He devours the ground with fierceness and rage, and is impatient when the trumpet soundeth. He uttereth among the trumpets, Ha! ha! He smelleth the battle afar off, the thunder of the captains and the shouting.

—Translation from the Book of Job,

By Dr. THOMAS SCOTT.

41299

For injured tendons, soft hocks, ring-bones, side-bones, and ailments that strong blisters have failed to cure, cauterization should be promptly resorted to; and for strain or injury to almost any part of the legs below the elbow or stifle, firing should be done before a blister is applied.—The Horseman.

Cavalry Bit. The regulation cavalry bridle, as used in the United States army, has two bits, a curb, two reins, and one headstall. Col. Battersby, in his work on the Bridle Bits, says the bridoon, or watering bit, has no guards, and is used with the curb bit as an auxiliary when the horse is mounted, but is used alone in going out to water. The bridoon has rings and a single loop-joint between the bars, the same as the snaffle. It has four distinct uses: 1. That of a watering bit. 2. For easing the mouth from the curb bit. 3. For certain uses of weapons in action, especially the sword. 4. For leaping.

Cavasson; Cavezon. A noseband of iron, wood, or leather. It may either have a separate headpiece, similar to the bridoon head of a double bridle, or have cheek-pieces which fasten on to the buckles to which the crown piece of the bridle is attached. It can be raised or lowered as required, and may be used with either snaffle or curb. A noseband or cavasson should not be attached to the headstall of a curb, as it might then interfere with the action of that bit.

Caveat Emptor. A legal term much used in cases regarding the purchase, sale, and warranty of horses. It means: Let the purchaser beware.

Cavort; Curvet. To cavort about. Said of a nervous, restless horse that is given to prancing and cantering about, especially when he is being led.

Cement. The external covering or tissue of the teeth. It is placed upon the enamel over the whole surface of the tooth, and fills more or less completely the cup of each. It is generally thicker in the lower than in the upper teeth, and in very old mouths is often formed in excess, furnishing a new wearing surface to replace the teeth which have been destroyed by use; hence it has great importance in determining the age of the horse. Its structure and composition is almost exactly that of ordinary bone.

Center of Motion. The center of motion in the anterior extremity of the horse, is in the scapula or shoulder, which is as high a bony base as could be reached.

While there is no bony connection between the anterior extremity of the horse and its trunk, therefore no fixed point of resistance and reaction, as in the posterior extremities, the center of motion is attained equally well, and it is difficult to conceive how it could serve its different relations to the trunk any better. The scapula,

4

if not anatomically so, is mechanically a joint, and corresponds to the hip joint of the posterior extremity, the shoulder to the stifle and the elbow to the hock. In this view there is no reversal in the joints but the same mechanical relation. The freedom of motion at its center in the limb is less than in the corresponding joint in the posterior extremity, but there is all that is required; it is placed considerably higher than in the latter, in order that more motion should not be required; and the restriction at that point is compensated for by the superior flexibility of the lower joints. The total result is that the stride of one limb is just equal to that of the other.—The Horse in Motion, J. D. B. Stillman.

Ch. f. In a summary or list of entries indicating a chestnut filly.

Challenge. An invitation to a contest of speed.

A challenge may be hedged around with conditions, so that its non-acceptance is no acknowledgment of the superiority of the challenger.—John H. Wallace.

Champion. The first among all contestants; holding the highest rank or record; that which is unexcelled or unbeaten. Applied to the greatest performers in the stallion, gelding, filly, and other classes of trotters and runners. See STALLIONS, TROTTING, and world's record under different time made, as TWO-TEN.

Change a Horse. [Eq.] To change hands; to turn or bear the horse's head from one hand to the other, from the left to the right, or from the right to the left.

Change of Color. The disguising of a horse in any way, or painting him for the purpose of concealing his identity that he may represent another or different horse is a fraud subject to fine and expulsion by the racing and trotting rules. The laws of many States have also made it a misdemeanor, punishable by fine and imprisonment. See LAW.

Change of Name. After starting in a public race the name of a horse cannot be changed without obtaining a record thereof from the secretary of the American Association, and paying a fee of $50. For a violation of this rule a fine of $100 may be imposed. If a horse has ever trotted in a public race, the last name under which it trotted shall be given with the new entry; and if the name has been changed within one year, each former name must be given; and if any horse has ever trotted a public race without a name, such fact must be stated when the entry is made, that the animal may be fully identified.

Channels. The small, shoal grooves made in the surface of a track by a dressing harrow or float.

Chant a Horse. To advertise a horse by qualities which on examination or trial are found wanting.

Charlier Shoe; Charlier Tip. An extremely narrow and very light steel quarter shoe or tip, invented by M. Charlier, an eminent veterinary surgeon of Paris, France. In preparing the foot for the shoe and sole, frog and bars are left absolutely untouched, and a groove is cut, or counter-sunk into the wall, not high enough to reach above the sole level, and less than the thickness of the wall in depth. Into this narrow groove the shoe or tip is sunk and nailed by from four to six conical-headed nails, the heads of which are counter-sunk in the shoe. By this system of shoeing the frog, bars, and a portion of the sole come to the ground the same as if the foot were unshod, and all participate in weight-bearing.

Charmed Circle. The 2:30 class of trotters. To obtain this record is said to get " within the charmed circle."

Chaser. [Eng.] A steeple-chase runner. He must be a thoroughbred; sound in wind and limb; of a generous, gamy disposition; well schooled, and well trained. He should possess good sloping shoulders; not overloaded, but with plenty of liberty when he moves. A horse with bad shoulders may be able to gallop up hill, but he cannot gallop down hill if defective in this respect. His propelling power behind must be great. He must have a powerful back and loins, with strong quarters; muscular, sound thighs, plenty of length from the hip to the hock; good ribs; deep through the heart, compact, and not too long in the back.

Check-rein; Bearing-rein. A short rein fastened from the bit of a headstall or bridle to the saddle of the harness to keep the horse's head in a particular line.

Very few horses require to be checked alike.—Horse Portraiture, Joseph Cairn Simpson.

Probably, if those who have to do with the harnessing of horses were better acquainted with the admirable mechanical apparatus for holding up the head in a natural and unstrained position, they would think it less necessary to supplement the cervical ligament by an external contrivance for effecting the same object; which, however, not being elastic, never allows the head, even momentarily, to be altered in position; which is generally fixed so tightly as to interfere greatly with the natural graceful curve of the neck, one of the horse's chief beauties; and which, being attached at one end through the tender corners of the mouth, must, if short enough to effect the object for which it is used, be a continual source of pain or irritation to the animal.—The Horse, William Henry Flower, C. B.

Cheekpieces. Those parts of the bridle which connect the crownpiece with the bit.

Chest. The cavity which occupies nearly the third part of the trunk, in which the lungs and heart of the horse are situated. It is divided from the abdomen by the diaphragm.

Chestnuts; Castors; Kerbs. Horny growths above and on the inside of the knees in the front legs, and on the level of the hock in the hind legs. M. Chauveau says they are composed of a mass of epithelial cells arranged in tubes like the horn of the hoof. Dr. George Fleming says: "In fine bred hôrses this horny production is much less developed than in the coarser breeds, and is always smaller in the hind legs." Dr. W. H. Flower regards them of the nature of epidermal glands. Some other authors make the distinction that these growths are chestnuts on the fore legs and kerbs on the hind legs, the latter being always smaller than the former. In grooming the outside flakes are habitually pulled off either with the comb or by hand.

Chin-groove. The smooth and rounded under part of the lower jaw, in which the curb chain should lie naturally, without pinching, when the rein is held lightly. The headstall should, in all cases, be of just sufficient length to allow the bit to lie exactly opposite the chin-groove.

Chinked in the Chine. A term used to describe what is called a "broken backed" horse. It is legal unsoundness.

Chromos. Pool tickets.

Chronograph. A split-second watch; a timer for track use in catching the time made by a horse in a heat or race; an instrument for measuring or recording the exact instant in which an event takes place. Applied to various kinds of watches so contrived that when a button is pressed the second hand stops, or one of the two second hands stops, or the second hand leaves a dot of ink upon the dial.

Chute. A straight, or nearly straight, extension of the home stretch of a running course; the track beyond the finish.

Cinch. [Local: Western United States.] A saddle girth made of leather, canvas, or woven horsehair. The ends of this tough cordage terminate in long, narrow strips of leather, called in Spanish, látigos—thongs—which connect the cinches with the saddle, and are run through an iron ring and then tied by a series of complicated turns and knots.

Cipher; [O]. In Chester's Trotting and Pacing Record, and in the summary of a race, a sign that the horse whose name it follows made a dead heat; as, for example, (3.0), signifies third heat dead.

Circuit. A tour; a journey from place to place for the purpose of attending race meetings. A union of two or more associations for the purpose of holding race or trotting meetings at different places and on different dates.

Circumduct. To move a limb around an imaginary axis in such manner that it describes a conical figure; the motion given to the fore foot and leg of a horse that paddles.

Class. The ranking together; a determination of the particular purse in which a horse may be entered, according to the record he has made; in racing, class is determined by the ability of the horse to go fast for a distance and carry weight. In some States the definition of class has been established by legislative enactment, as in Ohio, where the law says: "Class is determined by the public performance of a horse in any former contest or trial of speed, as proved by the printed rules of any society or association under which the proposed contest is advertised to be conducted." Other States have laws exactly similar to this. See LAW.

Classic Races. A term applied by universal consent throughout the turf world, to the five great races of the English turf, viz.: The Derby, founded in 1780; the Oaks, originated in 1779, for fillys only; the St. Leger, founded in 1776, in compliment to Lieut.-Gen. Anthony St. Leger of Park Hill, England; the One Thousand, and the Two Thousand Guineas, established in 1809.

Clay. One of the great American trotting families, founded by Andrew Jackson, 4, by Young Bashaw, a Barb, imported from Tripoli, in 1820; dam unknown. He was foaled at Salem, N. Y., in 1827, and died at Knightstown, Penn., in 1843. Among his most noted sons as trotting sires, were Henry Clay, 8, foaled in 1837; dam Lady Surrey, a pacing mare of unknown pedigree; and Long Island Black Hawk, a trotter and sire of high quality. After passing through many hands, Henry Clay went blind, and died in April, 1876. From him comes the line of sires known for a number of generations by the name of Cassius M. Clay. The Patchen branch of the Clays originated with George M. Patchen, 30, by C. M. Clay, dam by a son of imported Trustee. Other founders of celebrated branches of the Clays are American Clay, 34; Harry Clay, 45, and The Moor, 870.

Cleft of the Frog. The division in the middle line of the frog of the foot. In healthy feet it consists of only a single depression.

Clerk of the Course. The person who acts as Secretary to the board of judges during a race.

Clerk of the Scales. [Eng.] The weigher at a race.

Clicking; Forging; Over-reaching. The act of striking the toes of the hind foot or shoe, against the heel of the corresponding fore foot or shoe, when the horse is in motion. It is due to the imperfect conformation of the horse, or to improper dressing of the feet, and cannot be classed as a vice or an unsoundness.

Clip. A speedy gait; a spurt of speed for a short distance; as a 2:35 clip.

Clip. A projecting flange or claw on the upper edge or surface of a horseshoe which partially embraces the wall of the hoof, for its protection, and to assist in keeping the shoe in place.

Clip. A metal clasp or confining piece used to connect the parts of a carriage-gear, or to hold the hook of a whippletree.

Clipping; Clippers; Clipping-shears. The removal of the coat or hairy covering of a horse; clipping machines; shears for clipping horses. It is said that the practice of clipping horses was introduced into England in 1825 by the army officers who became acquainted with the art during the Peninsular war. In a most interesting work, published anonymously in London in 1831, it is said: "In regard to the newly discovered or invented practice of clipping and its supposed improvements * * * such deviations from nature rarely do any good." In former times clipping was done by ordinary hand shears, and two or three days was required to clip a horse. The new serrated clipping shears of the Newmarket, Brown, and Clark patterns, were invented in 1875, and began to be generally used in 1877. These clippers, or serrated knives or shears, consist of a plate upon which are highly tempered serrated teeth or fingers; to the flat surface of which is attached a duplicate movable plate having correspondingly fragile, comb-like teeth, this movable half being operated or moved by the hand, forming the upper arm of the shears, the stationary plate resting upon the skin of the horse while they are in use. These shears are now operated by hand, electric, and other motors—by hand, being understood as meaning crank and wheel power. The attachment of power to the shears is made by means of a series of small cogs and eccentric joints connected with a chain which plays through a rubber tube of indefinite length, running over pulleys, and attached to the movable arm or knife-plate of the shears, which are easily guided by the operator, who clasps only the arm of the under or immovable plate. By means of these power shears a horse can be clipped in two and a half hours.

The horse's coat should never be clipped until it is properly set. This is known by the appearance of long hairs known as "cat hairs." When they show these the coat may fairly be assumed to be ready for clipping; and if carefully done, and great care is exercised, the horse kept in a warm stable, etc., it is regarded as humane.—Through the Stable and Saddle Room, Arthur T. Fisher.

When you take a horse up out of his winter quarters, he will naturally have an excessive coat of hair, his flesh will be soft, and with very moderate exercise he will sweat more or less. If the weather is cold it is impossible to rub him dry, and he may sweat off the flesh a good deal faster than you may want him to. Under those conditions I invariably clip a horse, and the result has always been perfectly satisfactory to me.—Life with the Trotters, John Splan.

Will clipping have a permanent effect upon the horse's coat, making it come out earlier, or heavier, or coarser, the next autumn? Skilled opinions differ on this point, but, as a general principle, the cutting of hair certainly tends to affect its future growth. Still, clipping the coat once a year, probably has only a slight effect—at least, until it has been repeated for some years.—Road, Track, and Stable, H. C. Merwin.

Another reason which grooms advance for clipping is, that the horse moves much more freely after than before the operation, because it is relieved of the weight of superfluous hair. Mayhew, with all the caution of a man of science, does not actually deny that such an effect may be produced by clipping, but he very emphatically says that he never saw it.—Horse and Man, Rev. J. G. Wood.

Close on Him. When a driver or rider who has been trailing or following the running for half the distance, begins to approach, or comes up even with a contending horse in a heat or race, he is said to "close on him." Thus Mr. Splan, in describing one of his races with Rarus against Great Eastern, says: "As we rounded into the stretch Rarus began to close on him, and had got to his saddle skirts at the distance stand."

Clothing. Garments; covering; furnishings for the care of a horse. Horse clothing embraces: Sweat, cooling, stable and street blankets; hoods; working and walking suits, and waterproof covers — the materials being woolen, cotton-flannel and linen. A suit embraces the following pieces, viz: One kersey stable blanket; one sheet, (for summer); one cooler, (a light, square woolen blanket); one heavy square blanket, woolen; one light woolen hood for cooling out; one fancy suit for exhibition purposes, consisting of a nice blanket and hood to match, finely made and lettered with the name of the horse to which it belongs. In general there should be three suits for each horse—one of heavy, one of medium and one of light weight. Summer clothing should be of the same shape as winter clothing, but larger and wider on the quarter piece to give more protection from flies. The body cloth should come well over the withers, buckling in front of the chest, and extending back to the root of the tail or beyond. When a horse needs to be sweat out, use a heavy neck piece, crest or jowl hood, or a small blanket may be wrapped around the neck in its place. The uses of clothing are to keep the horse warm, to protect him from flies in hot weather, and against injury, and to reduce fat—especially on those horses where otherwise it could not be got rid of without so much work as would be injurious to their limbs.

Coarseness. An evidence of underbreeding with strength but without any redeeming features on the side of refinement. The characteristics are: Carty bone; soft muscles; want of symmetry and commanding presence; an unintelligent head; low and coarse withers; bull neck; a short top to the hind quarters coupled with droop, not to be compared to gentle obliquity which gives the muscular area and power in trotting and racing.

Coat. The external natural covering of hair upon the horse. The word especially refers to the color. To the investigation of this subject, Goubaux and Barrier of Paris, in their great work on the Exterior of the Horse, have given very minute studies, as a result of which they formulated a classification which has mainly been adopted, although in a modified form, in the presentation here given. A scientific description of the coats groups them in three classes, viz: 1, Primitive, or those already formed soon after the colt is foaled; 2, Derived, or those which appear some time after birth, and are due to the introduction of white into a primitive coat; 3, Conjugate, or those characterized by the presence upon the same animal of two primitive and two derived coats. I. In the first class there are three divisions: 1, simple coats as black, sorrel; 2, composite, as those formed of hairs of two colors—one black for mane, tail and extremities; others— yellow, red or gray for body, as Isabella, bay, mouse color; 3, mixed, formed by dark hairs upon each of which are found two different colors, the yellow more or less light at the base, the black at the summit. Of the blacks there is the true or ordinary black, and rusty black. The former is dark, uniform without any reflection; the rusty is dull, reddish in the sun, washed, hard to distinguish from brown. Sorrel or chestnut, which consists of golden, fawn, and reddish-brown hairs, (by some it is called coffee and milk color), fawn-sorrel; washed sorrel; cherry sorrel, (reddish tint); chestnut-sorrel; maroon- sorrel; burnt sorrel, or color of roasted coffee; Isabella, bay and mouse color. The Isabella has a coat of two distinct colors, on the body yellow or yellowish, on the extremities— from the knee and hock down—mane and tail, black. This color is also called dun. Bay differs from Isabella because the yellow hairs are replaced by red ones. The varieties are light bay; ordinary bay, (of a distinctly red color); cherry, blood and mahogany bay, darker than ordinary bay, and all essen- tially alike; chestnut bay, (the color of a ripened chestnut); maroon bay, deeper and fresher upon the upper parts of the body; dark bay, bordering upon brown; brown bay, almost black. Mouse color is formed by two colors, the body ashy gray, similar to the colors of a mouse, legs from the knee and hock down, black, as in the bay. II. Derived coats. These are four: Gray, white, flea-bitten, roan. Gray is composed of mixed hairs of white and those of a darker color, varying from the black to the brown. Very light gray resembles white, and shows but very few black or dark hairs. Light gray, with more dark in very light. Ordinary gray, almost equally composed of white and black hairs. Dark gray, with a preponderance of dark or black hairs. Iron gray, which has a bluish shade. Slate gray—a shade darker than iron gray. Clayey gray, which has a very light yellowish tint. Isabella gray, a mixture of white, yellow and dark hairs. Roan gray, a mixture of white, dark, red or reddish hairs, the latter less abundant than the former. White is a color easily recognized. It is a dull milk or pigeon white color, opaque, with no reflection. Porcelain white, has a tint of porcelain china. Dirty white, of a slightly yellowish tint. Rosy white, a color due to the absence of the cutaneous pigment and to the thinness of the hairs, leaving the discolored parts of the skin visible. Roan is composed of three kinds of hairs—red, white and black, or a bay modified by the admixture, more or less distinct, of white. The red is light, ordinary wine red, or strawberry, and the dark appears according to the predominance of the different colors. III. In the third class there are found two types: First, the Piebald or pied; second, conjugate gray and Isabella. The former is a union rather than an inter-mixture of the white coat with one or another of the above described derived coats. The animal presents a singular appearance, covered with large, irregular white patches, variously situated upon the body, but the colors do not blend. There are various examples of this singular combination, as, technically, rusty black pied; dark fox-color pied; flea-bitten rosy pied; burnt sorrel porcelain pied. The conjugate gray or Isabella is an extremely rare coat, which is termed spotted or marbled.

Cock Horse. A horse kept in the betting quotations to deceive public backers, though known to the private layers against him that he has no chance of winning.

Coffin-bone. The bone forming the end of the foot, and shaped like the hoof or horny box in which it is enclosed, and which it supports.

Coffin-joint. The joint at the upper part of the coffin-bone, made by the union of the small pastern, coffin and small sesamoid bone, or navicular bones, the latter being set behind and beneath the joint surface of the coffin-bone, in such a way as to largely receive the weight of the small pastern. The focus of weight in the foot is at this joint.

Collared. When a rider sees that he is beaten in a race, he is said to be "collared."

Cold. A cold, if neglected until it degenerates into some seated form, as for instance, nasal catarrh, is a cause of unsoundness.

Cold-blooded. Not thoroughbred; of common or mongrel stock; an animal showing only ill breeding.

Collect. To gather quickly in taking a fence, hurdle, wall or other obstacle.

The animal that is destined for chasing must learn to collect himself with the slightest possible diminution of speed, to fly his fences, to get away from them on the other side without a pause, and to do all this with the least effort.—The Badminton Library: Steeplechasing, Arthur Coventry and Alfred E. T. Watson.
To make a horse jump "big," pull him together, and make him bring his hind quarters under him by the pressure of the legs and touch of the whip.—Riding, M. Horace Hayes, M. R. C. V. S.

Collected. [Eq.] A horse is said to be collected when his head is in a perpendicular position, yields readily to the bit and has no disposition to go out of hand. His hind feet will be well in front of a perpendicular line dropped from the points of the buttocks, his fore feet will be brought back more than usual, and he will stand more or less over on them. His head and neck will be raised, and he will be looking to the front with ears pricked forward, ready for a move in whatever direction the rider wishes.

Color of the Coat. The old proverb that "no good horse is of a bad color," is manifestly untrue. Comparatively few horses of a bad color have ever been successful on the turf, and there is no doubt that those few would have been better animals had their color been good. It is said that records were kept of the colors of winners in the Phœnix stakes, Lexington, Ky., inaugurated in 1831, and that in fifty-four races, horses of a bay color won twenty-six times; chestnuts, fifteen; brown, two; black one. Statistics have also been published on this point from results of the English races. It is said that in about one hundred years of history of the Derby, Oaks, St. Leger and Doncaster races, in 3576 starters in 293 stakes the results were: Bays, 1826 starters, 159 winners, ratio of winners 11 1-2; chestnuts, 807 starters, 71 winners, ratio of winners; 11 1-3; browns, 699 starters, 54 winners, ratio of winners, 13; grays and roans, 127 starters, 6 winners, ratio of winners, 21; blacks, 109 starters, 2 winners, ratio of winners, 54 1-2; duns, 2 starters, one winner, ratio of winners, 1-2. The most objectionable colors are those which are weak and washy of their kind, and where the extremities are lighter than the rest of their body. Thus a very light bay or chestnut is liable to be of weak constitution, deficient in stamina, and when to this is added "mealy" legs, or legs lighter than the rest of the coat, and a lighter colored mane and tail, the weakness is intensified. Black legs are preferable in a bay, and with these the feet are generally more sound, and the horn is more enduring. White legs and feet are objectionable, but not so much so as mealy ones. Dark chestnut, bay, and gray are preferable to light shades of these colors. Black and roan are not so common. Bays, chestnuts and browns practically monopolize the turf, and the darker and more solid the colors are, the better are the animals. The bay is the best, most fashionable and highest priced color for a horse, because it is that which indicates the best breeding.

Colors. The custom of owners selecting their colors and publishing them, originated at Newmarket in 1762, the jockeys having before that worn colors but not as a proprietary distinction. In this country, the New York Jockey Club in 1842, required that riders should be dressed in Jockey style, viz: Jockey cap, colored jacket, pantaloons and boots; but colors as an owners' distinction are said to have been first adopted at Fleetwood Park, N. Y. Colors are a source of great individual pride on the turf in England and this country, and are a source of enjoyment in the race on the part of the public. The American rules require that colors selected by owners must be recorded by the secretary of the Congress, and shall not be used by others except in case of death or after five years' withdrawal from the turf. A list of all colors is obliged to be posted in the office of the clerk of the course.

Colt. A word specifically applied to a male foal.

Combination Horse. A term applied to the American saddler, or gaited horse.

The breeders of saddle horses have succeeded in producing a genuine combination horse—one which will go all the five recognized gaits under the saddle, using the rack, running walk and canter to the delight of the rider and the satisfaction of the horse, and will, when put in harness, forget for the time being, that they ever racked a rod, and will go a square, pure trot.—The Breeders' Gazette.

Combination Sale. A public sale, or sale by auction, in which several breeders, or owners, unite or combine a certain number of animals of their own, in order to make the sale more attractive, and to realize better prices at a less cost for commissions. The first American combination sale was held at New York in 1877, but they are now very common.

Coming. Said of a colt in training when he begins to understand his work and show speed. "He is a comer," or "he is coming," means that the animal is fast developing as a trotter.

Complaint. A charge made by one rider or driver against another for foul driving, or other misconduct during a heat. Such complaint must be made at the termination of the heat, and before the driver dismounts or leaves his sulky. By the racing rules, such complaint must be made to the judges either before or immediately after the jockeys in the race have passed the scales. For frivolous complaints owners, trainers or jockeys may, at the discretion of the judges, be fined or suspended.

Conditions. [Eng.] The conditions of the Grand National Hunt races are: Riders must not ride for more than one hundred yards at any one time on any road or lane; riders not passing the post within fifteen minutes of the winner to pay double entry; any rider examining the course before starting will be disqualified. By the American racing rules, the express conditions of a race always supersede the general rules, where they conflict.

Conditional Entries. A private understanding made between the owner of a horse and a society or association when the horse is nominated; an entry made outside the rules. The rules of both the National and American Associations attach severe fines to any member receiving conditional entries.

The great injustice of the conditional entry is that it practically abolishes the closing date for entries for one man, while it leaves it open for the other.—Spirit of the Times.

Conditioning. The fitting of the horse, in every part of his body, for his best performance upon the turf. It requires long, studious exercise, feeding and training, and a complete understanding of the disposition and peculiarities of the horse, that he may respond quickly to the wishes of his trainer, driver or rider. When a horse is in blooming condition he is fresh and healthy in appearance, clean and unloaded in his muscular system, bright in the eye, glossy in the coat, clean on the legs, and animated in expression. His muscles will feel hard and springy to the touch, and swell out, especially in the hind quarters, where they should seem divided and distinct from each other. The crest should be firm, and closely attached to the neck. When the hand is drawn along the ribs the skin should wrinkle up and appear loose and detached. In walking, his feet should strike the ground with a positive step, and his neck, held high, should rise and fall springily. The horse, in the best condition, has an inquisitive look, notices everything with pricked ears, and has a noble expression indicative of confidence and self purpose.

Cone. That part of the hub of a pneumatic sulky wheel which holds the ball bearings in place in the casing, or piece into which the bearings are set—which piece is fitted tightly into the ends of the hub. One of these cones is called the stationary cone, and the other the movable cone, the latter being used in adjusting the tension of the bearings, by means of a spanner wrench.

Conformation. External points; the particular texture or structure of outward form, and the arrangement and relation of the parts which compose it; general structure.

Congress. The sessions of the American and National Trotting Associations are held biennially, and are called a congress. At each officers are elected, the rules and laws revised, and other business pertaining to the good of the associations transacted. See AMERICAN TURF CONGRESS.

Consolation Race. A consolation match, or race, is a contest which can be entered only by those who have failed to win in the previous, or regular purses, or contests offered by a track or member, which have taken place within a given time.

Contending Horses. In any heat of a race it will very soon appear that several of the starters are dropping to the rear, and that the heat lies between two or three horses that are quite evenly matched. Such horses are called the contending horses, because the battle of the heat is narrowed down to them.

Contraction of the Hoof. A shrinkage of the tissues of the foot, by which the lateral diameter of the heels, in particular, is diminished. It affects the fore feet chiefly. It is of less moment if affecting the hind feet, because the hind foot first strikes the ground with the toe, and less expansion of the heels is necessary than in the fore feet when the weight is first received on the heels. Where produced by inflammation, accompanied by disease of the foot, or any change in its normal condition, though not producing lameness at the time of the sale of a horse, it is an unsoundness if lameness afterwards follows.

Converted Pacer. Many natural pacers have been so trained as to leave their natural gait and acquire the trotting gait. Such are termed converted pacers. The methods used to accomplish this are as varied as are the dispositions of the horses. Weighting in different ways, the use of the cross-strap, the placing of rails on the ground at such intervals as will compel the horse to put his feet down in the diagonal order, and many others. Charles Marvin, in telling how he trained Smuggler—Training the Trotting Horse—says: "I would start him up slowly, and rather suddenly throw him off to one side at a pretty sharp angle, compelling him to change his gait, and the new gait, (trot), he would keep for a few steps. As soon as he came back to the pace I would swing him off sideways again. Of course this was virtually driving around in a small circle until he began to go a considerable distance trotting. At each time he would remain at the trot a little longer, and one day struck a trot and kept it up for a quarter of a mile."

Cooling-out; Cooling Off. The walking exercise, light blanketing and personal care given to a horse after one heat, in order to fit him for the following heat.

Cooling-out Ground. The enclosed area between the stables and track, where horses are led to halter for cooling out between heats.

Coper. [Eng.] A broker in old horses; a dishonest horse dealer; a horse sharp.

Corded-up. A condition of the muscles of the back and loins very liable to follow a severe heat, in which they become distended, knotted, or partially paralyzed, requiring very careful attention and the application of hot lotions to bring them to their normal condition.

Corker. A rush; a hard heat; a fast brush; a heat that has required hard work to win; as "four corking heats;" "two corking miles."

Corner Teeth. The outermost of the front teeth, or incisors; those next to the tusks.

Coronet. The comparatively soft, but sharply defined line, or band, which runs round the foot, highest in front and becoming lower behind, immediately above the hoof, and which secretes the horn by which the wall of the hoof is formed. The coronet, or coronary bone, is the short, cube-shaped bone, between the coffin bone and the small cannon bone.

Corns proceed from an injury to the living horn of the foot, more commonly in the inner heel, and found, above all, in flat feet with low, weak heels. From the fact that they can seldom be cured they render a horse unsound.

Cough. However simple and however recent in origin a cough may be, while it lasts the horse is unsound.

Counting The Horseshoes. A custom founded upon the fact that Walter Le Brun, a London farrier, was granted a plot of land in the Strand, London, as early as 1235, upon which to set up a forge. For this privilege he was to render to the exchequer, each year, six horseshoes with the sixty-two nails belonging to them. This custom has continued ever since and from it originates the "counting of the horseshoes and hobnails" on swearing in the London sheriffs at the Court of Exchequer of the present day.

Coupling. That part of the sacrum where it joins the lumber vertebra; the point where the top of the ribs unite with the vertebral column.

While Flying Eaton had a strong, broad loin and excellent coupling, there was a graceful, downward curvature of the spine in front of the coupling which gave him in some degree the appearance of being slightly sway-backed.—S. W. Parlin.

Courage. That instinct or inbred quality of physical power which asserts itself in endurance and staying effort; the best evidence that a horse possesses high breeding and splendid ancestry.

Well-bred horses, properly broken, are more courageous than coarsely bred ones.—The Book of the Horse, S. Sidney.

Course. A track; the distance or direction laid out for a race course.

Courser. A racer or swift running horse. Hugh the Great of France, in the year 930, presented to Athelstan, one of the Anglo-Saxon kings of England, whose sister, Edelswitha, he had married, several running horses, the *equos cursores* of the chronicler. Coursers are also mentioned among the horses of Henry VIII. of England, in 1509; and Anthony Fitzherbert, who wrote the earliest English work on agriculture, 1534, speaks of the *corser* as a horse dealer.

Crack. Great; famous. A crack jockey, a crack driver —persons great in their respective lines.

Cracked; Crocked. To become tired; to give up; to quit.

In the stretch I called on Manzanita, and after trotting head-and-head for nearly a furlong with Belle Hamlin the latter cracked, and Manzanita won in 2:16¼.— Training the Trotting Horse, Charles Marvin.

Cracked Heels. Fleshy heels, the inflammation of which is due to a fungus, or grease; scratches, canker, or foot-mange. It is an unsoundness.

Cracker-jack. A horse with a very low record; a fast horse; a record-breaker.

Creep. When the pneumatic tire of a bicycle sulky wheel becomes loose from the felloe, it is said to "creep."

Crest. The upper part of the neck extending from the withers to the ears.

Cribbing; Crib-biting, is associated with the serious

vice of wind-sucking, which generally leads to tympany, impaired digestion, and rapid loss of condition. It is believed that in the early stages it can be cured and the horse rendered sound; but if neglected leads to serious results and becomes a vice, and in its more advanced stages the health and condition of the horse are affected, the digestive organs become impaired, and the horse is unsound because less valuable and less liable to perform his ordinary work. Hanover, in his Law of Horses, says: "As indications of approaching disease it would be difficult to say cribbing was not an unsoundness. A crib-biter will not retain his condition or be fit for constant work." In Massachusetts Reports, 8, Gray, [1861], 430, Washburn vs. Cuddihy, "Judge Briggs refused to rule as matter of law, that cribbing was not unsoundness in a horse."

Crop. [Eng.]· A short handled, stout hunting whip, having a hook at one end. It is generally held in the right hand about six inches from the loop, with the hook downwards, the lash coiled up and held in the same hand. This, of course, is when the crop is not in use.

Cropping. The barbarous practice of cropping or paring and clipping the ears of a horse, which was thought to be the proper thing for fashion, largely practiced in England about 1790–1800.

Cross. If a horse, in attempting to pass another on the homestretch, should at any time cross or swerve so as to impede the progress of a horse behind him, he becomes disqualified from winning that heat. This rule applies to the running and trotting turf, equally.

Cross-bar. A fore bar attached across the thills of a sulky or carriage, to which the whipple-tree is fastened. A splinter-bar.

Cross-country Riding. [Eng.] Steeple-chasing or hunting; riding across fields, over fences, brooks, ditches and hedges. The opposite from road riding.

Cross-strap. A hopple, or hobble. A leather and elastic attachment placed upon the legs of horses to assist in changing or converting the gait, or to prevent a horse from pacing. Attached to the horse for this purpose it must be crossed, or attached from left fore foot to right hind foot; and from right fore foot to left hind foot, or ankle.

Croup. That portion of the upper part of the body of the horse which is situated between the loins in front and the tail behind; the rump.

Crupper. That part of the harness extending from the

back strap to the end, a loop in the end of which receives and holds the horse's tail.

Cup. A vessel of precious metal, like silver or gold; or an elaborately wrought piece of plate offered as a prize to be contended for in a race.

Cup-races. Races in which horses start for a cup rather than for a purse or stake; a term applied to match races.

Cuppy. A cuppy track is a soft, sandy track, the surface of which is said to *cup* when the horse's foot leaves an impression upon it in the form of a small hollow, as though a cupful of earth had been removed; this condition being caused by the contact of the horse's shoe in going over it at high speed. A track that is cuppy is always a slow track.

Curb. A chain or strap attached to the upper ends of the branches of the bit of a bridle, and passing under the horse's lower jaw; used chiefly in controlling a spirited or vicious horse. The curb rein is attached to the lower end of the fauces of the bit, and when it is pulled the curb is pressed forward against the horse's jaw in such a manner as to compel obedience. The proper length for the curb is about one-fourth more than the width of the mouth; and it should be outside of the bridoon bit, for if placed inside of it the constant pressure of the bit on the curb would chafe and injure the under jaw bone.

Curb. A swelling in the median line of the hind limb just backwards of the back part of the hock, where in the normal state there should be a straight line, extending from the upper end of the point of the hock down to the fetlock. At first it is soft and doughy, later hard and resistant. Due generally to a sprain of the tendon which plays over the front of the hock, though in some cases the ligament beneath the tendon is injured. If large enough to be distinctly seen, or if it has been disfigured by treatment or otherwise, it is a blemish; but while forming, if the horse is lame, he is indisputably unsound.

Curb-bit. A form of bit for the bridle which by the exertion of slight effort can be made to produce great pressure on the horse's mouth.

It is impossible to ride well on any horse unless the curb-bit is properly made and properly adjusted.—The Saddle Horse.

Curb-chain. The curb-chain is made flat so that when twisted into shape it lies almost as smooth as a band of leather against the chin. It is attached by spring-hooks to the eyes of the upper ends of the levers of the bit.

Curby Hocks. A curby hock is one which is slightly bulged out behind. In some horses they are congenital and

5

cannot be regarded as a disease or an unsoundness, but rather as a distortion or blemish.

Cushion. A soft finish to a track; the surface to the depth of from one-half to three-fourths of an inch being made very light and soft by a fine finishing harrow, but yet so yielding as to be elastic.

The great point in track building is to get a perfect cushion — one that is smooth, springy, and clean, where there is a certain amount of yielding when the foot strikes. — Training the Trotting Horse, Charles Marvin.

Cut. To reduce; to take from. A term used by experts in judging a horse at exhibitions by means of a score card system, or scale of points. The work is generally done very rapidly by an expert judge, only the defects in the animal being marked, which are reduced or "cut," from the total number of points included in perfection, and deducted therefrom; thus showing the total number of points scaled by the animal in a possible 100.

Cutting, the result of faulty structure, is not an unsoundness, because the law cannot regard a horse as unsound merely from badness of conformation.

Cut Loose. A horse is said to cut loose when he jumps to an unprecedented rate of speed; to go uncontrolled and almost beyond all limit.

When they gave the word Edwin was going true as an arrow, and as he turned into the back stretch, he cut loose at a rate of speed that looked to me as though he was not only going to beat Rarus' time, but knock the watches out of their cases as well. — Life with the Trotters, John Splan.

D

Daisy-cutter. A horse that does not lift his feet much off the ground when trotting or galloping; a low, swift going horse.

> The trot is the true pace for a hackney; and were we near a town I should like to try that *daisy-cutter* of yours upon a piece of level road, (barring canter), for a quart of claret at the next inn.—Sir Walter Scott.

Dangerous Horse. An unknown horse of which one is afraid in a race; one of whose chances of success no information is to be had.

Dark. All racing and trotting rules forbid the making of a heat or race when it is so dark that the gait of the horses cannot be plainly seen from the judges' stand.

Dark Horse. A horse not known; one of which all contestants are afraid; whose capabilities are not known.

> Years ago there lived in Tennessee an old chap named Sam Flynn, who always had a nag or two, traded horses to some extent and who had a black horse called Dusky Pete, almost a thoroughbred, which he would straddle and ride into town in such a way as gave those who knew it the impression that Pete wasn't much of a "hoss." One day Sam came into town where there was a county race meeting and entered Pete at a post match. The people backed two or three local favorites quite heavily against him, not knowing anything of his antecedents. Just as the flyers were being saddled for the race, old Judge McMinamee, who was the turf oracle of that part of the State, arrived on the course and was made one of the judges. As he took his place on the stand he was told how the betting ran, and the folly of the owner of the strange entry in backing his "plug" so heavily. Running his eye over the track the judge instantly recognized Pete and said: "Gentlemen, there's a dark horse in this race that will make some of you sick before supper." The judge was right. Pete, the "dark horse," lay back until the three-quarter pole was reached when he went to the front with a rush, and won the purse and Flynn's bets with the greatest ease. This is the true origin of the saying "a dark horse." Wallace's Monthly, May, 1884.

> The first favorite was never heard of, the second favorite was never seen after the distance post, all the ten-to-oners were in the race, and a dark horse which had never been thought of rushed past the grand stand in sweeping triumph.—The Young Duke, Benjamin D'Israeli.

Darley Arabian. One of the three most remarkable horses of which equine history gives any record. It was during the reign of Queen Anne, 1702-1714, (famous in its history of the English thoroughbred racehorse), that this celebrated animal attained his greatest fame. He is supposed to have been bred in the desert of Palmyra, and was brought from Aleppo in Asiatic Turkey by the agent of an English commercial company trading there, about 1700. He was of bay color and was probably a genuine Arabian, although his exact lineage was never ascertained. His name is derived from his owner, Mr. Darley of Yorkshire. The Darley Arabian was the progenitor of some of the finest horses that have perhaps existed in the world, among them the Devonshire or Flying Childers, foaled in 1715, and named from his breeder, Mr. Leonard Childers; and the Bleeding, or Bartlett's Childers, a horse that was never trained, but which was the fleetest horse of his day, and the ancestor of Eclipse, one of the most remarkable horses of which there is any record. Common report affirmed that the Darley Arabian could run a mile in a minute, but there is no authentic record of this. His son, Flying Childers, ran over the round course at Newmarket, (three miles, six furlongs and ninety-three yards), in six minutes and forty seconds; and over the Beacon course, (four miles, one furlong and one hundred and thirty-eight yards), in seven minutes and thirty seconds.

Dash; Dash Race. A short race; as, a three-quarter mile dash; a mile and an eighth dash; a race decided in a single attempt instead of in heats. First run in the United States in 1864 at the Saratoga, N. Y., course.

For some years prior to 1864, heat-racing had been on the decline in England and dash racing growing in favor, and the people of New York followed England's lead until racing has come down from heats of four miles to dashes of five furlongs. Long-distance races are only a memory that lingers in the minds of a few turfmen of the old school who have survived the period of transition the sport has undergone.—The Horseman.

Dash Watch. A watch placed in a leather case made of the exact size to receive it, which is fitted to the dashboard or fender of the buggy, by means of a spring clasp, so that the driver can always have the time before him when driving.

Dawson, Thomas. Of Middleham, England, the most famous and best all-round trainer in England from 1830, till his death in 1881. He was the originator of the modern and improved system of training thoroughbreds. He was the first to see the fallacies of the old method, and to act upon his own well-considered opinions. He did away with the drenchings, profuse sweatings and short supplies of water, introducing in their stead plenty of old oats and hard work. He was an oracle on horse flesh, and the thanks of all owners of horses are justly due to him for the radical and salutary change he effected in the training world.

Daylight, Two Lengths of. There is an unwritten rule among some drivers that there must be " two lengths of daylight," (that is, a distance of twice the length of the horse and sulky), between the head of one's horse and the wheel of the other's sulky, before the attempt to pass can be made. But in practice this well understood rule comes down to the real law of the trotting turf that no driver shall pass another, when, by so doing, he causes him to swerve from his course, or in swinging in, impedes the stride of the horse passed.

Dead Heat. A dead heat, according to trotting law, is always counted, and is regarded as a heat that is undecided only as between the horses making it; and it is a heat that is lost by all the other contending horses. The time made shall be regarded a record or bar for the horses making the dead heat; and if for any other cause the heat is not awarded to either of the leading horses it shall be awarded to the next best horse, and no time shall be given out. By the National rules when two or more horses make a dead heat, the remaining horses start for the succeeding heat in the same positions with reference to the pole that they occupied at the finish of the dead heat. By the American rules whenever two or more horses have to their credit a sufficient number of dead heats, or heats and dead heats to have terminated the race if such dead heats had been won by either of them, only such horses shall start in the next heat. By the laws of the Turf Congress horses running a dead heat for a race, or place, shall be deemed winners of the race or place until the dead heat is run off, or the owners agree to divide; and if the owners agree to divide, each horse which divides shall be deemed a winner of the race or place for which he divides.

It is considered by many next to impossible that horses should run a dead heat, and, indeed, it seems as though there must be a slight difference between all horses in a close finish.—How to Train the Racehorse, Col. R. Warburton.

Dead Mouth. A dead, or non-sensitive mouth, is one of the most disappointing faults that a horse can acquire. It is generally occasioned by the horse, usually a tongue-loller, carrying his tongue over the bit, which produces that condition known as a dead mouth.

Dead Track. A track or race-course having a hard subgrade and an unyielding surface.

Rarus demonstrated his ability to pull a wagon in 2:15½ over a track that had just been made, and, in addition, was dead and damp from late rains.—Life with the Trotters, John Splan.

Deciding Heat. The last heat in a race; a heat of a race in which two or more heats have been performed, and which determines the final result by the starters in that particular heat. By the racing rules there is no distance in a deciding heat.

Declarations. The Turf Congress rules require that declarations must be made in purse races by 12 o'clock, noon, the day of the race. If a person having more than one horse entered in a purse, declares one out, he thereby declares all out. All declaration fees go—60 per cent. to second horse, and 40 per cent. to third horse; and in case one horse distances the field, in heat races, all entrance and declaration money must go with the purse.

Dental Star. A particular marking in the permanent incisors deemed an important factor in judging the age of a horse after he is eight years old. It is a discoloration of the dentine, (the ivory-like substance filling the cavity of the teeth, softer and darker colored than the rest of the tooth), which appears on the table of the tooth as the crown becomes worn away, in the form of a transversely elongated dark-yellow line.

Dentition. The act or process of cutting teeth. The horse has two sets of teeth, like all the other domestic animals. They are called those of the first dentition or temporary; and those of the second dentition, or permanent. See TEETH.

Derby. The most important annual race in England, possibly in the world, run on the Downs, a mile and a half south of the village of Epsom, Surrey, fourteen miles from London. The Derby stakes were founded in 1780, by Edward Smith Stanley, Twelfth Earl of Derby, the year following his establishment of the Oaks stakes. The stakes are 6,000 sovereigns—the winner to receive 5,000 sovereigns, the nominator of the winner 500 sovereigns, the owner of the second 300 sovereigns, and the owner of the third 200 sovereigns. The event is for three-year-olds, colts to carry 126 pounds, and fillies to carry 121 pounds. The first Derby was won by Diomed, owned by the celebrated Sir Charles Bunbury, which horse in a few years won over $38,000 in stakes, and was sold in 1798 for fifty guineas, and brought to this country. From the time the race was inaugurated up to 1784, the length of the Derby course was one mile. From 1784 up to and including 1871, the distance was one and a half miles. In 1872, and since, the start has been from the new High Level starting post, the distance being one and a half miles and twenty-nine yards. It is up hill for a quarter of a mile, tolerably flat for the next half, down hill for the next quarter, and undulating with a rise to the finish for the remainder of the distance. The Derby has been won by such great horses as Queen of Trumps, Bay Middleton, Smolensko, Surplice, Don Juan, St. Bevys, Plenipotentiary, Bard, Bend Or, Sainfoin, Pyrrhus the First, Mameluke, Orm, and greatest of all, the mighty Ormonde.

Derby Day. The day on which the Derby stakes are run for. It always occurs on the second day—Wednesday—of the great Epsom Spring Meeting in May, being the Wednesday before Whitsuntide. It takes place on this day, rain or shine, the precise minute varies only occasionally as when the horses are bad in coming into form for a start. Parliament adjourns till the race is run.

Every New England deacon ought to see one Derby day to learn what sort of a world this is he lives in. Man is a sporting as well as a praying animal.—Dr. Oliver Wendell Holmes, 1834.

The Derby has always been the one event in the racing year which statesmen, philosophers, poets, essayists and littérateurs desire to see once in their lives.—The London Field, May 29, 1886.

During the last twenty years the average time of the Derby, one and a half miles, is 2 min. 48 sec., or a mile in 1 min. 52 sec., the horses carrying 122 pounds.—The Badminton Library: Racing and Steeplechasing, Arthur Coventry and A. E. T. Watson.

The horses were brought out, smooth, shining, fine-drawn, frisky, spirit stirring to look upon —most beautiful of all the bay horse Ormonde. who could hardly be restrained, such was his eagerness for action. The horses disappear in the distance. They are off, not yet distinguishable, at least to me. A little waiting time, and they swim into our ken, but in what order of precedence it is as yet not easy to say. Here they come! Two horses have emerged from the ruck, and are sweeping, rushing, storming, towards us, almost side by side. One slides by the other, half a length, a length, a length and a half. Those are Archer's colors, and the beautiful bay Ormonde flashes by the line, winner of the Derby of 1886.—Our Hundred Days in Europe, Dr. Oliver Wendell Holmes.

As long as the Derby is run for at Epsom, which, for aught we know, may be to the end of time, so long will Epsom continue to fascinate the public, and people will flock to the Downs in the hope, or on the pretence, of seeing a race which not one man in fifty ever really sees, nor one in twenty cares about seeing.—The Badminton Library: Racing, The Earl of Suffolk and Berkshire, and W. G. Craven.

Description. An identification. All turf rules require an adequate description of every horse entered for any race, purse, or stake, which shall embrace name, color, sex, marks, and other facts required for identification.

Developed; Developing. To bring out; to perfect. It is said of a finished trotting horse that he is developed; the art of training a horse to develop his speed qualities. A horse that is in training is said to be developing; one that is getting his gait is said to be developing fast, or developing well; promising.

Developed Sires. Stallions in service that have been worked, trained and developed for speed, in distinction from those which have not been trained for speed. Upon the correctness of the theory that developed speed in sire and dam is an important factor in the transmission of speed, there are differing opinions. Many hold that the developed sires are not as successful in the stud as those which have never been developed, and instance Electioneer with one hundred and forty-four in the 2:30 list, never developed; and others believe that the complete 2:30 list is the most convincing argument that could be made, of the value of developing the speed qualities of horses from which it is intended to produce trotters.

Devices, of various kinds for the harness, stable, horse, and general business of the turf, have greatly multiplied of late, the finer and nicer work required in all departments demanding the use of a larger number of implements, contrivances, and equipments. Such as are of most value, not mentioned in other parts of this work under their proper heading, are named— *For the Harness:* Check rein holders for holding the check rein in place in the water hook, of various patterns; rein-snap or snap-hook for holding the reins in place; covering of fine lamb's wool, canvas lined, for applying to harness to prevent chafing. *For the Horse:* Elastic appliances of various kinds, as, hock compress or truss for blood spavin, fetlock support for colts with weak legs, shin brace, stockings, pastern brace, to prevent knuckling, curb compress; shoe pad of rubber and cork, held in place by a spring; calk cover, to be placed over the shoe when the horse is in the stable; ice creepers, adjustable, for preventing horses from slipping on icy roads; hoof expanders, for corns, contracted feet and quarter cracks; hoof pad springs, for holding in place felt packing upon the sole of the foot; double crupper, placed under or within the ordinary crupper for adjusting the position of the tail, so that a span may carry their tails uniformly when in harness; open saddle, for use in case of sore backs caused by saddle gall; supports and shields for stallions; anti-snowball pad for inserting in the shoe to prevent balling; rubber head bumpers, to be worn by the horse when being transported by rail, to prevent injury; bone and rubber rattles to prevent interfering. Simple and common stable equipments, the use of which is obvious, do not require mention. Devices for the track like jockey boards, score boards, electric bells, dials announcing successive races, boxes, electrical chronometers, etc., are generally described under their respective headings.

Diagonal Gait. The trot. The order of movement in the trot is: Left fore foot, right hind foot, right fore foot, left hind foot. Thus, the left fore and right hind foot move in unison, striking the ground together; then, in turn, right fore foot and left hind foot complete the revolution, and, therefore, the trot is most properly called the diagonal gait.

Diastema. The toothless interval in the lower jaw between the corner incisors and the molar teeth behind, called the bar, and upon which the bit rests. It is an interesting fact in zoological science that in the most primitive condition of dentition of the horse, there appears to have been no such interval, all the teeth having been in contact.

Diomed. First winner of the Derby. By Florizel; dam, by Spectator. He was no less celebrated as a sire than as a racer. He left famous stock in England, and when 22 years old was imported into Virginia where he laid the foundation for the best running stock in the South. Among his famous get in that State were: Sir Archy, Florizel, Potomac, Top Gallant, Peace Maker, Hamlinton and Duroc.

Directum. Black colt, foaled in 1889; by Director, 2:17, by Dictator; dam, Stem Winder, 2:31, by Venture. Holding the World's record for a four year old to the end of 1893, (race record), Nashville, Tenn., October 18, 1893, 2:05¼.

Dis. When occurring in a summary indicates that the horse against whose name it is placed was distanced in the heat where it occurs.

Disguising. Turf law inflicts expulsion from all tracks controlled by members, upon any person guilty of painting or disguising any horse to represent another or different horse, when entered for a race. Many states also have severe laws against the same. See Law.

Dismounting. By the trotting rules no driver can dismount at the close of a heat, or leave his sulky, without permission of the judges, and those deficient in bodily weight shall be re-weighed after each heat. During any delay in starting a race, occasioned by accident to any rider or his equipment, jockeys may dismount and give up their horses to an attendant; but at the close cannot dismount without permission of the judge.

Dismounting. [Eq.] In dismounting from the saddle, take hold of the mane of the horse and pommel of the saddle as in mounting. Bear the weight upon the straightened arms as the right leg is brought over the left side; hold the body for an instant in a position perpendicular to the side of the horse, the whole weight being supported by the arms, and drop gently to the ground at the shoulder of the horse. In dismounting when the horse is in motion, avoid the momentary rest as the leg is brought over the left side, and striking the ground prepared to take a few steps with the horse, whether at the gallop or trot, after which release the hold upon the mane and pommel of the saddle.

Disqualified. By the rules of the Turf Congress when a horse is disqualified, every other horse belonging wholly or in part to the same owner, is also disqualified; and if any transfer is made for the purpose of avoiding payment of forfeit orders or any disqualification, the person making and receiving such transfers may be fined or ruled off.

Distal Phalanx. The coffin bone.

Distance. The space measured back from the winning post or judges' stand which a horse, in heat-races, must have reached when the winning horse has covered the whole course, in order to be entitled to enter subsequent heats. By the rules of the trotting turf distances are: Races of mile heats, eighty yards; races of two mile heats, one hundred and fifty yards; races of three mile heats, two hundred and twenty yards; mile heats, best three in five, one hundred yards; heats of not over one mile, in which eight or more horses start, distance is to be increased one half, unless otherwise stated in the conditions of the race. In a fairly trotted heat, when there is no question as to the placing of horses, those whose heads have not reached the distance stand or post as soon as the leading horse arrives at the wire, are declared to be distanced. All horses distanced in the first heat are equal. If a heat has been won by a protested horse the judges are to waive the application of a distance as to all other horses except for fouls; and judges may waive distance, (except for fouls), to any horse for which they have substituted a rider or driver; also, in case of a dead heat, judges may waive the application of the distance rule. A horse distancing the field in one heat, closes the race and is entitled to the entire purse, stake or premium, unless otherwise stated. The American Turf Congress recognizes the following distances: In heats of three-quarters of a mile, twenty-five yards; one mile, thirty yards; two miles, seventy yards; three miles, sixty yards; four miles, seventy yards. In the deciding heat there is no distance.

Distanced. To be distanced in a heat or race, is to have no place. A horse which fails to reach the distance-post or stand before the heat has been won, or whose driver or rider is adjudged to have made certain specified errors, is regarded as distanced.

Distance Flag. The flag in the hands of the distance judge, the falling of which, as the winning horse reaches the wire, is the signal that horses which have not reached the distance post are shut out.

Distanced Horse. A distanced horse is out of the race, having no place.

Distance Judge. A person appointed by the judges to remain in the distance stand, or at the distance post during a heat or race, and, at the close, report to them the horse or horses that are behind the flag, and all foul or improper conduct, if any has occurred under his observation.

Distance Post; Distance Stand. The stand or post at the end of the distance.

Dock. The solid part of the horse's tail; the crupper of a saddle.

Docking. The act of cutting off or clipping the horse's tail, an operation which the dictates of fashion have caused to be inflicted, periodically, for the past two hundred years; the length of the dock or stump being a matter of mere caprice.

Dog. A mean horse; a quitter.

Domino. A phenomenal young thoroughbred racehorse, known as "the unbeaten." Bred by B. G. Thomas, Lexington, Ky. Foaled in 1890. By Himyar; dam, Mamie Gray, by Enquirer. Morris Park, September 29, 1893, won the Matron Stakes, six furlongs, carrying 128 pounds, in 1:09, the fastest time on record. Ilis winnings as a four-year old in 1893, were $176.730, no other American horse ever having won anything nearly approaching this sum in a single season.

Doncaster. In the West Riding of York, England, on the river Don. The seat of the great race-course which has a magnificent grand stand, and also a splendid noblemen's stand. Races were established here in 1703, and the St Leger, for three-year-olds, established by Col. St. Leger, is run in September of each year.

Doping. Drugging; from dope, any thick liquid. When a horse is said to have been doped, the inference is that he has been drugged or tampered with. It is punishable by severe penalties.

Double-bridle. A bridle with two bits, two headstalls and two reins, same as the bit and bridoon.

Double-gaited. A horse which, in motion, both trots and paces is said to be double-gaited. In general this change is made without apparent effort, but it is noticeable that when a horse changes from a trot to a pace he squats a few inches— some drivers assert from three to four inches—traveling closer to the ground, the back being perfectly level. The usual changes in gait are these: In starting from a walk the horse ambles, or goes at a slow pace, and in passing from this to a pace he usually consumes ten or a dozen steps in shuffling, skipping, hopping, before the settled pace is caught. In changing from a pace to a trot but two or three shuffling steps are required. The formula is this: It is easy for a horse to go from a trot to a pace; difficult to go from the amble to the trot, and hard to go from the pace to the trot.

Give Gus Glidden one of those double-gaited, shifty, pacing horses that are occasionally met with, and he could come nearer straightening him out and making him go on a straight trot, in less time than any man I ever saw.—Life with the Trotters, John Splan.

Double-harness. A harness for a span of horses driven abreast. Each one is usually lighter than a single harness, and contains nearly the same number of pieces, although in that intended for light carriage use the breeching or hold-back straps are discontinued.

Double-jointed Snaffle. A bit similar to the double-barred or Pantograph snaffle, intended for hard pullers, being a compromise between the single-jointed snaffle and the bar bit.

Double-pocket. A disadvantageous position for a horse in a heat, which may be the result of circumstances, or in part that of design. As an example: A horse may have the pole and another lapped on his outside wheel; when a third horse may come up behind the one at the pole and yet a fourth immediately lap on his outside. Hence the horse behind the leading pole horse would be in a "double pocket" with little chance of getting out, although he might have more speed than either of the others. See POCKET.

Double-reined Bridle. A bridle with a single bit and two reins, like the Pelham, having one bit, one headstall, and two reins.

Double-ringed Snaffle. A bit that may be used for horses which bore to one side, or which have at times to be turned very sharply.

Double-team, World's Record. To wagon, to the close of 1893: One mile — Belle Hamlin and Honest George, Providence, R. I., September 23, 1892, 2:12¼; in a race, one mile—Maxy Cobb and Neta Medium, Chicago, Ill., September 25, 1885, 2:18¼.

Down in the Dirt. When a horse that has been running or trotting badly suddenly recovers his form and improves all at once, the prophets who said he was a quitter, and those who layed on his opponents, are "down in the dirt," or floored.

Drawgate. The gate from the stables to the course, through which the horses in a race go upon the track.

Drawing. A term relating to feeding a horse for a race, but one having two meanings in this connection. It refers to the act of reducing the quantity of hay fed, or "drawing" away a portion of the regular ration. Mr. Splan, in telling how he fed one of his horses for a race, says: "She would get a light feed of hay after her work, and that was all the drawing I found necessary in her case." It also refers to the drawing up or reducing the size of the abdomen in order that the horse may not be cumbered with unnecessary bulk.

I am not in favor of drawing a horse as closely as many do, who, I think, err in making their restrictions too severe. There is a point to be reached in this preparation which it should be our aim to observe, viz.: That the stomach should not be encumbered, and yet the nourishment afforded by the food be sufficient to carry a horse through a race in which he would weaken unless the supply was adequate to meet the demands.—Joseph Cairn Simpson.

Drawing for Positions. When the horses are out the drawing for positions usually takes place in this manner: One judge with a pencil in hand, so that no one else can see, points to the name of a horse in the list of entries, and, with his back to another judge, asks, "What position shall this horse have?" The other replies, "second," "sixth," or any other number; and this goes on until all are drawn — number one having drawn the pole, and the highest number the outside place.

Drawn. A horse taken from a race after having been entered, is said to have been drawn; not a starter. But no horse can be drawn except by permission of the judges unless at or before 7 o'clock P. M., of the day preceding the race. By the old rules it had the same force as distanced.

Dress of Jockeys. The racing rules require that all riders must be dressed in proper costume — cap and jacket of silk or satin, white or colored breeches and top boots.

Dressed Mouth. A dressed mouth is one in which the tables or surface of the teeth have been filed down or bishoped, often for the purpose of complicating the determination of age.

Dressing. The scraping, cleaning, drying, bandaging, and blanketing of a horse after a race, or after a day's hunt or work, is called "dressing." The average time required is an hour and a half to each horse.

Dressing a Track. Fitting the surface for a heat or race by means of a light, fine harrow, float or brush.

Dressing Harrow. A wide harrow having sharp, fine teeth, adjustable in length, for the purpose of finishing the surface of a track.

Drive Him Out of It. A term used in training where the horse trots with his fore legs and at the same time runs behind. To balance such a horse, trainers recommend the use of light shoes behind, with heavier ones forward, and possibly a four ounce toe-weight. Drive at first at half speed, increasing it gradually. Radical treatment is to use spreaders and send the horse out brisk — in other words, "drive him out of it."

Drive Him Over Himself. To force a horse off his gait.

Driver. One who drives a race in a sulky, in distinction from one who rides a race in the saddle.

Driving Bit. The watering bit. An ordinary bridoon with rings, used with cart, car, truck, wagon, plow; and cavalry regulation bit. A bit, mild and harmless in general application.

Driving Rein. A rein in which the hand part consists of two strips or pieces instead of one; between which leather hand-loops are stitched at convenient distances apart ranging from six to ten inches, to meet the requirements of different kinds of service.

Dr'n. In a summary of the race, these letters mean that the horse against which name they are placed, was drawn from the race in the heat in which they appear.

Dropped Heat. Practically the same as a heat laid up, with this difference: The rules allow a heat to be laid up by permission of the judges upon having it announced from the stand, while a heat is often dropped to favor a fraud and not known to any but the parties interested. Thus a horse may ask permission to lay up a heat in order that he may be able to win the deciding heat of a hard race, while a horse able to win in straight heats may drop one to some other horse in order to insure him second money.

Dropping Anchor. [Eng.] Keeping back a horse in a race, or voluntarily losing it.

On the other hand, on remarking upon the mild way of riding, the visitor will, probably, be met with the retort, that if the jockeys did not flog their animals unmercifully, they would be accused of what is here termed in racing slang, "dropping the anchor." — Sporting Times.

No trainer of experience will attempt to deny the impossibility of detecting by ocular observation, whether the jockey whom he employs "drops anchor" or does his best to win a race.—The Badminton Library: Racing. The Earl of Suffolk and Berkshire, and W. G. Craven.

Dropping Behind. Knuckling or dropping behind with the pastern joint or joints, is caused by what is known as chinked or broken back; and is in all cases an unsoundness.

Dropsy. A distended, bulky stomach is too often an indication of dropsy, in which case the horse is unsound.

Ds. Small, semi-circular metal hoops which are attached by chafes, (short leather straps), to the front or back of the saddle for strapping on a coat, small case, or other personal effects.

Dumb Jockey. A device made of whalebone, gutta-percha, leather and rubber springs used in bitting and training colts. It consists of a saddle fastened by a belly girth, two arms extending upward from the saddle to which the ends of the reins and crupper strap are attached, the side checks being fastened to the lower part of the saddle on each side; the reins and straps being elastic and adjustable. There are various patterns.

D. V. S. Doctor of veterinary surgery.

Dwell. [Eng.] A short stop made by a horse at a fence before taking it; not refusing and bolting sidewise, but the act of considering. It is a fault in a chaser, as horses must fly to their fences and get away from them immediately.

Dwell; Dwelling Behind. When a horse has that faulty or erratic action in the hind members which is best described as being both too long and slow, he is said to " dwell behind."

E

Ears. The ears of the horse are expressive of many feelings, convey pleasure and pain as well as anger, and afford an excellent index of mind and health. The command which the horse has over them is marvelous. They can be thrown forward or backward at will. One can be thrown back to hear in the rear, while the other is thrown forward as the horse sees and hears in front. The normal position of the ear when the horse is inactive, is thrown backwards, but when he is at work it varies with conditions. When expecting orders it is vertical; when the horse is cross it drops back low; when listening or looking to the front it is thrown forward; when he is asleep one ear is always pointed to the front. When the saddle horse is in action he listens attentively to the least sound of his rider's voice, which he expects to hear, and by giving him the habit of listening to and obeying the voice, the use of the bit is reduced to the minimum.

The ear which has most admirers is the one which is composed of a mere shell of gristle enveloped in a layer of thin skin, which should be clothed with a coat of fine hair, that may, however, be somewhat meager on the inner surface, especially in the summer season. In shape it should taper from the base to a rather sharp point at the tip. Experience in selecting horses has led us to observe the movements of the ear with much care, and regard them to some extent as the index to the animal's character, for they not only indicate a well-balanced disposition, a vicious or sluggish horse, as the case may be, but they point to defective eyesight, or even total blindness, in which case the ever restless ear will be thrown first in one direction and then in another.—E. A. A. Grange, V. S., Michigan State College Experiment Station.

Easy Bit. [Eq.] In equestrianism what is termed an easy bit is the best for a horse, because, while a severe bit ought to enable him to do well and prevent him from doing ill, instead it often causes a severe restraint upon the natural action of the horse.

An easy bit is the best one by which to control the horse, and next to this a skillful hand—for the bit is the hand, and a good hand is the whole of the rider.—New Method of Horsemanship, F. Baucher.

Eclipse. The most celebrated horse in the annals of the turf. Bred by the Duke of Cumberland. Foaled April 1, 1764, the day on which occured the remarkable eclipse of the sun, from which event his name was given. By Mask, by Squirt, by Bartlett's Childers, by the Darley Arabian; dam, Spiletta, by Regulus, by the Godolphin Arabian. He was

80

chestnut in color, with a white blaze down his face and his off hind leg was white from his hock downwards. He had black spots upon his rump, a peculiarity said to be seen in his male descent to the present day. The very great size, obliquity and lowness of his shoulders were the objects of general remark; with the shortness of his fore quarters, his ample and finely proportioned hind quarters and the swelling muscles of his forearm and thigh. He was 15.1 hands high. His shoulders were so thick that, according to the observation of his time, a firkin of butter might have rested upon them; while he stood very high behind—a conformation suited to his great power of progression. Of his speed, no correct estimate can be formed, for he never met with an opponent sufficiently fleet to put it to the test. He was what is termed a "thick winded horse," and puffed and roared so as to be heard at a considerable distance. For this, or some other cause, he was not brought upon the turf till he was five years old. He run his first race at Epsom, May 3, 1769. In 1770 he beat Mr. Wentworth's Bucephalus, which had never before been conquered. Two days afterwards he distanced Mr. Strode's Pensioner, a very good horse; and in August of the same year he won the great subscription at York. No horse daring to enter against him, he closed his short turf career of seventeen months, by walking over the Newmarket course for the King's plate, on October 18, 1770, having run or walked over eighteen courses. He was never beaten, nor ever paid forfeit, and won for his owners over £25,000. Leaving the turf he entered the stud where his career was equally remarkable. He produced the extraordinary number of three hundred and thirty-four winners, which netted to their owners more than £160,000 exclusive of plates and cups. He died in February, 1789, at the age of 25 years. His heart weighed 14 pounds, which is said to have accounted for his wonderful spirit and courage.

In the language of honest John Lawrence, he "puffed and blowed like an otter, and galloped as wide as a barn-door." No sooner were his powers exhibited on the turf than every eye was set to scrutinize his form and he was then admitted to possess in perfection the external characters indicative of great speed. A volume was written on his proportions by M. Saintbel, a veterinary surgeon, whose investigations showed that his figure differed greatly from the conventional form which speculative writers had assigned as the standard of perfection. He was of an indomitable temper, and his jockeys found it in vain to attempt to hold him, but contented themselves with remaining still in the saddle while he swept along, his nose almost touching the ground. The fleetest horses of his time could not keep by his side for fifty yards together.—Domesticated Animals of Great Britain, Prof. David Low.

Mr. John Lawrence says his first race in 1769 aroused the curiosity of some persons who attempted to watch his trial. In his language: "They were too late, but they found an old woman who gave them all the information they wanted. On inquiring whether she had seen a race, she replied that she could not tell whether it was a race or not, but that she had just seen a horse with white legs running away at a monstrous rate, and another horse a great way behind, trying to run after him; but she was sure he never would catch the white legged horse, if he run to the world's end."—History of the Horse, London, 1831.

Edge. A horse is said to be on edge, when he is in splendid condition, and, after proper training, is eager for a race.

Elbow. A portion of the forearm; the large bony projection at the upper and front portion of the forearm.

Electioneer, 125. The great sire of trotters. Bred by Charles Backman, Stony Ford, N. Y. Foaled May 2, 1868. Bay; stout, and compactly built, standing 15.2½. By Rysdyk's Hambletonian; dam, Green Mountain Maid, by Harry Clay, 2:29. He was never trained, but as a three-year-old trotted in 2:42 with no fitting, and could trot in 2:23 or better, and for an eighth of a mile any day go at a 2:20 gait. His head was well proportioned, of fair size, and a model of great intelligence. He had good shoulders, splendid barrel, faultless back, and, says Charles Marvin, "simply the best quarters I ever saw on a stallion, possessing the perfection of driving power." His forearms and gaskins were heavily muscled, his joints clean and sound, and his legs and feet of first-class quality. He combined great power, elegant proportion and fine finish at every point. He died at Palo Alto, California, in 1890, the property of the late Leland Stanford. He stands at the head of all sires of 2:10 trotting speed, and, at the close of 1893 had one hundred and forty-four trotters and one pacer in the list of 2:30 performers.

Electric Chronometer. A device invented by Ritter Von Stockert of Vienna, Austria, which notes on regular telegram slips the speed shown by each horse in a field, to one-tenth of a second. It is set going as the word is given, and one person alone can control it and record the speed of each horse engaged in the race.

Electrical Appliances. The American racing rules punish by severe penalties the use of "drugs, electrical or mechanical appliances," or other means than the whip and spur for the purpose of stimulating the endurance or speed of a horse in a race.

Eligible. The American and National rules provide that a horse is not entitled to start in any race that has beaten the time advertised prior to the closing of the entries for the race in which he is nominated. A fraction is not a bar—that is to say, a horse having made a record of 2:29 and a fraction, is eligible to enter in the 2:30 class.

Elliott's Electrical Chronograph. A device for noting and registering the speed of horses in a race. It consists of a face seven feet high by sixteen feet long, having in the center a dial seven feet in diameter. On either end are indicators which show the number of the race, number of the heat and number of the winning horse; also the numbers of the horses occupying second, third and fourth places. On the other end is an indicator showing the time made to the quarter, half, and three-quarters, also the finish, in figures eight inches long, the time being given in sixtieths of a second. Upon the dial are three pointers—one revolving once in five minutes, another revolving every minute, and a third revolving once per second, and stopping on the sixtieth, as the dial is divided. The starting, indicating of the quarters of the course, and the stopping, is done by pressing buttons arranged on a small cabinet to be placed in the judges' stand or any convenient locality. As the connection is made by electricity, the distance or location of either the chronograph or buttons is a matter of no moment; only that the machine should be placed where the dial may be seen by the greatest number of persons interested in the race. The quarters, or any intermediate time, is taken without affecting the operation of the chronograph, by means of electrotyped dials having figures from one to sixty. Arranged alongside of these dials or discs is an inking ribbon and strip of paper. The pressing of the button by the timer strikes the electric hammer upon this paper, and by means of the inking ribbon the number of seconds or sixtieths of a second at that instant are recorded upon the strip of paper. The finishes are also recorded in the same way, in addition to the record which is made by the large dial outside; so that at the close of a day's racing the finish of every mile, half, three-quarters, and quarter of a mile, are accurately recorded upon the strips of paper, which may be kept for future reference. The device has a roof and sides of canvas to protect the operator and machinery from the weather, and its entire weight is 950 pounds.

Enamel. A texture of remarkable hardness forming the real protecting covering of the teeth, although laying under the cement or thin superficial covering. It is said to be of such extreme hardness that it will strike fire from flint. It resists decay longer than the dentine, or larger part of the tooth, and is always found in relief, or raised, on the surface of the table of the tooth.

Engagement. The appointment or nomination for a race; an entry. By all the turf rules the seller of a horse sold with his engagements, has not the power of striking him out. When a horse is sold with his engagements all penalties thereafter growing out of such engagements attach to the horse and his purchaser or purchasers.

Enlarged Joints; Soft Enlargements. Soft enlargements during their formation, and until their result is ascertained, render a horse unsound. But if, upon being fully developed, they do not impede the horse in his ordinary work, he is sound; but when they are so large as to be unsightly, they are blemishes.

Entrance Fee. A percentage of the premium or purse which is paid by the owner of a horse when entering him for a particular race, stake, or purse. The system was devised by John Trail of Shrewsbury, England, who is known as "father of the clerk of the courses." All entrance fees must be paid before a horse can become a starter, and horses and owners or drivers may be suspended for non-payment of entrance dues.

Entries. By the trotting rules entries may be made in writing, or by telegraph or telephone, and must be received before the advertised hour of the closing of entries, and all entries constitute an agreement "that the persons making them, owners, drivers, and horses" shall be subject to the rules, regulations, and by-laws of the association. The racing laws provide that on being entered a horse shall be named and identified, and after having started in a public race his name shall not be changed; and no alteration or condition shall be made in any entry after the time fixed for closing. Persons making entries become liable for the entrance money, stake, or forfeit; and every horse entered for a purse must start unless declared out. Entries and subscriptions do not become void on the death of the parties making them.

Epsom Downs. A mile and a half south of the town of Epsom, county of Surrey, England, where races lasting four days are run each year. Epsom is fourteen miles from London. The races were begun here about 1711, by Mr. Parkhurst, and have been held annually since 1730.

Equestrian. [Eq.] Relating or pertaining to horses, horsemanship, or saddle riding; consisting in or accompanied with performances on horseback; exercising or mounted on horseback.

Equestrian Feats. English turf history records the following interesting events: In 1758, Miss Pond undertook to ride one thousand miles at Newmarket, in one thousand hours, for a purse of two hundred guineas; which feat she performed in less than one-half the time. In 1759, Jennison Shafts rode fifty miles in one hour, forty-nine minutes, using ten horses. In 1761, Mr. Woodcock rode one hundred miles a day for twenty-nine days, using fourteen horses. In 1786, Mr. Hull's horse, Quibbler, ran twenty-three miles in fifty-seven minutes, ten seconds.

Equidæ. Latin for the horse family; *Equus caballus*, Latin for the horse. See HORSE.

Equilibrium. [Eq.] The perfect balance of the horse when under the saddle. Upon this depends his prompt, graceful and regular action. In equilibrium the weight of the rider and the forces of the horse are equally distributed. By means of this just distribution the different positions, the different paces, and the equilibriums that belong to them, are obtained without effort on the part of rider or horse.

Equine. Pertaining to the horse, or belonging to the horse kind.

Equine Bicycle. An equine bicycle was described in the papers in May, 1891, as having been invented by T. W. Moore, of New York. "It is made of steel tubing, like ordinary bicycles, and has similar wheels with ball bearings, rubber tires, etc., and is lighter than a sulky. The sliding of the sulky wheels on the curves of the track is overcome by the new sulky, in which the point of contact with the ground is in a line with the center of the propelling power. There is no side motion, and the driver is not obliged to lean toward the inside in going round a curve to balance the vehicle, for there is no side swing."

Ergot; Spurs. Natural structural growths of soft horn located behind and below the pastern joint, and generally concealed under the tuft of hair on the fetlock. In fine bred horses this growth is comparatively slight; in heavy, coarse ones it is very thick, often extending up the shank and giving origin to what is known as "feathers" in some breeds of horses. Dr. W. H. Flower believes that both by structure and position they are similar to the callosities on the palm of the human hand.

Erratic Gait. Any wrong, incorrect, or unnatural gait or action in a horse at motion, such as running behind and trotting in front; paddling; hitching; crossing, etc.

Event. A fixed date which arrives; an appointment that occurs; a trotting meeting. In the United States there is really no fixed national event excepting the Futurity and Real ization stakes.

Evolution of the Trotter. If evolution may be regarded as "the process of evolving or becoming developed, an unfolding or a growth," the word may not inaptly be used to express the development of the American trotter during the past half century. The accompanying table, compiled from the most accurate sources, will show at a glance the successive stages in this evolution of the 2:30 trotter:

Year.	Number of Horses with 2:30 or Better.
1844,	1
1850,	5
1860,	34
1870,	181
1880,	1,190
1890,	4,674
1894,	10,000

Exhibition Mile. A display of speed or action shown by a horse at a meeting, usually between heats of a regular race.

Expulsion. By the trotting law expulsion is construed to mean "unconditional exclusion and disqualification from any participation, either directly or indirectly, in the privileges and uses of the course and grounds of a member." It may be imposed for attempting to make fraudulent entries; allowing use of a member's track by an expelled person or horse; refusing to afford information; tampering with a horse; pulling; helping; breech of decorum or other just cause. All persons expelled for fraud from the trotting turf, stand, also, as expelled by all tracks under control of the Turf, or Racing Congress.

Extend. When a horse is put to his speed, and opens out freely, he is said to extend. Explained by the quotations:

" Well booted, the horse is not afraid of hitting himself when extended or put to his speed."
" Some horses will not extend themselves unless the rider has spurs on."
The complaint that a horse "can't extend himself" generally applies to a horse that can trot in about three minutes.—Wallace's Monthly.

Extension. A term commonly applied to all muscles whose action is to enlarge the angles and by so doing elongate the limbs—but their extension may be forward when the foot is in the air, or backward when the foot is on the ground.

Extreme Speed. The utmost limit of a horse's endurance at motion; the greatest effort of which a horse is capable. The extreme speed of the trotter previous to 1820 was at 2:50 to the mile in harness. In 1829, Topgallant went three miles in 8:11; in 1834, the gelding, Edwin Forrest went a mile under saddle in 2:31½; in 1839, Drover paced a mile in 2:28; in 1844, Lady Suffolk trotted under saddle in 2:26½; in 1844, Unknown paced to wagon in 2:23. In the next decade (1854), Flora Temple trotted in 2:19¾, and in the same decade the marvelous pacing mare, (for her time), Pocahontas, went the mile to wagon in 2:17½. The stars of the following decade, (1864), were: Dexter 2:17¾, and Lady Thorne, 2:18¼. In the next period, (1874), Goldsmith Maid 2:14: Hopeful, 2:14¾; Rarus, 2:13¼, and Lula, 2:14¾, represented the limits of trotting speed. In 1879, St. Julian trotted in 2:12¾, but reached his limit, 2:11¼, in 1880. In 1884, Jay-Eye-See trotted the mile in 2:10; and in 1885, Maud S. trotted in 2:08¾, which last was the best time in 1893, to the high-wheel sulky. In 1892 Nancy Hanks made the mile in 2:04; in the same year Mascot paced the mile in the same time, and in 1893 Flying Jib and Algona both paced the mile in 2:04, both against time.

Eye. One of the most beautiful organs of the horse and one giving a great insight into his disposition and character. It should be clear, the pupil black, the eyelids thin and comparatively free from wrinkles. A small eye is usually regarded as indicating a sulky disposition, or one wanting in courage, and is called a "pig-eye." Horses which show a good deal of white in their eyes are almost invariably vicious in temper. It has long been observed that before a kicker makes ready to "let fly" behind, he uncovers a portion of the white of the eye —on the side to which the head is inclined. In normal condition the eye of the horse usually shows but little of the white, except when it turns its head to the rear or inwards. The presence of deep hollows above the eyes is a defect, as it denotes that the horse is old and more or less worn out; or that either its sire or dam was well advanced in years when it was bred—hence such a mark indicates that the horse is somewhat wanting in vigor. It is thought by some that a reddish color to the white of the eye denotes a hardy constitution and staying power. When there is an absence of coloring matter to the eye, it is known as a wall or watch eye.

[Law.] Any disease of the eye, even from the slightest cold or inflammation, until it is completely cured, or until it has terminated in total blindness, stamps the animal as unsound. But while in some cases it has been decided that total blindness which does not unfit for work is only a blemish; in others, as in case of race horses, blindness is classed as an unsoundness.

The great index of character is the eye, and if this be dull, or give fitful flashes of animation in the excitement of coming on to the track, the horse will surely not be able to do what he ought to do. I never saw a horse that the brilliancy of the eye was not heightened by proper training. It may not show as much briskness, as there is a placid look acquired which might deceive you at the first glance; but as you look again, there is no glossy, unmeaning stare, and you look down into the clear depths till you cannot but resolve that such an organ must belong to more than an animal, and that it is a token of a being endowed with that reason which we haughtily arrogate as only belonging to man. When the horse is led up to start in a race, this placid look is changed to one as determined as ever flashed from beneath the brow of ancient knight attempting deeds that would either heighten his renown to that of the great Arthur himself, or consign him to an honorable grave. A fuming, fretty horse, that rears, and pitches, and refuses to come to the score when the time to start has been signaled, has rarely the look I have attempted to describe. He is either frightened at the remembrance of unmerited punishment, or is so sore from over or injudicious work, that he does not like to start.—Horse Portraiture, Joseph Cairn Simpson.

The eye is frequently regarded as the index of the animal's character, but I have been deceived so often by both kinds, the wild as well as the sulky looking, that I am now disposed to think it often over-estimated as a guide to future performances.—Dr. E. A. A. Grange, V. S., Michigan State College Experiment Station.

F

Face. That part of the front of the horse's head from the eyes to the nostrils.

Face of the Track. The surface of a track is called its face.

Facing the Flag. Said of the horses in a running race when they come up for a start, as in the expression, "as fine a field as ever faced the flag."

False Quarter. A lesion of the foot similar to sandcrack in appearance, but caused by an interruption of the secreting process at the top of the hoof, which causes it to become soft and spongy; a defect in the outer wall of the hoof. It is legal unsoundness.

Fancy Match. A cross match pair or span of horses, where no attention is paid to having them of the same color; as, black and white, or bay and chestnut, according to the individual fancy of the owner.

Farcy. Glanders. The two are one and the same disease, differing only in that glanders is applied to the disease when the local lesions predominate in the internal organs, especially in the lungs and air tubes; and that farcy is the term applied to the disease when the principal manifestation is an outbreak of the lesions on the exterior or skin of the animal. It is legal unsoundness. See GLANDERS.

Far Turn. The turn on the back stretch of the course.

Farrier. A word derived from the Latin *Ferrum*, meaning iron; hence a worker in iron; a smith who combines the art of horseshoeing with that of the veterinary profession. When the term was first applied it was a title of distinction, for very few had the skill necessary to be a successful farrier. It was a valuable gift, especially when the horse was so invaluable and necessary an adjunct of war, and in those early days the gift was confined in certain families the members of which were royal favorites. It is said the noble earls of Ferrier or Ferrers had such an origin.

Fashion. A famous racing mare of the early American turf. Bred by William Gibbons, Madison, N. Y. Foaled, April 26, 1837. By imported Trustee, by Catton; dam,

Bonnets o' Blue, by Sir Charles out of Reality, by Sir Archy. Chestnut, with star, 15.2 hands high. Fine in every point with a wonderful muscular development. She defeated Boston in the great race on Union Course, Long Island, N. Y., May 10, 1842, in a match for $20,000 a side; four mile heats—time of first heat 7:32½; second heat, 7:45.

Fashionably Bred. A term which has been rather promiscuously applied to a horse whose ancestors on both sides are of successful producing and prepotent blood, and of such breeding that his services and progeny meet with ready sale at high prices. But such a term is liable to many changes in its application, and often to some disappointment. It possesses little true significance.

Fasig Track. The kite track is often so called from the name of the person who built the first track of this kind in the United States, Mr. William B. Fasig of New York.

Father of the Turf. [Eng.] A term applied to Tregonwell Frampton, Esq., of Moreton, Dorsetshire, England, keeper of the running horses at Newmarket, to their majesties, William III, Queen Anne, George I, and George II. He died March 12, 1727, aged 86 years.

Favorite. The highest selling horse in a race; the horse most likely to win, in the opinion of the talent.

Feather Weight. A feather weight is seventy-five pounds.

Fee. The percentage of a purse paid by the person making an entry in such purse or race. The amount varies according to the rules. On the running turf, the fee to a jockey in all races not exceeding $500 to the winning horse, is $5 for a losing mount, and $15 for a winning mount; and in all other races in the absence of a special agreement, $10 for a losing mount, and $25 for a winning mount—this rule applying only to licensed jockeys.

Felloe. The outside circle of a wheel, of wood, or iron, around which the tire is fixed, and to the inside of which the spokes of the wheel are fitted. In some sulky wheels they are made of sheet steel, crescent in shape, to receive the tubular pneumatic tire; in others they are of wood, usually hickory.

Felt. A material of which many patterns of horse boots are made. It is an unwoven fabric of wool, short hair, or wool and fur, matted together by pressure, heating, and beating. Its close, inseparable quality is due to the uniting of the serrated edges of the wool fibres with each other, which are then compressed under heat and moisture.

Fencer. [Eng.] A term applied to a horse that has been trained to jumping or taking fences.

Feral. Unbroken. The colt, when untamed, is said to be in his feral state, or condition.

Femur. The thigh bone. In the horse it is comparatively short and stout, and placed very obliquely, the lower end advancing by the side of the body, and being so little detached from it that the knee-joint appears to belong as much to the trunk as to the limb.

Fetlock. The joint which the cannon-bone makes with the pastern; anatomically, the metacarpo-articulation. Fetlock signifies the tuft of hair growing behind the pastern joint, and also the joint itself, and the enlargement made by the bones which form it.

Fetter Bone. The great pastern or first phalangeal bone of the horse's foot, succeeded by the coronary and coffin bone and articulating with the cannon bone at the fetlock joint; the proximal phalanx.

Fettle. Condition; form; in fine order, as, "he is in splendid fettle to-day."

No animal ever came to the post in more superb fettle than Newmarket when he won the St. Leger of 1851.—The Badminton Library: Racing, The Earl of Suffolk and Berkshire, and W. G. Craven.

Field. All the runners or trotters in any race; the horses in a race as opposed to the favorite. To "chop the field" is said of a horse that outstrips the rest, literally beats them.

Field Marshal of Trainers. A term applied to the eminent driver, the late Hiram Woodruff.

Fielders. Those who buy on the field in the pools, against the choicest or favorites.

Fighting the Bit. The action of the horse in training, when dissatisfied with the bit or check, and becoming irritated by them; he is then said to "fight the bit."

Why some horses like an over-check and some a side-check, and why certain bits must be used on certain horses, it is often hard to explain; but the one fact confronting the trainer is that the mouth must be kept right, and the head rigged with check and bit which the horse will not resent and fight, if satisfactory results are to be accomplished.—Training the Trotting Horse, Charles Marvin.

Fighting the Flag. A horse is said to be fighting the flag which is trying by hard work to save his distance; that is, to get within the distance post before the flag drops.

Fileree. The common or trivial name in California for a plant known as Alfierilla, erroneously called a "grass." It grows rank and horses are very fond of it. Charles Marvin says: "I consider it far preferable to alfalfa for turf horses." It is the geranium, or *Erodium cicutarium* of botanists.

Filemaker. A celebrated jumping horse owned by Madame Marantette, Mendon, Michigan. He jumped 7 ft., 4½ in., at Taunton, Mass., October 7, 1891, the highest jump ever made over the bars in public in the world. Filemaker stands 17 hands high, weighs 1,370 pounds and in making this jump carried 149 pounds.

Filled Leg. A term applied to an enlarged or swollen leg, and when from any cause a horse has a trouble like this, he is said to *have a leg.* Thus Charles Marvin says: "Smuggler had a leg all through his campaign of 1876."

Filly. A female colt or foal; a young mare.

Find the Seat. [Eq.] This is a term used to express the acquiring of a firm, graceful, and proper seat in horsemanship. An amateur who rides well is said to have "found the seat."

Fine. A penalty or punishment imposed upon a rider, driver, or member, for a violation of rules. All fines are required to be paid on the day when imposed or when demanded, and are paid to the managers of the track, or member of the associations on whose grounds they were imposed, and by them paid to the National or American Association. Fines imposed by either association are recognized and enforced by the other, the same as though originally imposed by it. Fines paid to the American Turf Congress are held as a fund for the benefit of sick, superannuated, or injured trainers and jockeys in good standing in the Congress.

Finish. The end of a heat or race. The finish is the most vital point of a race, and it is here that the driver should display his best judgment. The attention should never, even for an instant, be diverted from his horse, as inattention to the horse at the finish has lost many a race.

Finished. Used to describe a horse of fine form and condition, as perfect in every respect; symmetrical; without fault; well finished.

Firing Iron; Cautery Iron. An instrument with which veterinary surgeons perform the act of cauterizing for sprains, wind-puffs, spavins, injured tendons, etc. The usual forms are line, point and needle surfaces — the former being used for superficial, and the latter for pyropuncture, or internal cauterizing. In the last named the needle attached to the iron is of platinum, nine-sixteenths of an inch long; and of the former there are various patterns. Internal or needle cauterizing is of quite recent introduction, although surface firing is one of the oldest arts in veterinary practice. Percivall, the father of modern English veterinary science, said of it: "By the firing irons have horses, originally worth their hundreds of pounds sterling, been raised from the knacker's price to their former value. By the iron has many a broken-down hunter, and many a racer, been joyously restored to his station and rank in the field, where his proudest laurels have been won." As to its value in modern practice *The Horseman* says: "Scarcely a string of campaigners goes home in the autumn without one or more of its members requiring a visitation of the firing iron. It is extraordinary that this efficacious adjunct to the veterinarian's kit of tools is not more generally used on the legs of light harness horses. Its benefits are lasting and it should often be resorted to as a preventive as well as a curative measure."

Flag, Dropping the. The signal for the start in all English and most American running races; also in shutting out horses at the distance post.

Flagged Out. The steeple-chase courses from point to finish of a fair hunting country are always flagged out, or indicated by a series or line of flags marking the course to be run.

Flagman. A distance judge.

Flank. That part of the side of the horse which is free from bone and which thinly covers the intestines. Placed between the loins above, the ribs to the front, the thigh and point of the hip to the rear, and the belly below.

Flat. [Eng.] The level part of a course, some parts of which are made on up and down grades.

In a race across the flat Clincher gave six pounds and an easy beating to Compass.—The Badminton Library: Racing, the Earl of Suffolk and Berkshire, and W. G. Craven.

Flat. A term sometimes used in announcing the time in a heat where there is no fraction, as 2:23 *flat*. But so used it is pedantic and has no significance.

Flexor Tendon. A muscle whose function is to bend or produce flexion, as opposed to extensor.

Flight. A single hurdle is called a "flight."

Flighty. Said of a horse that is uncertain and not to be depended upon in a race; unsteady.

Float. A single-cut file for dressing the surface of the teeth. It is usually made adjustable, having a removable file and hinged joint, so that the face of the file will rest on the table of the teeth.

Float; Flote. A light dressing-frame for finishing the face of a track. Usually made in sections twelve feet square, of 3 by 3 joist, the middle bar of which has two rows of sharp, fine teeth. Often three of these floats are attached together, one at the rear and outside of the other; and the float and harrow are often combined in one.

Floating. The act of rasping or filing the horse's teeth to give them a uniform and regular surface. When the teeth become irregular with ragged and sharp edges from uneven wearing, and they begin to cut and lacerate the cheeks on the inside, producing ulceration and inflammation, the horse does not gather or masticate his food properly, and is soon out of condition in consequence. To ascertain this, place the front finger of the right hand inside the horse's upper lip and shove it along his grinders of the upper jaw, and if they appear ragged and sharp on the inside corners, it is an indication that they should be repaired.

Fly-float. One who really knows little or nothing about racing, but who fancies himself thoroughly initiated in all its mysteries.

Fly the Track. When a horse in a race bolts instantly to one side, he is said to "fly the track."

Flyer. A fast horse.

Foal. The young of the horse kind.

Foot. The terminal part of the leg upon which the body rests. While from the standpoint of the comparative anatomist the foot of the horse includes all the leg from the knee and hock down, what is called the foot being in reality the last joint of the toe; from the standpoint of the practical horseman the foot is understood to mean the hoof. Its internal framework consists of the small pastern, or lower end of the coronet bone; the coffin or pedal bone which is within the hoof, and the small sesamoid or navicular bone extending across the back part of the coffin-bone. In the rear of the hoof is the supporting framework known as the elastic cushion or frog. Within this outward box or hoof the union of all the parts of the foot is secured by a series of from five to six hundred minute leaves, (laminæ), a complete fibrous network of secreting surfaces, soft, yielding and tough, the whole forming one of the most wonderful pieces of mechanism found in the whole animal economy. A description of all the parts of the foot will be found under their several names in different parts of this work. The defects of the foot may be severally due to wrong proportions of conformation or axis, and of the quality of the horn. Thus the foot may be too large, too small, too narrow, unequal, it may be flat; full; pumiced; having bunions; and with high, low, or sloping heels; it may be out-bowed; club-foot; cross-foot, or crooked; the foot may be soft; dry; brittle, or have weak heels. The sound, healthy, perfect foot is by far the most important part of the animal, and its care should receive the closest and most intelligent attention.

The unshod foot of a horse on favorable soil and sufficiently exercised, is a type of beauty and perfection. Compared to the foot that has been shod, it is large, strong, as wide as long, and in proper equilibrium—it constitutes a solid support. Viewed in front it is narrower above than below, more expanded externally than internally, and of equal height at its quarters. Viewed in profile, the line of toe has a mean inclination of about fifty degrees for the fore, and sixty degrees for the hind feet; the height of the heels is equal to at least one-half of the height of the toe. Viewed from behind, the heels of the standard foot are well separated, equal, of the same height, and fall vertically to the ground, especially the internal, which is sensibly more vertical than the external. Viewed from below, its sole is hollow and thick, the frog strong, healthy, and quite hard; the bars neither too high, straight, nor too much inclined; the toe and mammæ of the wall and the sole are perceptibly worn from usage. The horn of the sound foot is black or dark gray; the wall smooth and shiny, showing its fibrous structure. Such are the characteristics of the virgin foot. — The Exterior of the Horse, Goubaux and Barrier.

In the manifestation of his strength and the due performance of his useful qualities the horse must rely upon the soundness of his feet, as in them are concentrated the efforts created elsewhere, and on them depend not only the sum total of these propulsive powers being properly expended, but also the solidity and just equilibrium of the whole animal fabric. Hence it is wisely considered that the foot of the horse is the most important part of all the locomotory system; and that all the splendid qualities possessed by the noble creature may be diminished in value or hopelessly lost, if through disease or accident, natural or acquired defects, or other causes, this organ fails to perform its allotted task.—Horse Shoes and Horse Shoeing, George Fleming, LL. D., F. R. C. V. S.

Many persons believe that feet with dark colored horn are stronger and able to stand the wear and tear of hard work better than the light colored ones, but our experience has failed to demonstrate the truth of this idea. The white foot will show the invasion of the part by inflammation more perceptibly, which we think is the cause of disease often being noticed in the white one when a similar complaint would, and often does, pass unnoticed in the dark colored foot.—Dr. E. A. A. Grange, V. S., Michigan Agricultural College Experiment Station.

Foot-board. An adjustable platform which is confined to the rear of a break cart, upon which the driver can step and ride, before he has sufficient confidence in his colt to warrant him in mounting the seat. When not wanted it may be entirely removed.

Foot-scald. An injury caused by paring the sole too close and then shoeing with light, thin shoes, causing tenderness in the foot.

Force. That action between two bodies which changes or tends to change their relative condition as to rest or motion; or which changes any physical relation between them. The power exerted by a horse in motion, whether in drawing a load or in the performance of great speed.

The strongest propulsive force of either of the legs is given with the anterior one in each stride; indeed, it is so strong as to raise the center of gravity several inches above the horizontal line of motion. —The Horse in Motion, J. D. B. Stillman.

If the horse's nose is thrown up in the air it gives him a force of resistance equal to two hundred pounds; this force will be reduced to one hundred pounds when the hand is brought half way towards a perpendicular position; to fifty pounds when brought still nearer that position, and to nothing when perfectly placed. —Method of Horsemanship, F. Baucher.

Forearm. That part of the fore leg between the shoulder and the knee. It is generally conceded that long arms, comparatively speaking, are found in horses of great speed; and countless measurements by experts appear to indicate that in general the length of the arm is greater in the roadster than in the draft horse.

Forehead. The upper part of the face. It extends down to a line joining the inner angle' (canthus), of each eye, and reaches as high as the forelock and base of the ears.

Forehead Band. That part of the bridle which forms the browband or front, and goes across the horse's forehead.

Fore Leg; Fore Limb. The anterior or forward legs of the horse. All the joints of the fore leg from the shoulder downwards are simply hinge-joints, allowing free fore-and-aft flexion and extension, but scarcely any movement in any other direction. Some authorities regard the fore legs as weight-bearers, only; while others believe they have important functions as propellers.

Many have an opinion that the fore legs are merely supporters, like the spokes of a wheel. An English writer asserts that their only functions are to support the center of gravity and keep out of the way of the propellers; the hind legs. But the best authorities say that they are not only supports, but act as propellers in turn, although the anterior ones do the greater share of this work.—The Horse in Motion, J. D. B. Stillman.

Forelock. A tuft of hair which lies between the ears, and is a continuation of the mane. It naturally falls over the forehead between the eyes.

Foreign Horse. A foreign horse is regarded by the rules of the American Turf Congress, as one foaled out of the United States. No such horse can start in any race until proper certificates stating his age, pedigree, color, and other marks by which it may be identified, have been produced by its owner to the satisfaction of the association or racing club.

Forfeits. A forfeit is that to which the right is lost by one's own act or failure to act, or by a breach of conditions. By the trotting law failure to appear in all stakes and matches, refusal to answer protest, fraudulent entry, and collusion to violate published conditions of race, constitute forfeits. Forfeit money is not released by the death of the horse engaged. By the rules of the Turf Congress owners and horses may be suspended for non-payment of forfeits; no horse can start in a race against which a forfeit order is lodged until it is paid, and if any transfer is made for the purpose of avoiding payment of forfeit orders or any disqualification, the person making and receiving such transfers may be fined or ruled off.

Forge; Forging. Overreaching; clicking. The act by which the horse strikes the fore shoe, or heel or quarter of the fore foot, with the toe of the shoe of its hind foot, by reason of the fore feet not being taken up quickly enough when the horse is in motion. It rarely occurs except when the horse is going fast, and is most common with running and trotting horses, generally taking place when the animal breaks from a trot to a run. It is due to defective conformation or faulty shoeing. In the former case the stifle is generally set straight and the toes of their hind feet are inclined inward. To overcome this defect the action in front should be quickened. For this purpose use a scoop-toe rolling-motion shoe forward, beveled on the inside, with most of the weight in the toe, concaving the shoe on the ground surface in order that the hind foot may not strike under the toe when the foot is lifted. By shortening the toe of the fore foot it will be assisted in getting over early, and thus pass out of the way of the hind member. The shoe on the front feet should be short, so as to have as little ground surface as possible.

Forks. The upright guards or supports of the wheel to the pneumatic sulky, which extend from the ends of the axle-cone to the axle of the sulky. In a sulky which has been changed over from a high wheel to a "bike," they form the upright supports connecting the axle-cone of the wheel to the axle-socket of the sulky. With the braces which extend from the lower end of the forks to the thill or shaft, they form the support to the wheel and act as a guard in which the wheel plays.

Form. Condition; spirit; appearance. When it is said that a horse is in fine form it is meant that he is in excellent condition for his work or performance; and loss of the trotting or racing form is due to excessive racing or repeated fast heats. The word form is also used to denote age, as "in his three-year-old form," etc.

When we say that a horse is in form we intend to convey the idea that he is in high condition and fit to run. So, again, the word is used in still another sense; for we speak of a horse's form when we wish to allude to his power on the turf, as compared with other well known animals. Thus, if it be supposed that two three-year-olds, carrying

7

the same weight, would run a mile and a half and come in abreast, it is said that the form of one is equal to that of the other. — The Horse in the Stable and Field, J. H. Walsh.

Foul. The act of violating any rule or established usage; irregular or disorderly conduct; the act of fouling, colliding, or otherwise impeding one's motion or progress in a race; improper riding or driving. The trotting rules punish all offenses coming under the head of fouls, by fine, suspension, or expulsion; fouls applying to any act of a fraudulent nature, and to any unprincipled conduct such as tends to debase the character of the turf in the estimation of the public. Judges only notice or consider complaints of fouls which are reported by the distance flagman and patrol judges, and from owners, riders, or drivers in a race. By the rules of the Turf Congress persons guilty of foul riding are ruled off the course.

Foul Riding; Foul Driving. Any act on the part of driver or rider in a race which interferes with, or impedes the progress of another horse, causing him to change his course or shorten his stride, when by so doing an unfair advantage is gained. In such cases the offending horse is not given the heat, but is placed behind all the unoffending horses in the heat. Such acts are punishable by fine, suspension, or expulsion, according to the discretion of the judges. By the laws of the Turf Congress expulsion from riding for life is always the punishment for preventing a horse from winning in steeple chase and hurdle races, or in a clear case of fraud.

Founder; Chest Founder. See LAMINITIS.

Four-in-Hand. A team of four horses matched or harnessed for the purpose of being driven to a single vehicle. At Cleveland, Ohio, in September, 1882, the four-in-hand of Mr. W. J. Gordon trotted a mile in 2:26, and then repeated it in 2:28. This is probably the most remarkable performance of the kind that was ever made in the world.

Fox-trot. The gait of a horse which is a modification of the true trot. While it is not a true diagonal motion it departs from it simply in the fact that the fore foot touches the ground slightly in advance of the diagonal hind foot. It is, perhaps, the slowest of the distinctive or artificial saddle gaits, but it is above all others an all-day gait, and a horse possessing it to perfection will no doubt make a longer journey from sunrise to sunset, under saddle, than at any other gait, and at night neither horse nor rider will be seriously tired. The rate of speed is from six to seven miles an hour. The horse when going at this gait should always be ridden with a loose rein, as he generally carries his head low. [Local: Kentucky; Tennessee.

Foxhall. The famous American horse which won the French Derby, the Grand Prix of Paris, and the Grand Duke Michael stakes; also the Cesarewitch and Cambridgeshire handicaps at Ascot Heath, England, in 1881. By King Alfonso, by Phaeton, (sire of Ten Broeck, who, in his day, lowered the records at one, two, three, and four miles); dam, by Lexington Owned by Mr. Pierre Lorrillard, and at the head of the Belle Meade stud, Tennessee. In the great double event at Ascot, gave away weights to nearly every notable horse of his age in England, and some Derby winners of former years were behind him at the finish. In seven times Foxhall won as a three-year-old, £10,870.

Foxy. A term used to describe oats which have been heated in bulk when not perfectly dry and undergone fermentation to some extent. They have a pink, or reddish color, an unpleasant smell, and a bitter taste. When given to horses they act injuriously upon the kidneys causing diabetes and loss of condition.

Frank Forrester. The pen name, or *nom de plume*, by which Henry William Herbert, a celebrated writer on horses and horsemanship, is best known in the United States. He was born in London, Eng., April 7, 1807, and died at New York, May 17, 1858. His magnificent work on the " Horse and Horsemanship of the United States and British Provinces of North America," forms a fitting monument to his genius and ability; while his smaller and thoroughly practical books are yet regarded as trustworthy guides in every stable.

Free-for-all. A sweepstakes race open to all horses.

Free Handicap. A race in which no liability is incurred for entrance money, stake or forfeit, until acceptance of the weight allotted, either by direct acceptance or omission to declare out.

Free Track. Any track or course not in membership with the National or American trotting associations, where no rules are enforced, and where an expelled man can trot his horses as well as any man not expelled, is termed a "free track."

Frog. The triangular buffer which is in the center of the ground surface of the hoof, so called because when untouched by the knife it bears some resemblance to a crouching frog. The frog is divided into two equal parts by a deep fissure, extending from its apex in front to the base. The horn of the frog is produced in the same manner as the sole, but it differs from both the wall and sole, in that the horn is soft, moist, and elastic to a remarkable degree. There was an old opinion that the frog was intended as a protection to the inner part of the foot, and that it ought not, therefore, to touch the ground. This led to the practice of making the heel of the shoe high in order to protect the frog; but now the shoe is so set that the frog is allowed to touch the ground, its true function being to destroy the shock of concussion and prevent slipping.

The frog, on both hard and soft ground, is an essential portion of the weight-bearing face. In the unshod, healthy foot it always projects beyond the level of the sole, and seldom below that of the wall at the heels; indeed, it is found, in the majority of hoofs, either on a level with the circumference of this part, or beyond it, so that its contact with the ground is assured. Hence its utility in obviating concussion, supporting the tendons, and, on slippery ground, in preventing falls. In pulling up a horse sharply in the gallop, or in descending a steep hill, the frog, together with the angular recess formed by the bar and wall at the heel of the hoof, are eminently serviceable in checking the tendency to slip; the animal instinctively plants the posterior portions of the foot exclusively on the ground.—Horse Shoes and Horse Shoeing, George Fleming, LL. D., M. R. C. V. S.

[Law.] Until the frogs become bad or troublesome, or the heels become tender or fleshy, they should not be considered an unsoundness; but when the original structure of the frog has become so altered as to be perpetually tender, rendering the horse liable to drop at any step, he is then unsound.—The Law of Horses, M. D. Hanover.

Full Blood. An animal of pure blood. Usually synonymous with thoroughbred, although it is far from correct to so use the term as applied to horses.

Full Mouth. At from four and a half to five years of age the horse has what is termed a "full mouth," that is to say —the mouth is complete; the incisive arch is semicircular and regular in shape; the temporary teeth or nippers are all shed; all the permanent teeth have reached the same level, and while the anterior borders of the corner teeth are completely worn, the posterior borders are not yet worn.

Fullering. That crease in the lower face of a horseshoe in which the nail holes are placed; often called "twitcheling."

Furlong. A measure of length equal to the eighth part of a mile; forty rods, poles or perches; two hundred and twenty yards.

Furnishings. The appointments of a stable pertaining to the horse and his service, embracing harness, saddles, clothing, robes, whip, bridles, boots, bandages, sponges, and stable tools, but not including vehicles. See DEVICES.

Furniture. The fixtures to a riding saddle, including stirrups, girths, and surcingle with steel bridge.

Futurity; Futurity Stakes. A future event. A term applied to stakes to be decided in the remote future, generally speaking from one to three years after the event is opened for entries; and the usual custom is to call such stakes, especially where opened for young horses, "futurity stakes."

G

Gaining Break. A break made purposely, or one by which the horse making it gains in space on his contending horse; one by which the horse loses nothing in space in making it, and yet gains something by change of muscular action. When a horse breaks in a heat the driver is required to at once pull him to the gait prescribed for the race, but should the horse gain by this action, twice the distance so gained is taken from him, by the judges, at the finish.

Gait. The manner of walking or stepping; motion; the name given to the diverse modes in which progression is accomplished by the play of the locomotory members, or legs. The gaits are: 1, natural; 2, acquired. The former are the walk, trot, gallop, and at times the pace (amble), and the running walk; the latter are the amble, broken amble, running walk and racing gallop. Different names are often given to these various motions, as the rack for the pace; and some are known by other terms in local sections, as the fox-trot for the running walk, which is common in some of the Southern States. According to the forms which they assume the gaits may be described as: *Beautiful*—when they are energetic, regular, extended, harmonious, elegant. *Defective*—when they produce weakness and require great exertion. *Diagonal*—when the members in executing them move or succeed one another as diagonal bipeds, as the trot, the walk, the gallop. *Easy*—when they satisfy and accommodate the rider by their graceful motion. *Free*—when the motion is accomplished without undue effort. *Hard*—when they fatigue the rider by the violence of their reactions. *Heavy*—if the percussions of the feet are violent and resounding. *High-strained*—when the members are greatly flexed without passing over much distance. *Lateral*—when they evolve themselves by lateral instead of diagonal bipeds, as in ambling, racking. *Light*—if the percussion of the feet upon the earth produces little sound. *Long, elongated*—when their strides are as extensive as possible. *Low*—when the displacements of the body from the earth are slight. *Reacting*—when they are not only high but impress the center of gravity with strong, vertical displacements which separate the body from the ground at each step. *Regular*—when, for each gait, the evolution of the members and their manner of association obey the principles

101

of scientific analysis. *Repeated* — if the movements succeed each other with excessive rapidity, with or without an increase in speed. *Short* — when their strides are cramped and narrow. *Strong* — when the action is rapid, energetic, easy, high, extended and rhythmical. *Uniform* — resulting from equal length of steps.

Gait, Registering the. The methods of registering the motions of the horse known to science are called the graphic, hydrostatic, electrical, and photographic. M. Marey, principal of the College de France, was one of the first to study the locomotion of the horse by means of what he termed the graphic method. This was done by means of compressed air in two drums or metallic cases, each closed above by a rubber membrane to which was fixed a lever capable of executing to and fro vertical movements. These drums were connected by rubber tubes. When filled with air the pressure exercised upon one forced the air through the tube into the other drum, whose lever and membrane it elevated, and when the pressure ceased it relapsed. Hence this unity of action transmitted movements. These drums were again connected with a cylinder covered by a layer of smoked paper, which was made to turn regularly by clockwork. This moved a registering needle by which the least displacement left its trace upon the paper. The paper retained the tracing of vertical undulations corresponding to the pressure transmitted to the registering apparatus by the concussion and contact of the hoofs upon the ground — four recording needles corresponding to the four feet of the horse, each foot being provided with an India rubber pneumatic bulb, so that with each step the bulb was compressed, forcing a portion of the air into the registering drum or cylinder. When the foot was raised the bulb again became filled with the air which was expelled from the other when it resumed its original form. This device was not always practical in its operations, and M. Marey next invented a leather bracelet which was attached to the ankle of the horse, and upon which was a rubber bulb, and by an ingenious arrangement of copper plates and lead balls connected it by transmission tubes to a registry drum carried in front of the rider on the saddle, by which means the concussions were registered. He followed this with another invention which consisted of electric needles and conducting wires by means of which an apparatus closed and opened an electric current during the contacts and elevations of the horse's feet, and hence the notations of gait were obtained and registered. The hydrostatic method of registering the gaits in man was invented by H. Vierordt, and applied to the study of the gaits of the horse by M. L. Hoffman of Berlin, in 1887. The plan was to lay down white paper, over which the horse traveled. Attached to the external side of each hoof was a brass tube connected by means of a rubber tube along the legs to a reservoir placed in front of the rider upon the horse's withers. When the hoof touched the paper the pointed end of the brass tube, projecting downwards, deposited a small pool of colored liquid from the reservoir above, discoloring the paper. Thus the gait was registered by lengths. It is understood that M. Hoffman employed photography to obtain the positions of the legs when in motion. The electrical device of M. Marey was perfected in 1889 by Armand Goubaux and Gustave Barrier, professors in the Veterinary School of Alfort, and Central and National Society of Agriculture of France. By the use of a very ingenious instrument they succeeded in registering the gaits of the horse by electricity. So long as the horse's foot is in the air the two points of contact touch each other and complete the current; but as soon as the hoof touches the ground they are separated and interrupt it. At each rising and resting of the foot it is again closed and broken. This closing and breaking being instantaneous, and, moreover, the force of the spring and the projection of the leg being capable of modification at will, it is easy to give to this apparatus great strength yet with all the precision and sensibility desired. In short it is able to register with the utmost accuracy the periods of the change of contact, the rhythm of the beats, and the number, nature, and diverse bases of the complete step of any gait normal or pathological. By far the most complete and satisfactory method of registering the gait of the horse in motion is that of photography, originated by the late Hon. Leland Stanford of Palo Alto, California. Mr. Stanford had for many years entertained the opinion that by the use of the camera, instantaneous pictures could be obtained which would show the actual position of the limbs of the horse at each stride and in different gaits. In order to put this idea to a practical test, Mr. Stanford employed Mr. Eadweard L. Muybridge, a very skillful photographer of San Francisco, to institute experiments to this end. These were commenced in 1872, but were quite inconclusive in their results, and it was not until 1877 that Mr. Muybridge again took up the task, making his trials with a single camera. Subsequently the number of cameras was increased to twelve, which were arranged in a building, at intervals of twenty-one inches, with double shutters to each, which were opened by means of a machine constructed somewhat upon the principle of a Swiss music box, the arrangement being such that the whole series of exposures was made in the time occupied by a single complete stride of the horse. A difficulty was experienced in setting the apparatus in motion at the exact time required, and to regulate it to correspond to the speed of the horse. Accordingly, in later experiments, the following method was devised to better represent the gaits of the horse, because operated by his own movement. On the side of the track opposite the building where the cameras were placed, a wooden frame was erected, about fifty feet long, and fifteen high, at a suitable angle, and covered with white cotton sheeting divided by vertical lines into spaces of twenty-one inches, each space being consecutively numbered. Eighteen inches in front of this background was placed a baseboard twelve inches high, and on which were drawn longitudinal lines four inches apart. In front of this baseboard a strip of wood was fastened to the ground upon the top of which wires were secured at an elevation of about one inch above the ground and extending across the track. The wire was exposed in a groove to one only of the wheels of the sulky, being protected from contact with the horse's feet and the other wheel. Each wire was held in proper tension by a spring on the back of the baseboard, so arranged that when the wire crossing the track was depressed by the wheel it should draw upon the spring connected with it, and make contact with a metallic button and complete the electric current. These wires were placed at distances from each other corresponding with the cameras on the opposite side of the track, and with the spaces between the lines drawn on the background. Thus it will be seen that the depression of the first wire would complete the circuit and cause the magnet connected with the corresponding camera to move the latch and liberate the shutters, exposing the sensitive plate for a space of time, calculated by Mr. Muybridge at not more than the five-thousandth part of a second. In like manner, as the wheel passed over the second wire, the shutters would be liberated on the second camera, and so on until the whole series was discharged. This method was used in all experiments where horses were driven to sulkies; but when the wheels were not used this arrangement with wires under the track was modified, and a thread was drawn across sufficiently high to come in contact with the horse's breast, and strong enough to cause the contact and establish the circuit as before. The number of cameras was afterwards increased to twenty-four and they were placed at intervals of twelve inches to still closer analyze the movements of the horse. " These experiments," say the authors of the Exterior of the Horse, Messrs. Goubaux and Barrier, "effected a veritable revolution in the world of physiologists and artists." In 1889, M. Ottomar Anschütz of Lissa, Germany, somewhat modified and improved upon Mr. Muybridge's method, which was again improved by M. Marey at Paris, in 1882; and by Marey and Pagès at Paris in 1887. In 1879 Messrs. Vincent and Goiffon of the Alfort Veterinary School, Paris, applied the music notation to the scientific representation of the gaits of the horse; which was afterwards improved by M. Marey, and also by M. Lenoble du Tiel, in 1887.

These efforts are all in the direction of obtaining the accurate position and times of the gait of the horse. The animal has been always represented in an unnatural and false attitude, and in conditions of impossible equilibrium by artists and sculptors. Little by little the cause of equine realism will triumph over the old conventionalism which censures with disdain the innovators who assume the liberty of announcing its errors to the world.—The Exterior of the Horse, Goubaux and Barrier.

Gaited Horse. A saddle horse; a horse having the walk-trot-canter gaits, (including the walk, trot, rack, canter, running walk, fox trot, or slow pace), to perfection; a combination horse. See SADDLER; KENTUCKY SADDLER; NATIONAL SADDLE HORSE BREEDERS' ASSOCIATION.

Col. Dodge had a Kentucky horse which could walk flat-footed four and a half miles an hour; could running-walk five and a half; rack seven; single-foot up to twelve, and in harness or under saddle trot a forty gait as squarely as any horse ever shod.—Kentucky Farmers' Home Journal.

Gaiter. A device for trueing the gait; giving a steady, even, and quick motion, lengthening the stride, preventing a sidewise gait, breaking, bucking, or bolting, inducing correct knee action, and teaching the horse to travel wide. There are several different patterns. They are easily attached and adjusted; light in weight, and adapted for both slow and fast work.

Gaiting Bar; Gaiting Pole. A padded pole attached to the sulky, inside the shaft, for the purpose of keeping the body of the horse in straight line when in motion. One end is made fast near the point of the shaft, or to the shaft holder, and the other to the cross-bar above the whipple-tree or just under the sulky seat.

Gaiting Strap. A strap of strong leather, usually covered with sheepskin, attached to a sulky in the same manner as the gaiting bar, and for the same purpose.

Gaiting Wheel. A device for keeping the horse straight in the shafts, and for preventing hitching and sidewise action. It consists of a short metal arm attached to the shaft by means of an adjustable loop and set-screw, on which, plays a small wheel, which, when the horse goes to one side, presses against the flank, causing him to straighten the gait.

Gallop. The leaping or springing gait or movement in which the two fore feet are lifted from the ground in succession, and then the two hind feet in the same succession. The term is commonly used to denote the movement intermediate between the canter and the run, in which during the stride, two, three, or all the feet are off the ground at the same instant.

In the gallop the horse is supposed to be moving by a succession of bounds in which he rises as far as he falls. This would give one-fourth of a second as the time of descent equal to one foot of vertical fall to twelve and a half feet movement in a horizontal direction, and a consequent deflection of the center of gravity to that extent.—The Horse in Motion, J. D. B. Stillman.

This gait is wholly and radically different from the pace and trot; the order of action, and, necessarily, the mental organization governing the method of locomotion and use of the limbs are different. Hence no one horse is, or can be, possessed of great speed at the gallop, and also great speed at the trot or pace. To possess great speed of either one of these two orders he must inherit speed of that order.—Leslie E. Macleod.

The gallop is a fast gait, with three beats, and leaped, in which the synchronous beats of a diagonal biped are interposed between the successive beats of the opposite diagonal biped, which begins the step by its posterior member. The simultaneous beats of the second contact with the ground, (second biped), have the greatest tendency to become disassociated when the horse moves almost without advancing, when the equilibrium is bad, or when the speed is very great. In this case the ear can perceive four distinct beats. On the race course the gallop is an externally fast gait in which this separation of the diagonal beats is driven to its utmost limit. — The Exterior of the Horse, Goubaux and Barrier.

Galloping Courses. [Eng.] Courses devoid of obstacles like ditches, hedges, etc.

Gamy. Spirited; possessing undaunted courage. It is said of a courageous, spirited, staying horse, that he is "gamy;" will never quit.

Garter of the Turf. [Eng.] A term applied to the Oaks stakes, established in 1779. See OAKS.

Gaskin. That part of the exterior of the horse situated between the thigh and the hock, from which it is divided by a line drawn from the point of the hock, clear of the bony prominences of the joint.

Gathering. [Eq.] That art by which the rider, having mounted his horse, taken the reins in hand, is square upon his seat and his legs in position, collects all the forces of the horse in readiness for the execution of his will. By gathering or collecting, the horse is kept well upon his haunches, is guarded from crossing his legs, and has, all the time, as the phrase is, "a spare leg" to depend upon. The gathering, urging, and retaining, are the foundations of that obedience which it is the object of horsemanship to enforce.

Gelding. A male horse that has been castrated.

Gentlemen's Driving Race. A race open to horses kept for driving purposes only, driven by their non-professional owners, to road carts.

Gentling. A word used to denote the first acts of training, handling, and educating the colt. The term is one which should enforce the importance of gentleness in the first lessons of colt education, as bad habits come from bad early training, or first wrong impressions.

Gestation. The act of carrying or being with young. The period of gestation with the mare is eleven months; but tables show the shortest period to be 322 days; the longest period, 419 days; the mean period, 347 days. Records also show that three hundred mares went an average period of 343 days, with a range of sixty-one days between the shortest, (309 days), and the longest, (370 days), period.

Gift. [Law.] In order to legally transfer a horse by gift, the animal must be actually delivered to the donee.

Girdles. Used to denote that structural part of the anatomy of the horse by means of which the limbs or locomotory members are attached to the trunk.

These girdles are so called because a pair of them, when completely developed, nearly encircle the body; but it must be admitted that it is not a very happy expression, as, except through the intervention of the vertebral column, they never form complete circles, and very often the "semi-girdles" of each side are widely separated both above and below. These semi-girdles are sometimes called arches.— The Horse, William Henry Flower, C. B.

Girth. A leather strap passing under the belly of a horse for the purpose of securing the saddle or a part of the harness in place. The main saddle girth should be broad and soft with a reinforced backing.

Girth Line. A line encircling the body of a horse at a point just back of the withers, and four inches back of the fore legs.

Give and Take. An old term used to describe a race in which horses carried weight according to their height. The standard height was taken at fourteen hands, and the horse that height was obliged to carry nine stone, (126 pounds). Seven pounds were taken from the weight for every inch below fourteen hands, and seven pounds added for every inch above fourteen hands. A few pounds additional weight was regarded as so serious a matter, that it was said seven pounds in a mile race was equivalent to a distance.

Give Him a Repeat. A term used in working a horse when he is given a dash of two miles, the words meaning an exercise of a mile and repeat.

Given the Needle. It is said of a horse that has been doped or drugged, that he has been "given the needle"—meaning an injection by means of a hypodermic needle.

Glanders. The most loathsome disease to which the horse is subject. It was described by Greek veterinarians as early as A. D. 381, and in 1682, an accurate account of the nature of the disease was published by Sallysel, the stable master of Louis XIV., of France. Glanders is characterized by a peculiar deposit with ulceration, on the membrane of the nose and in the lungs; and farcy — which is one and the same disease modified by the cause which originates them—by deposits of the same material and ulcerations of the lymphatics of the skin. The former is the more active form of the disorder; the latter is the slow type fastening upon general debility. Each has its acute and chronic form, the former usually resulting from inoculation, and is always fatal—there is no known cure. Dr. James Law says the treatment in all its forms and of acute farcy with open sores, "should be legally prohibited because of the danger to man as well as animals." Always consult a veterinary inspector or official commissioner. It is without doubt the worst form of unsoundness in horses.

[Law.] The moment that symptoms of glanders appear in a horse—indications of the incipiency of the disease—that is, if he really have the seeds of it in him, he is unsound, although it may be some time before the disease becomes fully developed in its most offensive conditions, and it is the future history of the case which is to show whether it was the glanders or not.—Massachusetts Reports, 10 Cushing, (1857), 520.

Glomes of the Frog. The rounded projections or ends of the branches of the frog are called the glomes, forming the lower part of the heels.

Gloves. In the steel protected driving gloves the fingers are protected by small, flat steel staples. The gloves always continue soft and pliable, and they are very strong and durable.

G. N. H. [Eng.] The letters signify Grand National Hunt, a steeple chase run over different courses each year.

Go. The magic word that starts all the horses of the trotting field; one for which drivers listen with intense desire as it gives them the right to a fair race and no favor.

Go as They Please. A race in which it is held that the performance shall be in harness, to wagon or under the saddle; but after the race is commenced no change can be made in the manner of going, and the race is held to have commenced when the horses appear on the track.

Go to Pieces. A horse that is unmanageable in a race or heat, is unsteady, flighty, acts badly, and will not settle to a gait, is said to "go to pieces."

Go With His Horse. A phrase signifying that the rider should give himself up completely to the motion and spirit of his horse, on the great strides of the finish.

Godolphin Arabian. One of the three famous horses upon which rests the foundation of the modern English thoroughbred. He was a brown bay, stood about 15 hands high, with an unusually high crest, arched almost to a fault. He was probably foaled about 1724; and although called an Arabian, was unquestionably a Barb. Said to have been imported into England from France, and it is said he had actually been in use as a cart horse in the streets of Paris, from which ignoble position he was rescued by Mr. Coke, who presented him to Mr. Williams, keeper of the St. James Coffee House, by whom he was presented to Lord Godolphin, hence his name. He died at Gogmagog, Cambridgeshire, in 1753, being, as is suppcsed, in his twenty-ninth year. Despite his unknown blood and breeding, it is generally conceded that he contributed more to the quality of the thoroughbred horse, than any other stallion either before or since his time.

Going for the Gloves. Betting with utter disregard to means of payment.

Going Within Himself. When a horse is making high speed with perfect ease, he is said to be "going within himself."

Gameness and condition and all that won't prevail over a competitor that can throw dust in your eyes while going within himself.—Training the Trotting Horse, Charles Marvin.

Good Breaker. A horse so trained that he recovers quickly in breaking; one which instantly settles to his gait after a misstep in which he breaks.

Wedgewood was a good breaker.—Life with the Trotters, John Splan.

Good Day, Good Track. When a match is made "good day, good track," it means that all the conditions must be favorable or the race will not take place. Not only must the weather be fair but the track also must be in good condition. Even if the day be pleasant, and a rain on the previous day has rendered the track soft or unfit for the race, the match cannot occur.

Good Hands. [Eq.] Good hands in horsemanship may be described as the happy art of using the reins so as to restrain the horse by delicate manipulation and not by mere hauling at the mouth, and to enable the rider to conform to the movements of his mount in the best possible manner.

A very essential requisite in every man, in order to become a good horseman and rider, is the quality known as good hands; without this, most bits on awkward horses are ineffectual. Good hands with

almost any kind of bit, providing the horse gets a good amount of work, will generally have the effect of making him go quietly in time.—The Practical Horse Keeper, George Fleming, LL.D., V.S.
A light, yet firm, an elastic, yet steady hand on the rein is what is wanted.—Charles Marvin.

Goodwood Races. So called from Goodwood Park, the seat of the Duke of Richmond, in which they are held. The park is in Sussex, three miles from Chichester, Eng. The races begin the last Tuesday in July of each year, and continue four days, in which Thursday, which is called Cup Day, is the principal. These races, being held in a private park, are very select and are admirably managed. Goodwood Park was purchased by Charles, First Duke of Richmond, of the Compton family, then resident in the village of East Lavant, and the races were begun by the Duke, who died in 1806.

Gr. m. These letters in a summary or list of entries following the name of a horse, signify gray mare.

Grain Burnt; Burnt Up. Said of a horse in a shrunken, fevered, pinched condition, which has been caused by having been fed too much grain; the result of forced feeding of grain and too little hay; especially noticeable among horses kept in city stables. It is very seldom that the condition is due to constitutional defect.

Grand Circuit. A term applied to the great American trotting circuit which includes New York, Springfield, Buffalo, Rochester, Utica, Cleveland, Pittsburg, Detroit, and other cities, changes in the number being due from year to year to local causes. Originally called the Grand Central Circuit.

Grease; Canker; Scratches. A specific affection of the heels of horses, associated with the growth of a parasitic fungus; an offensive discharge from the numerous oil-glands, and often the formation of red, raw excrescences from the surface known as grapes. "It is," says Dr. Edward Mayhew, M. R. C. V. S., in his important work on the diseases of the horse, "a disgrace to every person connected with the building in which it occurs; it proves neglect in the proprietor, and want of fitness or positive idleness in the groom." Until cured, grease is an unsoundness.

Great Trochanter. A muscle situated in the haunches whose office is to give speed to the movements of the hind leg, abduct the thigh, and assist in rearing.

The length and volume of its muscular fibers enable it to keep up a sustained action from the time the hind foot takes the ground or in advance of the center of gravity, until it leaves it after completing its propulsive effect. When the foot is off the ground it furnishes the sinews of war offensive and defensive. The distance from the insertion to the fulcrum or head of the bone being so short, it causes the foot when free from the ground to move with great velocity.—The Horse in Motion, J. D. B. Stillman.

Green Horse. A horse that has never trotted or paced for premiums or purse, either double or single.

Grinding. A peculiar grinding motion of the hind foot upon the ground, which attends the articulation of the hind feet of some horses. Like stringhalt and cocked ankles, grinding is not only confined to the hind limbs and feet, but entirely among four footed animals to the horse. The action is a grinding motion of the heel sometimes outwardly, sometimes inwardly. It is performed through the agency of some of the ligaments that are not sufficiently powerful to act in opposition to the flexor and extensor tendons. All the methods known to farriery have been used to prevent it, but absolutely in vain.

Grogginess; Groggy Gait. A term applied to the peculiar knuckling of the fetlock joint, and the tottering of the whole of the fore leg. It is difficult to locate it in any particular joint, and it seems oftenest to result from a want of power in the ligaments of the joints generally, produced by frequent strains, severe sprains, or by ill-judged and cruel exertion. It is a legal unsoundness.

Groom; Grooming. One having the care of horses; the act of dressing or cleaning a horse. The grooming which each horse receives should be adapted to its individual peculiarities, and particular attention should be paid to the brushes and instruments used in the operation. Some horses can be rubbed with a stiff brush, others must have a very soft one—a wisp of straw or a soft cloth. After the dandruff and dirt have been removed, the best grooms rarely resort to anything else than the palms of the hands and sides of the arms up to the elbows —as nothing else will so make the coat smooth and glossy.

Grossness. Superfluous flesh; an undesirable quality or characteristic in a horse for speed or road purposes.

Grunting. A peculiar sound connected with the emission of the breath when the animal is suddenly moved, or started, or struck at. If the horse grunts at such times he is further tested for roaring. Grunters are not always roarers, but as it is a common thing for a roarer to grunt, such an animal must be looked upon with suspicion until he is thoroughly tried by pulling a load, or being made to gallop up hill.

Guaranteed Stake. A stake with a guarantee by the party or association opening it, that the sum shall not be less than the amount named; the prize being the total amount of money contributed by the nominators, all of which belongs to the winner or the winners; although such stake does not entitle the giver to any excess, unless so stated in the published conditions.

Guards of the Bit. The side-pieces or cheeks attached to the ends of the bit, connected with which are rings for receiving the reins and cheek pieces of the headstall or bridle.

Guard-rail. The pole around the inner circle of a race track; the hub rail.

Gullet-plate. The iron arch under the pommel of the saddle.

Gums. The fleshy parts of the sockets of the teeth.

Guy. Bay gelding; foaled 1880. By Kentucky Prince; dam, Flora Gardiner, by Seely's American Star. Holding the World's record to close of 1893; one mile to wagon, made at Detroit, Michigan, July 18, 1893, in 2:13.

H

Half Forfeit. As a definition of the half forfeit system in running races take the following example: A sweepstake for three-year olds, $50 each, half forfeit; $1000 added, of which $200 to second, $100 to third, etc. In such a race each horse that started would pay $50, and each horse that subscribed to the stake and failed to start would owe $25, (half forfeit); or in other words would owe a sum equal to half of the starting fee. At the East if not paid, the owner of the horse and the horse against which the forfeit existed would be put in the forfeit list, and the owner's entries and the horse's entry, if sold, would not be accepted to future races until the forfeit was paid. In the West an order would be issued against the owner and horse, and if the forfeit were lodged the owner could not start a horse nor could the horse start, until payment was made. As a rule, all entrance money and forfeits go to the winner. Thus, there is this difference to the forfeit systems East and West: In the East the clubs collect through the forfeit list for the winner; at the West orders are issued to the winner and he does his own collecting by lodging forfeits with the secretary when the horse or owner are starting in races. At the South the clubs have entirely discarded the forfeit system, and make the stakes entirely on the cash entrance plan.

Half-guards to a bit is a compromise between the snaffle and the common bridoon with rings only. Instead of full guards both above and below the rings to rest upon the cheek and prevent the bit from being drawn through the mouth, only that part or half of the guard below the ring or bar, is retained.

Half Mile Running. World's record to close of 1893: Geraldine, at Morris Park, West Chester, N. Y., August 30, 1889, 0:46. Heat race: Aged horses, Bogus, 113 lbs., at Helena, Montana, August 28, 1888, 0:48; 0:48. Four-year-olds, Eclipse Jr., Dallas, Texas, November 1, 1890, 0:48; 0:48; 0:48.

Halters are made in considerable variety, being plain neck of either leather or rope, and leather headstall with rope tie. These are of many patterns; plain, or with fancy trimmings in brass and nickel, in black or russet leather. Web halters are in scarlet, blue, and other colors. One of the best practical halters is the ordinary leather headstall, with forehead, throat and nose-bands, on which should be a ring under the chin for attaching a rope, chain or leather strap.

Halter-Breaking; Haltering. The act of accustoming a colt to the use and discipline of the halter; one of the first lessons in colt education.

Halter-Pulling. One of the very worst faults a horse can have, the result of defective and ignorant training. A person is never safe with a horse that has contracted this habit, and it is a habit very hard to overcome. The best method is to take an ordinary halter, having a lead sufficiently long to pass through the halter-ring, then back between the fore legs and under a surcingle, and attach to a strap around the ankle of one hind foot. Be careful that the halter-ring is sufficiently strong to resist the pull. As the colt pulls on the halter it draws both ways—upon the head in front, and also on the hind foot. The colt will find that by stepping forward the pull upon the hind foot will lessen, and he will rarely make more than two or three attempts to pull back. This treatment should never be attempted when the colt has the harness on, but always when in the stall or when hitched to a post. After this treatment, kindness and gentleness will complete the work of reform from this extremely bad fault.

Hambletonian, Rysdyk's. Founder of the greatest trotting family the world has ever seen. Foaled May 5, 1849, at Sugar Loaf, Orange County, N. Y. Bred by Wm. M. Rysdyk. By Abdallah, (son of thoroughbred Mambrino, by imported Messenger, and a trotting mare called Amazonia, pedigree unknown); dam, the Charles Kent mare, by imported Bellfounder, a Norfolk trotter; second dam, One-Eye, by Bishop's Hambletonian, a thoroughbred; third dam, Silvertail, by imported Messenger. He was a beautiful bay, with both hind feet white, and a small star in forehead. His shoulders and quarters were so massive that his exceptionally round barrel seemed somewhat light. His neck was short and straight, and he had a large, coarse head, though it was bony and expressive. He stood firm and solid, on feet perfect in shape and texture; and his legs were flat, clean, heavily muscled, and free from gumminess or swelling, even when he was old. His rump was rather round, than sloping, and his tail was set low and carried low. He stood 15.1 at the withers, and 15.3 at the rump. His knee was 13½ inches in circumference, his hock 17½ inches in circumference. From the center of the hip-joint to the point of the hock he measured

41 inches, and from the point of the stifle to the point of the hock, the length of his thigh was 24 inches. His chief points of excellence were his long, trotting gait, his muscular development, and the fine quality of his bones and sinews. He was never engaged in a race, and never had a record at any rate of speed; but as a three-year-old he trotted in public on Union Course, L. I., in 2:48½. Forty of his sons and daughters have made records ranging from 2:17¼ to 2:30, including Dexter, 2:17¼; Nettie, 2:18, and Orange Girl, 2:20. One hundred and thirty-eight of his sons are sires of eleven hundred and one trotters, and seventy-one pacers, with records ranging from 2:08¾ to 2:30; and sixty-nine daughters, (to the close of 1893), have produced eighty-seven trotters and two pacers, with records of 2:30 or better. "He is not only first as a sire of trotters, but as the progenitor of the producers of trotters, both male and female, he is incomparably above all others of his generation." He died at Chester, N. Y., March 27, 1876.

Hammering. Punishing a beaten horse; or whipping a horse at the finish when it is impossible for him to win, are acts known as "hammering."

Hamstring. The great tendon or sinew at the back of the hock on the hind leg of the horse.

Hand. A measure of four inches; the standard division of measurement for horses; a palm.

Hand-Gallop. [Eng.] Explained by the quotation: The hand-gallop is play; the pace of pleasure parties not hurried; of hunting men going to cover with a half hour to spare.—Book of the Horse, Samuel Sidney.

Hand-Loops. Loops attached to reins for the purpose of getting a better control of the horse, and managing him more easily. There are usually three hand-loops, or straps, to each rein, about one foot apart.

Handicap. An extra burden placed upon, or a special requirement made of, a superior competitor in favor of an inferior, in order to make their chances of winning more equal. In a horse race the adjudging of various weights to horses differing in age, power or speed, in order to place them all, as far as possible, on an equality.

Handicapper. An officer of the turf assigned to determine the amount of the handicaps in a race or contest of speed. It is said that an experienced handicapper can so weight two horses of different ages and different degrees of power, that they will run to a head-and-head finish.

Handicap Race. A race for which the horses are

weighted according to their merits, in the estimation of the handicapper, for the purpose of equalizing their chances of winning.

We never could see any object in handicap racing, except to enable a poor horse to beat a good one. To this we may add the opportunity to bet whether this horse can carry ten or twenty pounds more weight than that one, and beat him.—Wallace's Monthly.

Handler. One who breaks, educates or handles colts, giving them their first lessons in good service, as distinguished from a trainer or driver in races.

Handling Reins. Reins used in handling, or educating colts to the bit. They are usually made of hard rope line, about fifteen feet long, with loops, or handles made of double plaited rope the size of an ordinary clothesline. They are fastened by spring hooks to the rings of the bit, and pass through turrets on the pad of the surcingle, to the hands of the person handling the colt.

Hands on the Reins. [Eq.] A great English rider has said: "One ought to ride as though he had a silken rein in his hand as fine as hair, and that he was afraid of breaking it." The rider should never keep a dead pull on the reins, but "give and take," so that the horse may understand his wishes by the feeling of his mouth.

Hang out the Prizes. A term used in referring to the premiums, stakes and purses published in the programme of a race meeting. To "hang out," is to offer certain prizes.

Haras. A French term denoting a stud of horses, and applied generally to the stud establishment of the National government. These breeding establishments are governed by strict regulations, and a law of August 14, 1885, also provides for an inspection as to the character and soundness of the stallions in private ownership, which may be advertised for public use, and the law is rigidly enforced. It provides that a stallion cannot be employed without being first approved and authorized by the Administrator of the Haras—or master of the stud—and he must have a certificate that he is free from certain specified unsoundnesses. This certificate is in force for only one year, and is not issued until an expert official examination of the animal has been made. Violations are punished by fines imposed on the driver and groom. Every owner of a stallion advertising his horse for breeding purposes must notify the Prefect, and the animal is inspected by a committee, consisting of a veterinarian, a breeder and a government inspector. Terms like "the flower of the haras," "the gem of the haras," are often met with in turf journals or books, meaning the very choicest and finest bred of the animals in the stud.

Hard Mouth. When a horse has a confirmed hard mouth it is regarded as a serious vice.

Harem. A term applied to a collection of brood mares.

Harness. The working-gear, or tackle, of a horse, to connect him to a sulky or vehicle. It consists of the following parts: Crown-piece; cheek-piece; front; blinds; nose-band; bit; curb; check; throat-latch; rein; breastplate; martingale; trace-tug; trace; saddle; turrets; belly-band, (girth); turn-back, (back strap); crupper; breeching; breeching-strap; hip-strap. Track harness weigh from seven and a quarter to twelve pounds, all complete, the average weight being from eight to nine pounds.

Harness Meeting. A race to sulkies.

Harness Turf. A term used to denote the trotting turf as distinguished from the running turf.

Harrows, for dressing or finishing the surface of a track. Track harrows are made in two forms—square and triangular, of the best wagon timber, and generally twelve feet on each side. The square harrows are made of three pieces one way, and four the other, each of two by four inch material. In each of the four cross-pieces are thirty teeth, or one hundred and twenty in all. Within the outer frame of the triangular-shaped harrow are braces forming a smaller frame of the same shape, but exactly reversed from the larger or outer one, the points of the smaller one being at the centre of the outside pieces. The outside pieces of this harrow are two by eight inches; and the inside pieces two by four inches. In the outside pieces are three rows of teeth, one hundred and four teeth to each piece; and in the inside pieces are two rows of teeth, or thirty teeth to each piece, making a total of four hundred and two teeth. These teeth are 60-penny, forged, steel wire nails, six inches long, set so firm in the frame work that they may be adjusted to depth as required, the general rule being to have them so set as to make channels one-half an inch apart, and from one-fourth to three-fourths of an inch deep on the face of the track. When more than one harrow is used with the same team in dressing a track, as is usually the case, they are drawn diagonally, so that one will not follow directly behind the other, but behind and outside of the other; hence once around the track will dress a section of from twenty-four to thirty-six feet of its width. Such a triangular harrow as is described will weight 300 pounds.

Haunch. The upper thigh of the hind leg of the horse; situated between the gaskin, or lower thigh, below; and the point of the quarter, above.

Head. The head of a horse, by a side view, is divided from the neck by a line proceeding from the back of the ear, along the rear edge of the lower jaw, to its angle. It embraces the following named regions, or parts, viz.: Ear, poll, forehead, face, nostrils, muzzle, mouth, cheek, eye, jowl, lower jaw, inter-maxillary space.

Head, Lead of the. In speeding, the horse should be allowed to follow its instinct in fixing the position of the head —there can be no safer or more successful rule in training than this; indeed, it is one of the golden rules in horse discipline.

Headstall. The name given to the leather work of the upper part of a bridle when in collected form, and to which the snaffle or bit and bridoon is attached.

Heat. An act requiring intense and uninterrupted effort; great activity; as to do a thing at a heat; one part of a race, or once around a course in a race. In trotting races, heats best three in five; a horse not winning a heat in the first five trotted cannot start in the sixth unless he shall have made a dead heat. In running races of heats best two in three, a horse that actually wins two heats, or distances the field, wins the race; and a horse running in two consecutive heats, without winning, or running a dead heat, cannot again start in the race. In a running race of heats best three in five, a horse that wins three heats, or distances the field, wins the race; and a horse running in any three consecutive heats, without winning, or running a dead heat, is not allowed to again start in the race.

Heaves. Broken wind; asthma; a disease of the organs of breathing caused by the rupture of the air cells, which prevents the animal from expelling air from the lungs without a double effort. A legal unsoundness.

Hedge. To protect by betting on both sides; or, in other words, after having bet on one side, to bet also on the other side, in order to guard one's self against loss whatever the result may be.

No bet is good till it is well hedged.—Blue Ribbon of the Turf, Louis Henry Curzon.

Heels. The posterior part of the horse's foot, formed by the angles of inflection of the extremities of the hind portion of the hoof.

Heels of the Shoe. The rear part of the web or plate of the shoe protecting the heels of the foot.

Helper. A groom; rubber, or assistant; one who helps in the care of a horse at a race, in a subordinate position.

Helping. A term used to designate any action by an offending horse, rider or driver, by which any horse is enabled to come to the wire in an unfair manner, and by which the progress of another horse is impeded. The trotting rules demand that no horse, rider or driver shall jostle, cross, or strike another horse, rider or driver, during a heat; nor swerve, carry him out, sit down in front of him, or do any other act coming under the head of "helping," under liability of fine, suspension or expulsion.

Heredity. In breeding, the influence of parents upon their offspring; the fact or principle of inheritance or the transmission of physical and mental characteristics from one generation of ancestors to those following them.

Hero of Chester. A term universally applied to the great sire, Hambletonian.

Herod Blood. In the English thoroughbred pedigrees, founded by the Byerly Turk, a celebrated charger owned by Capt. Byerly of Ireland, in the time of King William's wars, in 1689.

Hidden Quality. An element of speed in many pedigrees which trace to unknown sources, but one of uncertainty at best, and in the formation of a family of trotters its evolution must ever be a matter of doubtful experiment.

High Blowing. A term applied to a noisy breathing made by some horses, produced wholly by the action of the nostrils—a distinctly nasal sound, and by no means to be confounded with roaring. It is a habit; not an unsoundness.

High-bred. A meaningless term in common use, one applied alike to the trotting horse, the cross-bred Percheron, or any other class, by which people are often deceived at the hands of the horse sharp, regarding the pedigree or value of an animal. It possesses no significance, and has no proper place in the turf vocabulary.

High-jump. In the high-jump, photographs show that the fore feet first strike the ground after clearing. All high jumpers, as distinguished from broad or hurdle jumpers, land on their fore feet first. At the Madison Square Garden, (New York), fair of 1891, the mare Maud got over a fence seven feet high and landed on her fore feet so nearly perpendicular that had not the grooms laid hold of her, she must have completed a somersault.

High-wheel. The old standard sulky.

Hind Action. Perfect hind action in the trotter is just sufficiently wide to prevent interference with the fore legs and feet; and yet, brought as nearly as it can to approach to a straight line with the forward action, without interference, or the least loss of muscular power.

Hippodroming. An old term, said to have been first used by George Wilkes in 1857, to denote the plan of taking two well known horses together through the country to trot for purses and divide the profits. The plan met with great opposition when first started. Flora Temple and Lancet were the first horses to trot together in this way, which they did at Elmira, N. Y., September 2, 1857. Now termed "campaigning."

Hippometer. A French term for a standard adjustable instrument for measuring the height of horses—consisting of an upright standard, an arm to rest on the shoulder, and registering the height in centimetres.

Hippometric Cane. A cane which pulls out in segments, one within the other, being a metallic rod within a hollow rattan staff or cane, and fastened in, when closed, by means of springs. Used for measuring the height of horses.

Hippophagy. The consumption of horse meat as human food.

Hippophile. A horse fancier; one who has a special love or fondness for horses.

Hip-Straps. The pieces of a harness attached to the back straps, on each side, which hold the breeching-straps and breeching in place.

Hiring Horses. [Law.] When a horse is let out for hire for the purpose of performing a particular journey, the person letting warrants it fit and competent for such journey; and the owner of the horse is liable for any accident which may befall it when used with reasonable care by the person hiring it.

History. The three great periods into which the history of the English turf and the breeding of horses is naturally divided, are: 1. From the beginning of history to the end of the reign of Queen Elizabeth, (1603), or before the times of the thoroughbred horse; 2. from the ascension of James I. in 1603, to the year 1791, the first publication of the Stud Book, the period of the making of the thoroughbred horse, and; 3, from 1791 to the present day. Races were known in very early times. In the reign of Henry II., (1154-1189), tournaments began to be of frequent occurrence, and one writer, Fitz-

Stephen, mentions the delight taken by the people of London in this diversion. In 1326 Edward III. purchased running horses, and in the ninth year of his reign received a present of two running horses from the King of Navarre. Henry VIII., (1483-1485), took great pains to improve the royal stud, and imported horses from Turkey, Naples and Spain. In 1602 the first Arabian horses were imported, and races were run for silver bells at many places. Oliver Cromwell, (1653-1660), kept a racing stud and patronized the turf. During the reign of Charles, (1660-1685), he imported horses of Eastern blood, which was continued by his successors, and led to the establishment of the thoroughbred horse. During the reign of this monarch it was proclaimed that persons in His Majesty's service in riding should not use any snaffles but bits. This was probably because bits were more becoming and better suited to the troops, as snaffles were in general more fit for "times of disport," by which racing and the chase were undoubtedly meant. During the reign of George II., 1727, statutes were enacted: That no plates or matches were to be run for under £50 in value, except at Newmarket and Black Hambleton, on a penalty of £200 to be paid by the owner of each horse running, and £100 by the person who advertised the plate; that no person should run any horse at a race but his own; that every horse race was to be begun and ended the same day. The objects of these statutes were "the preventing the multiplicity of horse races; the encouragement of idleness, and the impoverishment of the meaner sort of people." An act for the suppression of races by ponies and weak horses was passed during the reign of George III., 1739. At this time races were held in one hundred and twelve cities and towns in England. During the latter half of the eighteenth century racing declined very much and numbers of meetings were discontinued, this result being due to the wars then raging. But from the beginning of the nineteenth century, and especially after the conclusion of the French war of 1815, racing again revived. A great number of matches and stake races were established, records of the latter having occurred as early as 1828. The royal stud was sold on the ascension of Queen Victoria, in 1837. Just when racing began in America, is not easy to determine; but it is a well attested fact that pacers were bred and paced, especially in Rhode Island, during the last decades of the seventeenth century. Pacing races took place between the gentry of Rhode Island and Virginia, in and about Philadelphia, early in the eighteenth century. In 1665, Governor Nichols established a race course at Hempstead Heath, L. I., N. Y., and ordered that a plate should be run for every year.

In 1669, Governor Lovelace, who succeeded Governor Nichols, ordered races to be run on Hempstead Heath, but from that time for nearly a hundred years, history is quite silent on the subject of horse racing. Then it revived, and one historian says "there was no end to scrub and pace racing in all parts of the middle and southern colonies, and particularly on the good and shaded roads of Manhattan Island." As wealth and leisure increased in the country, after the close of the Revolutionary war, the sport of racing grew so rapidly that laws for its suppression were passed. Pennsylvania passed such laws in 1794, 1817 and 1820; New Jersey in 1797, followed by the States of New York, Connecticut, and probably all the other New England States. The first recorded trotting performance in this country was by the horse Yankee, at Harlem, N. Y., July 6, 1806, over a track said to have been short of a mile, in 2:59. At Philadelphia, in 1810, the Boston horse trotted a mile to harness in 2:48½. The earliest organized effort in behalf of trotting in this country was started at Philadelphia in 1828, by the establishment of the Hunting Park Association. See, SPORT OF KINGS, QUEENS OF THE TURF, TROTTING FAMILIES, EXTREME SPEED, and celebrated individual horses.

Hitch. To hobble; an unsteady gait which crosses and jerks.

Hitch. A team; a horse or horses harnessed to a buggy is said to be a "hitch," and if fine, is properly called a nice hitch; a good hitch.

Hock. The hock is placed between the gaskin and the hind cannon bone, from which it may be separated by a line drawn across this bone at the point at which its head begins to enlarge in order to form a joint with the lower bones of the hock. The hock in the horse represents the heel in man, and the elongations of bones and corresponding tendons are necessary modifications of the plan for the development of speed.

The hock joint is unique in construction. The interlocking grooves of this joint are not direct, as in other hinge joints of the body, and as the corresponding joint in man is, but oblique, so that when flexion takes place at that joint, the lower ray is carried obliquely outward, and when the other leg is passed, and the extension takes place again, its action is reversed and the foot is returned to the position required to support the center of gravity. By this simple contrivance the danger of accident is placed beyond the will of the animal, and in well formed horses beyond the possibility of accident. Some horses circumduct the hind feet more than others, and in others the stifle action is most marked; but it is not common to see both excessive in the same horse. There is often considerable difference in different horses in the length of the hock. The long hock gives the greatest power, for the reason that the leverage is greater; but what is gained in power is lost in speed. —The Horse in Motion, J. D. B. Stillman.

Hock, Point of. The bony projection at the back and

top of the hock. The parts of the hind leg below the hock are similarly named to those of the fore leg below the knee.

Hock Strap. A spreader used to prevent the hopping or sidewise gait of the horse. It is a stout, elastic band of rubber webbing, one and a half to two inches wide, with two small straps and buckles at the ends used to tighten it. Attach this to the leg just above the hock, (not the leg with which the horse hops, but the one carried out), draw moderately tight, and its use will tend to regulate the action of the leg which the horse uses out of line.

Hog on the Bit. A hard puller, and especially a borer or puller to one side, is said to "hog on the bit."

Hogging. The custom of cutting off the mane of the horse in a sort of pompadour style, so that the hairs are about the length of hog's bristles. The delineations of horses in Egyptian, Persian and Grecian monuments and sculpture, represent them with the mane hogged; and this fashion prevailed to a considerable extent in England, in the early part of this century, "when," says Rev. J. G. Wood, "a sham classical mania reigned in the fashionable world." It is not harmful to the horse; it may not come under the head of mutilation, but it is both unnatural and unnecessary.

Hold Over Them. A term used to denote that the horse of which it is said has more speed than his opponents. Thus John Splan says: "Lady Thorne was pitted against George Wilkes, Dexter, Lucy, Goldsmith Maid, American Girl, Mountain Boy and George Palmer, and held over them in nearly all her engagements."

Hold the Horse Together. Used to denote the art of saving a horse at the finish, especially in a running race, from overdoing himself when there is no occasion for it; the act of easing up on the horse at the bit, an inch at a time, as the situation of the finish among the contestants allows; to drive without forcing the horse.

Holders. Hand loops attached to the reins for the purpose of better holding and controlling the horse, particularly if he is a hard puller.

Have the reins made the right length. and don't have three or four yards of leather hanging down behind the sulky. Have the holders on the reins good length and wide, and be sure that you have them in exactly the right place, so that if the horse, from any cause, either from breaking or otherwise, should take an extra hold of the bit you are ready and in the right position to handle him with ease. I drive all my horses with holders on the reins, and I think no man should ever drive in a race without them.—Life with the Trotters, John Splan.

Hole in Him. A defect. "That horse has a hole in him," means that he has an out, an unsoundness, a fault.

Hollow of the Pastern. The hollow at the back and lower part of the pastern joint.

Home. The goal; the ultimate point to which the horse runs; the line which every rider or driver hopes to reach first.

Homestretch. That part of the track between the last turn and the wire, usually wider and more level than any other section of the trotting course; the real battle ground of the contending horses in a race. The rules governing horses in a race on the homestretch, are, perhaps, more carefully made than those covering any other part of the track, with a view of protecting every horse and giving to each the best possible chance to win. They provide that when the foremost horse or horses come out on the homestretch they shall each keep the positions first chosen, under penalty of being ruled out. The hindermost horse or horses, when there is sufficient room to pass on the inside, or in fact, anywhere on the homestretch, without interfering with other horses have the right to do so, and any one interfering to prevent such passing is ruled out by the judges. If in attempting to pass another horse, however, a horse should at any time swerve or cross, so as to impede the stride of a horse behind him, such horse is not entitled to win the heat.

Hood. A protective covering for the horse's head. Hoods are used for both sweating and cooling-out purposes, and are made of various patterns. They embrace long hoods which cover the face in front and extend to the withers; shorter ones which drop just below the eyes and cover half of the crest; throat hoods or jowl sweaters; cooling hood, both long and short; goggle hoods, etc. They are usually made of Canton flannel or California wool goods in plain and fancy colors; heavy or light weight, according to the purpose for which they are used, and in a wide variety of styles and patterns of texture.

I do not believe in getting flesh off a horse with a sweat-blanket or hood—work it off in the natural way.—Training the Trotting Horse, Charles Marvin.

Hood. A canvas covering which buttons upon and closely envelopes the skeleton body or foot-rest of road and speed carts, as a protection to the legs of the driver from mud or dirt. It is adjustable, and taken off when not wanted.

Hoof. The horny box which encloses the horse's foot. In general terms the front part of the hoof near the ground surface is called the toe, the two sides of which are designated as outside and inside toe; the lateral or side portions constitute the quarters; the rear parts on the ground surface the heels. The general shape is that of the half of a cylinder-cut obliquely across its middle, and resting on the surface of this section. In nearly all feet, however, it is slightly conical. Specifically the hoof is separated into these portions, viz: the wall; the sole; the frog. The wall is the outer portion of the hoof, and is divided into a hard, fibrous covering called the crust; and a soft, inner layer of non-fibrous horn. The sole is a thick horny plate between the border of the wall and its reflected prolongations, occupying what is termed the inferior face of the hoof. The frog is a mass of horn, pyramidal in shape, situated between the two re-entering portions of the wall, having a base, four sides and a summit. Within this box or hoof is contained the coffin, navicular and part of the small pastern bones; the sensitive laminæ; the plantar cushion, and the lateral cartilages. Generally the hoofs of the fore feet are broader and rounder in front; those of the hind feet narrower and more pointed. The right and left hoofs of either leg can be distinguished by observing that the inner edge of the wall is flatter and the outer edge more convex.

The hoof grows more rapidly in warm, dry climates, than in cold, wet ones; in healthy, energetic animals, than in those which are soft and weak; during exercise, than repose; in young, than in old animals. In winter it widens, becomes softer and grows but little; in summer it is condensed, becomes more rigid, concave and resisting, is exposed to severer wear, and grows more rapidly. This variation is a provision of Nature to enable the hoof to adapt itself to the altered conditions it has to meet—hard horn to hard ground; soft horn to soft ground.—Horse Shoes and Horse Shoeing, George Fleming, LL.D., M. R. C. V. S.

In a state of nature the hoof preserves its form and qualities under the following conditions: 1. Its elasticity is complete when the frog is in full relation with the ground; 2, its constant use maintains a proper length and a regular axis; 3, the sole has all its thickness, all its strength, and prevents contraction of the heels; 4, the hairs of the coronet cover and protect the cutidure, the varnish of the wall, (periople), protects the horn against alterations of dryness and humidity; 5, the moisture of the soil, the dew, and the freshness of the pasture maintaining it in a state of humidity favorable to the preservation of its form. It requires about eight months for the production of a completely new hoof. All loss of substance to the wall is therefore reduced very slowly; whence the lesson is taught that we should avoid this loss as much as possible. The healthy foot is a very beautiful object.—Exterior of the Horse, Armand Gouboux and Gustave Barrier.

Hopping. Wobbling; the motion of going crooked behind. In doing so the horse shortens the stride of one hind foot, places it under or between his fore feet and carries the other one out, thus causing the hip to hop or wobble behind. Some horses will hop and go sideways to avoid scalping, hitting shins or quarters. The remedy then consists in skillful shoeing and proper booting. Some horses will hop when their heads are checked out of a natural position, either too high or too low. Radical changes in shoeing, such as changing light shoes for heavy ones, and *vice versa* will sometimes cure hopping. Difference in the length of stride of fore feet, arising from faulty conformation or other irregularity, will often cause the horse to go crooked behind. In such cases it can be remedied by adding more weight to the foot which steps the shortest.

Hopples; Hobbles. A device used for changing the gait of a horse from a pace to a trot; from a trot to a pace, or for holding a horse steady at either gait. There are several patterns. They are usually made of leather, covered with lambswool, with elastic connections by which to draw the leg back to the gait desired. They are changable, and may be so adjusted as to act as cross straps, or in a straight line from fore to hind legs.

Horny Sole. A concave plate contained within the lower margin of the wall of the horse's foot covering the lower face of the pedal bone. It is thickest around its outer border where it joins the wall, and thinnest in the center where it is most concave. It is less dense and resisting than the wall of the hoof, and is designed more to support weight than to stand wear. It has a characteristic of breaking off in flakes on the ground face when the fibers become long.

Horse. A well known and most noble domestic animal of the genus *Equus;* family Equidæ; sub-order Perissodactyla, (odd-toed); order Ungulata, (hoofed); class Mammalia. The name of a genus corresponds to the surname or family name of persons of civilized nations, but in the language of science it always precedes the specific name, which corresponds to our given or Christian name. The horse is distinguished from all other members of the Equidæ, by the long hairs of the tail being more abundant and growing from the base as well as from the ends and sides; and also by possessing a small bare callosity on the inner side of the hind leg, just below the hock, as well as one on the inner side of the forearm above the knee, common to all the genus. The mane is longer and more flowing, the front part of it drooping over the forehead, forming the forelock; the ears are shorter, the limbs longer, the feet broader and the head smaller. By the agency of man horses are now diffused throughout almost the whole of the inhabited portions of the globe, and the great modifications they have undergone, in consequence of domestication and selection in breeding, are well illustrated by comparing such extremes as the Shetland pony, dwarfed by scanty food and a rigorous climate, standing from 9.2 to 10.2 hands high; the thoroughbred race-horse of 16.2 hands high, and the gigantic London

dray-horse of from 17 to 18 hands high. There are seven
modifications of the horse type, at present existing, sufficiently
distinct to be reckoned as species by all zoologists. There
were in the United States at the close of the year 1893
16,081,139 horses of all ages, valued at $769,224,799. The
four leading horse producing states are: Iowa, with 1,367,329;
Illinois, with 1,308,771; Texas, with 1,183,895; Missouri,
with 1,008,361. Aside from the recognized trotting bred and
running bred horses in this country the generally recognized
breeds or sub-families are: Clydesdale, Percheron, French
Coach, Yorkshire Coach, Cleveland Bay, English Shire,
Suffolk Punch, Hackney.

In the choice of a horse and a wife a man must please himself.—G. J.
  Whyte-Melville.

Horse. [Law.] The legal definition of a horse is: A
hoofed quadruped of the genus Equus, (E. caballus), having
one toe to each foot, a mane, and a long flowing tail. The
term horse embraces generally all the classes and sexes. It has
been decided that a ridgling is not a gelding, but a horse.—
Chattel Mortgage. It has been decided that a colt born of a
mare which is held under mortgage belongs to the holder of the
legal title, the mortgagee; but to make a chattel mortgage good
to hold the colt he must show that it was conceived prior to the
date of his mortgage.—*Exemptions.* The exemption of a horse
from execution under the exemption act in Texas, includes
everything absolutely essential to its beneficial enjoyment, as
bridle, saddle and martingale. It has been held that a horse
standing at a farrier's to be shod, is exempt from distress on
the plea of public utility.—*Leaving at an Inn.* The tendency
of modern cases, says the American and English Encyclopedia
of Law, xi, 23, (1890), is to hold that merely leaving a horse
at an inn cannot of itself suffice to constitute one a guest,
though, according to the earlier cases, and others which have
followed their views, it is not essential, in order to constitute
one a guest, in legal contemplation, that he should receive personal entertainment at the inn; but it may be enough that he
leave his horse, particularly if he be a traveler in the strict
sense. The older doctrine that the mere leaving a horse at an
inn may constitute the owner a guest, is supported in the leading American case in which this view is taken, by an early
English decision, recognizing, by a divided court, the lien of an
inn keeper in regard to a horse left at his stable by a traveler
who did not himself put up at the inn, and is further sustained
by judicial declarations and statements of legal writers. It
also receives qualified support in this country from a modern
leading case, where the point does not seem to be directly

involved · and from a recent case in which a preference is given to the view cf the older authorities, and it is held that a traveler or wayfarer journeying over the country becomes a guest by obtaining and paying for entertainment for his beasts at an inn; but in both these cases the doctrine is apparently confined to those who are travelers or wayfarers as distinguished from residents. But where one leaves his horse with an inn keeper with no intention of stopping at the inn himself, but stops at a relative's house, he is not a guest of the inn, and the liability of the landlord is simply that of an ordinary bailee for hire.

If a person who is traveling over the country from place to place, or from one place to another and returning, has occasion to seek entertainment for his horse or horses, alone, and obtains it for them upon consideration of reward or pay charged him by the host or landlord, he is in the legal sense a guest, as much as if he had himself received personal entertainment, and while such entertainment for his beasts continues, if any damage or injury happens to them, or they be stolen, he is absolutely liable for them to the same extent as if he had undertaken against the particular damage by a special arrangement.—Atlantic Reporter, Vol. 8, Rochester, N. Y., (Del.), 228

The existence of an inn involves, in legal contemplation, a stable attached to it also, and travelers with horses and carriages are not to be presumed to put them up at an inn otherwise than as inn stables strictly, whereas those not travelers, but merely putting up their teams at the inn stables as a livery, (as in the case with persons residing near towns, who use such stables as mere conveniences), are not to be considered in the light of guests and entitled to the same degree of protection as travelers are.—Atlantic Reporter, Vol. 8, Rochester, N. Y., (Del.), 260.

If a guest goes to an inn and leaves his horse there with the host and goes away himself for a time, and in his absence the horse is stolen, the host is chargeable on account of the profit arising from the keeping of the horse.—American Decisions, A. C. Freeman, San Francisco, 1880, 254-259.

By the rules of the American Turf Congress the word horse is understood to include mare or gelding.

Horse Breeders' Registry, The, for the registration of trotting and pacing horses, according to established rules and classes. Headquarters, Boston, Mass. Rules governing admission to registry:

First: Any stallion that has himself a trotting record of 2:30 or better, or pacing record of 2:25 or better, provided any of his get has a trotting record of 2:35 or better, or pacing record of 2:30 or better, or provided his sire or dam is already standard.

Second: Any mare or gelding that has a trotting record of 2:30 or better, or pacing record of 2:25 or better.

Third: Any horse that is the sire of two animals with a trotting record of 2.30 or better, or pacing record of 2:25 or better, or one trotter with a record of 2·30 or better, and one pacer with a record of 2:25 or better.

Fourth: Any horse that is the sire of one animal with a trotting record of 2:30 or better, or pacing record of 2:25 or better, provided he has either of the following additional qualifications, viz: (a), a trotting record himself of 2:35 or better, or pacing record of 2:30 or better; (b), is the sire of two other trotters with records of 2:35 or better, or pacers with records of 2:30 or better, or one trotter with a record of 2:35 or better, and one pacer with a record of 2:30 or better; (c), has a sire or dam that is already standard.

Fifth: Any mare that has produced a trotter with a record of 2:30 or better, or pacer with a record of 2:25 or better.

Sixth· The progeny of a standard horse when out of a standard mare.

Seventh: The progeny of a standard horse when out of a mare by a standard horse.

Eighth: The progeny of a standard horse when out of a mare whose dam is standard.

Ninth: Any mare that has a trotting record of 2:35 or better, or a pacing record of 2:30 or better, provided either her sire or dam is standard.

Class Rules: I. This includes only horses standard under either rule 2, 3 or 4, and mares standard under rules 2 and 5. Every animal in this class must be either a performer or producer.—II. This includes only the produce of mares in class I., when by stallions in class I. Every animal in this class must have a performer or producer for both sire and dam. —III. This includes only the produce of a mare in class I., when by any standard stallion not in class I., also the standard produce of any mare not in class I., when by a stallion belonging to class I.—IV. Includes all standard bred animals not embraced in the other three classes.

Horse-leap Church. A church near Kilbeggan in the county of West Meath, Ireland, which takes its name from a remarkable leap that was made near it by a horse while hunting with hounds. It was over a narrow road, on either side of which there was a stone wall. The horse took both walls and the road in one leap thus clearing all from field to field. The extreme distance was thirty-six feet.

Horseman. One who has thorough skill in the knowledge of horses, and in their management under all conditions; a person who fancies, sells, buys, drives and handles horses; a rider on horseback.

Horsemanship. The art of equitation. It generally refers to riding on horseback, and the management of horses under the saddle.

9

In horsemanship art and science are combined, and so closely connected in any critical performance that they are inseparable for success. The theory and practice must be united, as well in the horse as in his rider, for in equestrian feats these are the exercise and power of mind over matter, and when theory and practice are united and in proportion, and the material and opportunities good, success follows.—The Bridle Bits, Col. J. C. Battersby.

Horse Measurement. In taking the measurement of a horse, length is obtained from the point of the buttock to the point of the shoulder, and height both at the croup and the withers. Other measurements are: Length of head from the poll to the muzzle; length of crest, or arch of neck from the poll to the withers; length of back from the withers to the croup; width of chest at the shoulder points; width of hips; width of forehead. These are made with a rule having two short arms; one fixed at one end, the other moveable and sliding along the face of the rule to the point of contact. Other lines of measurement are: The girth; length from dock to stifle; length from hock to whirlbone; size around the gaskin; size around the forearm; size around the shank; size around the front cannon; size around the coronet. These latter are best made with a common tape measure.

Horse Motion. That peculiar jerking, jogging, or up-and-down motion of a sulky, road cart or other two wheeled vehicle whereby it partakes of the motion of the horse in whatever gait he may be going, is termed "horse motion."

Horse Racing. The practice or sport of running or trotting horses; a race by horses; a match of horses at trotting or running.

Horse-sharp. A term applied to a person who practices deception and fraud in the sale of a horse; a pedigree-swindler; a horse-leech; one who claims fraudulent records of speed, and deceives in regard to the age and soundness of horses which he sells.

The horse-sharp is in general a very versatile rascal. In the village bar-room or around the stable doors he talks loud and persistently, and can crowd more lies into a given number of words than any other specimen of degraded humanity. In short, whether he misrepresents his own horse's pedigree or slanders his neighbor's horse, he is a wholly dirty individual whom an honest man instinctively feels that he soils his hands by touching, and who is a good fellow to keep wholly clear of.—Wallace's Monthly.

Horse Tax. [Eng.] The horse tax in England was imposed in 1784, and was then levied on all saddle and coach horses. Its operation was extended, and its amount increased in 1796, and again in 1808. The existing duty is upon "horses for riding" only.

Horsy. A word used to indicate that a person is fond of, or interested in horses; especially devoted to, or interested in horse-breeding or horse-racing; relating or having to do with horses and turf matters.

Hot Fitting. Fitting the shoe to the horse's foot while the shoe is hot—a practice almost universally followed, formerly, but now rarely used; a method obsolete with the best farriers.

Hour. Trotting races are started at two o'clock P. M., from the first day of April to the 15th day of September, and after that date at one o'clock P. M., until the close of the season.

Housings. A covering. The name derived from a coarse sort of tapestry or carpet work, used in the East for housings or coverings of saddles; hence, the trappings or caparison of a horse; the leather fastened at a horse's collar to turn over the back when it rains. A pad which covers the horse's back under the harness saddle; a lay.

Hub. The center or stock of a wheel in which all the spokes are set, and through which the axle-arm is placed. In England it is called nave. The best hubs of wood are those made of American Elm.

Hub Case. That part of the wheel of a pneumatic sulky which receives the cone containing the ball bearings.

Hug the pole; Hug the Track. Said of a horse that trots close to the pole or guard-rail, or that trots low; as in such case he "hugs" or goes close to the pole, or hugs the ground in a square, level, uninterrupted gait.

Hunting Seat. [Eq.] In horsemanship, as distinguished from a riding seat in racing contests.

The race riders mount for other people's pleasure, and the large sums of money at stake; the hunting man rides for his own pleasure, and is only answerable to himself for his expenditure of horse flesh.—Seats and Saddles, Francis Dwyer.

Hurdle. A movable fence; a bar or frame placed across a race course to be cleared by the horses in a hurdle-race. Hurdles are usually made three feet high; of plank, rods or narrow boards, with an additional foot in height of cedar brush placed above that. The sections of hurdles are placed upon feet, braced, in order to make them stand in position.

Hurdle Race. A race in which the horses are required to jump over hurdles or similar obstacles. Although this style of racing was abandoned throughout the South and West about 1882, the American Turf Congress still maintains rules for hurdle racing. No such race shall be of less than one mile, if a dash race, or over less than four flights of hurdles; and in races longer than one mile there must be an additional flight of hurdles in each quarter of a mile. Winners of hurdle races are not considered winners in steeplechasing, but are considered winners in flat racing. The term "winning horse," with reference to those liable to carry extra weight, or to be excluded from any race, applies only to winners of hurdle races, value $100 and upward, not including the winner's own stake. In the absence of conditions welter weights are carried in hurdle races.

Hurdle Racing. This style of racing is said to have had its origin in the time of King George IV., when, in the absence of better sport a royal hunting party on the Downs near Brighton, amused themselves by racing over some flights of sheep hurdles. The sport was thought to be so good that regular races over hurdles were organized. In the early days of the sport the close-wattled hurdle made of hazel was always used. These were between four and five feet in height and so firmly fastened into the ground that it was not easy to knock them down. In more recent times the hurdles were fixed loosely in the ground, so that a mere tap would throw them over. The cross-country horse that is a good hurdle-racer is regarded as an undeveloped steeplechaser. The hurdles are always to be jumped, not run through or knocked down. The well trained hurdle-jumper will always judge his distance, prepare for the jump, and glide over it, or "take off," easily.

Hypodermic. A term pertaining to parts under the skin; relating to a remedy, or drug, introduced under the skin of the horse by means of a needle or hypodermic syringe.

I

Identification. Facts, testimony, certificates, pedigrees, which help to distinguish a person or horse from all other persons or horses. By the trotting rules, when a horse is nominated for a stake or purse, his color, sex, name, age, class, and whether entered singly or in a double team, must be given. Applied to a person making the entry it includes name, residence, post office address, and other facts to establish his identification, where personally unknown to the officers of a course. Heavy fines and penalties are imposed for refusing to comply with such rules, or for making wrong answers to questions. Similar rules are enforced by the Turf Congress governing all running races.

Illegitimate Racing. [Eng.] An absurd formula used by the sporting press as a synonym for steeplechasing, hurdle-racing, and hunters' flat paces. Previous to the establishment of the Grand National Hunt committee, these sports were unregulated by any code of law, and unrecognized by any racing tribunal, and were then properly regarded as illegitimate. They are now, however, as much under rules as flat racing; notwithstanding, the term continues to be applied to them though it has lost its significance.

In-and-out Horse. A horse that is one day good, and another off, and not to be depended upon; either from being sick, sore, or from some unknown cause trotting a poor race.

J. Q. was a peculiar horse and often trotted in-and-out races, and sometimes the public imagines of such a horse that his driver is not honestly trying to win, when the facts of the case are otherwise.—Life With the Trotters, John Splan.

Inbred; In-and-in Breeding. To breed from animals of the same parentage, or from those closely related.

Infield. The ground or lawn inside of the track or course.

In-hand. [Eq.] A horse is said to be "in hand" when he is sensible to the movements of the rider's legs; bears the spur without becoming excited; does not displace his head or neck, thus wasting his force, the reins bearing upon the sides of his neck, and is ready for the word of the rider, being in perfect equilibrium.

In Harness.   A trotting race in harness means that the performance shall be to a sulky.

In Line.   A term used in attaching pneumatic wheels to the old high wheel sulky.   The wheels must be in exact line in order for the best results as to speed, and also for the life of the wheel.   If not properly placed in line with the point of draught, they will be slower, the stress upon them will be greater, and their life will be shorter.

In-line Trotter.   A horse whose stride is in a straight line, or the print of whose hind foot at speed, is in line with that of his fore foot.   It is said that Martha Wilkes goes so near to line that a person standing in front of, or behind her when at speed, only sees one set of legs.   Her stride at a 2:09¼ gait is eighteen and a half feet.

Incisors.   The twelve front teeth of the horse.   There are two dentitions of the incisors, the first, known as the milk or deciduous teeth ; and the second, or permanent teeth, which replace the former at from two and a half to five years of age. They are known as the pincher or front teeth ; the intermediate teeth, and the corner teeth.

Indications.   [Eq.]   The principles of horsemanship require that the horse should instantaneously obey the indications of the legs and hands of the rider.

Individuality.   That quality, or distinctive characteristic which distinguishes one horse from another ; peculiarity of disposition or make-up.   In no animal is this characteristic more positive than in the horse.   Indeed it may be said with truth that every horse is different from every other horse ; that in almost no respect are they at all alike.   In conformation, disposition, gait, ability to acquire knowledge, gift of speed, quickness of perception, readiness to obey the driver's or rider's will, horses are most unlike.   This individuality is a matter for the closest study, as it must determine the use of the over-draw or side check ; open or blind bridle ; the sort of weights, boots and bits ; the manner of shoeing, and a score of other details of training and management.   Some horses have an abundance of speed for every race, others have only one burst of speed in a mile.   Not only do horses differ widely from each other in the matter of gait, but the different feet of the same horse must often be shod with peculiar shoes to meet peculiar conditions. Hence the mastery of individuality is the first business of the trainer, as success can only come from a full understanding of the horse's peculiar characteristics, and the means of utilizing them to the utmost in the best lines of his service to man.

Indivisible Prize. An indivisible prize is one in which a dead heat is again run for second place, and in which the horses running agree to divide the money or run for an indivisible prize.

Inflate. The act of inflating the pneumatic tire of a bike sulky previous to a heat, by means of an air-pump. There is of course more or less leakage to these tires, consequent upon their age, use, etc., hence the act of inflating must be performed often or less frequently as circumstances require.

Inherited Qualities. Explained by the quotation:

Flexibility of articular ligaments may be acquired by early training and regular exercise, but the proportions of the body are inherited. —The Horse in Motion, J. D. B. Stillman.

Inspectors. Under the old racing rules, a term applied to those officers of the course now known as patrol judges.

Interchangable Gait. A horse that both paces and trots, is said to have an "interchangeble gait."

Interfering. An animal is said to interfere when one foot strikes the opposite, as it passes it, in motion. The inner surface of the fetlock joint is the part most liable to this injury, although it may occur to any part of the ankle. It takes place more often in the hind than in the fore legs. It causes a bruise of the skin and underlying tissues, and is generally accompanied by an abrasion of the surface, causing lameness, dangerous tripping and thickening of the injured parts. The trouble is chiefly due to deformity or faulty conformation, and when arising from this cause is not easy to overcome. But in many cases it may be prevented by special shoeing. In general, the outside heel and quarter of the foot on the injured leg should be lowered sufficiently to change the relative position of the fetlock joint, by bringing it further away from the center plane of the body, thereby allowing the other foot to pass by without striking.

Interphalangeal Articulation. One of the joints of the foot or leg of the horse, situated between any two successive phalanges of the same leg.

Intermaxillary Space. A name given to the V-shaped channel, or groove, formed by the spread of the branches of the lower jaw,—which should be sufficiently deep to make its presence quite perceptible. Where this groove is not well defined, but clothed with a thick tissue, the head has a coarse appearance. This space should be broad between the angles of the jaw, in order that the top of the windpipe may have abundant room for its action at whatever position of the head.

Iroquois. A remarkable horse, descended from the best and most successful racing families in England and America. Foaled in 1878. By imported Leamington, son of Faugh-a-Ballagh; dam, Maggie B. B., the dam of Harold, by imported Australian; second dam, Madeline, by Old Boston, out of Magnolia, dam of Kentucky by imported Glencoe. His color is brown, stands 16 hands, with white stripe in the face, white on the left fore foot; he has a well placed, oblique shoulder, good barrel, fine hip and loin, and sound, good legs and feet. He has been a fine success in the stud. As a two-year-old he won the Chesterfield stakes at Newmarket, and Levant stakes at Goodwood, England; as a three-year-old he won the Burwell stakes, Derby at Epsom, Prince of Wales stakes, Doncaster, St. Leger, Newmarket Derby, and other important events in England, winning, in nine races, the sum of £16,805.

Irregular Race. The trotting rules provide that any public race at a less distance than one mile, and exceeding half a mile, is an irregular race, and time made in any such race is a bar.

Isabel. A family of celebrated pure cream-colored horses in Hessenhausen, near Hanover, Germany, from which the famous cream-colored horses used by Queen Victoria on state occasions are obtained.

Isabella; Isabelle; Isabelline. A name applied to a horse of a pale brown, or buff color, similar to that of a hare. The origin of the color is given by two French writers, Bouillet and Littré, but better by Isaac D'Israeli, in his Curiosities of Literature. At the beginning of the seventeenth century Ostend was being besieged by the Austrians. Isabella, daughter of Philip II, and wife of the Archduke Albert, Governor of the Netherlands, vowed not to change her body linen till Ostend was taken. The siege, unluckily for her comfort, lasted three years—1601-1604—but the fair princess kept her oath; and the supposed color of the Archduchess's linen gave rise to a fashionable color called *l'Isabeau*, or the Isabella—a kind of whitish-yellow-dingy.

J

Jack-saddle. Small saddle; the saddle which supports the lugs of a harness, and which, with the back-band, or back-strap, is the real keel of the harness.

Jady. Tired; worn out; reduced in condition.

Jadish. Said of a horse that is skittish, vicious, tricky.

Jibbing. Restiveness; unsteady. A vice.

Jimmy. A bad break.

Jockey. The saddle tree of a harness.

Jockey. A professional rider of race horses; often applied, though erroneously, to drivers in harness races. The Turf Congress rules provide that jockeys cannot ride without first having obtained a license, and the requirements governing the issuing and recording of licenses are exceedingly strict. All licenses are for one year, and expire December 31. Fees are regulated by the Congress, [see FEE], and a heavy penalty attaches for receiving or offering fees for riding, in excess of those stipulated by the rules. If a jockey refuses to ride for the fee allowed, he may be fined, suspended or ruled off. If a jockey should own, in whole or in part, a race horse in training, he is not allowed to ride horses other than his own.

That corporate body of men and boys to whose skill, judgment and honesty is ultimately entrusted the issue of all turf contests, and who are, therefore, the arbiters of each racing man's destiny.—The Badminton Library: Racing, The Earl of Suffolk and Berkshire, and W. G. Craven.

Jockeying. Trickery; a term applied to any fraudulent transaction concerning a race; deception in recommending or selling a horse.

Jockey Seat. When he comes to the finish of a race, the jockey sits down to ride his horse just as the cavalry soldier should.

Jockeyship. The science and art of race riding.

Jog; Jog Trot. An idle, listless motion; a slow trot, in which the space which the body of the horse passes over with its center of gravity unsupported, is very short.

Jogging. The act of exercising, or working a horse to keep him in condition, or to prepare him for a race. There is no development in jogging, and it is wholly a preliminary exercise to bring the muscular organization to the point of sustained, determined action. In jogging, the horse is generally attached to a jogging cart, or sulkyette, which is easier for both horse and driver than a sulky. There is more motion to a bike, in jogging, than to a high wheel sulky, but at speed the former rides easier. Eight miles an hour is the usual jogging gait.

Jowl-piece; Jowl-wrap. A sweat bandage about four feet long, one foot wide at one end, tapering to six inches at the other end, for binding around the throat and neck.

For sweating out the throat, or for any purpose that a hood answers, I prefer a jowl-piece. The use of heavy sweat-hoods is, I am sure, often weakening and injurious, and, if used at all, it should be with great discrimination and care.—Training the Trotting Horse, Charles Marvin.

Judges. Every race is under the management of three judges, one of whom may be the starter, or a starter may be chosen, in addition to the judges. The judges may act as timers, or timers may be appointed, independent of the judges. Judges must be in the stand fifteen minutes before the time for the starting of every race, and they have absolute control over all horses, drivers, riders and assistants during a race, with authority to appoint assistants, remove or put up drivers or riders, and to fine, suspend or expel whosoever fails to obey their orders or the trotting rules. The functions of the judges cease when they have placed the horses in a race, announced the time—subject to objections that have not been decided—and affixed their signatures to the clerk's record of the race, which must be done before leaving the stand.

Judging Pace. A trick of the rider or driver, by means of which he knows at just what pace his own horse is going, compared to that of his opponents; and by which he is able to regulate his speed so that he may have the best possible chance of getting home successfully, and selecting the exact point from which he ought to make his closing effort at the finish.

Jump. The act, on the part of a horse, of taking or clearing a fence, ditch, hedge, hurdle or other obstruction. "Throw your heart over the fence," says the maxim, "and the horse will follow if he can." It is said that horses can jump walls and timber highest and safest when they are just well into a canter, or when they have had a trot of twenty yards, before approaching a fence, to give them a chance to see something of the kind of obstacle they are to get over, and have got into their second or third stride of a canter. But the writer in Badminton says it is curious to note, in a steeple-chase, that however straight a horse is put at fence, he never jumps quite straight, but always lands a little to left or right. From various sources in English turf history, accounts of remarkable jumps are given, some of which, it must be said, do not appear to be absolutely authentic. The horse Proceed is said to have cleared thirty-seven feet while running a steeple-chase in 1847. A horse called Culverthorn is reported to have jumped thirty-three feet on one occasion; and Lather, a hunter owned by Lord Ingestrie, is said to have jumped thirty-seven feet five inches, over a pit. Sir Charles Knightley's horse, the black thoroughbred Penvolio, jumped thirty-one feet over a fence and brook below Brigworth Hill, in the Patchley Hunt. A jump over a brook was made by Old Chandler, a famous steeplechaser, ridden by Captain Broadley, in March, 1847, while running in the Leamington Cup, Warwick, which meas-ured thirty-nine feet, from the hoof-marks on the taking-off to the hoof-marks on the landing, from actual measurement.

K

Keeping with One's Horses. A term used to denote what has been called the easiest of all tactics in a running race—that is, to keep with one's horses, the contestants, until the finish, and then to come away if one can.

Kegging. A form of restiveness; a vice. A restive horse is one, under the saddle, that is fidgety and uneasy, yet refusing to go on. To overcome the habit, give the horse a good shaking up; a cut or two with the whip, a few digs of the spurs, pull him round and round to one side, then to another, rein him back, and thus tire him out.

Kentucky Saddler. A family of celebrated horses, native of Kentucky, founded by breeding the thoroughbred four-mile race horse, Denmark, by imported Hedgeford, to the native or Canadian cross-bred mares of that State; hence, the modern Kentucky saddler is a cross between the thoroughbred and the pacer. The horses are very handsome, of good disposition, weigh about 1,200 pounds, and are good jumpers. They are trained to the flat-footed walk, or ordinary walk; the running walk; the amble; the rack, or single foot; the trot; the canter, and the gallop.

Keratogenous Membrane; Keratopyllus Tissue. The name of a membrane of the horse's hoof which embraces the coronary cushion; the velvety tissue, or formative organ of the sole and frog, and the laminal tissue.

Kerbs; Chestnuts. Epidermal glands on the curb, or level of the hock joint; and on the inside of the knees. See CHESTNUTS.

Kicking. A serious vice.

Killing Big. Making a fortunate strike in the pool-box.

Kindergarten. The training ground for young colts.

Kings of the Pacers. To close of 1893: One mile by a gelding—Mascot, by Deceive, Terre Haute, Ind., September 29, 1892, (race record); and Flying Jib, by Algona, Chicago, Ill., September 15, 1893, (against time), 2:04. One mile by a stallion—Direct, by Director, Nashville, Tenn., November 8, 1892, 2:05¼. One mile to wagon—Roy Wilkes, by Adrian Wilkes, Independence, Iowa, October 30, 1891, over kite track,

2:13. One mile under saddle — Johnston, by Joe Bassett, Cleveland, Ohio, August 3, 1888, 2:13.

Kings of the Runners. To close of 1893: One mile—Salvator, four-year-old, 110 pounds, Monmouth Park, August 28, 1890, (against time, straight course), 1:35½; Chorister, three-year-old, 112 pounds, Morris Park, June 1, 1893, 1:39¼. Two miles—Ten Broeck, five-year-old, 110 pounds, Louisville, Ky., May 29, 1877, (against time); and Newton, four-year-old, 107 pounds, Washington Park, Chicago, July 13, 1893, 3:27¼. Four miles—Ten Broeck, four-year-old, 104 pounds, Louisville, Ky., September 27, 1876, (against time), 7:15¾. See RUNNING.

Kings of the Trotters, Stallion. During the period between 1858 and 1894, thirty-six years, there have been fifteen stallion kings of the American trotting turf which have had their share in reducing the time of one mile from 2:30 to 2:05¼, viz: 1858: Ethan Allen, foaled 1849, by Black Hawk, dam, Holcomb mare; New York, October 28; 2.28.—1859-'67: George M. Patchen, foaled 1849, by Cassius M. Clay, dam, Sickles mare; New York, July 7, 1859; 2:26½; May 16, 1860; 2:25; May 16, 1860; 2:24; July 2, 1860; 2:23½.—1868: Fearnaught, foaled 1859, by Morrill, dam, Jenny by the French horse; July 29; 2:23½.—1868: George Wilkes, foaled 1856, by Hambletonian, dam, Dolly Spanker, by Henry Clay, Providence, R. I., October 13; 2:22.—1871-'73; Jay Gould, foaled 1864, by Hambletonian, dam, Lady Sanford by American Star; Buffalo, N. Y., August 11, 2:22; August 7, 1872; 2:21½.—1874-1884: During this period the crown was held by Smuggler, with the exception of one month in 1874, when it was held by Mambrino Gift. Smuggler was foaled 1866, by Blanco, dam, the Irwin mare; Buffalo, N. Y. August 5, 1874, 2:20¾; Boston, Mass., September 15, 1874; 2:20; Philadelphia, Pa., July 15, 1876; 2:17½; Philadelphia, Pa., July 15, 1876; 2:17; Cleveland, Ohio, July 27, 1876; 2:16¼; Rochester, N. Y., August 10, 1876; 2:15¾; Hartford, Conn.; August 31, 1876; 2:15¼. Mambrino Gift, foaled 1866, by Mambrino Pilot, dam, Waterwitch by Pilot Jr.; Rochester, N. Y.; August 13, 1874; 2:20.—1884: Phallas, foaled 1877, by Dictator, dam, Betsy Trotwood, by Clark Chief; Chicago, Ill., July 14; 2:13¾. The above are all records obtained in races; the records obtained below, with the exception of the last race made by Directum, are races against time. 1884-'88: Maxie Cobb, foaled 1875, by Happy Medium, dam, Lady Jenkins by Black Jack; Providence, R. I.; September, 30; 2:13¼.—1889: Axtell, foaled 1886, by William L., dam, Lou, by Mambrino Boy, Terre Haute, Ind., October 11; 2:12.—

1890–'91:   Nelson, foaled 1882, by Young Rolfe, dam,
Gretchen, by Gideon, Kankakee, Ill., September 20, 1890;
2:11½; Terre Haute, Ind., October 9; 2:11¼; Cambridge City,
Ind., October 21; 2:10¾; Grand Rapids, Mich., September 17,
1891; 2:10. Allerton, foaled 1886, by Jay Bird, dam, Gussie
Wilkes by Mambrino Boy, Independence, Iowa, September 4.
1891; 2:10; Independence, Iowa, September 19, 1891; 2:09¼.
—1891:   Palo Alto, foaled 1882, by Electioneer, dam, Dame
Winnie by Planet, Stockton, Cal., November 17; 2:08¾.—
1892:   Kremlin, foaled 1887, by Lord Russell, dam, Eventide,
by Woodford Mambrino, Nashville, Tenn., November 5;
2:08¼; Nashville, Tenn., November 12; 2:07¾.—1893:   Directum, foaled 1889, by Director, dam, Stemwinder, by Venture,
New York; September 4, 2:07; Chicago, Ill.; September, 15;
2:06½; Nashville, Tenn., October 18; 2:05¼.

Kite.   The kite-shaped track.

Kite Track.   A track so called because in shape it
resembles a kite, having only one turn, the stretches bearing
towards each other instead of running parallel, and finally converging at a point.   On such a track the horses are started
from a wire stretched from one side of the judges' stand to the
opposite side of the track; and finish under another wire
stretched from the opposite side of the judges' stand from that
by, or from which, they are sent away.   All kite tracks are
one mile between these two wires.   It is said that kite-shaped
tracks were laid out on the ice in Canada as early as 1870;
but the first one in the United States was devised by William
B. Fasig of New York, and built by him for C. W. Williams
of Independence, Iowa.   Work upon it was commenced in the
fall of 1889, and it was completed in the spring of 1890, the
first meeting over it having been held in the fall of 1890.   To
the close of 1893 kite tracks had been built at Independence,
Iowa; Rockford, Ill.; Sturgis, Mich.; Columbia, Tenn.;
Meadville, Penn.; Newark, N. Y.; Chillicothe, Ohio; Stockton, Cal.; Old Orchard, Maine.

I claim it is the fastest form of a track, because there is but one turn
to make, and that a long, easy one, rendering it nearer a straight
mile than can be secured by any other arrangement.   In addition
to the increase of speed to be obtained incident to making one turn
instead of two, every horse in a race, except the pole horse, would
trot a shorter mile than on the regulation track.   Assuming the
second position on a track to be six feet from the pole—and it is
undoubtedly more than that distance—a horse in second position
trots, on a regulation track, thirty-seven and seven-tenths feet
further than at the pole.   On the kite-shaped track, in second
position, he trots but twenty-two feet further, making a saving in
distance of fifteen and seven-tenths feet.   It has but one disadvantage that occurs to me, and that is, that no heat longer than one
mile could be trotted upon it.   But for fast time at mile distances
it would certainly eclipse any other form.—W. B. Fasig, in Spirit of
the Times, December, 24, 1887.

Knee. The carpal articulation, or proper wrist-joint of the horse; the joint between the two principal parts of the fore leg.

Knee-pads. Pads or rolls placed on the flaps of a saddle to help prevent the rider's knees from going too far forward.

Knees, Swollen. A legal unsoundness in a horse.

Knock. To "take the knock," is to lose more money to the bookmakers than one can pay, and thus to be incapacitated from approaching the ring.

Knock the Knees. A knee-knocker; a horse which in speeding fast hits the right knee with the inside, or toe, of the left front foot; or the left knee with the right front foot. In shoeing, the outside of the foot towards the toe should be lowered, with most of the weight on the inside, and the knee-joint should be properly booted.

Knuckling Over Behind. A stumble with one of the hind feet. The trick can generally be cured by lowering the foot if it be too long, and reducing it under the toe, so as to set the slope of the hoof at an angle of about 55 deg. Until cured it is a legal unsoundness.

Koomrah. The wild horse of Northern Africa.

L

Lameness. All lameness, whether of a permanent or temporary character, is a legal unsoundness.

Lamina; Laminæ. A thin scale, leaf or membrane; the lamellar structure of the horse's foot. There are from five to six hundred of these leaves in each foot. They run parallel to each other, and are separated by deep channels, into which are joined, by a dovetailed arrangement, similar leaves on the inside of the wall of the hoof. They extend from the white zone, between the coronary cushion, to the plantar border of the foot, terminating in large prolongations lodged in the horny tubes at the circumference of the sole. While these leaves are exceedingly tenacious, they have great expansive capacity. Mons. Bouley, an eminent French hippopathologist, affirms that their elasticity is equal to one-fourth of an inch, both in the lateral and the longitudinal directions; the entire laminæ, therefore, have a combined capacity of more than one hundred and fifty inches of expansive force.

Laminitis. An inflammation of the sensitive parts of the foot; formerly known as founder, and chest-founder. It is chiefly confined to the sensitive laminæ, or leaves, which unite the wall of the hoof to the parts within; and of these, the leaves in the front of the foot are most seriously affected, although generally the entire fleshy portion of the foot is involved. While the fore feet are those most frequently affected, the hind feet may also suffer, and, in certain instances, all the feet may be inflamed. Among the chief causes of this terrible affliction are a sudden chill from drinking cold water when heated and fatigued, and overloading the stomach with grain; though why certain kinds of grain will cause it has not yet been clearly ascertained by the best veterinarians. The disease is always insidious in its attack, and destructive to the horse. It is a legal unsoundness.

Lampas. A congestive and swollen condition of the fleshy lining, or soft parts, of the roof of the mouth, immediately behind the upper front teeth.

Landing. Referring to the finish of a heat or race, as in the expression, "the horses made a fine landing."

Lapped. It is said of horses in a finish, when so close to each other that only a length separates some of them, and when others are so near their opponents as to have their heads over the other's backs, that they are "lapped."

They all finished lapped on each other.—Life with the Trotters, John Splan.

Lapped Track. A short track. Time made on a lapped track is accepted, provided it is lapped a sufficient distance to make the horse trot a full mile three feet from the pole.

Lateral Cartilages. Tissues attached to each side of the wings of the coffin bone, whose function is to assist the frog and its connected structures to regain their normal position, after having been displaced by the weight of the body while the foot rested on the ground.

Lateral Gait. The pace. The pacer, like the trotter, moves two feet in the same direction simultaneously, then alternates with the other two; but in place of the fore leg and the hind leg of opposite sides, he moves in unison the fore and hind leg of one side, then the fore and hind leg of the other side. Hence the pace is called the "lateral gait."

Lateral Strain; Lateral Stress. A stress at right angles to the strain which produces it, or at right angles to a line of motion, or strain; the sidewise strain which comes upon a sulky wheel in going around the curves of a track.

Lavender. [Eng.] "In lavender" is said of a man or a horse to denote that he is ill; unfit; out of condition.

Law. The racing, or speeding, of horses is not illegal, or against public policy. This is evident from the fact that State legislatures expressly authorize it to be done by certain corporate bodies. The offering of a premium, or reward, to those competing in such races, when such premiums or rewards are not a mere cover or disguise for betting, is not illegal. The party entering a race, if a winner, may recover the premium, though he paid an entrance fee which went to make up such premium. Where the judges of a horse race had discretionary power to exclude a horse violating a certain rule from further participation in the race, their decision allowing the horse to proceed after a violation should not be set aside, except upon the grounds of clear proof of fraud affecting such decision. These points are well established by the case, Porter *vs.* Day, *et al.* [Reports of Cases in the Supreme Court of Wisconsin, Chicago, Ill., 1888; Vol. LXXI, p. 296-304.] In a race over the Eau Claire Driving Park Association in September, 1885, trotted under National Rules, Porter entered a horse,

10

Sorrel George, in a $150 purse, paying an entrance of $30. The defence was that the plaintiff did not comply with the rules, as his horse paced instead of trotted, and could not have won had he trotted instead of paced. Verdict for plaintiff. Defendants appealed, and contended that the contract was void as against public policy. Only two points were considered: 1st. Was the contract void or illegal under common law. 2d. Was there sufficient evidence of fraud on the part of the plaintiff to avoid the decision of the judges of the race in his favor, by allowing nim to keep in the race. Finding of the full bench: 1st. The speeding of horses is not illegal, as the Legislature would not allow corporate bodies to do that which was against the policy of the State. 2d. No case is made out for setting aside the decisions of the judges at the time of the race. The plaintiff's horse fairly won three of the five heats. The only doubt as to the right of the plaintiff to the money, is that in the third heat, (when the plaintiff's horse did not win), he was so managed by his driver that he violated the rules governing the race, and should have been excluded from further competition for the reward. There is nothing in evidence to show that the judges were, in duty bound, to exclude the plaintiff's horse; and the decision of the judges cannot be overruled in order to give the reward to some other competitor, except by showing a clear case of fraud. In the third heat the plaintiff's horse paced most of the way, but admitting this, it was within the discretion of the judges to permit him to go again. This discretionary power to exclude the horse must be exercised by the judges before the next heat is run, and having exercised that power and permitted the horse to go again and win the race, nothing but the clearest case of fraud, on the part of the owner of the horse, should be allowed to set aside the decision of the judges of the race. No fraud was shown, and the decision of the judges of the race must stand. Judgment of the Circuit Court affirmed.

Books of veterinary practice cannot be read to a jury in argument. In the case of Washburn *vs.* Cuddihy, in Massachusetts Reports, 8 Gray, p. 430, 1861, counsel for the plaintiff proposed to read from Dadd's "Veterinary Surgery," a description of the habit of cribbing, in horses, as a better mode of showing the jury what cribbing was, but the opposing counsel objected, and the court sustained the objection. In sustaining the objection, Judge Briggs said that where such books are thus offered, they are, in effect, used as evidence, and the substantial objection is that they are statements wanting the sanction of an oath; and the statement thus proposed is made by one who is not present, and therefore not liable to cross-examination. If the same author were cross-examined, and called to state the grounds of his opinion, he might, himself, alter or modify it, and it would be tested by a comparison with the opinions of others. Moreover, the range of subjects in the veterinary art are not open to persons of common experience, hence they are not qualified to judge regarding them, and it is not competent for counsel to use them in argument against the objection of the other side.

In the New York Supreme Court, Justice Gaynor, of Brooklyn, rendered an opinion, May 28, 1894, that horse racing is not a lottery. The opinion was given in the case of Philip Dwyer, President of the Brooklyn Jockey Club, accused of "contriving, proposing and maintaining a lottery." Acting for the association, of which he was president, the defendant advertised and organized a horse race to be run May 15, 1894. The race was to be open to all thoroughbred horses three years old and upwards, which horses, in order to run, had to be duly entered on the books of the association. An entry fee of $250 was charged, part of which was to be remitted in the case of horses withdrawn before the race. The race was to be for a stake of $25,000, of which $18,000 was to go to the winner, $5,000 to the second horse, and $2,000 to the third horse. The stake was to be made up by the association adding to the total of the entry moneys a sufficient sum for that purpose. This is what the complainant calls a lottery; and in rendering his opinion, Justice Gaynor said: "There is no foundation for his contention. It is not a lottery, either in common speech or within legal definition. A lottery depends on lot or chance, such as the casting of lots, the throwing of dice or the turning of a wheel. Human intelligence, judgment or skill plays no part in the determination of the result. In the scheme of this race, horse owners do not pay a sum to win a larger sum by lot or chance, but in order to enter into the contest of skill, endurance and speed upon which the stake depends, in which intelligence, sagacity and good judgment play a very important part in the determination of the result." Racing horses for stakes was made penal by the New York statute of 1802, and the same provision, coming from the beginning down the distinct lines of legislation, known as "Lotteries" and "Gaming," is now found in Section 352 of the Penal Code, which, in so many words, makes all racing or trials of speed between horses or other animals for any bet, stake or reward, a misdemeanor; and it indisputably covers the facts of this case, viz.: The racing of horses for contributed stakes. But by Chapter 479 of the laws of 1887 the operation of this section is suspended during thirty days in each year on the grounds of the said association, and all like associations, and the day of the race on which the alleged offense is predicated was one of those days.

Law. Compendium of the laws and statutes of the different States in regard to racing, trotting, ringing, disguising, welching, betting, book-making, pool-selling, fraudulent entries and change of name of horses:

Alabama: Race tracks must be licensed; towns and cities of less than five thousand inhabitants pay $100 annually; those of over that number $200.

Arkansas: A race course is prohibited within three miles of any institution of learning, under a fine of not less than $50, nor more than $1,000.

Connecticut: For entering any horse, mare, gelding, colt or filly for any prize, stake, purse, premium or sweepstake under an assumed or false name, or out of its proper class; or for misrepresenting the previous performance of a horse when he is entered, is punishable by a fine not to exceed $1,000, or imprisonment not exceeding three years, or both. Bets on horse racing are void. Pool-selling or book-making on any race is punishable by a fine of $500, or imprisonment not more than one year, or both. Horse racing within two miles of any public assembly or religious meeting in a field, is punishable by a fine of from $8 to $50, or imprisonment for thirty days.

Delaware: Stallions kept for service must be licensed; betting on a horse race is punishable by a fine of $30.

Florida: Associations for the purpose of driving, racing, or otherwise improving the speed and breed of horses, duly incorporated, or which shall be incorporated in the future, are allowed the privilege of selling pools, except between the first day of November and the first day of May of each year; and all pool-selling shall be confined to the track, and on days only on which the races take place. All associations shall pay to the State three per cent. on the gross receipts for admissions to the tracks or grounds. Racing within one mile of a camp-meeting is punishable by a fine of $20.

Georgia: Entering a horse in a race under a false name, or out of his proper class or division, is punishable by a fine not to exceed $1,000; imprisonment not to exceed six months, or to work in the chain-gang on the public works not to exceed twelve months.

Idaho: To mark or brand any horse, mare, colt, jack or other animal not belonging to the person so marking it; to change such brand, or to steal such animal, is punishable by a fine of from $25 to $300, or by imprisonment six months, or both.

Illinois: There shall be no racing within one mile of a camp meeting, or on the public highway, under a penalty of a fine of $100.

Indiana: Making a false entry for any purse, prize, premium, stake, or sweepstake, offered by any agricultural society, association, person, or persons, is punishable by imprisonment in State prison not less than one, nor more than three years, or in the county jail in the county where convicted not less than six months, or by a fine not exceeding $1,000. The name of a horse shall not be changed after once having contested for a prize, except as prescribed by the code of printed rules of the society or association. Registry of the pedigrees of stallions kept for service must be made with the county clerk. Betting or buying pools on any trial of speed is punishable by a fine of from $5 to $100, or imprisonment from ten days to three months.

Iowa: To enter or drive any horse, mare, gelding, colt, or filly, for any prize, purse, premium, stake, or sweepstake, under an assumed name or out of its proper class, is punishable by imprisonment in the penitentiary not more than three years; in the county jail where convicted not more than one year, or by a fine not exceeding $1,000. Provisions with reference to pool-selling, or book-making, do not apply to races taking place upon grounds or within enclosures controlled by agricultural societies and driving associations duly incorporated.

Kentucky: For entering a horse in any race under an assumed name or out of its class, or for fraudulently misrepresenting the public performance of a horse as to time made, is punishable by imprisonment in the county jail not more than one year, in the penitentiary not more than two years, or by a fine not exceeding $1,000. The name of a horse shall not be changed after he has made a public performance except in accordance with the rules of the racing association. No minor shall ride a race, practice a horse to run, or break a horse to ride, under a fine of $100 paid by his parent, master or guardian.

Maine: Ringing, disguising, or making false entries of a horse in a race is punishable by a fine of $500, or by imprisonment not exceeding six months. Stallions kept for service must be recorded in the county registry where kept, by giving name, color, size, and pedigree. Failure to so register, or for making a false entry of pedigree for record, is punishable by a fine of $100.

Massachusetts: For making an entry of a painted or disguised horse, or a horse different from the one purported to be entered or driven, for the purpose of competing in a class or for a purse or premium in which he does not belong, the law imposes a fine not exceeding $500, or imprisonment not exceeding six months. Pool-selling on races is punishable by one year's imprisonment, or by a fine not exceeding $2,000, or both. The owner of a stallion kept for breeding purposes must file a certificate giving the name, color, age, and size of the same, with his pedigree, with the clerk of the city or town for record. Failure to do so is punishable by a fine of $100; and for a false pedigree or false certificate of registry the penalty is ninety days in jail, or a fine of $300, or both.

Maryland: Stallions kept for service must be recorded with the clerk of the Circuit Court of the county where kept, such record giving the name, age, pedigree, and record of the stallion. Failure to record, or the recording of a false pedigree is punishable by the recovery of such damage " as may be shown to have been sustained by reason of such false and fraudulent representation." For entering any horse under a false name, or out of its proper class, is punishable by imprisonment in the penitentiary not less than one nor more than three years, in the county jail not less than six months, or by a fine not exceeding $1,000. Book-making, pool-selling, or betting on horse races is allowed on the grounds of any agricultural association in the State during the days on which the fairs of such associations shall be actually held, or upon any race course or driving park. For book-making, or pool-selling on races other than as above provided the penalty is a fine not exceeding $500.

Michigan: The giving of premiums by societies and associations for running or trotting at fairs and regular appointed meets shall not be illegal or unlawful; but all running, trotting, or pacing, unless allowed by special laws for that purpose, are misdemeanors, punishable by a fine of $500, or by imprisonment one year, or both. The entering of any horse, mare, gelding, colt, or filly under an assumed or false name, or out of its proper class or division, for any prize, stake, purse, premium, or sweepstake, offered by any agricultural society or driving club, is punishable by imprisonment in the State Prison not exceeding three years, or by a fine not exceeding $1,000, or both. " The class or division in which an entry is made shall be determined by the rules and regulations of the society, organization, or association, under whose auspices the contest is to be conducted, and the published terms and conditions under which the prize, purse, premium, stake or sweepstake is offered, opened or announced." " The name of any horse, mare, gelding, colt, or filly shall be the name by which it is known under and according to the rules and regulations of such society, organization or association; and the name by which such horse has once competed for any prize, shall be regarded as its true name unless changed as provided by the rules of the associations or societies."

Minnesota: To enter for competition, or for any prize, premium, sweepstake, purse, or stake, by any agricultural or other association; or to drive or handle any horse, mare, gelding, colt, or filly, out of its proper class, is punishable by imprisonment in the State Prison not less than one nor more than five years. Persons misrepresenting or fraudulently concealing the public performance of the animal which he, she, or they, propose to enter, in any former contest, is liable to the same penalty as above, " irrespective of success as to the entry offered."

Missouri: Book-making and pool-selling on races, except when done within the grounds where such races occur is a felony punishable by fine or imprisonment.

Montana: No race ground shall be opened on the first day of the week.

New Hampshire: The registry of stallions kept for service must be made with the Secretary of the Board of Agriculture; and for failure to make such registry, (giving name, age, color, and pedigree); or for giving a false statement in such pedigree, the penalty is a fine of $100.

New York: All racing is a misdemeanor except such as is allowed by special laws to societies and associations; and all parties engaged in racing, other than when so allowed are subject to a fine of $500, and all public officers are empowered to prevent such races. The penalty for contributing to a plate, stake, or purse, not authorized by such special law, is a fine of $25. Racing in the town of New Utrecht, whether for a stake or not, is a misdemeanor, subject to fine and imprisonment. To enter a horse in a race, under an assumed name, or out of its proper class, is punishable by imprisonment in the State Prison for a term not more than three years, or in the county jail in the county where convicted, not more than one year, or by fine not exceeding $1,000. [Class is determined in the same manner, and the change of name of a horse in the same way, as by the law in Michigan.] The act of fraudulently concealing the result of any public performance of a horse in any former contest of speed, is punishable in same manner and amount, as above.   Pool-selling or book-making outside of any race track or grounds on which racing is had, conducted by racing associations duly incorporated for the purpose of improving the breed of horses, is a felony, punishable by imprisonment in State Prison not less than one, nor more than five years.   A tax of five per cent. on the gross receipts of admissions to the race grounds on race days, is payable to the Comptroller of the State.   The number of days upon which races may be conducted is limited to thirty days in each year.   All racing and pool-selling shall be confined to the period between the 15th day of May, and the 15th day of October, of each year; and all pool-selling shall be confined to the tracks where the races take place and on the days when the races take place.   The tax on receipts, paid to the State, is applied as a fund for purses "for improving the breed of cattle, sheep, and horses at the various county fairs throughout the State."   It is a felony to engage in pool-selling except as before stated.

New Jersey: Race courses must be licensed; owners, jockeys, and trainers must be allowed the privileges of the race course unless they have been ruled off for fraud; no person or persons can make up stakes or purses, except those connected with the management of fairs or agricultural societies duly incorporated or authorized by law, under a penalty of six months imprisonment or a fine of $100, or both; it is unlawful to maintain a race course not used prior to January 1, 1893, unless a resolution is filed with the Secretary of State, adopted by three-fourths of the members of the board of chosen freeholders of the county in which such race course is proposed to be maintained,that it is a public necessity.   Book-making is not a misdemeanor when carried on within the exterior enclosures of the grounds of any race course, of any agricultural society or other incorporated body, provided such book-making is carried on only on the days of the races of said society or body. It is unlawful to permit the racing, running, trotting or pacing of horses between the first day of December of any year, and the first day of March of the succeeding year, under a fine of $1,000 or not over $10,000, or imprisonment from six months to two years, or both—this law to be enforced by the state police or the militia of the State.   "Welching" is made a penal offence.

North Carolina: For entering a horse under an assumed name or out of his proper class, for any purse or stake, a fine of from $200 to $1,000 is imposed, or imprisonment in the penitentiary from one to five years, or both, at the discretion of the court.

North Dakota: Racing on the Sabbath, or near any religious meeting, is prohibited; and all racing is a misdemeanor unless authorized by special laws.

Ohio: For entering a horse under an assumed name, or out of his proper class, for any purse or in any race, is punishable by imprisonment in the penitentiary not less than one, nor more than three years. The same punishment as the above is imposed for painting or disguising a horse; and also for concealing the real performance of any horse in any former contest or trial of speed. [Class is determined, and names of horses can only be legally changed, the same as by the law of Michigan.]

Pennsylvania: For entering a horse out of his class for any purse, prize, stake or premium, the penalty is imprisonment not exceeding. six months, or a fine not exceeding $500, or both. Stallions must be recorded in the records of the clerk of the court of quarter sessions of each county, under penalty of the forfeiture of the service fees, and the recovery of such damages as may be shown to have been sustained by reason of such false and fraudulent representation, where a false pedigree has been presented for registry.

South Dakota: Whoever enters a horse for any race under an assumed name, changes the name of any horse entered in any race, except by virtue of the code of printed rules of the society or association opening the purse or stake, or enters any horse out of his regular class, [determined the same as by the law of Michigan], shall be guilty of a misdemeanor and so punished, at the discretion of the court.

Tennessee: It is unlawful gaming to bet or wager in any way upon any race track, (applying to trotting and pacing, as well as running horses), unless the race track upon which the race is run, trotted or paced, be enclosed by a substantial fence, and the bet or wager to be made within said enclosure, upon a race to be made within said enclosure. It is unlawful to sell pools or make any betting book or combination upon any race, unless the same be conducted by the authority of a lawfully chartered or incorporated blood-horse or turf association, and then only in the county in which the association or fair may be located.

Texas: Penalty for giving a false pedigree of a horse, or a false certificate of sale.

Vermont: Agricultural societies, corporations and associations authorized to hold public fairs, are authorized to offer premiums, or purses, for success in competition of horses or horse kind in respect to speed, under their own rules and regulations publicly advertised, not in conflict with the laws of the State; and to establish and designate classes of horses or horse kind, with respect to the previous exhibitions of speed of such animals, or to any other reasonable and lawful grounds of classification, as set forth in such publicly advertised rules and regulations. Whoever enters or drives any horse, or animal of the horse kind, that shall have been painted or disguised, or shall fraudulently represent any animal of the horse kind to be another or different animal from the one it really is, or enters or drives any horse or animal of the horse kind in a class where it is not entitled to be entered, under the rules and regulations of the society or association offering such premium or purse, and upon conviction, shall be punished by a fine of not more than $500, or imprisonment not exceeding six months.

Virginia: It is unlawful for any person, or persons, or association of persons to make, write or sell books, pools or mutuals on the result of any trotting race or running race of horses, under a penalty of not less than $200 nor more than $500, or imprisonment not less than thirty nor more than ninety days.

Washington: Any corporation duly formed to establish, maintain and manage any driving park, (the same as any association for improving the breed of domestic animals), may have grounds for improving and testing the speed of horses, and may offer and award prizes for competition; but no racing for any bet or wager shall be allowed.

Wisconsin: To enter any horse, mare, gelding, colt or filly under an assumed name, or out of its proper class, in any purse or stake, is punishable by imprisonment for not less than one nor more than three years; or six months in the jail of the county where convicted; or in any sum not exceeding $1,000. The name of any horse shall not be changed, except as provided by the rules and regulations of the association or society opening and offering the purse or stake. Class shall be determined by the public performance of said horse in any former contest or trial of speed, as provided by the printed rules of the society or association under which the proposed contest is advertised to be conducted.

Wyoming: Grants the right to establish and maintain parks, grounds or race courses for the trial of speed, and the development or training of horses, with the right to offer and award premiums.

Law of Motion. The law of perfect locomotion in the horse, as in all other quadrupeds, requires uniform support to the center of gravity, and continuous propulsion by each extremity or leg, in turn.

Law of the Track. The rule, or law, of the road is reversed on the track; that is, horses meeting always pass on the left side. Horses working on a track usually jog several miles before they are called on to go fast. As all races are trotted with the horses going around the track to the left, or, in other words, they are started from the left of the judges' stand, it has come to be called the right way of the track; and horses going the other way, or to the right, the wrong way of the track. Hence, it has long been recognized that all horses working at speed, in order to prevent collisions and accidents, shall go the right way of the track, next to the pole, and have the right of way. This causes the horses jogging to take the wrong way of the track, or the outside, hence the rule of the road is reversed. If horses were allowed to speed both to the right and left of the track, confusion and innumerable accidents would result.

Lay. A felt or fancy leather housing to place under a saddle pad on the back of the horse.

Lay. To stake, or wager; to put down, or deposit a bet on a contingency or future event.

Lay Up; Laying Up Heats. The act of driving so as not to win; being in the field with the starters, but going easily the entire heat. Laying up takes place for many reasons. A driver may quietly lay up a heat, that he may have his horse fresh for a succeeding heat; or he may lay up the first part of a heat, that he may have some speed left for the stretch and finish. But it is believed that no driver can lay up a heat successfully unless he has the ability to evenly rate the mile. It was formerly a National rule that a driver could lay up one heat in a race, with the consent of the judges; but such rule has been stricken from the code. In reality, it was always meant that each horse should trot to win each and every heat, and the only departure ever intended to be allowed was, that the winning of the race being the primary object, a driver could only favor his horse sufficiently to save his best efforts when the pinch became necessary to secure that end. Most of the great drivers object to this device. Mr. Marvin says: "The laying up of heats is seldom necessary, and should never be done unless one is sure it will materially better his chances of winning the race, and this will not be the case as often as some seem to think." Mr. Splan says: "I have seen men go out to lay up a heat and lay it all up in the first half mile, and then have to drive the last half as fast as they could, and in that way make the heat as hard on the horse as though they had tried to win the heat with him."

Lay Over Him. To have more speed than an opponent; to hold over him.

Leaded Saddles. Weighted saddles for use when dead weight is to be put on; or for trials when the trainer does not want his jockeys to know more than he can help.

Leading Horse. The pace-maker in a heat. Such horse is entitled to any part of the course, in a heat, with the exception of the homestretch. See HOMESTRETCH.

Leap. The projection of the body off the ground by means of the hind limbs, after the forehead has been raised. As the horse approaches a barrier at a run, the instant it is observed he begins to shorten his steps, and, apparently, measure its distance, preparatory to taking it. The leap cannot be considered as a pace; for although it is a mode of progression, it is not a continuous one.

Leg, A Good. Indications of a good leg are: The shape of the bone should be broad and flat; good size below the knee; large sized cannons, with strong, clean, back sinews and suspensory ligaments. They should be firm and hard, smooth to the touch, indicating an entire absence of adipose tissue; the joints large and well defined, entirely free from abnormal appendages; firm, elastic cords; a short pastern, and short from hock and knee to pastern.

The ordeal of the race course, and more especially the trotting course, is very trying upon the legs and feet, and here soundness and quality of the highest order is essential. The turf horse that is always troubled with " a leg " is a nuisance.—Horse Breeding, J. H. Sanders.

Legs. Swollen legs, from whatever cause, are an unsoundness until cured.

Leggins. A part of a jockey's rig; also worn in hunting and when riding. Of various patterns and styles, both full length and short or half-size, the former extending above, and the latter fitting below the knee.

Lesion. Any wound or injury to the physical system; a morbid change in the structure of the bodily organs, not outward changes only, but those which are indicated by an interruption of any of the normal functions of the system.

Let Him Out. To give a horse his head; to let him go at speed.

When I gave Kansas his head he went to them without an effort, and won the heat by a neck with something to spare.—Life with the Trotters, John Splan.

Letters. Worn on the arms of drivers, equally with figures, to indicate the positions of the horses they drive or ride in a heat or race.

Level. A horse is said to trot level when he goes square and perfect, with no forging, cutting, interfering or striking; the perfection of the trotting gait.

Levers. The branches of a bit.

Liability. [Law.] A horse breaker or trainer is liable for any damage which, through his negligence, may happen to the horse which he is handling.

Lien. [Law.] It has been held that where a horse was sold, payment being made by check, and the horse placed in the hands of a third party till the check was cashed, as it was dishonored, the vendor had not given up possession. No conditional or temporary arrangement by which the buyer gets possession of a horse will forfeit the seller's lien. An auctioneer has a lien on the price of a horse when paid for his charges and commissions, and may bring an action in his own name therefor. Where the rules of a repository or mart provide that in certain cases of dispute the horse shall be tried by an impartial person, and the expense of trial in case the horse does not answer his warranty is to fall on the seller, the keeper of the repository has a specific lien on the horse until such expense is paid. A farrier has a lien upon a horse for his charges, which covers, however, only the work done at the particular time. It does not cover any previous account. The horse breaker, by whose skill the horse is rendered manageable, has a lien upon him for his charges, which is favored by the law, being consistent with the principles of natural equity. A stable keeper or trainer has a lien for the keep and exercise of a horse sent to him for the purpose of being trained, and the lien extends to the labor and skill employed on a race horse by a trainer; but if, by usage or contract, the owner send the horse to run at any race he chooses and select the jockey, the trainer has no continuing right of possession and consequently no lien. A stallion is entitled to a specific lien on the mare for the charge of service. A livery stable keeper cannot detain a horse for his keep, as an inn keeper may, because he is not obliged to take it. An agister has no lien on horses taken to pasture on a contract at so much per head per week; but where there is an agreement to that effect he has a lien.

Where a party went to an inn with two race horses and a groom, in the character of a guest, and they remained at the inn for several months, taking the horses out every day for exercise and training, and being occasionally absent for several days together at races in different parts of the country, but always with the intention of returning to the inn, it was held that in the absence of evidence of any alteration in the relation of the parties, that of inn keeper and guest must be presumed to have continued; and that the occasional absences did not destroy the inn keeper's lien upon the horses for his bill.—Reports of Common Bench, (English), new series, Vol. 12, 638-644.

Lie-off. To make a waiting race by keeping some distance in the rear of the other horses. A jockey is said to "lie out of his ground," when he pushes the lying-off tactics to excess, and gets so far behind that he has little or no chance of recovering the lost ground.

Light-harness Horse; Light-harness Race. Terms applied to the trotter, and to a trotting meeting.

"The only guide to the scientific breeding of the light harness performer, is the standard rules."

Limited Heats. A race in which the heats shall not exceed a given number.

No high-class, resolute, game horse should be forced to continue a supreme effort for more than five heats; beyond that number it ceases to be manly and dignified sport. It is cruel to trot a horse mile after mile every thirty minutes until from sheer exhaustion the very best drop several seconds back from their first heats.—H. D. McKinney, in The Horseman.

Line-trotter. A square trotting horse; a horse, whose hind and fore feet in trotting, are in the same line; undoubtedly the fastest trotter, and one which goes easiest to himself.

The truest kind of action is what we may call line-trotting. The horse does not sprawl to get his hind feet outside of his front ones. The hind foot goes low, and the fore foot is lifted just high enough to let the hind one go under, not outside of, the front one.—Training the Trotting Horse, Charles Marvin.

Lips. The lips of the horse are remarkably sensitive and flexible, and can be extended in various directions. Any one who has seen a horse take a small piece of sugar from a child's hand will appreciate the delicacy and efficiency of these organs as agencies of prehension. The lips should be clean and comparatively thin. A slack or drooping condition of the lower lip indicates want of vigor; and a long or large upper lip is a very objectionable conformation, and usually, with the presence of a thick tuft of hair on the upper lip, are indicative of coarse breeding.

Lipstrap. A small leather band that passes through a loose ring in the curb-chain, and buckles to the lever of the bit on each side. Its use is to prevent the horse from taking the branch of the bit in his teeth and thus destroy the effect of the curb.

List. A dark stripe running along the spine of some horses, and occasionally extending to the shoulders and legs. It was a theory of Mr. Charles Darwin, the great naturalist, that this stripe—which is found in the Cleveland Bay and the

Exmoor breed of ponies—might have indicated "a descent of all the existing races from a single dun-colored, more or less striped primitive stock, to which our horses occasionally revert."

Liverpool Slide. A coach or carriage bit the bar of which slides or plays within the guards.

If the checkrein be used on a bit with the Liverpool slide, the slide cannot act, for the check is supposed to be always on the strain, and this would keep the bit always tight up against the corners of the mouth. The check, therefore, should never be used on this bit if the slide is intended to operate.—The Bridle Bits, Col. J. C. Battersby.

Loaded Boots; Leaded Boots. Quarter boots or ankle boots having a pocket on the inside for weight—usually small pieces of sheet lead. In some styles the boots are provided with a series of two or more rings into which shot is placed, the shot being kept in position by means of cotton wool, in order to distribute it evenly around the boot, and to keep it flexible. Generally used in place of toe and side weights, or weighted shoes.

Locomotion. The expenditure of animal force in the act of progression; bodily movement.

The points of attachment between the active principles of locomotion, the muscles, and the passive principles, the bones, appear in the form of sometimes an eminence, sometimes a depression, sometimes a border or an angle, or, again, as a mere roughness, but each perfectly fulfilling its purpose, while the necessary motion is provided for by the formation of the ends of the long bones into the requisite articulations, joints or hinges. Every motion is the product of the contraction of one or more of the muscles, which, as it acts upon the bony levers, gives rise to a movement of extension or flexion, abduction or adduction, rotation or circumduction. The movement of abduction is that which passes from, and that of adduction that which passes towards the median line, or the center of the body.—Dr. A. Liautard, Principal American Veterinary College.

Length of muscular fibers and acute angles of the levers on which they act, give sweep of limb, and strength depends upon the number of them, and the effective power of both depends upon the will or courage; but all these qualities would be vain if the motions of the extremities were not so co-ordinated that their functions should be performed without interference one with another. Though difficult of demonstration, it may be taken for granted that, at full speed, the adduction and abduction of all the muscles in action counterbalance each other; if they did not, either the feet would interfere, or they could not be brought to support the center of gravity, and in either case the animal might fall. But the Master Mechanic, in forming the anatomy of the horse, attached great importance to using every available means to enable the fore foot to reach the ground as far in advance as possible, that no time might be lost in giving support to the center of gravity.—The Horse in Motion, J. D. B. Stillman.

Loins. That portion of the spinal column which is devoid of ribs, and which is in front of the highest point of the pelvis. They are placed between the back and croup at the front and rear, with the flanks at each side.

Some writers describe the back and loins as separate parts, but it always appears to the writer that the latter is only a continuation, or part of the former; for when we come to consider roach and hollow backs, we find the anterior and posterior part of them so intimately concerned in the peculiar conformation, that it is somewhat difficult to tell where one begins and the other leaves off; that is, in the living creature; though in the skeleton the line of demarcation is well marked, so much so that there is good reason for those who prefer to describe them as separate regions to do so. —E. A. A. Grange, V. S., Michigan State College Experiment Station.

Long-distance Racing. A term referring to the three and four mile heat races formerly run on the American turf, as distinguished from the short, or dash races of more recent years. See DASH.

Long Pasterns. When long pasterns do not impair the horse's action by causing weakness, he is sound; but if the length of the pasterns arises from the rupture, or unnatural elongation of the tendon, the horse is then broken down and is unsound.

Long Shots. To "take the long shots" is to back a horse which is not in popular favor at the moment, and against which the book-makers, therefore, give a larger rate of odds. It is, in fact, a form of speculation for the rise.

> How oft, at morn, we've laughed to scorn
>   A *long shot's* chance to win;
> How oft, at eve, we've had to grieve
>   O'er our departed tin.
> We've had the tip, and let it slip,
>   What's done we can't retract,
> And we've had to pay on the settling day,
>   O'er the winner we might have backed.
>   —The Sporting Times.

Long-waisted Daughter of Alcyone. Cognomen of the famous mare, Martha Wilkes, 2.11¼.

Longeing. [Eng.] The act of teaching a colt obedience; the first lessons of colt education. Often spelled allongeing.

Look-over. The last rapid, but trained and careful examination which is always taken of horse, sulky, boots, buckles, straps, nuts, bolts, before coming out for a heat.

Looking On. A term implying that a horse is not intended to do his best in a race; is not a winner; is in the race just to look on; a cock horse.

Loop. The scoring ground of a kite track, occupying a space about one hundred and sixty by four hundred feet. This space is often in the form of an oval course, with a small green in the center; and in other cases it is all graded to a level.

Loops. Rein holders.

Loops. Keepers attached to a bridle, or other part of the harness, used with buckles to retain the ends of the billets and straps.

Lope. A long stride; loping gait; a leisurely canter with a somewhat long, easy stride; the gallop slowed down.

Losing Horse. A beaten horse in a performance; a horse that is not a winner.

Luck. The origin of the superstition that a horseshoe brings good luck, can be traced back to the thirteenth century. It is left on record by the monk, Gervaise, of Tillbury, that at that time there was a kind of demon in England, which appeared as a horse rearing on his hind legs, and with sparkling eyes, whose presence foretold conflagrations and disaster. As a charm to allay his fearful deeds, a horseshoe nailed against a building prevented it from catching fire; and the finding of a horseshoe was regarded as a sign of good luck.

Lug. When a horse is heavy-headed, drives on one rein' bears down or pulls, he is said to " lug," or to " lug on the bit.'

Whenever Sunol showed an indication to lug I would let her have her head, talk to her, and have her go along as easily as possible, without being hard held, and she gradually forgot to pull.—Training the Trotting Horse, Charles Marvin.

Lugs. Straps attached to each side of the saddle of a single harness, having a strong loop near the end to receive and hold in place the thills of a sulky or carriage.

Lugging. A term used to denote that one of the horses in a span or double team, which does not do his share of the work, is being lugged, or pulled along by his mate.

Lunette. A tip, or half-shoe, claimed to have been invented by Lafossepere, the great French veterinary authority, in 1756, but which, it is said, he really derived from Fiaschi, his great Italian predecessor, who devised it so early as 1556. It is a tip, or plate, ending at the quarters, where it is drawn thin, leaving the wall, bars and frog at the heel to bear upon the ground.

Lunge. A quick stride; a plunge; to dash off in a frantic, unmanageable way; the plunging or jumping of a horse held by a long rein for training or exercise.

Lungs. All diseases affecting the lungs of the horse are causes of unsoundness.

Lunk-head. An ignorant, awkward, stupid horse; one incapable of being educated or taught, having a dull eye, big belly, banged tail, and no spirit; with a large head, lolling tongue, and an aimless, lazy gait.

11

M

Made to Rule. A term referring to the legitimacy of records, indicating that they must conform to the rules of the associations, or they will not be received for registry.

Maiden. By the rules of the Turf Congress a maiden horse is one that has never won a race in any country. The English rules define maiden as a horse which has never won a public race; therefore the winning of one or more matches does not disqualify a horse from being entered as a maiden for subsequent events. The term is not used on the trotting turf, the equivalent being "green horse," or a horse that has never trotted or paced for premiums or money, or against time, either double or single.

Maiden Stakes. The money contested for in a race between young horses that have never run before. It is a term exclusively used in connection with the racing turf.

Making a Mouth. A term used by trainers in accustoming the young colt they are handling, to the bit. The term, "My colt has no mouth yet," means that he has not been sufficiently trained to the bit.

Making the Pace. The leading horse in a heat or race is said to make the pace for all the contending horses engaged; hence, at his highest speed, the horse is said to be "making the pace."

Making the Running. Where a rider urges his horse from start to finish, or in other words forces the pace, he is said to be "making the running."

The jockey should never make his own running except when he is on a horse that frets or goes unkindly when there is anything in front of him, or when he cannot get any other rider to force the pace fast enough. It may be good policy, when the ground is heavy, for a light weight to make the running, as weight tells far more through "dirt," than when the horses can hear their feet rattle. — Riding, M. Horace Hayes, M. R. C. V. S.

Mallenders. Normal structures, or patches on which no hair grows, existing at birth and equally developed in both sexes, upon the inner surface of the fore limb, but nearer the hinder than the front border; and constituting one of the characteristic distinctions by which the species *Equus caballus*, is separated from the other member of the genus. On the fore limb the mallenders are placed upon the inner surface above the carpal or knee joint. They are about two inches long and three-fourths of an inch wide, pointed at each end, and situated obliquely, so that the long axis has its lower end pointed backwards nearly to the hind border of the limb. Their natural color is dark slate, and their structure is much like that of a wart or corn.

The signification and utility of these structures are complete puzzles. If they teach us nothing else, they afford a valuable lesson as to our own ignorance, for if we cannot guess at the meaning or use of a structure so conspicuous to observation, and in an animal whose mode of life more than any other we have had the fullest opportunity of becoming intimately acquainted with, how can we be expected to account, off-hand, for the endless strange variations of form or structure which occur among animals whose lives are passed in situations entirely secluded from human observation, and of whose habits and methods of existence we know absolutely nothing?—The Horse, William Henry Flower, C. B.

Mandate. A proclamation; an official paper announcing the terms of agreement by which members of the trotting associations are bound to be governed, and to carry out, in all meetings, engagements and performances.

Mane. The long hair growing on the neck and neighboring parts of the horse, as distinguished from the tail and shorter hair on the body. It grows on the middle line of the neck or crest and falls naturally on the near or off side.

Mane Pulling. A cruel practice once fashionable in England, by which the hairs of the mane were thinned out for the purpose of giving it a thin, graceful, fleecy appearance.

Manège. A French term denoting the art of breaking, training and riding horses; a school for teaching the whole art of equestrianism.

Mange. A disease of the skin caused by parasitic acari, or lice. A mangy horse is unsound.

Manger. The crib from which a horse eats in the stable; a feed-box in which to give the horse oats, bran, or roots.

Mare. The female of the horse kind.

Marey's Law. A law first affirmed by M. Marey, an eminent French veterinarian, and now universally acknowledged; stated in these words: The muscles of speed in the horse are long and slender, and those of strength short and thick.

Mark of Mouth. The mark of the mouth in horses extends to the commencement of the ninth year, and from that period to old age the wearing away of the crowns of the teeth is such, that the fact of determining age by them is so uncertain that the horse is said to be past the "mark of mouth."

Market Horse. [Eng.] A horse simply kept in the betting lists for the purpose of being betted against. The market is the turf exchange at Tattersall's.

Markings. The markings of white upon the forehead and face of bay or dark colored horses, are defined as follows: Blaze — if the white spreads over the forehead; reach — if the white runs down the nose in the form of a line of no great width; snip — a white or pink patch on either lip; star — a small patch of white more or less in the center of the forehead.

Master of the Horse. In Roman history, an official appointed by the Dictator to act as his chief subordinate. He discharged the duties of the Dictator during the latter's absence. An equerry. The third great officer in the British court. He has the management of all the royal stables, with authority over all the equerries and pages, coachmen, footmen, grooms, etc. In state cavalcades he rides next to the sovereign.

Martingale. A strap fastened to the girth of the saddle or harness, passing between the horse's fore legs, and ending in two rings through which the reins pass. Its uses are to aid the hands in keeping the horse's head in position; to increase the power of the rider in holding his head straight; to retain the reins in their places, and to prevent either of the reins from getting over the neck.

When the bridoon bit is drawn straight to about one inch above the pommel of the saddle, the rings of the martingale should just hang easy on them when the horse holds his head in its normal position. If he attempts to throw his head up the martingale will, at this length, check him. In leaping, the martingale must be lengthened and wholly powerless, else the horse may be thrown over the fence. The curb and martingale have no fellowship with each other. They belong to two different bits or reins, for, while the curb cannot be used on the bridoon, the martingale should not be used on the curb rein.—The Bridle Bits, Col. J. C. Battersby.

Match. A pair of horses; a span; to mate together, as, "the horses are an exact match in height, color, gait and disposition."

Match Race. The trotting rules regard match races as performances against time, and time made in such races is so treated and designated. By the rules of the Turf Congress a match is a private sweepstakes.

A match against time is a bet that a horse will beat a certain time, or, in other words, is a bet against individuals.—J. H. Steiner.

It is said the first match between two horses took place in 1377, between Richard Fitzallan 14th Earl of Arundel and the Prince of Wales, afterwards Richard II. The horses were ridden by their owners. The Earl's horse subsequently became the property of Richard at a price which would be represented to-day by $20,000. The first match against time upon record occurred in the year 1604. John Lepton, a groom in the service of James I., undertook to ride five times between London and York from Monday morning until Saturday night. He actually performed the task in five days.

Median Phalanx. The coronary bone, or small pastern.

Medicine. For a horse to require a dose of medicine is an evidence of unsoundness; therefore, until the effects of medicine are removed, the horse is unsound.

Meeting; Meet. A race or trotting event. The word originated from the English term "meet," to meet for the chase or hunt on horseback; hence, it came to be applied to the events of the running turf, and subsequently to trotting races. By the rules of the Turf Congress a meeting begins at 10 o'clock A. M., of the first day, and ends one hour after the last race of the last day.

Member. Any driving park association, society fair ground, or race track owned or leased by a corporation or by an individual, upon which races are trotted or paced under the rules of either the National or American trotting associations, is known as a "member" of such association.

Members. The legs of a horse are called its members.

Messenger. One of the greatest horses of all history, and the foundation source of the American trotter, the fleetest and stoutest breed of horses in the world. Foaled in 1780. Bred by John Pratt, of New Market, England. By Mambrino, by Engineer, a son of Sampson, by Blaze, by Flying Childers, by the Darley Arabian—the celebrated horse imported into England from the Levant in the reign of Queen Anne, (1702-1714); dam, by Turf, by Matchem, by Cade, by the Godolphin Arabian. His color was gray; he stood 15.3 hands high, a plain, somewhat coarse animal, having a large, bony head, low in the withers, upright shoulders, and a rather short, straight neck. He had large knees and hocks, and his windpipe and nostrils are described by contemporary writers to have been nearly twice as large as ordinary. Whether in motion, or at rest, his legs were said to have been always in a perfect position. He was an animal of great vigor and soundness, and although running bred was a natural trotter. Messenger was imported in May, 1788, by Thomas Benger, of Bristol, Pa., and when he landed at Philadelphia, said Hiram Woodruff, "the value of not less than one hundred million dollars struck our soil." He never went out of the States of Pennsylvania, New Jersey and New York, and died on the farm of Tounsend Cock, near Oyster Bay, Long Island, N. Y., January 28, 1808, being twenty-eight years of age, and "having attained such a height of equine reputation that he was buried with military honors, and a charge of musketry was fired over his grave." Messenger's three greatest sons were: Winthrop Messenger, taken to Maine in 1816, the founder of that sterling family known as Maine Messengers, of which Sanford Howard said, in 1852, "Maine has, until within a few years, furnished nearly all the trotting stock of any note in the country;" Bishop's Hambletonian, foaled on Long Island in 1804; Mambrino, foaled in 1806, from whose loins came two of the greatest families in all history—the Mambrino Chief, and Hambletonian, the latter "by far and away the greatest of all trotting progenitors."

Metacarpus. The cannon bone. It extends from the hock in the hind leg, and from the knee in the fore leg to the fetlock. It stands nearly perpendicular, and is somewhat cylindrical in shape, though it should be flat from side to side.

Mexican Derby. First run in the city of Mexico, N. A., December 3, 1893. Won by R. R. Rice, of Arkansas, his entry, Francis Pope and Castanet, finishing in first and second position. Distance: one mile and one-fourth; time: 2:24¼.

Mile. A distance of eight furlongs, or five thousand two hundred and eighty feet.

Mitbeh. A term used by the Arabs, applying to a point of the horse which they esteem of great importance. Explained by the quotation:

Next to the head and ears, the Arabs value the manner in which the head is set on the neck. This point, or rather form of juncture, they call the mitbeh. It especially refers to the shape of the wind-pipe, and to the manner in which the throat enters or runs in between the jaws, where it should have a slight and graceful curve. This permits of an easy carriage of the head, and gives great freedom to the air passages.—Road, Track and Stable, H. C. Merwin.

Mixed Gaited. When a horse has two ways of going at speed, and changes from the trot to the pace, and from the pace to the trot, it is said that he is "mixed gaited."

Change of gait is only possible when all the feet are clear of the ground. If the attempt should be made while one foot is on the ground, the result would be a misstep and a fall. This opportunity is afforded when the extraordinary propulsive force, given by the fore leg that leaves the ground last, projects the body upward, giving a time equal to one-fifth of a stride for the hind foot of the same side to take the place of one that would have followed had the same order continued.—The Horse in Motion, J. D. B. Stillman.

Mixed Meeting. Those meets at which both trotting and running races take place.

Molars. The molar teeth of the horse appear in two dentitions, or groups — the temporary and permanent. The first consists of twelve teeth, six in each jaw, three on each side. The second consists of twenty-four teeth, twelve in each jaw, six on each side. They are designated by numbers, from front to rear, as first, second, and so on. The first three, which replace the temporary molars, are known as pre-molars, and the last three as post-molars. The permanent molars have the shape of quadrangular prisms flattened from side to side, with the exception of the first and sixth, which are triangular.

Mongrel. A mixed breed; an individual of a breed, or a breed of animals resulting from repeated crossings, or mixtures of several different varieties; the progeny of artificial varieties, as distinguished from those which are a cross between two different species.

The greater variability in mongrels than in hybrids does not seem at all surprising. For the parents of mongrels are varieties, and mostly domestic varieties, and this implies that there has been recent variability, which would often continue and be added to that arising from the act of crossing. — The Origin of Species, Charles Darwin.

Monkey. [Eng.] Five hundred pounds. The cry not unfrequently heard in the ring, of "the field a monkey," means that the layer is willing to bet £500 even, against one horse in the race.

Morgan. A New England family of trotters of great excellence. Founded by a horse foaled in Springfield, Mass., in 1793, and purchased when two years old by Justin Morgan of Randolph, Vt. after whom the horse, and the family he founded, were named. He was said to be by True Briton, by Lloyd's Traveller, by imported Traveller; and out of a mare of Wildair blood, (Wildair, a horse of the very highest excellence imported into this country from England and subsequently purchased at a high price and carried back to that country.) Other accounts represent the dam of Justin Morgan as having been a descendant of the Lindsey Arabian, a famous horse which stood in Connecticut and subsequently in Maryland. Justin Morgan became famous as a sire of splendid driving animals, the branches of his family being the Black Hawk, old Vermont Black Hawk, the grandson of Justin Morgan, and the sire of Ethan Allen—the first stallion to beat 2:30, taking a record of 2:28 as early as 1858; the Lambert, founded by Daniel Lambert, a horse ranking little inferior as a producer of speed to any sire in recent times; the Fearnaught, a family founded by a son of Young Morrill, by Old Morrill, and through the Jennison horse a son of Young Bulrush Morgan, by Bulrush to the fountain head, Justin Morgan; the Golddust, the founder of this branch being by Vermont Morgan, by Barnard Morgan, by Gifford Morgan, by Woodbury Morgan a son of Justin Morgan; the Knox, founded by Gen. Knox, a son of Vermont Hero, by Sherman Black Hawk, by Vermont Black Hawk. "The popularity of the Morgan family," says Mr. J. H. Sanders, "at one time was unbounded; and no blood, excepting that of the thoroughbred, has been so generally disseminated and so highly esteemed throughout the United States."

Motion, Center of. A point of the horse's back directly over the fourteenth vertebra, or in other words, half way between the withers and the coupling, or top of the ribs. It is the central point from which the forces of the horse when carrying weight may be said to radiate; and is the point on which weight can be most easily carried, the least motion being imparted to it, and where its distribution will be most equal over all four of the horse's feet—hence it is over this point that the rider's center of gravity should fall.

The only muscular power required to keep a body in motion, at whatever speed, is that which is necessary to resist the action of gravity and overcome resistance. It is plain, that in order to maintain a uniform support of gravity, and a continuous impulse in the direction of motion, the limbs must move, at whatever pace, in such manner as best to attain that end; that the more rapid the motion, the more uniform must be the support.—The Horse in Motion, J. D. B. Stillman.

Mount. [Eq.] The act of gaining the seat in horseback riding. Stand opposite the cantle of the saddle with the face to the front, the right hand holding the rein sufficiently taut to feel the horse's mouth over the right side of the cantle; with the left hand hold the stirrup-strap while placing the left foot in the stirrup; give a spring upward and forward, throwing the weight of the body as evenly as possible on the left foot and right hand, so as to avoid turning the saddle; grasp the lower part of the mane with the left hand in rising, stand erect in the stirrup with the feet touching each other; throw the right leg, without bending the knee, over the horse's croup, and settle into the saddle; at this instant, as the right hand is raised from the cantle, let go of the mane, grasp the reins between the fingers of the left hand, and adjust them with the aid of the right hand which has just been released from the cantle. The stability of the seat is dependent upon the weight of the body, the erect balance and the grasp of the saddle with the inside of the thighs. The horse should be taught that the act of mounting is no signal for him to go on. The pressure of the legs and shortening of the reins are signals that the rider is ready for the horse to move.

We are all taught to mount and dismount exclusively on the left or near side of the horse, because the military horseman, whether Oriental or European, ancient or modern, requires to mount and dismount with his sword or spear in his hand ready for attack or defence.—The Book of the Horse, Samuel Sidney.

We commend readiness in mounting, for this reason, that the rider, as soon as he is seated on his horse, is in every way prepared for action if it should be necessary to encounter an enemy on a sudden. —Xenophon.

Mount. A horse, his rider and appurtenances are often collectively referred to as a mount; as in the expression "a fine mount," meaning a beautiful horse, saddle and rider's outfit.

Mount. A jockey's outfit. This includes the saddle; racing bridle and martingale; surcingle; girth; stirrup-straps and stirrups—the weight of the whole varying from one to three pounds. The ordinary riding saddle has underneath the leather a wooden or iron stock or frame—but the stock of the running saddle is a very thin piece of the very best sole leather, hammered to wonderful density and toughness, or else it is of tenacious steel. The best leather is in the saddle and bridle. The surcingle is of silk; the girth of pigskin; the stirrup-straps of linen web, and the stirrups of light spring steel. The English running saddles are made chiefly at Newmarket, Eng. Saddles cost from $37 to $58; and a complete mount will cost from $85 to $110.

Mouth, Hard. A hard mouth is one in which is a thick, fleshy tongue, protruding over its channel and not only filling it up but rising high above the level of the bars.

Mouth-piece. The mouth-piece of the bit consists of three parts—the port, to give freedom to the tongue, and the two canons, which are the parts that come in contact with the bars of the jaw or mouth.

Mouthing Bit. A large sized snaffle having one joint in the center between the bars, the use of which is to gradually teach the colt submission, and accustom him to the use of bit and bridle. The bars are an inch thick at the guards, and taper slightly to the joint, from which a flat oval piece of steel about an inch and a quarter long, is suspended by two small rings, and from three holes in the lower edge of the plate are suspended small steel tags or pendants.

M. R. C. V. S. These letters stand for: Member of the Royal [England] College of Veterinary Surgeons; and indicate that the person whose name they follow is a graduate of that Institution.

Muddler. [Eng.] A clumsy horse; one which easily gets in a muddle.

Muscles. Organs in the physical structure of the horse which are known as the active elements in locomotion, the bones with which they are connected being known as the passive elements. They vary greatly in quantity as well as quality; some contain a larger proportion of fibrous or cellular tissue than others; and, also, other things being equal, have less power. The force of the muscles is not always concentrated at both extremities, but is distributed over the face of their levers at different angles and different distances, as well as at each change in the position of the levers. The sweep of the limb is dependent on the length of the muscular fibers and the acute angles of the levers on which they act; while strength depends upon the number of them, and the effective power of both is dependent on the courage or will.

When the time comes for a thorough revision of the names of the muscles of the horse, (which must soon come), it is to be hoped they will be determined by their mechanical action without reference to the action of corresponding muscles in man.—The Horse in Motion, J. D. B. Stillman.

Mustang. The wild horse of America.

Muzzle. The lower end of the head, including the nostrils, upper and lower lip, and the bones and teeth covered by them. The Arabs have a saying that while the head must be broad above, it should taper down to a nose or muzzle fine enough, and sufficiently pointed, to allow the horse to drink from a pint pot.

Muzzle. A guard or cage for the horse's mouth, made in various patterns and of different material, and used to prevent eating the bedding, tearing the blankets, cribbing, and also used on vicious horses that are addicted to biting. Among the forms are the common leather shipping muzzle; the wire muzzle; the anti-cribbing muzzle for preventing crib-biting; the Spooner muzzle to prevent eating of the bedding— this muzzle having an adjustible bottom; Low's muzzle, which can be changed into a closed or open bottom, allowing the horse to eat hay or grain, but can be closed to prevent his eating the bedding or tearing the blanket; Gillespie's link-apron muzzle—having a band fastened to a headstall with a chain-apron or net at the bottom, which does not prevent eating or drinking but prevents tearing of the blanket.

N

Nag. A name applied to a mean, ill-bred horse, one having no characteristics of value; specially applied to a horse that has been docked.

Name. Every horse entered in a race must be correctly named. The trotting rules require that if a horse has ever trotted in a public race, the last name under which such horse trotted shall be given when the entry is made; and if the name has been changed within one year each name the horse has borne during that time must also be given. Not only must all horses be named, they must bear distinctive and characteristic names, as no such appellations as gray mare, bay horse, unknown, no name, can be accepted. Fines accompany the violation of this rule. The Turf Congress rules require that where a name has been changed both old and new names must be given with the nomination, until the horse has once run under the new name over the course of an association in membership in the Congress.

Narragansett Pacer. An early breed or family of saddle horses said to have been originated on Point Judith, Narragansett bay, Rhode Island. They were at the height of their fame about the middle of the eighteenth century, and long since became extinct. The real origin of this family of horses is lost in obscurity, but they appear to have very closely resembled the Palfrey of the Middle Ages, and were brought into use for the same purpose, that of riding on horseback from place to place, before the days of good roads and easy carriages. They were celebrated in their day for fleetness and endurance, transporting the rider with great ease, pleasantness and safety of foot. Marvelous stories of their speed and endurance are found in the early historic annals of the American colonies; and it is said they were capable of pacing seventy miles a day, and going a mile in but little over two minutes.

Nasal Gleet. A primary form of catarrh; and in any stage of its progress an unsoundness.

National Saddle Horse Breeders' Association. Organized at Louisville, Ky., in 1892. At the close of the year 1893, it had a membership of two hundred and seventeen, representing twelve States. Its objects are to advance the interests of the breeders of the saddle or gaited horse, and maintain its purity by the establishment and publication of a stud-book for the registry of animals coming within the recognized standard of the Society. The foundation stallions are: Denmark, by imported Hedgeford; Brinker's Drennon, by Davy Crockett; Sam Booker, by Boyd McNary, thoroughbred; John Dillard, by Indian Chief; Tom Hal, imported Canadian; Coleman's Eureka; Vanmeter's Waxy; Cabell's Lexington, by Gist's Black Hawk; Copperbottom, pacer; Stump the Dealer; Texas, by Comanche; Prince Albert, by Frank Wolford; Peter's Halcorn; Varnon's Roebuck, (a Missouri horse); Davy Crockett. The Society recognizes the following gaits as required to secure the registry of animals: 1, walk; 2, trot; 3, rack; 4, canter; 5, running-walk, or fox-trot, or slow pace. These gaits constitute Rule 1, of the standard for admission to registry. The other rules are: 2. Stallions and mares tracing on both sides to registered or foundation stock. 3. Mares that trace on either sire's or dam's side to registered or foundation stock, and go the gaits required in rule one. 4. Mares that trace on either sire's or dam's side to registered or foundation stock and have produced two performers under rule one. 5. Geldings that go the gaits required by rule one. 6. Progeny of a registered horse when out of a registered mare. The Society has published two volumes of its stud-book, embracing the pedigrees of about two thousand stallions and mares.

National Trotting Association, The. This association was organized in February, 1870, under the name of the "National Association for the Promotion of the interests of the American Trotting Turf;" which name was changed in 1878, to the one it now bears. It was chartered by a special act of the Legislature of Connecticut, approved March 18, 1884. It has for its object, the "improvement of the breed, and the development of horses, by the promotion of the interests of the American trotting turf; the prevention, detection, and punishment of frauds thereon, and uniformity in the government and rules of trotting and pacing." It is managed by a board of officers having a board of appeals and a board of review; holds a biennial congress on the second Wednesday in February, and to the close of 1893, had a membership of five hundred and fifty-two.

Natural Gaits. The natural gaits of the horse are the walk, trot, and run, or canter. In the walk one foot is not raised until its fellow is upon the ground; or in other words, there is always two feet upon the ground while the diagonal ones are being advanced. In the trot the off fore foot and the near hind foot strike and leave the ground exactly together, followed by the near fore and off hind foot. In the canter the horse gallops on one foot, fore or hind, while trotting with the others.

Navicular. The small or lower sesamoid bone, situated between and behind, or at the back of, the distal phalangeal articulation of the foot; or between the coronary and coffin bones. It is related to the great development of these bones, and to increasing the mechanical advantage of the flexor tendon which passes over it. Navicular disease is an ulceration of the lower surface of this bone, its synovial sac and ligaments, and the flexor tendon which plays over it. It is an unsoundness.

Near-side. The near side of the horse is the left side, or that which is approached to mount or handle; as the off-side is the right side. The distinguishing parts are: Near fore leg; off hind leg; off ear; near eye, etc.

Neck. That part extending from the poll to the withers along its upper border, and from the throat to a point somewhat above the anterior point of the breast-bone on the lower border, or line. These general forms are recognized among horsemen, viz: The straight neck; clean-cut neck; ewe neck; bull neck, and peacock neck. 1. The straight neck is one in which both the lower and upper boundaries, or lines, are practically straight, tapering gradually from the chest to the throat. 2. The clean cut neck is best described as the neck of the thoroughbred horse. 3. The ewe neck is described as one "put on wrong side up." In other words, it is one, the upper line of which is concave instead of convex, while the under line bulges out more or less in an ungraceful way. 4. The bull neck is thick, short and heavy. 5. The peacock neck is one in which the crest is unduly arched, prominent and elevated. When not too pronounced it gives the horse a showy appearance.

In the clean-cut neck the muscles and other parts stand boldly out, the crest is prominent and whipcordy, or wiry, the sides are marked by hard muscles, the lower border, including the windpipe, stands out perceptibly, leaving a prominent groove, the jugular gutter, between it and the neck above, gracefully incurvated near the throat, and attached to the head in a manner that leaves a line of demarcation between the leaving off of the head and the beginning of the neck, doing away with the appearance of a plastered-on head. The posterior part usually terminates perceptibly just in front of the withers, so that one can tell where the neck leaves off and the withers begin—a point that is not always easy to determine.—E. A. A. Grange, V. S., Michigan State College Experiment Station.

Needle. A hypodermic syringe used for making injections under the skin; a trocar. Injections of cocaine are made directly over or under the part to be operated upon so as to produce an immediate local effect. Medicinally, injections are usually made at the point of the shoulder or in the breast or neck, as at these points the skin is very flexible and can be easily taken up. Inter-venous injections, (those directly into the circulation), are also sometimes resorted to, for the purpose of obtaining a more immediate effect.

Negotiate. [Eq.] To handle; to manage; to take. In equestrianism, to negotiate a leap hold the bridle-hand loose, grasp the horse firmly with the legs and thighs, the toes being up and outward, the back inward, and the neck steady. As the horse rises meet his crest with the body, being careful not to bear on the bridle which might pull him backward. The instant his forequarters descend, and his hindquarters ascend, keep time with him in an appropriate, but opposite motion and throw the body sufficiently backward to be found firm in the seat at the conclusion of the leap. Success depends upon the perfect coolness of the rider, leaving everything to the discretion of the horse, freedom from all support of the bridle or stirrups, on the firm grasp of the legs and thighs, the instantaneous performance of the alternate motions forward and backward, and the preservation of a perfect equilibrium.

Negotiate a Race. To accomplish or perform a race.

We have been over one hundred years producing but a single trotter that can negotiate a mile in 2:04.—Dr. George H. Bailey, December, 1893, in American Horse Breeder.

Nerving; Neurotomy. The operation of nerving a horse for navicular disease, and frequently for ringbone. It is the act of dividing the planter nerve above or below the ankle —called high or low operation, as the case may be—and is only practiced as a last resort in what are regarded as incurable cases. A horse upon which the operation of nerving has been performed, has been declared as legally unsound.

Newmarket. Once the racing center of Great Britain, if not of the world. On the border of the counties of Cambridgeshire and Suffolk, England, twelve miles from the old university town of Cambridge. Racing was established here by James I., in 1605, who erected a hunting seat called the "King's House." The races, discontinued on the ascension of Charles I., and the civil war, were revived on the advent of Charles II., who was a munificent patron of the turf. He built a stand-house here, for the sake of the diversion, and re-established the races about 1667. During the races on March 22, 1683, Newmarket was nearly destroyed by an accidental fire, which occasioned the hasty departure of the company then assembled, including the king, queen, the Duke of York, the royal attendants and many of the nobility; and to this disaster historians have attributed the failure of the Rye-house plot, the object of which is said to have been the assassination of the king and his brother on the road from Newmarket to London, if the period of their journey had not been thus anticipated. The races are held on the beautiful heath west of the town, and the course is upward of four miles, being considered the best in England. The training ground, on a slope south of the town, is very fine. Seven race meetings each year are held here, of three days each. They are: 1, the Craven; 2, first spring; 3, second spring; 4, July; 5, first October; 6, second October; 7, the Houghton. The old course was said to have been kept elastic by the action of earth worms. It was divided into eighteen lengths, each having a different name adapted to the different class of race run on them with regard to weight, age, etc. Among these names were those known as Ditch in; Across the Flat; Beacon Course, etc. One of its most noticeable features was " the Ditch "—an embankment running from the Cambridge fens to Wood Ditton, which, in old times, all riders were accustomed to salute in passing. See SALUTE THE DITCH.

Nick. To unite; the act of coupling. In breeding, said of the crossing of one strain of blood with another, where satisfactory results are reached, " it nicks or unites well."

Nicking. The nicking or docking of the tail, by incisions in the lateral and depressor muscles, that the erector muscles may keep the tail in a forced position more or less erect according to the whim or fashion.

Nighted Colors. The black outfits or rigs worn by jockeys.

Nippers. The incisor or front teeth of the horse, twelve in number, six in each jaw, three on each side. Although the incisors are all included in the term " nippers " as generally used, only the middle teeth are properly so called.

Nobble. [Eng.] To incapacitate a horse from starting in a race, or from winning a race, by previously drugging, laming, or otherwise injuring him, is to " nobble " him.

No Heat. A heat not awarded. If, in the opinion of the judges, a horse has been helped in coming to the wire by another horse, rider or driver, they have the power to declare the heat to be " no heat," and have the same trotted over again.

Nominator. The person naming or making entry of a horse in a race. If the nominator is not the owner of the horse, the real name and residence of the owner shall be given when the entry is made; and all persons making entries are obliged to establish their identity, if unknown, to the officers of the course. In making the first payment the nominator thereby binds himself to pay the balance of the entrance fee, or he is liable to suspension. In courses under the rules of the Turf Congress a horse cannot be entered in the name of any person or company unless such person or company has an interest or property in the horse; persons entering become liable for the entrance fee, stake or forfeit; entries in purses are not void by the decease of the nominator, and in no case is the entrance money refunded if the horse fails to start.

Nonesuch Palace. [Eng.] A royal palace built at Epsom by Henry VIII., (1509-1547), which was a marvel of magnificence, erected on purpose for the reception of the court attending the races.

Northern King. The stallion Nelson, 2:09. Bay horse, foaled 1882, by young Rolfe, 2:21¼, (son of Tom Rolfe, 2:33½, and Judith, by Draco, 2:28½); dam, Gretchen—in the great brood mare list—(the dam of Susie Owen, 2:26¼; Daisy Rolfe, 2:26¼, and the pacer Edna, 2:24), by Gideon, (son of Rysdyk's Hambletonian and Dandy, the dam of Silver Duke, 2:28¾, by Young Engineer); second dam, Kate, by Vermont Black Hawk, 2:42, son of Sherman Morgan, by Justin Morgan. Trotting inheritance and development are both represented in Nelson's breeding. Holding the world's record to the close of 1893 for best mile over a half mile track, made at the Inter-State Fair, Trenton, N. J., October 6, 1892, 2:11¾. At Rigby Park, Portland, Maine, August 12, 1893, 2:09. Owned by C. H. Nelson, Waterville, Maine.

In 1889 Veritas dubbed the good horse Nelson, "the Northern King," and despite the slings and arrows of outrageous fortune, through days dark with disaster, and days when his mighty powers were frittered away in useless efforts on country cow-path courses, the Northern King he still remains. There are many good horses, but few great ones; Nelson has proved himself one of the greatest.—The Horseman, December 14, 1893.

Nose. The continuation of the forehead which ends opposite the nostrils, at an angle formed by the line of the face and of the muzzle.

Nose Him Out. Said of a horse, when, by a spurt of speed at the close of a heat, he finishes a nose's length ahead of his competitor; "It was a close call, but I nosed him out."

Not Traced. When occurring in a pedigree, these words indicate that the line of ancestry to which it refers has not been followed back, or traced; unknown.

Numbers are worn on the arm of the jockey or driver, corresponding with the number of the horse ridden or driven, on the programme of the day; or indicating their position in the heat. By the racing rules if a horse does not start and run the course after his number has been exhibited, and no reasonable explanation for such withdrawal can be given the judges, they have the authority to fine, suspend, or rule off such horse.

Nursery. The quarters in the stable assigned to weanlings.

Nut Bone. The navicular, or small sesamoid bone of the foot.

O

Oaks. "The garter of the English turf." The celebrated stakes for three year old fillies, established by Edward Smith Stanley, 12th Earl of Derby, May 14, 1779. The stakes received its name from Lambert's Oaks, in the parish of Woodmansterne, formerly an inn. The house was erected by the Hunter's Club, and was rented to the Lambert family. It afterwards became the residence of Gen. Burgoyne, from whom it passed to the 11th Earl of Derby. It is the most important fixed event of the English turf, for fillies only, and consists of fifty guineas, forfeit forty guineas. It is run on the fourth day—Friday—of the great Epsom races over the Derby course. The Earl of Derby, originator of the stakes, died in 1834.

Oats. Oats are regarded as the best and healthiest of all the grains as a food for horses, because the ingredients necessary for the complete sustenance of the body exist in them in the most perfect proportions. They are easily digested and a large proportion of the nutritious elements which they contain are absorbed and converted into the various tissues of the system. Oats should have a sweet, flowery smell; thin, smooth skins that slip quickly through the fingers, and a sweet taste. White oats are generally thinner in the skin than black; and short, plump oats are better than large, long ones. New are chiefly distinguished from old oats by the smell, which, in the former, is somewhat earth-like; the husk of the new oat is also bright, while its taste is more sweet and milky than that of the old oat. Light oats are composed of more skin or husk than flour. Oats badly saved, mouldy, sprouting, or otherwise damaged, will destroy the condition, if, indeed, they do not cause disease in the best horses. In the case of most horses, oats are better fed whole, although crushed or bruised oats are preferable for old horses, and those having defective teeth. Old oats, old corn and old hay are better than new for feeding. In all the States the legal and standard weight of a bushel of oats is thirty-two pounds, excepting in Maryland, where it is twenty-six pounds; in New Jersey, where it is thirty pounds, and in Oregon, where it is thirty-six pounds.

Objections. An objection is an opposition to a ruling or decision; a complaint against a horse, driver or jockey.

178

Objections must be made before the conclusion of the meeting at which the race is run, and shall be heard and determined by the judges of that race, except in cases where a longer time is given for their consideration. They must be made by the owner, trainer or jockey of some other horse engaged in the same race, or by the officials of the course, or by some creditable person. On the days of the race they must be made to one of the judges of the race, or to the clerk of the course; and at other times to the officers or the clerk. Objections must be made in writing, if required; and when so made cannot be withdrawn without leave of the officers of the association. In all cases where a decision cannot be made during the meeting at which the objection was presented, it must be made in writing and placed in the hands of the clerk of the course. Objections may be made to a horse on the ground of his not having run the proper course, or for other causes. If an objection to a horse which has won or been placed in a race be declared valid, the horse shall be regarded as distanced in heats of races. If an objection is made as to the age of a horse, the judges shall demand proofs which are deemed satisfactory, of his correct age. Where a dead heat is run for second place, and an objection is made to the winner, it shall be run over, or the horses shall divide or draw lots for an indivisible prize. An objection on the ground of fraudulent entry, willful misstatement or on representation that the horse which ran was not the horse entered, may be received any time within one year after the race. Pending the settlement of any objection, any prize or money may be withheld until such matter is decided. If an objection is made to a horse in a selling race and after the horse has been bought, if the objection is sustained, the buyer may have the option of returning him; but if the objection is made before the sale, the time of delivery, but not of selling, may be postponed at the option of the judges. If the objection is declared valid, the person who bought the horse shall have the option of returning him.

Occipital Crest. The bony prominence which constitutes the top of the horse's head, and rises, more or less prominently, between the ears.

Odds. The proportion or amount by which the bet of one party to a wager exceeds that of the other; as to lay or give odds.

Odometer. A device designed to register the distance traveled by carriages. The machinery is contained in a small metallic case fastened to the axle, and is operated by means of a steel pin inserted on the inner end of the hub, which propels the mechanism of the odometer with each revolution of the wheel. The dial contains three indexes, each of a different color. A red index registers a mile every time it makes a complete revolution, and, as the dial is divided into forty spaces, each space represents one-fortieth of a mile, or eight rods. A yellow index revolves once every forty miles, and each space represents a mile. A blue index revolves once every 1,600 miles, so that each space represents forty miles in relation to this index. Around this dial are three rows of figures which register the distance, and with each mile passed the fact is announced by one sharp stroke of a small bell. When designed for attachment to sulkies for training or trotting purposes, a bell strikes each quarter mile.

Off. Dead-off. Spoken of a horse when out of condition, as off his feed, if ailing; off his feet, if lame; off in going, when he does not do his best.

Off-and-On. A term used to describe the leap in the hunt or cross-country riding; the taking-off and landing in passing a fence or ditch.

The mare I rode on the journey carried me over the raised watercourses by the Euphrates in the cleverest way in the world; off and on, without the least hanging or hesitation, and always with a foot ready to bring down in case of need.—The Bedouin Tribes of the Euphrates, Lady Anne Blunt.

Off Side. The right hand side in driving or riding; the side most remote from the driver or rider when on the left side of his horse or team. In English countries the left hand side is the off side, when meeting teams on the highway.

Offending Horse. A horse, which in the hands of a driver or rider is guilty of disobeying any of the turf rules. The National and American Associations prescribe that if an offending horse violates any of the restrictions, he shall not be entitled to win the heat, but shall be placed behind all the unoffending horses in the heat; and under certain conditions the judges have the right to rule the horse out and impose a fine upon the rider or driver.

On-and-Off. Used in describing a safe landing when jumping on horseback.

A good, hard bank on which to land in jumping a ditch or brook, (which is usually taken at a half speed gallop), so that the rider can land upon it and be off without danger.—The Practical Horse Keeper, George Fleming, LL. D., M. R. C. V. S.

On His Balance. Said of a horse in good trotting or running condition.

Open Bridle. A bridle or headstall having no blinds or blinders.

Open Gait. A square gait; a pure gait. An open-gaited trotter is one that places his hind feet outside of the forward ones when in action — said to be the fastest mode of locomotion a trotter can possess.

Open Out; Open Up. To speed or exercise a horse, before a race in which he is entered, takes place.

Open Out. A term applied to that process of fitting the heels of the feet by cutting the horn between the bars of the foot and the frog.

Orders. The orders given riders, drivers or jockeys by the owners of the horses they handle in a race, in regard to the points of the race and what they are to do when making it.

Oregon Wonder. The horse Linus, foaled at Marion, Oregon, May 20, 1883. Clyde and French, chestnut color, 16.2 hands, weight 1,450 pounds. At five years of age his tail and mane began to grow, and in 1889 dragged several feet upon the ground when both were braided and put in sacks. From 1890 to 1892 they increased in length at the rate of nearly two feet each year. He was shown at the Columbian World's Fair in 1893 as one of the most wonderful horses ever known in history. He died in August, 1894.

Orloff. A breed of Russian trotting horses founded by Count Alexis Orloff - Ortov - Tchesmensky, an enthusiastic horseman, about 1770 or 1772. He imported a gray stallion from Arabia named Smetanska, which was bred to a Danish mare, the produce being a horse known as Palkan I; and from a union of this half-blood with a Dutch mare sprang a stallion known as Barss I. All the modern trotters of Russia trace their leinage back to him and to daughters of Smetanska out of English and Arabian mares. It took thirty years to establish the Orloff as a distinct type. Their trotting performance is remarkable, and their size is equal to their speed. A monument was erected to Count Orloff in 1876.

Ormonde. A noted English race horse, bred by the Duke of Westminster at Eaton Hall, near Chester, England. Foaled in 1883. In color a rich, solid bay; 16.1 hands high. By Bend Or, (son of Doncaster and Rouge Rose, by Thormanby), dam, Lily Agnes by Macaroni; second dam, Polly Agnes by The Cure; third dam, Miss Agnes by Birdcatcher. Ormonde has a shoulder, arm and muscle that are of the grandest proportions; a plain, sensible head; short back; large, powerful stifles, and grand legs. He is the sire of Orme, one of the most remarkable horses that ever appeared on the English turf, and of itself alone, honor enough for a world's horse. He was sold in 1886 for 2,000 guineas; in 1889 he was sold to Señor Bocan for $75,000 and taken to Buenos Ayres, S. A.; in 1890 he was sold to Baron Hirsch for $70,000 and again taken to England, and was purchased in 1893 by Mr. W. O'B. Macdonough, of San Francisco, Cal., for $150,000 — the highest price ever paid for a horse in the world. Ormonde was never beaten.   He is probably the greatest race horse ever bred in Great Britain, or anywhere else.   He flourished in an age remarkable for great race horses, such as Minting, Paradox, Melton, Bendigo, Bard, St. Gatien — and beat them all.   He always beat all the Derby and St. Leger winners, and they beat everything else, showing how great they were.   Even when his wind was touched they could not beat him, showing how great he was, how indomitable his heart and muscular power.   He is one of the few horses that have won the Derby, St. Leger, and the 2,000 guineas; and is said to be the only horse that ever won the great Hardwicke stakes at Ascot Heath, twice.

Ormonde is the horse of the century.—M. Horace Hayes, M. R. C. V. S.

Osslet.   A hard substance growing on the inside of a horse's knee.

Large, coarse osslets show cold, mongrel blood. — General Grant's Arabian Horses, Randolph Huntington.

Out.   Horses in a race often do not all appear for the second or subsequent heat; but those which come on the track at the sound of the bell are said to be "out."

Outfit.   The outfit of a rider or jockey in running races consists of cap, jacket, knee-breeches, boots, spurs and whip. The cap and jacket, or blouse, are made of satin; the breeches, (which are always white), of undyed merino; the boots of calf skin; the spurs of spring steel, and the whip of whalebone with a gut covering.   The entire outfit does not weigh more than two pounds.

Out for an Airing.   [Eng.]   Said of a horse that is backward, or of one not meant to win.

Out of Form.   A horse that gets a bad start in a heat or race, either by a jump cross-legged, or in some way which makes it plain that the race or heat is lost to him at the start, is said to be "out of form."

Out of Hand.   Hand to hand; a system of private betting from out the hand, or between one person and another, the wager being placed in the hand of a third party.

Oval Track.   A track the sides of which are longer than the ends; or one where the sides, or stretches, are ninety rods long; and the ends, or turns, seventy rods long.

Overhead Rein; Overdraw Check. A check or bearing rein that passes over the head of a horse between the ears, and thus to the bit, used with an overcheck bridle. The use of such a check is altogether a matter to be regulated by the disposition of the horse. Judiciously used, an overhead check need be no more distressing or injurious to the horse than a side check; while some drivers assert that it is impossible to handle some horses without the overhead rein, and that such a check is especially necessary for a mixed gaited colt.

Overreach. Where the shoe of the hind foot strikes and injures the heel or quarter of the fore foot. It rarely occurs except in trotting and running horses, and in trotters generally takes place when the animal breaks from a trot to a run. It results from the faulty conformation of the horse and is neither an unsoundness nor a vice.

The hind foot should be the last to leave the ground. The early start of the fore foot enables it to clear the way for the hind one on the same side to advance to the support of the center of gravity in its turn without being hit by it, or overreached, as it is technically termed. The fore foot being dilatory, or having a more circuitous route to travel, or the disproportion in the length of the body to that of the legs, exposes the fetlock and heel to injury from the shoe of the hind foot; but generally the hind foot is pushed under the forward one as the latter rises.—The Horse in Motion, J. D. B. Stillman.

Over the Sticks. Running a hurdle race.

Overweight. The law of the trotting turf provides that if the weight of any driver exceeds twenty pounds the conditions or rule of the race, the judges may, if they have reason to believe that such extra weight was imposed on the horse for an improper purpose, substitute another driver of suitable weight. By the American racing rules a horse is not qualified to run with more than five pounds overweight; and if he carry more than two pounds which has not been duly declared and announced by the clerk of the course, he is disqualified.

Owner. By the rules of the American Turf Congress, an owner includes part owner or leasee of a horse, and proof of ownership must be given when required, or the horse becomes disqualified. If a jockey is an entire owner of a horse or horses he shall only be permitted to ride his own horses.

Owners' Handicap. A race in which the owner fixes at the time of entry the weight his horse is to carry.

Owners Up. A term denoting that in the race to which it is applied, the owners of the horses entered for it, are to ride

P

Pace. A word constantly used as a general term to describe all the different gaits and modes of progression of the horse; hence, a fast horse, one showing remarkable speed, is almost invariably spoken of as "going at a great pace," although his gait may be the trot and not the pace.

Pace. A gait in which the horse moves two legs on the same side at the same time, and both feet strike as one — then the limbs on the other side are advanced and strike as one foot. The two strokes: One, two, complete the revolution. To the ear, therefore, as well as the eye, the motions of the pace are, one, two; one, two; at regular and distinct intervals, the horse appearing, by the sound, at least, to have but two feet. The lateral motion of the pacer is without doubt as old as the diagonal motion of the trotter, and the two gaits were contemporaneous centuries ago, just as they are in this country to-day; at least it is clear that the exact motion of the pace now, is like the motion of the amble in England described two hundred years ago by the Duke of Newcastle. The pacing gait is more favorable to a high rate speed with the same expenditure of vital force, than the trotting gait.

While in the trot the center of gravity falls near the intersection of the two straight lines drawn through the diagonal footprints, in the pace it is shifted from side to side, as the right or left feet alternately support the weight. The effect of this is to give a rolling motion to the body like that of a ship with the wind abeam. It is an easy pace for the rider, being free from the short undulations of the trot. * * * The necessity which exists of rapidly changing the base of support from side to side, makes it practicable in the horse only when the speed is considerable and quite impossible in the rate pursued in the walk.—The Horse in Motion, J. D. B. Stillman.

Pacer. A horse whose natural gait is the pace. All families of pacers lack hock action and go close to the ground; hence the pacer is utterly unsuitable for cross-country riding. He is not a jumper and his action is too much of the gliding nature, and too near the ground, to ever think of his becoming a hunter.

Pacers are ordinarily not as handy in recovering from a break as are trotters, but even at that it is only once in a long time, that, with ordinary care on the part of the driver, a pacer that has the speed of his field need be distanced simply because in some particular heat he is unsteady.—Wallace's Monthly.

Pacers. In the Year Book, and in all correctly printed summaries of races, the names of pacers are placed in *italics.*

Pacers. To the close of 1893, there were fourteen pacers with records of 2:08, and thirty-two with records of 2:10; while the number with records of 2:30 or better, was about two thousand.

Pace-maker. The leading horse in a heat is said to be the "pace-maker," as he sets the pace for the field.

Pacing-blood. It is generally believed that pacing blood is an element of great speed in the trotter; in support of which is cited the case of Blue Bull, the great pacing sire of trotters, who never showed a disposition or ability to trot at any rate of speed, yet he maintains his position as one of the three or four great progenitors of trotters. This is believed to be evidence of the oneness of the trotting and pacing gaits. There are multiplied evidences that a horse may be trotting bred and his natural habit of action may be the lateral motion —the pace; or he may be pacing bred, and his habit of action may be the diagonal gait—the trot. It is true that if the horse move the two legs on one side at the same instant, he is a pacer; and if he moves the diagonal legs at the same instant, he is a trotter, however he may have been bred. If one desires to know where the trotting colt gets his pacing action, he has inevitably to go back to his pacing ancestors.

No colt has ever been foaled a natural pacer that did not have a pacing inheritance or ancestry from some source.—Wallace's Monthly.

Pacing Standard. The following rules embrace the pacing standard for registry in the American Trotting and Pacing Register:

First: Any pacing stallion that has a record of 2:25 or better; provided any of his get has a record of 2:30 pacing, or better; or provided his sire or dam is already a standard pacing animal.

Second: Any mare or gelding that has a pacing record of 2:25, or better.

Third: Any horse that is the sire of two pacers with records of 2:25.

Fourth: Any horse that is the sire of one pacer with a record of 2:25 or better, provided he has either of the following additional qualifications—1: A pacing record of 2:30 or better; 2: Is the sire of two other animals with pacing records of 2:30; 3: Has a sire or dam that is already a standard pacing animal.

Fifth: Any mare that has produced a pacer with a record of 2:25, or better.

Sixth: The progeny of a standard pacing horse when out of a standard pacing mare.

Seventh: The female progeny of a standard pacing horse when out of a mare by a standard pacing horse.

Eighth: The female progeny of a standard pacing horse when out of a mare whose dam is a standard pacing mare.

Ninth: Any mare that has a pacing record of 2:30, or better, whose sire or dam is a standard pacing animal.

Tenth: The progeny of a standard trotting horse, out of a standard pacing mare, or of a standard pacing horse, out of a standard trotting mare.

Pacing—World's Record. [To the close of 1893.] One mile—Mascot, by Deceive, Terre Haute, Ind., September 29, 1892, (race record); and Flying Jib, by Algona, Chicago, Ill., September 15, 1893, (against time), 2:04. Fastest mile by a stallion—Direct, by Director, Nashville, Tenn., November 8, 1892, 2:05¼. Fastest mile to wagon — Roy Wilkes, by Adrian Wilkes, Independence, Iowa, (kite track), October 30, 1891, 2:13. Fastest mile under saddle — Johnston, by Joe Bassett, Cleveland, Ohio, August 3, 1888, 2:13.

Packing. The act of stopping, or stuffing a horse's foot when in stable, by covering the sole with some moist and soft material, which is often fastened in place by means of a thin steel spring inserted under the rim of the shoe. Various materials are used—moist clay, a wet sponge, damp moss, (peat), petrolatum, (a packing saturated with petroleum), and felt pads, which are made to fit the sole, and are fastened by means of a metallic toe-piece and a strap which buckles around the foot. As a winter packing, tar and oakum is often used.

Pad. A pad-horse; a road-horse.

Pad. A small lay, or cushion, made of leather, felt or deer skin, kersey-lined, placed under the saddle of a harness, to prevent it from resting directly on the back of the horse.

Pad. The saddle on the top of a surcingle, used in giving the colt his first lessons in bitting; to which the turrets through which the reins play are fastened, thus keeping the colt's head in line with his body, preventing accidents and securing an evenly made mouth and carriage.

Pad-tree. A soft cushion, or stuffed part of a saddle or harness; used to fill up a hollow, to relieve pressure, or as a protection from a saddle gall.

Paddling. An erratic action of the forward feet by which the horse goes very wide, and swings the near or off, and sometimes both forward feet, outward, when at speed. In general, paddlers are bad scalpers, are liable to hop, and should never be used without scalpers and hind ankle boots with pastern attachments.

Paddock. An enclosure near the stable in which horses are turned out for exercise, or when not required for work; or for aid in restoring to health and soundness those which are recovering from lameness or sickness. It should have a supply of water, and also an open shed under which the horses may go during showers or in the heat of mid-day. A paddock is not a pasture, and it must not be regarded as, in any sense, a grazing ground.

Palfrey. A breed of saddle horses of the best type, such as kings and the nobility who had large studs kept for their own personal use when they rode privately, without state, or made short journeys. These Palfreys were under the peculiar charge of a private officer of the king's household, while the other horses of the stud fell to the care of the master of the horse, or officer of the stable. They were perfectly white, with round barrel and Barb head, originally from Spain or Barbary, and rarely exceeded the size of a Galloway. The breed is now nearly extinct.

Pannel. The lining of the saddle which lies between the tree and the horse's back.

Pantograph Snaffle. A double-barred snaffle bit. The joints of the bars are not in the center, but that of one bar is at a point one-third of its length to one side, that of the other one-third of its length to the opposite side; so that, in operation, it has a double converging action, and is a very severe bit. It is designed for a hard puller, or a horse liable to take the bit in his teeth.

Paralysis. A horse liable to attacks of paralysis, from having eaten ergoted hay, is unsound.

Parker. A fashionable saddle horse.

Parotid Gland. A gland situated under the horse's ears. When from any cause it becomes ulcerated, it is an unsoundness.

Passage. A French term, signifying a short and very light trot, in which each fore limb, in its turn, when it is raised to the highest point, is poised in the air for an instant, and is bent at the knee and fetlock. Similar to the Spanish walk, and Spanish trot.

Pastern. The short column of bones which is placed between the fetlock and the hoof; in comparative anatomy corresponding to the first phalanx of the middle finger of the human hand, or the first phalanx of the toe on the human foot. When the pastern joint of one or both of the fore legs is perpendicular to the rest of the leg, instead of sloping backward, if this defect arise from work, the animal is unsound. With the hind legs this does not obtain, for a horse may be quite upright in the joints of the hind legs, and yet be perfectly sound.

The pastern is the most important part of the leg. If the horse is to be used under the saddle the kind with long oblique pasterns are more elastic and graceful in their movements, than the short, upright sort, which are often unpleasant to the equestrian on account of the concussion produced by the more or less upright columns of bone. Very straight pasterns are not desirable on account of the concussion they are liable to produce, but even the long, oblique kind may be, and often are, overdone; in them the strain upon the parts is liable to produce an irritation that in its turn will cause ringbone. The pasterns of the fore leg are usually a little more upright than those of the hind leg.—E. A. A. Grange, V. S., Michigan State College Experiment Station.

Pastern-bone. Either one of the two proximal phalanges of a horse's foot; the first phalanx being the great pastern, articulated, (or united), above with the cannon-bone at the pastern joint; and the second phalanx, the small pastern, united below with the third phalanx, or coffin-bone, inclosed in the hoof.

Pastern-joint. The joint, or articulation of a horse's foot, between the great pastern-bone and the cannon-bone.

Patrol Judges. Persons appointed by the judges of a race to inspect the back turns and stretches of a track during a race; to observe that the heats are trotted honestly, and to report to the judges any foul or improper conduct on the part of riders or drivers, if any has come under their observation. A patrol judge, while an agent of the judges, is, to all intents and purposes, a judge. Should there be one patrol judge at each of the four turns, then, if a claim of foul was made, the judges would be in a position to ascertain, from their official aids, the exact truth of the matter in each instance.

Peat Moss. Used largely in city stables for bedding. It is free from odor, incombustible, lasting, and is never eaten, even by the most inveterate bedding-consuming horse.

Pedigree. The line of descent; ancestry. A writing, or copy of records, giving the names, dates, etc., concerning the progenitors or ancestors of a certain horse, and establishing his descent from certain famous sires and dams; an evidence of breeding.

Pelham. A combination bit of snaffle and curb, or a single bit with two pairs of reins, which acts either as a plain bar or curb—less severe than the true·curb bit, and a bit which is much esteemed by jockeys, as it allows them to have complete control over their horses. The best racing bit.

Penalties. Added weight. As an illustration, take the following example: "Purse of $500, of which $70 to second and $30 to third. For three-year-olds; winners of two races to carry five pounds extra; those that have not won a race allowed seven pounds. One mile." In all races exclusively for three-year-olds, the weight is 122 pounds. Now, if a horse was entered that had won two races, it would be obliged to carry 127 pounds; or, in other words, would carry a five pound penalty. Hence, a penalty is an added weight to the better horse. Penalties are invariably obligatory, but are not cumulative unless so declared by the conditions of a race.

Performance. That which is accomplished; as a heat, or race; any contest on a race course or track, between horses, or singly, for a prize or against time.

Performance Against Time. A performance in which a horse starts to equal or beat a specified time; now regulated by rules of the National and American trotting associations. Performances against time are marked with a star, (*), in the Trotting Register, to distinguish them from records obtained in a race. See AGAINST TIME.

Periplantar. The Charlier method of shoeing, by which the sole, frog and bars of the foot are left untouched by the knife; the toe and front quarters of the crust, or wall of the hoof, is beveled into a groove, or recess, into which the thin plate of steel, or shoe, is fitted. Its object is to take the place of the perishable horn forming the circumference of the foot, and which is being constantly worn and broken away, replace it by a more durable material, and leave the parts of the foot to perform their natural functions unimpaired. See CHARLIER SHOE.

Phalanges. The digital bones of the hand or foot beyond the metacarpus or metatarsus. The knee of the horse corresponds to the back of the wrist of man, and everything below it corresponds to the hand proper. The phalanges of the horse's foot are connected by hinge joints, allowing only motions of bending backwards and forwards; viz: The large pastern, small pastern, and coffin-bone.

Phenomenal Trotting. Remarkable; unusual. The extreme speed attained during the decade, 1882 to 1893, the rapid and marvellous reducing of the trotting records, and the fast time made by individual animals, have been phenomenal —hence the term is one that has obtained recognized currency in turf language,

Piaffer. [Eq.] A passage without gaining ground. A French term meaning the graceful position of the body of the horse and the harmonious precision of movement of the legs and feet. The most brilliant kind of piaffer is when the movement is slow, lofty, in true cadence and with a well-marked pause as each leg is raised to its highest point.

Picking Up, is the short for a driver's expression of "picking a horse up and setting him down in front;" which means the act of pulling the horse together; rallying him for a great effort; going to the lead.

Pigeon Toed. A defective conformation whereby the feet point inwardly. Where the defect is such as to impede the horse in his work, but not otherwise, he is unsound.

Pigskin, The. A jockey's saddle.

Pinchers. The two front incisors of the upper and lower jaw of the first, and also of the permanent dentition, are called the "pinchers" or "pincher teeth."

Pink-eye. A contagious influenza of horses; a febrile disease closely allied to scarlet fever in man, so named from the pink color of the conjunctiva, (the mucus membrane which lines the inner surface of the eyelids.) Until cured, an unsoundness.

Pipe-opener. A brisk exercise given the horse for the purpose of starting up his wind; to open him out at a corking brush for the benefit of his breathing; to clear out his pipes. Mr. Marvin says of his training of Sunol: "We trained her as usual, driving no more miles, but speeding fast quarters, with an occasional pipe-opener at a half."

Place. The word place in racing means first, second or third. When a horse is decided by the judges to be first, second or third in a race he is said to be "placed," or gets a place; but in the betting a horse must "to win" be first; "for the place" be second or better; and "to show" be third. Horses are placed in the race in the position in which they passed the judges in the deciding heat. A horse not placed in a deciding heat has no place in the race, nor is he entitled to any portion of the prize or purse; provided there is no third money, in which case the third horse in the race of heats is not to be deprived of third money if ruled out for not winning a heat in two, three or more heats, as the case may be.

Placing Horses. In placing or ranking horses other than the winner in a race, the trotting rules require that those that have won two heats shall be regarded as better than those winning one; a horse that has won a heat is better than a horse making a dead heat; one winning one or two heats and making a dead heat, better than one winning an equal number of heats but not making a dead heat; one winning a heat or making a dead heat and not distanced in a race, better than one that has not won a heat or made a dead heat, and one that has been placed "second" one heat, better than a horse that has been placed "third" any number of heats.

Planer. A track building and finishing machine made of several patterns, all similar in construction and operated much alike. In general they consist of a body or framework of wood and iron, upon four small iron wheels. Under this framework and between the forward and hind wheels are two cutters placed diagonally to the body of the machine and to the track, operated by means of levers controlled by screw purchase, and by which they are raised or lowered being thus properly adjusted to the work they have to do. The cutters are each about thirteen feet long, placed two feet apart; the forward one usually has a serrated edge and is called a harrow; the rear one is a plane scraper. When at work these machines dress or plane a section of the track from seven to nine feet wide. The usual weight of such planers or track machines is about two thousand pounds.

Plantar Cushion. A thick pad of fibrous tissue, situated behind and under the navicular and coffin bones, and resting on the sole and frog of the foot. It is wedge-shaped, the narrow, pointed end which is turned forwards and reaches to the middle of the under surface of the foot, causes the center triangular prominence known as the frog. The plantar cushion is one of the most important divisions of the foot, its office being to receive the downward pressure of the column of bones in the leg, and to destroy the concussion occasioned by rapid motion. See FROG.

Plate. A light shoe, or protection for the foot, for running horses; a bar plate. They are made of steel or aluminum and weigh from one and three-fourths to four ounces, according to the size and also to the weight the horse is to carry. They have no calks and are each fastened with six small nails.

Plate. A cup, flagon or other article of precious metal awarded to the winner in a contest, or to the owner of the winning horse; a sum of money offered as a prize in a speed contest, as the "king's plate," "members' plate."
The trotter should be bred to trot just as the thoroughbred runs in plates.—American Horse Breeder.

Plater; Selling Plater. A horse that competes for a plate; "selling plater," is a horse of medium quality or what might be termed a low class race horse, such as start in selling races where the weight is graduated by the price. Class is determined by ability to go fast for a distance and carry weight, but the want of class makes the "plater." Still, many good horses go in such races, their owners backing them heavily and then buying them in.

Play or Pay. An imperative ruling. In all match performances where the amount of the match is placed in the hands of the stakeholder one day before the event comes off, the race becomes play or pay; that is, whether the match comes off or not the stake is forfeited and all the money goes as wagered. All English races are so declared, and it applies to all trotting and racing matches under American rules.

Plebeian-Bred. Coarsely bred; of cold, mongrel blood.

We thought nothing great could come from her plebeian-bred dam.— Training the Trotting Horse, Charles Marvin.

Plug. A common term for an old or used-up horse; an awkward, untradable horse; a lunk-head.

Plugging. The act of stopping horses' ears with cotton in order to render them more steady when in training or at work; and to make them less liable to become rattled by the noise and confusion often occurring on tracks when horses are at work, or during a race. It is a method that does not succeed with all horses, and must be employed with great caution.

A great many horses treated in this manner will act as though they were dumb—will not try to go, and will stop to shake their heads when asked to trot. If you have a horse that you think will do better with this treatment commence with him gradually. That is, in his work put just a little cotton in his ears at first, or, what is still better, put it in his ears while he is in the stable, and let him get used to it in that manner.—Life with the Trotters, John Splan.

Plunge. A sudden and violent pitching forward of the body, in which the horse throws himself forward and extends the hind legs upward; the exertion of great force upon the propellers to plunge the body forward in an erratic manner. Mr. Marvin says of one of the horses which he trained: "At times she plunged violently."

Plunger. To lay large stakes; a dashing, reckless better; a venturesome speculator.

Plunger. That part of the interior construction of the valve-stem in a pneumatic sulky wheel, which prevents the escape of the air. It consists of a small piston the head of which is beveled in cone-shape, which plays within the cylinder and is fitted between sections of rubber and felt packing. When the air is forced into the tire through this valve-stem by means of the air pump, the piston is forced back, or down against a minute spring fixed at the base of the stem; and with the cessation of each stroke of the pump, this spring forces the piston up, the cone-point being pressed against the packing where it is kept in place, thus preventing the escape of the air.

Pneumatic Sulky. A sulky having a rubber air-inflated, or pneumatic tire. See SULKY.

Early in 1892, Sterling Elliott, a bicycle manufacturer of Newton, Mass., took the large wheels off an ordinary sulky and substituted a pair of 28-inch pneumatic bicycle wheels, (in exactly the same manner in which thousands of sulkies have been altered since.) This sulky was taken to a private track and a trainer there employed was asked to hitch a horse to it and give it a trial. * * * He had not ridden the distance from the barn to the track before he began to look serious, and after the first half mile he made this earnest statement: "If I were going into a race for my life I would take that sulky in preference to any on which I ever sat." During the next few days his opinion was endorsed by other horsemen, and Mr. Elliott at once took steps to secure such rights as he was entitled to under the patent laws.—Pneumatic Wheels and How to Apply Them.

I have understood that the pneumatic tire sulky was first used in some place in New England. Its real adoption, however, was at the Detroit Grand Circuit meeting in 1892. There was one sulky sent to Budd Doble who would not use it for Nancy Hanks. He loaned it to Ed. Geers who trotted the horse Honest George in it winning his race. At Cleveland, the week following, there were two sulkies, and it was at the Cleveland meeting at which their superiority was positively demonstrated and admitted. From that on everybody got them as fast as it was possible to have them built and rigged.—Letter of Wm. B. Fasig, New York.

Pneumatic Tire. A rubber tire fitted to contain air, attached to the outside of the felloe or rim of a sulky wheel. There are different patterns, some of which are one-piece tires, while others are fitted with a second or inner tire, smaller than the outer. They are molded whole, and are generally one and three-fourths inch in outside diameter. In the center of some tires, between the outer and inner sections of vulcanized rubber, is a section formed of two layers of Sea Island cotton, one-sixteenth of an inch in thickness, for the purpose of giving greater strength, and to which the inner tube is vulcanized. They are attached to the rim by means of shellac or a high grade of coach varnish, or by a cement, the composition of which is a manufacturers' secret.

Pocket. A horse is said to be in a pocket when he is in a race, and is so confined behind a leading horse and between the pole and another horse, or with a horse on each side of him, that he cannot get out of his position. The act of his getting in such pocket may be a perfectly natural one, or it may have been aided by some one to get a competitor bottled up, or out of the way, or for the purpose of helping.

Point Pockets. Small pockets in the saddle in which the ends of the points of the tree rest.

13

Points. Exterior conformation. All those outward features or sections of the horse's form, which have different names
and different functions, the union or combination of which
make up the whole exterior of beauty and perfect service.
The term points has commonly been used to describe the members, or legs of the horse, as in the phrase : " Bay with black
points," meaning black legs; as though they were the only
points possessed by the horse. In fact, however, every part of
the exterior of the horse form a joint, point, or line to some
other line or distinctive feature in his exterior conformation, is
a point equally with his members or legs. Hence, the error of
applying the word point only to them. The more correct
expression to use in this instance, is : " Bay, with black extremities ; " or, " bay, with black members ; " the word points should
not be used in this connection.

Points. A system, scheme or schedule of points covering the conformation, breeding, health, and performance of a
horse, each point represented by an equivalent number, the
sum total of which is perfection; used in scoring or judging,
and by the test of which system an animal will score a certain
number of points, the range of judgment extending from a
cipher [0] up to the figures indicating perfection in each point
—the sum total of each being cut for defects, or retained at or
near perfection for the presence of excellencies. There is no
one accepted standard of points; there are several distinct
ones each of which have material differences. In some there
are as few as thirteen points on structure or conformation; in
others as many as twenty or more, in each case the total scale
reaching 100. Some schemes include educational points, or a
given number for the good discipline of a saddle horse—others
exclude this; some include a health scale for soundness and
freedom from vice; while all embrace historical points which
relate to pedigree, performance and quality or merit of offspring.

SCALE OF POINTS.

Structural Points.	Perfection.	Judgment.
1. Head,	7	
2. Neck,	5	
3. Shoulders, chest, and forearms,	8	
4. Barrel and coupling,	8	
5. Quarters, croup, stifles and gaskins,	10	
6. Hocks,	8	
7. Knees,	6	
8. Canons and pasterns,	6	
9. Feet,	10	
10. Color and coat,	6	
11. Size and substance,	10	
12. Symmetry and style,	8	
13. Action without speed,	8	
Total,	100	

Historical Points.
1. Pedigree, 40
2. Performance, 30
3. Character of progeny, 30

Total, 100

Point of the Hip. The bony surface, more or less prominent, which is a little to the rear of the last rib; the anterior point of the pelvis.

Point of the Shoulder. The prominent bony angle, on each side of the chest, a little below the junction of the neck and shoulder.

Point of the Tree. The wooden continuations of the gullet plate of a saddle.

Point to Point. [Eng.] A phrase describing a race to take place from one point of a fair hunting country, to another given point; which is not to be named till the time of starting, and is then to be named by a committee previously selected for the purpose.

Pointer. An item of important information on a race, obtained in some surreptitious manner, which may be used with advantage by the person to whom it is communicated.

Pointer. Any unnatural position assumed by the horse's foot, when standing, or any altered action which indicates lameness, is said to be a "pointer," or indicator of such trouble.

Pole. The guard-rail on the inside of the track or course, often called the hub rail. When a horse is given the pole, he has the inside when the field starts. Posts erected at the quarter on a half-mile track, and at the quarter, half, and three-quarters on a mile track, for the purpose of catching the time made by horses at those points in a race. On many courses, poles or posts are erected at each furlong—eight to the mile.

Pole Horse. The pole horse brings the field down to the wire, after which he has no rights over the other horses; but he has the right to the pole, provided he can keep it. The horse winning a heat takes the pole, or inside position, at the succeeding heat, and all other horses in the field take their positions in the order assigned to them in judging the previous heat, and so on until the race is finished.

Poll. That part of the horse's exterior which is on top of the neck, immediately behind the ear.

Poll Evil. Whether resulting from an injury, or a disease between the bones of the neck, it is a legal unsoundness.

Pommel. That part of the saddle, often called the head, which goes over the withers.

Pony. [Eng.] The sum of £25.

Pool. The combination of a number of persons, each staking a sum of money on the success of a horse in a race, the money to be divided among the successful layers according to the amount put in by each. The box in which tickets on a race are placed, is called a pool-box.

Port. The tongue-groove of the mouth-piece of a bit. Its use prevents the horse from taking the pressure on his tongue, as he might do if the bit were straight, and thus become heavy or dull in the hand.

Port-bit. A bit having a curved or open place in the center of the bar. In a perfect bit this groove or opening should be about two inches wide at the bottom and one inch at the top.

Position. The station of the horse when standing attention, or awaiting the rider's or driver's orders and signals.

Position of Horses. Placing, or ranking. The position of horses in a heat or race has reference both to their position as starters and at the finish. As starters, positions are given by the judges, the place of each horse being determined by lot. This is overruled, however, on the racing turf by giving the judges the right to place an unruly or a supposed vicious horse, where he cannot injure others. At the finish the winner of a heat has the inside position in the following heat, and the others take their positions on his right in the order in which they came out in the previous heat. See DRAWING FOR POSITION, and PLACING HORSES.

Post. [Eq.] The act of rising and sinking on the saddle, (when the horse is at the trotting gait), in accordance with the motion of the horse.

Post. A pole or post marking a boundary, or certain division or point of the course; as starting post, distance post, winning post.

Post Stake; Post Race; Post Match. By the old rules of the turf, those by which the New York Jockey Club governed its races fifty years ago, a post stake was an amount or sum named at the starting post; and a post match for horses of a certain age, was one in which the parties had the privilege of bringing any horse of that age to the post, ready for starting, without having previously named him. The Turf Congress rules define a post race as one for which the subscribers declare at the usual time before a race for declaring to start, the horse or horses they intend to run, without other limitation of choice than the racing rules and the conditions of the race prescribed.

Post to Finish. A term applied to the whole heat or race, especially on the running turf, and referring to the course of the race from start to wire; as, "an honest race from post to finish;" a square, handsome race all through. Also embracing the rules relating to the trotting or running of a match or heat, as to riders, drivers, starting, fouls, finish, etc.

Posterior Extremity; Posterior Member. That which is situated behind; the opposite of anterior, meaning before. In scientific language its meaning is the hind leg or hind limb of the horse.

P. P. [Eng.] These letters in the announcements or programmes of the Grand National Hunts, indicate that the race advertised takes place from "point to point" of a fair hunting country.

Prance; Prancing. The rearing or capering motion of a horse; said of a horse in high fettle, that he is prancing; riding with a proud step.

Prepotency. The power of transmitting; ability to produce; superior influence.

The clear and uninterrupted succession of trotting qualities is what makes prepotent sires.—Wallace's Monthly.

When one parent alone displays some newly-acquired and generally inheritable character, and the offspring do not inherit it, the cause may lie in the other parent having the power of prepotent transmission.—Animals and Plants under Domestication, Charles Darwin.

Private Sweepstakes is one to which no money is added, and which is not publicly advertised previous to the engagement being made. The racing rules say: "One made by the owners of the horses engaged without having been publicly open to any others."

Produce Race. A match for which horses are named by whose produce the race is to be run; the entries for such race specifying the dam and sire or sires.

Propellers. The hind legs of the horse in distinction from the fore legs, which are termed the weight-bearers. Each limb is required to support the body and act as propeller in turn, and Prof. Stillman says the anterior one does more than its share of both offices.

Propping. A form of restiveness similar to kegging. It is a vice.

Prophet. [Eng.] A tipster; one who obtains information concerning horses, races and probable winners, in advance of the occurrence of the race. A business which was formerly a regular profession carried on by means of disguises by men, (and women too), who were able to assume a variety of characters. Prophets now form a regular craft who work for a weekly fee, or for percentages on successes; they use the telegraph, and send letters to the sporting press.

Propulsion. The act of propelling or driving forward; the rapid stride of a trotting or running horse.

There is no act of extension further than the extension of the body upon the thigh. It is not until the center of motion, or head of the thigh has passed over the foot that extension is possible. * * * The act of propulsion begins from the moment that the hind foot takes the ground and its contraction begins.—The Horse in Motion, J. D. B. Stillman.

Protecting a Horse. A term referring to the act of the judges in protecting the pole horse, when the field is scoring, in not allowing any horse to come to the wire in advance of him.

Protest. Any complaint or charge made against any horse, rider, driver or owner, or against the decisions of the judges, upon any feature of the race or heat; whether complaining of a fraud or foul, or for the violation of any rule. The protest may be made verbally before the purse or winnings are paid, and reduced to writing when required; charges to be filed with the evidence, under oath, when so demanded.

Public Race. A public race is defined to be any contest for stake, premium, purse or wager, and involving admission fees, on any track or course, in the presence, and under the direction of duly appointed judges and timers.

Puffiness. Softness. An indication of a strain or injury to the tendons of the legs.

Pullers. Horses that pull hard on the reins; those having hard mouths. It is believed to be contrary to the facts to say that a horse cannot pull hard and last. That they fail to stay is often the fault of their riders and drivers.

There is no cure for a pulling horse, however, like that of not pulling against him.—Joseph Cairn Simpson.

When a horse pulls I do not think it at all expedient to get rid of the pull by means of punishing bits, bridoons, or such like devices. The trotter that goes at his best rate, while pulling hard, had best be borne with. If you get rid of the pull by means of the appliances just alluded to, you will soon get rid of some of the trot.— The Trotting Horse of America, Hiram Woodruff.

Pulling. The act of slowing or lessening the speed of a horse during a heat, by the driver. If such act is performed with a design to prevent his winning a heat or place which he is perfectly able to win; or for the evident purpose of aiding or perpetrating a fraud, such driver shall be taken from his sulky and another driver substituted, the offending horse punished, and the driver fined, suspended or expelled, at the discretion of the judges.

Pull to the Gait. The act of catching a horse, and bringing him to his gait, after a break. The trotting rules are very severe on a driver who neglects to instantly pull a horse to his gait should he break during a heat. If he does not do so, the horse is liable to be distanced, and the driver punished by fine or suspension. Different means are used by drivers to accomplish this, which must depend upon the disposition of the horse and the manner in which he has been trained.

Pulled Together. [Eq.] A phrase indicating that the horse is well collected, or gathered.

It is a very expressive term.—The Book of the Horse, Samuel Sidney.

Pull Up. To stop in riding or driving; to pull up at the close of a heat when beaten; the act of sawing the reins when a horse has the bit between his teeth, to make him dislodge it.

If you find you are beaten easily, pull up; spare your horse, and avoid the cruel and unsportsmanlike practice of flogging a beaten horse all the way home.—The Book of the Horse, Samuel Sidney.

Pulp of the Teeth. A soft substance furnished with blood-vessels and nerves, constituting the central axis of the tooth, and affording the means by which its vitality is preserved. In teeth which have ceased to grow the pulp occupies a comparatively small space, which, in the dried tooth, is called the pulp-cavity; while with advanced age it often becomes obliterated, and the pulp itself converted into bone-like material.

Pulse. The circulation of the blood through the heart, which, in the horse, is taken at the angle of the jaw where the artery crosses the bone. The normal beat is from thirty-six to forty-six times a minute, according to the breed, disposition and temperament. The various characteristics of the pulse are: *Slow*—where the number of beats is less than normal; *soft*—where the beat is rather weak, but not over-rapid; *small*—where the sensation conveyed to the finger is one of lessened diameter of the artery; *full, strong*—where there is a bounding sensation as though from an over-distention of the artery with each beat; *weak, feeble*—where the beat is hardly perceptible; *quick*—where the beats are more rapid than normal; *hard*—where the beats are tense, incompressible, vibrating and more frequent than normal; *irregular*—where several pulsations come in quick succession, and are then followed by a pause; *intermittent*—where the beat is lost at regular intervals.

Pumice Sole; Pumice Feet. An inflammation of the feet, which results in an excessive growth of soft, spongy horn in front of the laminæ of the toe, separating the coffin-bone from the hoof-wall. Its presence stamps the horse as unsound.

Pumping. The act of lifting a horse by the bit, or pulling back on him, when in a race, then letting him out, and repeating the operation constantly, to induce speed; urging a horse by the reins, as, "in the last heat Vet. Hanscomb pumped Honest John half the way round."

Punishment. Any fine, or other penalty imposed by the judges upon a horse, rider or driver, for any improper conduct or attempted wrong during a heat or race. All such punishments may be inflicted without notice or warning. The unnecessary or unwarranted flogging of a horse during a race or heat.

Punter. [Eng.] One who lays a wager against a book-maker.

Pure Gaited. A horse that trots squarely, without hitching, crossing, overreaching or swinging out; a perfectly balanced trotter—such a horse is said to be "pure gaited."

Purse. A specified sum of money, or other prize, offered by an association for a race, to which an entrance fee may, or may not, be required. Where an entrance fee is required, it is not returnable on the death of the horse or his failure to start.

Push; Push Him. A term used to indicate that a driver or rider is urging, or forcing his horse; when such extra force is being used, it is said that he is "pushing him," or "pushing his horse."

Put Up. When judges are dissatisfied with the manner in which a horse is being ridden or driven, they have the right to put another rider or driver in the saddle or sulky; and this is termed to "put up," or putting up. For such act no interference can be made by the owner, rider or trainer; and any driver or jockey who refuses to be put up, may be at once ruled off the course.

Q

Quality. A high degree of excellence in breeding; good blood; hence, a good horse is one of quality; a blooded one; one giving evidence of character in the form and expression of the head, the symmetry of the limbs, and the velvetlike softness of the hair and skin. More specifically quality is shown in the manifest superiority of texture, both of bone and muscle—the bone being compact, not cancellated; the muscles free from adulteration—that is, free from adipose and cellular tissue, fat, etc. Quality is mentally dependant on nerve-tissue, the source of all muscular motion, sensation and intelligence. Quality in individual points embraces a neat, expressive head; a countenance indicative of ability; neat legs; strength, with refinement of make; ample bones; quality in the tendons; courage and superior physical power.

It is this quality of organism in its greatest perfection which enables the horse to stand up, under preparation and training, year and year, profiting by his education and improving with age, that makes the really valuable turf horse. It is a quality more valuable than speed, because whatever measure of speed it possesses can be depended upon and improved. In short, it is the quality which distinguishes the thoroughbred from the dunghill. The number of heats and races won, and the number of successful years upon the turf, are more reliable lamps by which the breeder may guide his footsteps than the record of colt stakes and mere tests of speed.— Horse Breeding, J. H. Sanders.

Quarters. Those parts of the body which embrace the fore and hind quarters—the former including the part from the withers and shoulder to the arm; the latter from the hip and flank to the gaskin, or, in other words, including the entire thigh and haunch. Both quarters should have that fulness and roundness which good judges so much admire in these parts of the horse. The quarters of the foot are the names given to the two sides, or lateral regions of the wall between the toe and heel, and known as the outer and inner quarters.

Quarter Blanket. A blanket which reaches from the tail to a point just forward of the saddle, and is intended only for street use.

Quarter Crack; Sand Crack. A crack or fissure, generally extending from the coronet downward, for a variable distance, in the direction of the horny fibers of the foot. Often caused by allowing the foot to grow long and the horn to become dry and hard, when the expansion of the foot at the coronet cracks the inelastic hoof below it. It is a legal unsoundness. See SAND CRACK.

Quarter Cut; Quarter Grabbing. The act of the horse when at speed, by which he grabs, or cuts the quarters of the fore feet by one or the other of the hind feet. This may be due to faulty conformation, but it is often caused by a misstep or a break. It is generally the outside quarter that is most liable to injury, and the special use of quarter boots on the fore feet is to prevent them from being cut by horses that are quarter grabbers.

Quarter Horse. A horse that is good for a dash for a quarter of a mile at high speed; a sprinter; not a stayer for a long distance; a quitter.

Quarter Mile. World's running record to close of 1893: Bob Wade, four years old, at Butte, Montana, August 20, 1890; 0.21¼.

Quarterstretch. The homestretch of the course.

Queens of the Turf. The queens of the trotting turf, to the close of the year 1893, have been: 1. Lady Suffolk, gr. m. foaled in 1833; by Engineer 2d, (3); dam, by Don Quixote, by Messenger; Hoboken, N. J., October 7, 1844, 2:28.—2. Highland Maid, (a converted pacer), b. m. foaled in 1847; by Saltram; dam, Roxana, by Hickory; Centerville, N. Y., June 15, 1853, 2:27.—3. Flora Temple, b. m. foaled in 1845; by Bogus Hunter; dam, Madam Temple, by the Terry Horse; East New York, N. Y., September 2, 1856, 2.24¼. She had a reign extending from 1856 to 1867, her best time being 2:19¼, at Kalamazoo, Michigan, October 15, 1859.—4. Gold-smith Maid, b. m., foaled in 1857; by Abdallah, (15), by Abdallah (1), Milwaukee, Wis., September 6, 1871, 2:17. She reigned from 1871 to 1878, her best time having been made at Boston, Mass., September 2, 1874, 2:14, when she was seventeen years old.—5. Maud S., ch. m., foaled in 1874; by Harold, (413); dam, Miss Russell, by Pilot. Jr., (12). In 1880 she lowered the world's record, but her time was beaten the same year by St. Julien. At Rochester, N. Y., August 11, 1881, she trotted in 2:10¼, and from that time to 1891 her reign was undisputed, except for a single day, (August 1, 1884), when Jay-Eye-See beat her at Providence, R. I., by three-quarters of a second. Her best time was made at Cleveland, Ohio, July 30, 1885, 2:08¾.—6. Sunol, b. m., foaled in 1886; by Electioneer, (125); dam, Waxana, by General Benton, (1755); Stockton, California, October 20, 1891, 2:08¼.—7. Nancy Hanks, br. m., foaled in 1886; by Happy Medium, (400); dam, Nancy

Lee, by Dictator, (113); Terre Haute, Indiana, September 28, 1892, 2:04.

In a career extending from 1838 to 1851, Lady Suffolk won a total of eighty-three races. Flora Temple had ninety-six winning races to her credit, and her turf career extended from 1852 to 1861. The career of Goldsmith Maid was largely made up of exhibition races. From 1867 to 1877 she won one hundred and fourteen contests, and made three hundred and thirty-two heats in 2:30 or better—a triumph never approached by any other animal. Her earnings during this time were over $250,000. Her public career closed the year she was twenty years old, but in that year her campaign comprised twelve victories, in which she trotted seventeen heats better than 2:20, including one in 2:14½. "The day she was twenty-one years old," writes John Splan, "Budd Doble drove her for Governor Stanford a mile in 2:26—a performance I never expect to see any other animal make under similar conditions." Maud S. was nine years old when she trotted in 2:08¾. The distinction, "Queen of the high wheel sulky," is claimed for her, by her record of 2:08¾ at Cleveland, Ohio, July 30, 1885, the record of Sunol, at Stockton, California, October 20, 1891, of the same mark, 2:08¼, having been made over a kite track. When Nancy Hanks trotted at Independence, Missouri, August 31, 1892, in 2:05¼, the trotting and pacing records were placed on an equality for that period.

Queer. A term applied to a horse that is a kicker. To say that he is "queer behind," means that he kicks and must be looked out for; as in the term, "this horse is queer."

Quidding. The act of partly chewing the hay and allowing it to drop from the mouth. It is a habit generally due to irregular teeth. In cases where, from irregular teeth, the sides of the mouth become lacerated, quidding is an unsoundness while it lasts.

Quietness. A warranty of soundness does not imply quietness on the part of the horse sold.

Quintet, The. [Eng.] The five mighty reunions or meets of the English turf, viz: Epsom, Doncaster, Goodwood, Ascot and York, are known as "the quintet."

Quit. To stop in a race.

It is my idea that the more finely organized and better bred a horse is, the more liable he is to quit when out of condition.—Life with the Trotters, John Splan.

Quitting. The act of giving up a heat or race. It is said of a horse that lacks courage that he is a "quitter;" the term denoting not so much want of training and work, as lack of real courage or nervous force.

True quitting is a mental quality — cowardice, faint-heartedness.—Training the Trotting Horse, Charles Marvin.

Some quitters are fair campaigners. This fact may tend to show that quitting is a mental, and not a physical infirmity; a lack of courage and perseverance rather than of hardiness, which I believe to be the general opinion of horsemen.—Wallace's Monthly.

Quittor, may be described as a number of abscesses, in most cases at the coronet, towards the quarters or heels, giving great pain and causing much lameness. It indicates a very serious condition of the feet, and is a legal unsoundness.

R

Race. A race includes any purse, match, stake, premium or sweepstakes for which a contest of speed is made by horses, over any course or track. The term includes both trotting and running contests, and whether in harness, to wagon or under the saddle. Hence racing means the sport or practice of trotting and running horses. A public race is understood to mean a race for any prize, for which an admission fee is charged, and at which judges and timers take direction of the trial.

Race Record. A record obtained in a regular race, as distinguished from a record made against time.

Horses with race records bring the best prices.—The Horseman.

Racer. The thoroughbred English or American horse; a running bred horse.

In a work published at London in 1836, entitled "Comparative View of the Form and Character of the English Racer and Saddle Horse During the Last and Present Centuries," embellished with eighteen fine plates of famous horses, a celebrated racer called Old Partner, foaled in 1718, is represented as galloping in clothing which greatly conceals his form. So also in the portrait of the famous racer, Sedbury, foaled in 1734, (both painted by Seymour, a noted animal painter), the horse's body is much concealed by clothing—a large blanket being strapped closely about his body, extending up on the neck one-third of the way to the poll, with an apron fastened around his breast and dropping nearly half way to the knees. Both horses are represented at full running speed.

Racing Calendar. A stud book; a registry of the pedigrees and performances of running horses. It is said that the first English racing calendar was issued by John Cheny in 1727. The English Jockey Club, which had been established seven years previous to this period, had taken an active part in preserving pedigrees of horses, which were probably published in this first calendar. In 1751 the records that had appeared in this old calendar and other sporting publications, were compiled and published in a collected form, but it was not until 1791 that the English Stud Book appeared in its present shape, since which time it has been continued to this day.

The publication of the Stud Book marked an era in the science of breeding. It was the first effort to establish special books for recording animal pedigrees for preservation and for purposes of study; and the practice has spread to every land where thoroughbreds are bred, and the method has been extended to every important breed of live stock. English racing first showed that superiority could only be maintained by purity of blood. It took a hundred years or more to establish that doctrine so as to be generally accepted. The annual publication of tables of " winning sires" began many years before the Stud Book appeared. We have now such annual tables extending back for more than a hundred years, and, from a careful study of the earlier ones, men came to see that success, as shown by winnings, came from purity of blood, and not from wide admixture.—Dr. W. H. Brewer, Yale College.

The standard of admission to the first volume of the Stud Book appears to have been simply creditable performance upon the turf, as shown by the Racing Calendar, it being taken for granted that no horse could be a creditable performer that was not well bred—an assumption that has never yet been found at fault.—Horse Breeding, J. H. Sanders.

Racing Plate. A very narrow, light rim of steel or aluminum, weighing not more than from two to three ounces, about half an inch in width, and used as a shoe for running horses. The rules of the Turf Congress forbid the use of shoes in races, but allow that of a plate.

Rack; Racking. A gait which is a modification of the pace, and is often very appropriately called single footing. In racking the fore feet move as in a slow gallop, while the hind feet move as in a trot, or pace. When the horse is going at this gait, we hear the four distinct strokes of the four different limbs, for each foot strikes the ground singly, and independent of the others. In making the complete revolution, therefore, the count is—one, two, three, four—one, two, three, four; while in either trotting or pacing the count is—one, two; one, two. The confusion of terms regarding this gait is occasioned by the fact that the gait itself is somewhat varied according as the horse which racks carries the one or the other fore foot foremost in the galloping action of the fore feet. Hence many have confounded the rack with the pace and used the words synonymously. A horse which racks after a slower trot, is esteemed much inferior to one which only changes to this gait after moving at a greater speed.

Rank of Distanced Horses. When horses are distanced in the first heat of a race, their rank is equal; but when they are distanced in any subsequent heat, they rank as to each other in the order of the positions to which they were entitled at the start of the heat in which they were distanced.

Ranks, The. A term used to describe that portion of the field not up to par; those far in the rear of the contending horses; the "rank and file," or common members of the field.

Rarey Cord; War Bridle. A simple halter used in giving colts their first lessons in harness where they have not been well broken to the halter, or not handled till two or three years old. It is made of a piece of sash-cord fourteen feet long. Tie a good knot at the end by putting the end through twice before tieing down. Tie a half-knot, (a regular halter knot), about one foot from this and put the end knot through, making a small loop that will fit the colt's under jaw. This knot and loop should be wound with soft cloth or leather before being used. Standing on the near side, put the small loop over the neck, pass the long end through the loop and draw down to about the size of a headstall. Pass the right hand under the jaw, and take firm hold of the nose on top, with the left hand slip the small loop on the under jaw, place the rope on top of the neck close to the ears. In two or three lessons with this cord, any colt, however high tempered, can be taught to lead in any place, or in any manner desired by the trainer.

Rarey System, The. The system of educating horses generally known as the Rarey System, and practiced with so much success by Mr. John S. Rarey, its originator, is based upon these three simple principles: 1. That any young horse can be taught to do anything that a horse can do, if taught in a proper manner. 2. That no horse is conscious of his strength until he has resisted and conquered a man; therefore, that the colt should always be handled in such manner that he shall not find out his strength. 3. That as seeing, smelling, feeling and hearing are the senses by which the horse examines every strange object, we may, by allowing him to exercise these senses, reconcile him to any object or sound that does not hurt him. It is, undoubtedly, the recognition of these principles and their practice in horse management, to which is due the success of the various systems of educating colts, and handling or subduing vicious horses, in use by many horsemen and professional trainers of the present day.

Rating Driver. A term applied to the driver in a race who comprehends at each step the rate at which his horse is going, and is able to so gauge and control him in such manner as to make him do his best, save himself and yet win. Such a driver, however, is unable to rate the speed of any horse in the race but his own.

Crit Davis I call a rating driver: he seems to know about how well his horses can go before they start, and then rates them along to accomplish the mile in that way.—Life with the Trotters, John Splan.

Ration. Fodder; provender; the daily feed for a horse. Hay and oats form the "staff of life" in the keep of the horse. The only hay that should ever be given is clean, pure Timothy. Old hay is always preferable to new. If possible it should not be used till a year old; crisp, clean, fresh, free from dust, of a greenish color, and possessing a sweet, pleasant smell. New hay is hard to digest, is liable to produce excessive salivation and purging. A normal ration is four pounds at a feed, three times a day. Of the grains, oats always take the lead. The usual ration is from ten to twelve quarts a day in three equal rations. Barley is frequently used for work horses. Corn is a heavier food than oats, more fattening, but may be given in cold weather, in small quantities, cracked and mixed with oats, (in some cases), but generally preferred whole. A bran mash serves to keep the bowels open and may be given once or twice a week, according to condition. Always give it at night. Of the roots, potatoes and carrots are most esteemed. These are the general essentials, to be varied according to the condition of the horse, the work he is doing and the work required of him in the future. The subject of feeding is a whole study in itself, and one which the groom should master in all its details, according to the individual peculiarities and different constitutions of each of the horses under his care. See BRAN MASH and OATS.

Rattled. When a horse becomes confused or unsteady in a race, is obstinate and unmanageable, he is said to be "rattled," to have his head turned.

In the confusion Palo Alto became rattled and made a very bad break. —Training the Trotting Horse, Charles Marvin.

Readying. [Eng.] Explained by the quotation:

Trial in a horse case. Question: Do you mean to say that you don't know what was meant by "readying" Success? Answer: Of course I know what it means. It means pulling.—London Standard.

Rearing. When a horse rears furiously the rider should bend well over the horse's neck, lower the hands and pull him vigorously to one side or the other. Rearing is a serious vice.

Record. A fact written down officially for preservation and future reference; the time made in a race; the best recorded achievement of speed. Every public performance for a purse, stake or premium must be timed, and the time thus made written down in a book and attested by the signatures of the judges. This writing in the book is the record, and when once made must remain till blotted out. When one horse trots against another the time made by the horse first to pass under the wire is recorded against him. When a horse trots against time, say to beat 2:28, and the time is recorded as 2:28¼, that time is officially ascertained and must be officially recorded. The common theory that because a horse fails to win he fails to make a record, does not hold. In hundreds of instances a horse is first in a heat and is distanced in the next, and fails to win a dollar. But he has made a record.

Record Breaker. Any horse that lowers a record; a horse making faster time than that which has previously stood as the record for age, class or distance.

Recovery. A catch at breaking which brings the horse to his gait. When the horse at such time catches his gait and goes to speed, he is said to "recover"; to have recovered.

Everybody knows that pacers are ordinarily not as handy in recovering from a break as are trotters.—Wallace's Monthly.

Rectangular Course. A rectangle is a plane having all its angles right angles, and its opposite sides consequently equal. Hence a rectangular track or course is one commonly called a four-cornered track, with four short stretches and four turns; of which the track at Terre Haute, Indiana, on which Nancy Hanks made her record of 2:04, is an example.

Reefing. Driving for every inch of speed the horse has in him; using the whip; urging; hard driving; forcing the pace by every known means; rallying the horse by voice and rein to his best effort.

Refuser. A horse that refuses an obstacle or a hurdle, either from fear, contrary disposition, having been badly educated, is afraid of forcing his bit, or of hurting himself when taking-off. By the turf rules, a refuser having been led over an obstacle, is disqualified from winning, although he comes in first.

Registry Certificate. A certificate from any established or well recognized registry association for recording either pedigrees or records, that the pedigree or record of which it is a copy, has been duly received and is eligible to registry and publication.

Regular Meeting. A regular meeting is construed to mean a meeting advertised in a public journal not less than one week before the commencement of the same, and at which meeting no less than two regular events, (purse or stake), take place on each day, to which an entrance fee is paid or a subscription made; entries must be made as provided in all cases, and matches or races must take place over the tracks of the National or American Associations.

Regulation Track. A regulation track is one generally understood to mean a track the stretches and turns of which are each eighty rods long; again it has been taken to mean one in which the stretches are shorter and the turns longer. But the shape of a track will always depend much upon the lay of the land. That at Springfield, Mass., has stretches one hundred rods long, and turns correspondingly shorter; the track at Rigby Park, Maine, has seventy rod stretches and eighty rod turns, and the track at Terre Haute, Ind., has four stretches and four short turns — yet they are all regulation tracks. On a regulation track the horses start from a wire stretched across the track from the judges' stand, and finish at the same point. In another sense a regulation track has come to mean a track in membership with the National or American Trotting Associations, as distinguished from a free track, or one not in membership with either association.

Reins. That part of the harness consisting of leading-lines or straps, passing through the Ds on the gig-saddle, and fastened to the bit on each side, by which the horse is guided.

Rein-back. The act of moving a horse backward by the reins.

Rein-holder. A clasp or clip on the dashboard of a carriage by which to hold the reins after the driver has alighted.

Rein-holders. Devices in the form of adjustable metal buttons or clamps, to prevent the slipping of the rein in the hand, thus enabling the driver to obtain a better hold upon the reins in controlling the horse.

Rein-hook; Water-hook. A hook on the gig-saddle or jack-saddle of a harness for the purpose of securing the check or bearing rein in place.

Reinsman. A person skilled in managing horses; an expert driver.

Reinforced Girth. A saddle girth having a double thickness or backing of strong leather is called a "reinforced girth." Long before the use of the bike sulky, John Splan wrote: "Be sure and have a good, strong saddle and an extra wide, soft girth, as there is where most of the strain comes on a track harness." This is even more true with the pneumatic sulky than before, and the need of reinforced girths is consequently greater.

Reinstatement. The act of restoring one to a position from which he has been removed. All persons who may have been suspended by the judges of a race from any cause, have the right of appeal from such decisions or rulings, which appeal, with a statement of all the facts in the case, goes to the Board of Review or Board of Appeals of the governing association, where it is carefully considered, and in many cases the horse, party, or track suspended, is again reinstated to full privileges.

Repeat. To give a horse an additional exercise of a mile, after he has already been driven one mile; as "a mile and repeat."

14

Repeater. A watch that, on the compression of a spring, indicates the seconds and fractions of a second; a watch often known as a split-second watch, by which horses are timed in a race.

Resilience. Resistance backwards; a term denoting the resistance which a horse and sulky meet in passing through the air at a high speed.

Responding. A term describing the act of the horse in understanding and yielding to the wishes of his rider or driver; more especially used in speaking of the action of a horse under the saddle.

Some men inspire confidence so readily that a horse will take hold and do all he knows the first time the man drives him. For another man the same horse will not trot a yard.—Hiram Woodruff.

Rest. It is an interesting fact that a horse never rests on two legs, but always on the two anterior or forward, and one posterior or hind leg, so that the center of gravity always falls within a triangle.

The tendinous fibers or tissues, (serratus muscle), of the fore legs are incapable of fatigue, hence the horse has no occasion to rest them, and will stand in his stall all day without resting either of his fore legs; while in the hind leg the labor falls upon the triceps of pure muscular fiber and he will be observed to rest his hind legs alternately.—The Horse in Motion, J. D. B. Stillman.

Resting Break. A change of gait made quickly by a horse at high speed for the purpose of giving an instant of rest to the muscles of locomotion; very different from that made by the unsteady, hard-mouthed, repeated breaker in a race.

Sometimes a horse seeks relief in a break, but as to the ultimate benefit of "resting breaks" I am skeptical. I think the steady horse makes the mile with greater ease than the one that engages in the rather violent exercise of "breaking and catching."—Training the Trotting Horse, Charles Marvin.

Restiveness stands at the head of all the vices of the horse, for it includes many different vices and assumes forms which are dangerous to rider and groom. Among the different forms are pawing, or striking with the fore feet; rearing; plunging; kegging; gibbing, or backing; propping, and kicking. Generally these various forms of restiveness are the result of bad temper and worse education, and like most habits founded on nature and confirmed by education are inveterate.

Review, Boards of. The board of review of the National Trotting Association is made up of one member from each district of the board of appeals, and possesses the authority and performs the office and duties which belong to the board of appeals, and has jurisdiction on such matters relating to the turf arising in their respective districts, "as may be delegated to them by the board of appeals." Of the American

Trotting Association there is a board of review in each state, district and territory of the United States, and in each foreign state or country in which there is one or more members, which has "original jurisdiction of all matters relating to the turf arising on the grounds of members in such state," as well as all cases of appeal brought to it under the by-laws of the association.

Rheumatism. A form of inflammation attacking the fibrous structures, (tendons, joints, muscles, etc.), of the body; largely dependent on constitutional predisposition transmitted from ancestors to offspring. It is an unsoundness only when it has become a determined and constitutional complaint; and where no relapse of it has occurred for some time, and it may be considered a permanent cure has been effected, the animal may be given a certificate of soundness.

Ribs. The region of the ribs of the horse is bounded by the shoulders in front; by the flanks behind; by the back above, and by the belly and brisket, (sternum), below.

Ribbons. Reins; leading-lines to a harness by which the horse or horses are controlled. To "handle the ribbons" is to drive; to hold the reins.

Jim Keegan handled the ribbons over the six fine grays when President Grant was received in Augusta, in fine style; and many a man on the street no doubt thought him a more important person than the President. —Daily paper.

Ride; Rider. To be carried on the back of a horse; to sit in a, sulky or buggy and manage a horse in motion; to ride a race. Hence a rider is a person who rides on horseback; one who is skilled in horsemanship.

Ride and Tie. A method of riding by two persons having but one horse between them, much practiced in early times by those travelling. The plan was for one person to ride half a mile or more, according to the agreement, then dismount, hitch the horse and walk. The second person coming up on foot would take the horse and ride his turn, going ahead of the one walking, and tieing the horse for him for his next turn at riding, and so on the entire distance.

Riding a Race. The four different methods or tactics to be used in riding a race are denominated: 1. Waiting; 2. Making the running; 3. Waiting in front; 4. Keeping with one's horses. See particular definitions under each heading.

Ridgling; Ridgel; Riggot. A male animal having one testicle; a horse half castrated; a nag. The courts have decided that a ridgling is a horse; not a gelding.

Rig. A jockey's outfit. The colors worn by jockeys are often gorgeous and brilliant. Generally the oldest stables have the simplest and least variegated colors; the newer ones the most complex. Among the former are the blue jacket with orange sleeves and blue cap; and the blue jacket, orange sleeves and orange cap. In some, stripes of color run in rings around the body of the jacket, or around the sleeves, or the cap; in others the colors are in vertical or diagonal lines. There are over two thousand running stables in the United States, the riders of no two being rigged in precisely the same colors or combination of colors.

Rim. The felloe of a sulky wheel, of wood or steel, which forms the support of the tire, and into which the spokes are inserted. Hickory is the wood most used for this purpose; and when the rim is made of steel, for holding the pneumatic tire, it is rolled cold, united with a brazed joint.

Ringbone. Bony growths which usually begin as inflammation of the membrane covering the bones at such points in the structure as give attachment to ligaments, viz: on one or both pastern bones, and which sometimes extend to the interphalangeal joints. In cases where the flexibility of the cartilage is altered or lost, it is an unsoundness; but where it is only in front of the pastern bone, and not in the way of any joint, or approaching the heels, it is a blemish.

Ringer. A horse that has been painted or disguised to represent another or different horse, with the intent to have him concealed in identity, in order that he may be taken in different circuits and entered in a class slower than that in which he belongs, and thus win races and obtain purses in a fraudulent manner. Consular rules have been adopted by England and Germany prohibiting the importation of horses from this country, for racing purposes, unless the owner lodges with the secretary of the track a certificate of identity, pedigree and record, from the secretary of the National Trotting Association of the United States. All turf rules have severe punishment for a horse that is a ringer, and many of the states have enacted laws making the operations of a ringer a crime punishable by imprisonment of its owner, agent or driver. See LAW.

The man who starts out with a ringer, starts out to steal.—Spirit of the Hub.

Roach or High-back, the reverse of low-back, or saddle back, is held to be a blemish.

Road Cart. A jogging cart; a sulkyette; a half-sulky for road purposes. Built somewhat heavier than a speed sulky, weighing from seventy-five to eighty pounds, having a low foot-rest, and dasher for protection of the legs from mud and dirt.

Roadster. A carriage horse as distinguished from a speed or draft horse; a gent's driver; a horse used in driving for pleasure. He should weigh 1100 pounds, be handsome in every outline and point; showy; sound. He should have his nose above the line of his back; be well proportioned; well "set up"; kind; fast. The best color is bay.

The ideal roadster starts slowly, gradually warms up to his work, and after ten miles or so; (just as the inferior horse has had enough), begins to be full of play. Such pre-eminently is the habit of the Morgan family.—Road, Track, and Stable, H. C. Merwin.

It requires a combination of qualities rarely met with in any animal to make a perfect road horse. I find it much easier to select and buy a first-class race horse than a road horse which would please the ordinary road driver. It will be impossible to find one that will be perfect in three or four different positions, or in other words you cannot expect to use your horse in the ordinary family carriage five days in a week and then have him able to go at a high rate of speed the other two. In picking out a road horse, always be sure and buy one that is perfectly sound. Test the horse thoroughly as to kindness and ability to draw weight at a high rate of speed.—Life with the Trotters, John Splan.

Roaring. A wheezing, or hoarse rasping sound made in the upper part of the windpipe, (larynx), in breathing, and especially when excited, or galloped up a steep hill, or put to rapid work. It is generally due to paralysis and wasting of the muscles on the left side of the larnyx, which opens the channel for the air, and in such cases the roaring is only produced in drawing air in. Roaring is an unsoundness.

An animal that is a roarer should not be used for breeding purposes, no matter how valuable the stock. The taint is transmissible in many instances, and there is not the least doubt in the minds of those who know best that the offspring whose sire or dam is a roarer, is born with an hereditary predisposition to the affection.— W. H. Harbaugh, V. S.

Rolls. Devices used upon the ankle of the horse for various preventive purposes. The calking roll is to prevent him from standing in the stable with one foot on another; the shoe-boil roll is to prevent the horse from getting the calk of the shoe under the arm while lying down, causing a shoe-boil; the shin roll is used as a protection to the legs between the knee and ankle. They are made of buckskin or enameled leather, web or kid, and often stuffed with hair to render them soft.

Rolling-motion Shoe. A shoe specially fitted for horses inclined to stumble, or for those having a peculiar motion of the fore legs, to assist them in a more balanced action. The shoe has four calks, and is of great convexity on the ground surface. It is designed to give the horse more action and make him raise his feet high, so that, in placing them down, there is nothing to impede his movements or cause him to stumble, as is often the case with horses shod with shoes having the ordinary toe-calk.

Roomy. A term used in describing a perfectly shaped brood mare; as a horse having a long, deep, wide middle, with a well-developed pelvic boundary.

Rosettes. Metal ornaments attached to the upper parts of the side pieces of a headstall; embossed and plain; containing fancy device, initial or monogram.

Rough-gaited. A horse is said to be "rough-gaited" when he travels in a hitching, unbalanced way; a horse that hobbles, falters and breaks in his ordinary gait, or when put to speed.

Rounding To. A term used to denote the art of again getting a horse into condition after a hard race. It takes some horses a long time to recover, others will do it more quickly. Mr. Marvin says: "On returning from the East, I found Wildflower and Manzanita somewhat broken up, and both were some time in 'rounding to' again."

Round-course. What was, without doubt, the first round, circular or oval race track ever built, was that established at Newmarket, England, in 1666. It was three miles, four furlongs and one hundred and seventy-eight yards long.

Rowel. One of the short, pointed arms on the circle, or wheel of a horseman's spur.

Rowley Mile. Where the two thousand guineas stakes is run—the important opening three-year-old event of the year on the English turf. The distance was formerly one mile one yard; but is now one mile eleven yards.

Rubber. A person who rubs down, dresses or cares for horses; especially one who rubs a race horse after he has trotted or ran a heat or race; a person who has graduated as a stable-boy and is apprentice to a trainer.

In attending to a horse as famous as Rarus, the head rubber must be, on every day of the trotting season, prepared to act as a reception committee to thousands of people, many of whom have, apparently, no idea of the responsibilities that are involved in the care of such an animal. Morrel Higbie was the best rubber I ever saw. He remained with me until the day Rarus was sold, and afterward rubbed for me the pacer Johnston.—Life with the Trotters, John Splan.

Rubber Tire. The term generally used in describing the pneumatic tire of the bike sulky. A rubber tire is described by Mr. Samuel Sidney, in his "Book of the Horse," published in 1880, which is, undoubtedly, the first mention of such a tire having been used for carriages in England or America. He says: "India-rubber tires are a great luxury; they give to a wheeled carriage the smoothness of a sledge on hard snow, and subdue nearly all the rattle and noise of wheels. But they are usually made on a wrong principle. If india-rubber is stretched, every cut continually widens, and the tire is speedily destroyed. Tires made on a directly opposite plan will endure for an unlimited period; that is, a thick, hollow tube of india-rubber shrunk on an iron core shorter than the rubber, and coiled round a wheel grooved to receive it. This kind of india-rubber has been used for many years on two carriages, by Mr. Ransome, the agricultural implement maker, of Ipswich."

Ruck, To Come in With the. To come in with the ruck, is to arrive at the winning post among the unplaced horses.

> I once knew a chappie not famed for his luck,
>   Who to punting was muchly addicted;
> But the horses he backed, to a place "in the ruck"
>   Were, with scarce an exception, restricted.
> —Bird o' Freedom.

Rudder and Compass. [Eq.] In horseback riding, the head and neck of the horse are said to be at once the rudder and compass of the rider.

Rules. When an appeal to the rules is made, or the rules are referred to, it means, for the trotting turf to the rules of the National or American associations; for the running turf to those of the American Turf Congress.

Rule of the Track. In all driving on the track, or course, the rule is to turn to the left in meeting, not to the right, as in driving on the highway. See LAW OF THE TRACK.

Ruled Out; Ruled Off. A term used to imply a punishment to an offending horse, rider or driver. Horses may be ruled out for interfering with other horses or failing to keep positions, and an offending horse may be ruled out in case of collisions or break-downs, for which he is responsible. A horse ruled out for fraud retains his record, or bar. Drivers and riders may be ruled out for improper, corrupt or fraudulent practices. In the summary of a race the letters "R. O.," following the name of a horse at any given heat, mean that such horse was ruled out of the race on that heat.

Rumbling. A low, rattling, rumbling sound of the bowels, technically called *borborygmus*. It is an unpleasant fault in a horse, not an unsoundness.

Run. The leaping, or springing gait of a horse; an acceleration, or quickening of the action of the gallop, with two, three, or all the feet off the ground at the same instant during the stride; a race, as "the horses were matched for a run at Morris Park."

The run is the perfect gait of the horse, for it is that which displays most perfectly the play of all his locomotive organs, and by which he attains his greatest speed.—The Horse in Motion, J. D. B. Stillman.

Run Big. A horse that runs when quite fat, and yet in good training, is said to "run big." The term applies more particularly to the English turf.

Run Fine. For a horse to "run fine" is to carry no superfluous flesh; trained fine; in high form.

All race-horse men will tell you that some horses run big, and others run fine—that is, that some are at their best when rather stouter than what, on the average, is regarded as perfect condition, while others show the highest form when trained pretty "fine," but the latter are in the minority. That some horses are at their best when very fine is true beyond question; but I know that in the great majority of cases a horse, to be in the pink of condition, must carry a quite fair degree of flesh—a good smooth coating over the ribs, not feeling gross and thick to the hand, but amply covering the bones.—Training the Trotting Horse, Charles Marvin.

Run-in. A term used more especially in the hunt and steeplechase, where the horses come in in fine style at the close; but also used in describing the finish of a running race, as, "a fine run-in," "a fine finish." That part of the course on which the finish of a race takes place; the last quarter; the straight.

Run off; Run out. [Eng.] The habit which many horses have of turning away from fences, when in the chase, and, instead of taking them, turn rapidly and run along their side. To break a horse of this habit nothing is so effectual as a secundo bit, which, though quite severe, is much used with horses that refuse.

Running Horse. The thoroughbred race horse. The exterior conformation of the running horse may be summed up in these words: He should have a high chest and long members; a short body and strong loins; the neck, shoulder, croup, thigh, buttock, leg and forearm should be long, without being too heavy in the upper part; the members strong, clean, free from blemishes; he should have wide and thick articulations, closed in the superior angles, open in the inferior; a deep chest, abdomen slightly full; fine skin, hair, mane and tail; an animated and expressive physiognomy; he should be graceful, nimble, elegant, excitable, energetic, impetuous, and of great endurance.

Running Races. [Eng.] During twenty years coming down to about 1890, the average time of the English Derby at Epsom, has been 2m. 48sec.; the Grand National at Liverpool, has been for the same time, 10m. 13sec. The Derby is one and one-half miles; the Grand National is four and one-half miles. At Epsom one mile has been run in 1m. 52 sec.; at Liverpool in 2m. 16sec. The Derby horses carried an average of eighty pounds; the Liverpool horses carried nearly eleven stone—one hundred and fifty-four pounds. On the Liverpool course there are about thirty jumps of formidable size, the going on the turf is worse than at Epsom and there are some ploughed fields to be crossed.

Running, Remarkable. In October, 1741, at the Curragh meeting in Ireland, Mr. Wilde engaged to ride 127 miles in nine hours. He performed it in six hours and twenty-one minutes. He employed ten horses and, allowing for mounting and dismounting, and a moment for refreshment, he rode for six hours at the rate of twenty miles an hour. Mr. Thorndike, in 1745, rode from Stilton to London, and back again to Stilton, 213 miles, in eleven hours and thirty-four minutes, which is, after allowing the least possible time for changing horses, twenty miles an hour on the turnpike road and uneven ground. Mr. Shaftoe, in 1762, with ten horses, and five of them ridden twice, accomplished fifty and one-fourth miles, in one hour and forty-nine minutes. In 1763, he won a more extraordinary match. He was to procure a person to ride one hundred miles a day, on any horse each day for twenty-nine days together, and to have any number of horses not exceding twenty-nine. He accomplished it on fourteen horses; and on one day rode one hundred and sixty miles, on account of the tiring of his first horse. Mr. Hull's Quibbler, however, afforded one of the most remarkable instances on record, of the speed of the race horse. In December, 1786, he ran twenty-three miles round the flat at Newmarket in fifty-seven minutes, ten seconds.

Running Rules. By the rules of the Turf Congress a horse when in the hands of the starter shall receive no further care from his attendants. He must be started by the jockey. With the consent of the starter a horse can be led to his position, but must then be let loose. The horses are started by a flag, and there is no start until, and no recall after the assistant starter drops his flag in answer to the flag of the starter.

Running. World's record to close of 1893. It is noticeable that in races on the running turf the time record has been lowered but slightly in recent years and that only in short races; the long distance races having been changed but little as but few long races have been run. The fastest one-half mile up to 1880, was 0:47¾; it was reduced by Geraldine, four-year-old, carrying 122 pounds, at Morris Park, (straight course), August 30, 1889, to 0:46. In 1880, the fastest five furlongs was 1:02¾; reduced in 1889 by Britannia to 0:59; reduced by Correction, five-year-old, carrying 119 pounds, at Morris Park, September 29, 1893, to 0:57. In 1880, three-fourths of a mile, fastest time was 1:15; reduced by Domino, two-year-old, carrying 128 pounds, at Morris Park, September 29, 1893, to 1:09. The fastest seven furlongs is Bella B's, five-year-old, carrying 103 pounds, at Monmouth Park, July 8, 1890, (straight course), 1:23½. The fastest one mile in 1880 was by Ten Broeck, 1:39¾; reduced by Salvator, four-year-old, carrying 110 pounds, (straight course, against time), at Monmouth Park, August 28, 1890, to 1:35½. One mile and twenty yards, Maid Marian, four-year-old, carrying 101 pounds, Washington Park, Chicago, July 19, 1893, 1:40. One mile and seventy yards, Wildwood, four-year-old, carrying 115 pounds, Washington Park, Chicago, July 5, 1893; and Faraday, four-year-old, carrying 102 pounds, Washington Park, Chicago, July 21, 1893, each 1:44. In 1880 the best time for one mile and one-eighth was 1:54; reduced by Tristan, six-year-old, carrying 114 pounds, New York Jockey Club, June 2, 1891, to 1:51. One mile and a quarter, Banquet, three-year-old, carrying 108 pounds, Monmouth Park, N. J,. (straight course), July 17, 1890, 2:03¾; Salvator, four-years-old, carrying 122 pounds, at Sheepshead Bay, N. Y., June 25, 1890, and Morello, three-year-old, carrying 117 pounds, Washington Park, Chicago, July 22, 1893, each 2:05, on circular courses. One mile and five hundred yards, Bend Or, four-year-old, carrying 115 pounds, Saratoga, N. Y., July 25, 1882, 2:10½. One mile and five-sixteenths, Sir John, four-year-old, carrying 116 pounds, Morris Park, N. Y., June 9, 1892, 2:14¼. One mile and three-eighths, Versatile, five-year-old, carrying 100 pounds Washington Park, Chicago, July 7, 1893, 2:19¾. One mile and a half, Lamplighter, three-year-old, carrying 109 pounds, Monmouth Park, (straight course), August 9, 1892, 2:32¾. Of the long distance running, Ten Broeck's two miles, Louisville, Ky., May 29, 1877, 3:27½ and his four miles, Louisville, September 27, 1876, 7:15¾ yet stand as the best.

If the time occupied by a running horse in going a mile be one minute and forty seconds, and the length of stride twenty-five feet, (as represented by some horses), it would follow that he must be off the ground a full half second at each bound, and according to the law of falling bodies, he would, if he moved horizontally, during that time, fall a distance of four feet.—The Horse in Motion, J. D. B. Stillman.

In 1889, Prof. W. H. Brewer of Yale College, published a tabulated analysis of the records of one thousand and thirty-seven running horses, whose performances extended over a period of nineteen years, having records of one mile in 1:45 or better, made on ninety-three tracks in twenty-eight different States. This table showed that there was but one best horse; six within one second of the best; fifty-three within two seconds of the best; one hundred and ninety-two within three seconds of the best; four hundred and sixty-six within four seconds of the best, and one thousand thirty-six within five and one-fourth seconds of the best. "The results," says Professor Brewer, "illustrate in an impressive manner that low records are due to the qualities of the breed rather than to any local excellence of track, climate, jockeys, or training."

If we would improve our horses we must lengthen the distances run. By means of these short selling races, handicaps and penalties and allowances, good horses either cannot enter or are crushed out by weight, and bad ones are left in with feather weights. What is wanted in a race horse is one with speed and endurance which enables him to cover a distance of ground with little distress to himself and in the quickest time.—The Horseman.

Running Rein. A device used by riders where the horse has the habit of carrying his head so high as to cause the bit, when drawn upon, to ride up into the corners of the mouth instead of bearing against the lower jaw. It is of the width of an ordinary bridle-strap and about eight feet long. One end is furnished with a buckle at the end of a tongue-strap eighteen inches long. Buckle this end through a staple or D-ring on the left side of the saddle near the pommel. Then pass the other end of the rein through a smooth iron ring about two inches in diameter, in front of the horse's breast like the ordinary martingale; then through an iron ring an inch or more in diameter attached to a strap under the horse's chin about nine inches from the bit, then back again through the same breast-ring and up to the rider's right hand. This gives the rider more power to draw the horse's head down to its proper position than any other device. When this rein is slack the horse has perfect freedom, but when necessary the least pull acts with double force and brings the head at once in the right position.

Running Rein. One of the greatest scandals in the history of the English turf is known as the Running Rein swindle in connection with the Derby of 1844. This was a scheme for "ringing the changes" by exchanging a three-year-old for an English four-year-old called Running Rein, and also for running a German bred horse called Leander, a four-year-old. In the race Leander fell, broke his leg and was buried the same night. The changeling Running Rein won, Orlando being second. The secret became known, payment of stakes was refused, and an action brought to recover them. At the trial the justice adjourned the same for one day in order that the best and most important witness, Running Rein himself, could be produced. When the trial again came on the horse was not to be found, so a verdict went for the defendants and the stakes were awarded to Orlando. Some curious people dug up the body of Leander to look at his mouth, but found him headless.

Running Walk. A gait which is a modification of the trot. In this gait the head is generally carried higher than in the fox-trot or the ordinary walk, and the hind foot takes the ground in advance of the diagonal fore foot, which breaks the concussion. It is a more showy gait than the fox-trot, and in it

the poise of the horse is such as to give him more of a climb-
ing action in front.   At this gait the sound of the footfalls is
not unlike that of the ordinary walk quickened, and the feet
take the ground in the same order.   A closer rein is generally
held with this gait than in the fox-trot, and the pace is a faster
one and may be carried to a three minute gait before the horse
is forced out of it.

S

S. Following the name of a horse, in Chester's Trotting and Pacing Record, indicates that the horse went to saddle.

Saddle. That piece of horse furnishings, which, secured to the back of a horse, makes a seat for the rider. The parts of the saddle are: Pommel or head—that part which goes over the withers. Cantle — the hind part. Seat — that on which the rider sits. Tree—the wood and iron framework. Gullet plate — the iron arch under the pommel. Points of the tree — the wooden continuations of the gullet plate. Bars of the tree — the narrow front portions of the wooden side pieces of the tree. Bellies of the tree — the broad boards on which the rider sits. Waist — the narrowest part of the seat about midway between the pommel and cantle. Pannel — the lining which lies between the tree and the horse's back. Point pockets — small pockets in which the ends of the points of the tree rest. Spring bars — which allow the stirrup-leathers to be attached to or detached from the saddle. Knee-pads or rolls — placed on the flaps to help prevent the rider's knees from going forward. Skirts — small flaps that cover the bars on which the stirrup-leathers are suspended. Sweat flaps — pieces of leather which are placed under the girth straps on each side to prevent the sweat working through. Ds — small semicircular metal hoops which are attached by chafes, (short leather straps), to the front or back of the saddle for strapping on a coat, or small traveling case. Staples — somewhat similar in size and shape to Ds but which are firmly fixed to the tree.

Saddle-back; Cradle-back; Hollow-back; Low-back. These terms denote a horse having a back lower than is generally seen. When such ill formation prevents him from carrying a reasonable amount of weight, it is an unsoundness for saddle purposes, but not for harness purposes.

Saddle-blanket. A small and coarse blanket folded under a saddle; used almost exclusively in the Western United States, in place of any special saddle-cloth.

Saddle-cloth. A cloth put under the saddle and extending some distance behind it to preserve the rider's clothes from becoming soiled from contact with the horse; and also used to save the pommel of the saddle from being soiled by sweat.

Saddle-cloths of felt are most useful when the saddle stuffing has become thin, or when the horse's back has become sore. Leather saddle-cloths chiefly preserve the lining of the saddle; but as a rule, a saddle looks better, is lighter, and less liable to give a horse a sore back, when well stuffed, than when a saddle-cloth is used.— The Practical Horse Keeper, George Fleming, L. L. D., F. R. C. V. S.

Saddle-girth. A band which is passed under a horse's belly and secured to the saddle at each end, being fastened by buckles.

Saddler; American Saddler; Gaited Saddler. A saddle-gaited horse, having the natural gaits, the walk-trot-canter, to perfection. The conformation of the saddler consists of a good forehead—a "horse in front of you;" good, serviceable withers; a strong, springy back and loin; quarters of pleasing shape; "set" hocks; short canons; having a long, easy stride that conveys but little motion and is agreeable to the rider—and all these points set off by a flowing tail and mane, and controlled by a gentle yet spirited temper, make up the ideal saddler.

St. Leger. The great English race run at Doncaster, York. Inaugurated in 1776, but did not receive its present name till 1778, in honor of Colonel St. Leger who founded the stakes, since which time it has been run annually. The course was originally two miles. In 1813 the distance was changed to one mile, six furlongs, and one hundred and ninety-three yards. In 1826 the distance was reduced sixty-one yards, and has remained since that date, one mile, six furlongs, and one hundred and thirty-two yards.

Sale. [Law.] Where there is no warranty in the sale of a horse, the rule *caveat emptor* applies, and except there be deceit either of fraudulent concealment or fraudulent misrepresentation, no action lies by the vendee against the vendor upon the sale of the animal.

Salivation. Slobbers. Frequently caused by the irritation of the bit; and often by diseases of the teeth, or wounds and ulcers of the mouth. In such cases consult a veterinarian.

Sallenders; Sellanders; Sellenders. Epidermal structures or eruptions, upon the hind legs of the horse, the upper end of which is about four inches below the point of the hock or ankle joint. Its posterior margin is nearly straight or regularly convex, while its anterior margin is excavated in its upper third, being, therefore, more pointed above than below. Its natural color is dark slate, but when much dry epidermis gathers on the surface it has a lighter or yellowish appearance. Similar to mallenders which appear on the fore legs. See MALLENDERS.

Salute the Ditch. [Eng.] The ditch at Newmarket, Eng., was an object of regard with old turfmen. It is supposed to have been the remains of an ancient Roman fortification, or an entrenchment which divided the Eastern and Western Anglican tribes. From the historic associations connected with it this ditch became an object of regard, and in by-gone times it was the custom with all turfmen in passing by it to "salute the ditch."

Salute the Judges. At the close of a heat all the drivers and jockeys return to the front of the judges' stand and salute the judges, receiving in return their recognition, before dismounting. While all the rules prescribe that no rider or driver shall dismount without the consent of the judges, this salutation is a graceful act of mutual recognition.

Sandals. [Eng.] A plate or bar shoe made to buckle upon the foot of the horse, in case of accident by which a shoe was thrown, serving as a very good substitute for the lost shoe when on the road or in the field. In earlier times it was the custom for riders and hunters to carry one or two of these sandals in the pocket when starting out for the hunt.

Sand-crack; Quarter-crack; False Quarter. Fissures or lesions in the horn of the wall of the foot. Quarter cracks on the lateral parts of the wall nearly always affect the fore feet. The inside quarter is more liable to the injury than the outside one, because the crust is thinner, and when in motion it receives a greater part of the weight of the body. Toe cracks are more common in the hind feet. All fissures of this kind constitute an unsoundness.

Sandwiched Race. A race, the heats of which are sandwiched in between those of another class. Such sandwiching of heats is allowable, but in these cases one race of the two must be finished before another can be started.

Sash. When two horses from the same stable run in a race, the jockey riding the secondary horse is distinguished by a sash.

Save the Distance. For a driver to land safely within the distance flag when he cannot win, or for any reason does not want to win the heat, is to "save his distance"; to save his horse from being shut out.

I drove my mare all this time with a view of simply saving her distance, and I noticed that most of the other drivers were hustling their horses as though they were in a hurry.—Life with the Trotters, John Splan.

If you drop so far back in the first quarter or half that you will have to drive fast in the last half to save your distance, you have not gained anything. Get away well with the field and drop back gradually, say about twenty yards in each quarter, so that you will land safely inside the distance flag after going an easy, evenly rated mile well within your horse's capacity at every stride.—Training the Trotting Horse, Charles Marvin.

Saved Him. A term used to denote the act of saving a horse from breaking, in a heat. Before breaking, most horses give some indication to the driver, either by a pull on the bit, an error in gait, or by some other motion that they are to break their gait; and the driver, by understanding his horse, can usually tell what these signs mean, and can often, by instantly taking advantage of them, save the horse from a break. Hence it is a common thing to hear a driver say: "He wobbled, but I saved him."

Scalp; Scalping. The act of cutting the coronary band or quarters, when the horse is at extended speed; although some horses scalp when at a slow gait. Generally due to faulty conformation, but may be remedied in many cases by proper shoeing.

Scalpers; Scalping Boots. Light toe-boots, made of thin leather and padded, worn only on the hind feet. They are especially needed for use on a half-mile track, to prevent scalping or cutting of the coronary band, when the horse is on the sharp curves.

Scalping a Track. The act of taking a thin shaving off from the surface of the track, either for the purpose of evening its face, or for removing a slight layer of sand and replacing with loam or clay, or *vice versa*. This scalping is done with a track planer.

Scapula. The shoulder-blade, or bladebone. In the horse there is practically but one action at the shoulder joint— a fore-and-aft hinge motion. The scapula and the leg attached to it are not in any way joined to the rest of the skeleton by bone, but only by the muscles which pass from one to the other. The trunk is, in fact, only slung between the two shoulder bones.

Scars upon the horse from wounds or sores, and all unsightly enlargements, from whatever cause, not affecting the soundness of the animal, are blemishes.

School for Trainers, Jockeys and Drivers. It has been the hope of many gentlemen interested in turf matters, and who desire to see the business raised to a more intelligent level based upon special education, and knowing that drivers and jockeys come up from stable boys, who, in most cases, have but deficient education; to see established in this country a school for the education and fitting of young men who wish to become trainers, riders and drivers of speed horses. The scheme of instruction at such a school has been formulated to embrace the following: The theory of breeding on scientific principles; history of the race and trotting horse; the sources from which speed has been derived; characteristics of the different types and families; results of crossing strains, of inbreeding and outcrossing as demonstrated by performances; the handling, feeding and care of colts; preparation of colts to show their greatest flights of speed without injury to themselves or to their development; expedients and appliances necessary for colts of different conformation and disposition; the management of horses before, during and after a race; the driving and riding of horses in a race; the proper judgment of pace or gait and how to place the horse in a race so as to give him the best chance to bring out his power of speed; study of the rules of racing; propriety of deportment on the turf.

Schooling. The art of teaching a horse; training, educating and developing the trotter, chaser, jumper and racer; a horse in training is said to be "at school."

Score; Scoring. A mark or line; the act of bringing a field of horses to the score or starting point, in order for them to make a fair start in a heat or race; getting in position and coming down to the judges' stand for the word. The trotting rules provide that any horse in scoring, which unnecessarily delays the race, may, after notice to the driver, be started regardless of his position or gait. No field is ever sent away when any of the horses are running under the wire. One of the contending horses, usually the pole horse, is selected by which to score or govern the other horses; and no driver must come down for the word in advance of the governing or pole horse, nor can any driver hold back from the governing or pole horse, without the infliction of severe penalties.

In many years of experience we have never seen one of these "incontrollable" horses that could not be taken back when an adequate fine was imposed on the driver for improper scoring.—Wallace's Monthly.

There is a great difference in the behavior of the different horses in scoring. Some pull and tug on the bit, despite the signal to return, carrying their drivers down to the first turn in the track before they can be stopped; whereas others, old campaigners as a rule, will slacken at once when they hear the bell, stop, and turn around of their own accord.—Road, Track, and Stable, H. C. Merwin.

A horse scoring two hundred and twenty yards at each score, in scoring two times trots one-fourth of a mile; four times, one-half mile; six times, three-fourths of a mile; eight times, one mile; ten times, one and one-fourth miles; twelve times, one and one-half miles; fourteen times, one and three-fourths mile; sixteen times, two miles. The pole horse trots three feet from the pole. Allowing three feet more to his outer wheel, one foot between his outer wheel and the inner wheel of the second horse, then three feet to the horse, makes seven feet between the pole and second horse, and so on to the extreme outside horse. The second horse trots forty-four feet further in trotting the mile than the pole horse; the third horse, eighty-eight feet; the fourth horse, one hundred and thirty-two feet; the fifth horse, one hundred and seventy-six feet, and a horse forty feet from the pole trots two hundred and fifty-one feet over the mile.

Score Board. The sign-board in front of the judges' stand upon which the positions of the horses and time made, is hung out by the judges at the close of each heat. In the

2:23 CLASS.	A	B	C	D	E	F	G	H	I	J	K	TIME.
FIRST HEAT.	4	2	5	1	3	7	6					2:23¼

DIAGRAM OF SCORE BOARD.

accompanying diagram representing the first heat of a race, there were seven starters represented by the letters A to G, attached to the arm of each driver, respectively. In this heat the horse D came in first; the horse B came in second, and so on, as indicated.

Score Card. A printed card having upon it the names of the horses entered in each class, at a race meeting, with blanks for the purpose of recording the time made in each heat.

Scratch. A scrub race; a race without conditions; often put in to fill up the time, on a free track, where a class did not fill; a scurry.

Scratch. To scratch; to strike a horse's name out of the list of runners in a particular race. The rules of the Turf Congress provide that if any person offers or receives any amount of money for scratching an entry in purse or stake, the person so offending shall be ruled off the course.

Scratches. Grease; a disease of the heels of the horse, and until cured, an unsoundness. See GREASE.

Screw. A common stable term for a used-up horse, or one having an ill-shaped or unsound foot; a plug.

Seat. That part of the riding saddle on which the rider sits.

Seat. [Eq.] The principles of a correct seat in equestrianism are, that the flat thigh should grip the saddle with the lower leg free to give impulse, direction and control to the horse; the body erect and moving in instinctive harmony with the horse's motion, and the hands entirely independent of the body.

The seat on horseback is one in which the crotch and hips are as firmly attached to the saddle as it is possible for them to be; the legs below the knee as free and independent as possible, and the body from the waist upward, perfectly supple and pliable. Whatever movement the horse makes, the hips must conform, moving to the right or to the left, or tipping backward or forward, as the case may be. The legs from the knees downward, must be free to move in obedience to the rider's will, the upper part of the trunk keep perfect balance and move easily on a flexible spine, accommodating itself to every movement.—The Saddle Horse.

Seated Shoe. A horse-shoe fitted into a groove or beveled edge of the crust or wall of the foot; a Charlier shoe.

Second Favorite. A horse thought to possess the ability of winning second place; the second choice of the field.

Second Thigh. A group of small muscles located on the outer face of the thigh and below the stifle or knee, and in front of the calf.

Sectional Shoe. A shoe for contracted feet, quarter cracks and tender feet. It consists of a plate and overshoe, the shoe being adjustable and removable from the plate as often as desired, without drawing the nails from the foot.

Secundo. The name of a very severe English bit used for pulling horses; for those that refuse the jumps; that run out at their fences, or which are at times liable to take charge of their riders.

Selling Race. A race the conditions of which require that the winner must be offered for sale at public auction, unless otherwise stipulated. Any horse running in a race "to be sold," shall be liable, if the winner, to be claimed for the selling price; and if it is a condition of the race that the winner is to be sold by auction, the sale takes place immediately at the close of the race, one-half of any surplus over the selling price going to the second horse, and the remainder to the association. In selling races the horse's engagements are included in the sale. Any person offering or entering into an agreement for a consideration to bid or not to bid on a horse winning a selling race, shall be deemed guilty of a fraud and shall be ruled off.

Send-off; Sent Away. A start in a race; a good send-off is a fine uniform and fair starting of all the horses in a heat or race.

Sensitive Laminæ. The thin plates of soft tissue covering the anterior surface of the coffin bone. They number from five to six hundred, extend parallel to each other, and by fitting into corresponding grooves on the inner surface of the horn of the wall, the union of the soft and horny tissues of the hoof is rendered complete and perfect.

Sent to Stable. A horse sent to the stable is a horse that is ruled out by the judges. A horse may be sent to the stable for any misdemeanor, foul driving, or fraud of any kind. In heats of one, two, three or four miles, a horse not winning one heat in three cannot start in a fourth; and in heats best three in five, a horse not winning one in five cannot start in a sixth—unless such horse, in either case, shall have made a dead heat.

Sesamoids; Sesamoid Bones. Bones developed in tendons where they play over joints. In each foot of the horse there are three; a pair of nodular form, placed side by side over the metacarpo-phalangeal articulation, or behind the fetlock joint; and a single, large, transversely extended one, called the navicular bone. The sesamoid bones of the hind and fore feet are exactly alike.

Set Back. When an offending horse is placed behind other horses of the field for breaking, running or foul driving, he is said to have been "set back," or punished.

Settles to his Work. When a horse trots low, or hugs the track, he is said to " settle to his work."

This technical expression is intended to represent the idea that when the horse is speeding the centers of motion are nearer the ground, in order that the muscles should act to the best advantage, and that in propulsion the act shall be most direct and longer sustained; or, in other words, the points of action and reaction are in a line forming a more acute angle with the ground.—The Horse in Motion, J. D. B. Stillman.

Shaft. A thill; one of a pair between which a horse is harnessed to a sulky or buggy; the pole, or tongue of a carriage used with a span of horses.

Shaft-holder; Shaft-rest. A device for supporting the ends of the shafts projecting in front of the horse's breast. Leather sockets are made to fit the ends of the shafts, and a strap on each side of the horse's neck extends therefrom to the strap supporting the breastplate over the neck; so that a part of the weight of the shafts is borne by the shoulders, instead of the entire weight being borne from the back.

Shag-trot. [Eng.] Jog-trot: a slow trotting gait.

The shag-trot is practiced on the way home by every huntsman, every whip, and every hunting man, after a long day, if he has any consideration for his horse.—The Book of the Horse, Samuel Sidney.

Shake Him Off. To come away from a contending horse. "He came up to my wheel but I shook him off," means that the horse of which it is said did not have speed enough to go past his leader, or pace-maker.

Shank. That part of the hind leg of the horse above the fetlock and below the hock, corresponding to the canon of the fore leg. It generally, however, is somewhat longer than the canon, flatter and measures greater in circumference. It should be flat and deep from the front backwards, the skin lying close to the bone and tendon.

Shifting Gait. A horse that changes from a trot to a pace, and from a pace to a trot, is said to be of "shifting gait." A fast trotter will make a fast pacer, and *vice versa*.

Shirt. [Eng.] To put one's shirt on a horse, is to lose all one's money on a horse.

"Now the word shirt," said the teacher, "is a common noun, and means an undergarment for men." "And for horses, sir," put in a sharp youngster. "For horses!" roared the teacher, "what do you mean?" "Father says he is going to put his on Friar's Balsam for the Derby, sir." There was trouble in that class.—Bird o' Freedom.

Shoe; Shoeing. A horse shoe; a protective support to the horse's foot; a plate, or rim of metal, generally iron, nailed to the horse's hoof to protect it from injury; the art, or business of shoeing horses; farriery. There can be little doubt that the first shoes were of leather, attached to the feet with thongs, as were sandals to the human foot, and from the use of leather, or socks made of rushes, the transition to metal was very natural. It is believed that horseshoes were originated by the Romans and came into use in Cæsar's time, as Catullus, a Roman who was contemporary with Cæsar, speaks of them. In the East there was no necessity for an artificial protection to the hoof, as, from the dryness of the soil and even temperature, the hoofs became firm and tough. During the period of the Crusades, when knight-errantry was at its zenith, the horses were heavy and carried great weights. They wore shoes which were fastened with clamps, so they could be easily detached. Some writers have asserted that horseshoeing was not practiced in England until the time of William the Conqueror, in 1066; but, on the other hand, it has been shown from illuminated MSS. that the custom was practiced by the Anglo Saxons as early as A.D. 600, and there is a statement in history that horseshoes were found at Tourney, in the tomb of Childeric, the Frankish king, which refer us to the date of 480 A.D. There is historic evidence that iron shoes were nailed to the hoofs of war horses in the ninth century. In general form and manner of attachment horseshoes have undergone very little change during hundreds of years; it is in the evolution of shoes for trotting horses, within the years 1869-1893, that the greatest change has been noticeable. In 1869 American Girl, 2:19, carried shoes weighing eighteen to twenty ounces in front, and fourteen or fifteen ounces behind. Goldsmith Maid, 2:14, in 1874, carried a sev enteen ounce bar shoe. Smuggler, 2:15¼, 1874–1876, wore, at one time, two-pound shoes on each front foot; and it is said that the little mare Lula, 2:15, 1875, carried a shoe of even greater weight. In 1889 the shoes of Axtell, 2:12, weighed five ounces in front and three ounces behind. Shoes of reasonable weight are those of from eight to twelve ounces, although the range of weight in 1893 would be eight ounces forward, and from five to six ounces behind, nailed with four nails on the outside, and three nails on the inside. Aluminum is now much used for horseshoes. It is a metal of silver-white color, about as hard as zinc, very malleable and ductile, and very light. Horseshoes are made in a great variety of styles; but the old, standard, plain shoe with beveled edges, bar or open heel, has always been, and, without doubt, will always be, the most in use, and the best suited to the greatest number of horses. From the records of the United States patent office down to the close of the year 1893, it appears that in Class No. 168, sub-class No. 6, Farriery, four hundred and thirty-five patents had been granted on horseshoes alone. The parts of the shoe are: The toe; the two heels; the quarters between the toe and the heels; the calks, or projections from the lower part of each heel; the toe calk; the clip, a sort of claw, usually at the upper edge of the toe, for protecting the hoof and assisting in keeping the shoe in place; the fullering, or crease in the lower face, in which the nail holes are punched; the bar, which is the entire body of the shoe. The following principles should govern the shape of the shoe and the art of shoeing: 1. The foot surface of the shoe should be flat, so that the outer portion of the sole may aid the wall in bearing weight; 2, in order that the frog may bear weight, the shoe should, generally, be as thin as possible consistent with its standing wear and retaining its shape; 3, the shoe should, as a rule, be of uniform thickness at the toes, quarters and heels, so that the proper bearing of the foot be not disturbed; 4, the shape of the foot surface should follow the general form of the weight-bearing surfaces of the wall and sole; 5, the heels of the shoe, on their foot surface, should be perfectly flat, or sloping slightly outward, to prevent the tendency to contract; 6, shoes should project slightly beyond the ends of the heels, (without risk of the fore-shoe getting caught by the hind-shoe), so that the heels of the shoe may rest on the solid pieces of horn that are found immediately behind the angle formed by the wall and bar; 7, the ground surface of the shoe should be beveled, to increase the foothold of the horse, and also to lessen the weight of the metal employed. These are the generally approved principles—when it comes to balancing the trotting action it is a matter of individuality, for no two horses can be shod exactly alike.

Keep the foot level, and the frog untouched and on the ground.—Robert Bonner.

[Law.] Whenever bar or round shoes are required, even for a temporary purpose, the horse is unsound; for no disease is cured, whether sandcracks, corns, thrushes, or whatever else it may be, so long as these shoes are necessary.—The Law of Horses, M. D. Hanover.

The unpared sole and frog of the healthy foot need no protection on any kind of soil. The more the frog is exposed to wear, the larger and sounder it grows, and the better it is for the foot and limb. What is required in shoeing is merely protection from undue wear, with the least possible interference with, or disturbance to, the functions of the foot and limb. Not a grain of iron more than is absolutely necessary, should be allowed as a protection.—George Fleming, LL.D., F. R. C. V. S.

The ideal shoe, regarded simply as a means to locomotion, is the lightest, simplest, smallest piece of metal that can be contrived to protect the wall of the foot. When it is a question of balancing a trotter by means of weight in his shoes, another problem is introduced. —Road, Track and Stable, H. C. Merwin.

The first thing to be decided upon is how little weight you can possibly use in the horse's shoe to protect the foot, and, at the same time, balance the horse so he will be able to go at his highest rate of speed on a trot. What makes it more difficult than anything else to give rules to shoe a horse by is the fact that no two horses can be shod alike. All horses are formed differently, gaited differently, and have different dispositions.—Life with the Trotters, John Splan.

Shoeing is unnecessary to the horse in his wild, natural state; it is artificial and unnatural, because the domesticated horse is kept in an artificial and unnatural state. It must, therefore, be regarded as a necessary evil. But the foot of the horse, unprotected, will not stand the battering of turf-training; therefore, the prime and sole object of shoeing is to afford the wall of the foot protection against the terrific concussion of fast trotting on more or less hard tracks. * * * I want to enforce the necessity of non-interference with the expansion and contraction of the hoof from the quarter to the heel, according as the foot bears weight or is relieved of it. As a rule, use six nails, three on either side; but never put a nail back of the widest part of the hoof, the quarters, thus leaving the heels free. The foot should be trimmed so that the frog will lightly touch the ground, but take little or no weight. In shoeing, the aim is to keep the foot elastic, yielding and natural. Be careful with the knife, cutting only the horn of the wall. Leave the frog, the sole and the bars alone. They will care for themselves. Shoeing, like everything else, should be looked at from a common-sense standpoint. There are no wonderful and unrevealed mysteries about it. Keeping in view what nature intended, remembering that the sole purpose of shoeing is to afford protection, the simpler the better, steering clear of quack smiths that know it all and recklessly slash and rasp—these are the most important precautions to be kept in view concerning shoeing.—Training the Trotting Horse, Charles Marvin.

Short of Work. It is often said of a good horse when he fails to do his best in a race, that he is "short of work"—a term which also embraces many apologies for a poor horse; although it is no doubt true that being short of work has much to do with defeats on the turf.

The gamest horse will stop if short of work, and if you do not know that he has had sufficient work, that he is not sick or sore, how are you going to know whether he stops from physical causes or from true quitting.—Training the Trotting Horse, Charles Marvin.

Shoulder. The withers form the upper boundary of the shoulder. The rear border of the shoulder may be taken from behind the swell of the muscle which is just below the withers to the elbow.

It is one of the most indispensable conformations in a race horse or jumper to have an oblique shoulder. No straight shouldered horse could be a successful racer or steeple chaser. A straight shoulder means a short stride, and racers with short strides are distanced and get run off the turf.—The Bridle Bits, Col. J. C. Battersby.

Shuffling. A word which most appropriately describes any gait which is dull, awkward, inelegant; the motion of a lazy, used-up, worthless horse.

Shut Out. Left behind the distance flag.

Shut Up. A horse which fails to respond to rider or driver, or which refuses his jumps, is said to "shut up."

Shying. A dangerous and disagreeable characteristic in a horse. Often a horse shys at naught, in which case he is governed by illusion of sight; it is frequently due to near-sightedness; to a bad-fitting bridle, or other cause that may be remedied. Where it results from nervousness it is a vice; but if it results from disease in the eye, it is an unsoundness.

Side Check. The check-rein in ordinary use.

Side-pulling. A very disagreeable habit, due in many cases to the presence of painful wolf-teeth; or, in colts before they have a full mouth, to sore and swollen gums on one side of the lower jaw, between the incisors and molars; often due to the sharp edges of the grinders coming in contact with the cheek. In some instances it is due to the use of too long a bit, in which case the bit may need side-washers of leather or chamois skin of several degrees of thickness to prevent the bit from pulling through the mouth.

Side-reiner. Said of a horse that is a side-puller; he "side-reins," or drives on one rein.

Side-weights. Often attached to the outside of the hind hoofs to obviate defective or narrow hind action. The side-weight is frequently combined in the shoe, the outside bar of which is much heavier than that of the inside.

Side-wheeler. A pacing or racking horse. See PACING and SINGLE-FOOTING.

Sight. Any disease which causes obscurity or dimness of sight, and prevents a horse from seeing common objects, renders him unsound.

Sinew. Any cord or tendon of the physical structure.

Single-footing. An irregular pace of a horse in motion; the single-footed rack; a strictly lateral gait. The full revolution is this: The hind foot, on the right side, strikes the ground a little before the fore foot strikes it, then with the legs of the left side making the same movements, there are four strokes in the revolution.

The single-foot is an irregular pace, rather rare, and distinguished by the posterior extremities moving in the order of the fast walk, and the anterior ones in that of a slow trot. These mixed paces are quite compatible, as they are of the same kind and move in the some diagonal order.—The Horse in Motion, J. D. B. Stillman.

The single-foot is intermediate between a trot and a pace; or in other words is such an exaggeration of the fox-trot as to bring it half way to the rack; or *vice versa*. Each foot appears to move independently of association with either of the others, and the same interval of time elapses between each footfall. It is a fast gait, generally not less than ten miles an hour, which can be increased to a three-minute gait. It affords the smoothest seat of all the gaits, because that portion of the animal which supports the saddle apparently glides evenly forward, while each quarter, moving separately, causes none of that bounding or jolting that accompanies the trot or pace.—Randall's Horse Register.

Sir Archy. One of the best bred horses ever produced in England or America. Bred by Col. John Tayloe, Mt. Aery, Virginia. Foaled in 1805. By imported Diomed, by Florizel, one of the best sons of old King Herod; dam, Castianira, by Rockingham, son of Highflyer, by Herod. Sir Archy, although bred in Virginia, was from imported English sources on both sides—Diomed was one of the best racers on the English turf, and unquestionably the finest formed horse ever imported into this country; Castianira, his dam, was imported when three years old, by Colonel Tayloe, in 1799, and ran successfully in Virginia. Sir Archy was a blood bay 16 hands high, his shoulders were unexceptional, very deep in his girth, back short and strong, arms and thighs long and muscular, and bone large. He was possessed of both speed and bottom, and was not only distinguished on the running turf, but also famous as a producer of great horses. He died June 7, 1833, "meriting," says Mr. S. D. Bruce, "the sobriquet of the Godolphin Arabian of America."

Sit Down in Front. A term describing the act of stopping or pulling in front of a contending horse, for the evident purpose of impeding him, or to help, or aid another horse in the race. An offense punishable by fine, suspension or expulsion.

Sitfasts; Horny Sloughs. Pieces of dead tissue, or small tumors, otherwise known as wartles, generally caused by saddle-galls, or by irritating masses of sweat, hair, and dirt under the saddle, which would be thrown off but from the fact that they are firmly connected with the fibers of the skin beneath. Whenever they become ulcerated, and are in such position as to prevent the ordinary use of the harness or saddle, they constitute an unsoundness.

Sixty-mile Race. A famous race made in Deer Lodge county, Montana, between a horse owned by Colonel Thornton, and a "little short-legged horse called the Lizzard," owned by Bailey & Hammond. Run in 1890. Distance sixty miles continuous running. The large horse took the lead from the start, and held it up to the thirty-second mile, when Lizzard commenced to close on him, had everything his own way after the thirty-third mile, and won in four hours, forty-five minutes.

Skeleton. A track wagon of four wheels, the wheels being of the high or old style, and also bike style with pneumatic tire.

On the Beacon and Centreville courses, wagons, in distinction from sulkies or match-carts, must weigh 250 pounds.—Rules of the New York Trotting Club, September, 1841.
I have lately seen in a Boston warehouse a skeleton wagon that weighs but fifty pounds. Such a vehicle might almost be described as a work of art.—Road, Track and Stable, H. C. Merwin, 1892.

Skin. The external covering of the horse. It is composed of two quite distinct sections, each, however, intimately connected with the other. The first or inner part is called the derm, a layer of interlacing filaments of fibrous tissue to which the nerves and blood vessels are copiously distributed; and the second or outer section called the epidermis, non-sensitive, containing no blood vessels, soft in its deeper or newly-formed part, but dry and hard at the exposed surface. The hairs covering the skin grow from minute projections, cylindrical in form, seated in the outer surface of the derm, the roots of which form little follicles or pits. The outer part, or epidermis, is continually being worn away at the surface, but is also continually being renewed from the inner surface of the derm; or, as is the case with the hairs, thrown off entire. See COAT.

Skin the Lamb. [Eng.] When a non-favorite wins a race, bookmakers are said to "skin the lamb," under the supposition that they win all their debts, no person having backed the winner.

Skipping Break. A break in gait that is not continuous; the act of quickly recovering, on the part of the horse, at the very instant any change in gait occurs, from whatever cause, and at once striking the former gait; a skip with one foot, while the next takes its regular step.

Skirts. Small flaps that cover the bars on which the stirrup leathers are suspended to the saddle.

Skittish. Said of a horse that shies; is disposed to start quickly, and at times to run; is over-timid; tricky; deceitful in action. Skittishness is a vice.

Slew; Slue. The turning of a body upon an axis within its own figure; to swing around; the outward motion of a sulky wheel in going rapidly around the curves of a track.

Sling. A device in which to suspend a horse in case of broken or injured limbs, where it is necessary to take all the weight of the body from off the feet.

Slip-him. A term used to describe the act of giving a horse his head; letting him out; the opposite from pulled.

Slow Track. A track is said to be slow when from any cause horses cannot make their usual speed upon it; a heavy track. This slowness may result from some peculiarity of construction, or kind of soil that renders it slow at all times; or it may be temporarily slow, although a good track, from poor drainage, and being heavy from rain.

Slow Trot. A trot in which the undulations are greater than in the fast trot, and therefore one very hard for the rider. These slow undulations diminish as the speed is increased.

Smell. The sense of smell in the horse is one which is most acutely developed; and many good students of the horse are of the opinion that this sense has far more to do with his general intelligence and ability for education than any special endowment of brain power.

Connoisseurs in horse flesh prefer plenty of space between the eyes, and some even go so far as to say that a broad forehead is indicative of intelligence; but as this part of the bone does not cover the brain, (the seat of intelligence,) it is hard to conceive how its shape can control such an important feature in an animal. When the space between the eyes is well developed that portion of the interior of the head to which the nerve of special sense of smell is distributed would naturally be larger in proportion, on that account the smelling power of the animal with the broad forehead may be increased; and if it be true that the horse is capable of judging of the quality of things by their odour, we can then explain why the horse with the broad forehead and well developed organs of special sense of smell, may appear more intelligent than his less fortunate neighbor with the narrow one.—E. A. A. Grange, V. S., Michigan Agricultural College Experiment Station.

Snaffle. A bridle having one plain bit, jointed or stiff, and one pair of reins, without guards. Its action is to restrain the horse by pressure on his tongue, bars of his mouth, (the part of his gums which are between the tushes and grinders), and the corners of the mouth. It is simple in its operation and less apt to confuse the horse than any other bit used.

The snaffle, in its various sizes and forms is the most useful bit, and were I restricted to one pattern that would be the one chosen.— Horse Portraiture, Joseph Cairn Simpson.

This bit is the same as the bridoon with the exception of the guards. It was originally used on the saddle horse, while the bridoon with plain rings was always used alone or in common with a carriage harness bit, or the curb bit for riding. For the light buggy horse and harness, and head stall without blinds, it is a most desirable bit. It is the king of hunting bits.—The Bridle Bits, Col. J. C. Battersby.

Snaffle Lay. An old term used to describe the hold or clutch of a thief or highwayman who stopped horseback riders by laying hold of the horse's bit or snaffle.

Snip. [Eng.] Information as to the certainty of a horse winning a race.

Soft. Out of condition; wanting in stamina; not fitted for a race.

Many have said that Johnston was a soft horse. Out of condition he is about as helpless a horse as can be imagined; but this is not his case alone. Some of the gamest horses that I ever saw when in condition, were the most helpless when out of form.—Life with the Trotters, John Splan.

Soft-hearted. Faint; faint-hearted; wanting in courage; the quality characteristic of a quitting horse.

In Flanders, where the air is humid, and the pastures are moist and rank, horses grow large, but they have flat feet, inferior sinews, lymphatic temperaments and soft hearts.—Road, Track and Stable, H. C. Merwin.

Sojer-toed. A horse that is a knee-knocker is said to be "sojer-toed."

Sole. That portion of the ground surface of the foot included between the wall, bars and frog. Its front and side borders, where it comes in contact with the inner surface of the toe and quarters of the wall, form nearly two-thirds of a circle. Its rear concave border is bounded on each side by the bars, and in the middle it is deeply grooved to receive the point of the frog.

The sole binds the frog and wall together. The horn of which it is made is very different from that of the wall or frog. It is formed of a number of extremely hard and strong horny plates laid one above the other, and curved so as to form a sort of dome surrounding both sides and the front of the frog. The sole has another object besides connecting the frog and the wall. It is intended to defend the sensitive parts of the interior hoof from stones, sharp points of rocks, etc. When the sole becomes worn out, it has the faculty of reproducing itself in a manner quite distinct from that of the wall and the frog. Instead of being rubbed away by friction like the former, or throwing off little flaps like the latter, it exfoliates in flakes, a new flake being secreted above before the effete one falls below.—Horse and Man, Rev. J. G. Wood.

Soliped. According to the old classification of Cuvier, a family of solid-hoofed animals, including the domestic horse.

Sons of Horses. An Arabian half-bred horse. Explained by the quotation:

The Bedouins of Arabia, in general, keep their mares, but sell many of their horses, and it is from the horses thus sold, crossed with infer-lor mares, that the animal known in England and in India as an Arab, is bred. The Bedouins call these half-breds "the sons of horses," and they look upon them as mongrels, or "kadishes."— Road, Track and Stable, H. C. Merwin.

Sore. Until cured, sores are a cause of unsoundness.

Sound; Soundness. Free from defect or injury. A horse is sound when he is free from hereditary disease, is in the possession of his natural and constitutional health, and possesses no alteration of structure in any part which impairs, or is likely to impair, his natural usefulness.

Soundness. [Law.] A horse is defined to be *sound* when he is free from hereditary disease, is in the possession of his natural and constitutional health, and as much of his bodily perfection as is consistent with his natural formation.

The word "sound" means sound; and the only qualification of which it is susceptible arises from the purpose for which the warranty is given. If, for instance, a horse is purchased to be used in a given way, the word "sound" means that the animal is useful for that purpose; and "unsound" means that he, at the time, is affected with something which will have the effect of impeding that use. The word "sound" does not mean perfect, but means just what it expresses, viz.: That the animal is sound and free from disease at the time he is warranted.

The rule of unsoundness is, that if, at the time of the sale, the horse has any disease which actually does diminish the natural usefulness of the animal, so as to make him less capable of work of any description, or which in its ordinary progress will diminish the natural usefulness of the animal; or if the horse has, either from disease or accident undergone any alteration of structure, that either does at the time, or in its ordinary effects will diminish the natural usefulness of the horse, such horse is unsound.

Soup. A term used to denote any drug, mixture or lotion administered to a horse by means of an injecting needle, for the purpose of affecting his speed or spirit, either one way or another.

The danger of doping a horse was again illustrated lately at Gloucester, when Gray Forest, who had been given the needle, ran away about two miles and had to be withdrawn. Oregon, who had a liberal quantity of the soup, was caught Tuesday about a mile from Gloucester, after he had run away.—The Horseman.

Spanner. A small pocket wrench for clasping and turning a screw coupling. Made with a projecting end or claw to fit into a hole in the cone or coupling in order to give it a hold or purchase. Used for adjusting the axle cone of a pneumatic sulky wheel.

Spanish Walk; Spanish Trot. High stepping paces of the horse. When each fore leg is advanced in its turn it is poised for a moment and left more or less straight out, and about as high as the elbow, before it is placed upon the ground.

Spavin. Inflammation and ulceration of the small flat bones in the lower and inner part of the hock joint, often involving those of the outer side as well. *Blood* spavin—a dilation of the vein which runs over the seats of the bog and bone spavins. *Bog* spavin—An excessive secretion of joint-oil, from over exertion, into the cavity of the joint, producing a swelling. *Bone* spavin—A bony swelling which may be more to the front, or more backward on the inner side of the hock, or it may even show mainly on the outer side; while in bad cases it may extend up to the true hock-joint and even prevent its movement. In some cases these are known as high and external spavins according to location.

Spavin. Inflammation and ulceration of the small flat termed enlargement on the seat of spavin, the disease being determined, and not likely to increase, if the horse goes sound he is sound, in common sense. But the courts having decided both ways it is best, as in case of curb and other diseases, to except spavin in the warranty. See CURB.

Blood, bog and bone spavin are unsoundness. Bone spavin is not a curable disease.—The Law of Horses, M. D. Hanover.

Speech. [Eng.] Private information on a horse, and what he can do in a race, used in such phrases as "get the speech;" "give the speech."

Speed. Speed may be defined as comparative rapidity, whether fast or slow; the rate of motion; haste in progression; to advance towards a goal. Interesting tables compiled from accurate sources are given. The evolution of the fast individual trotter is thus shown by the records—

In 1806, Yankee, trotted in,	2:50 ;	one mile.
" 1810, the Boston horse,	2:48½ ;	" "
" 1834, Edwin Forest, (under saddle),	2:31½ ;	" "
" 1844, Lady Suffolk, (under saddle),	2:26½ ;	" "
" 1859, Flora Temple,	2:19¾ ;	" "
" 1867, Dexter,	2:17¼ ;	" "
" 1879, St. Julien,	2:12¾ ;	" "
" 1885, Maud S.,	2:08¾ ;	" "
" 1893, Directum,	2:05¼ ;	" "

The table of average extreme speed from 1820 to 1890, in the United States, is thus given; the distance being one mile:

1820 to 1830,	2:42
1830 to 1840,	2:35¼
1840 to 1850,	2:28½
1850 to 1860,	2:25
1860 to 1870,	2:18¾
1870 to 1880,	2:14
1880 to 1890,	2:10¼

A horse in trotting a mile in three minutes, covers a distance of 29 ft. 3 in. and 15–16 of an inch in one second of time; at a 2:30 gait, 35 ft. 2 in. and 4–16 of an inch is covered in every second; at a 2:20 gait, 37 ft. 9 in. and 1–16 of an inch is covered; at a 2:10 gait, 40 ft. 7 in. and 8–16 of an inch is

covered; at a 2:08 gait, 41 ft. 3 in. is covered; at a 2:04¾ gait
42 ft. 3 in., and 14–16 of an inch is covered, and at a 2:00 gait,
44 feet is covered.

Emphasize the possession of speed certainly, but do not let us lose
sight of the fact that speed without brains is not worth trying to
produce.—Wallace's Monthly.

We have no more right to conclude that no horse will ever beat Nancy
Hanks' mark of 2:04, than we had to conclude that Goldsmith Maid's
record of 2:14 would never be broken.—Kentucky Stock Farm.

The record of 1893 is surpassingly brilliant, and every page evidences
the progress of the trotting breed toward that time when it will be
as purely a breed and a type as is the thoroughbred to-day, and
when 2:00 trotters will be no more rare than thoroughbreds that
can run in 1:40.—The Horseman.

If speed is desired we must look for those mechanical conformations
of parts that determine speed, but speed is always at the expense
of power. The anterior limbs must conform in their mechanical
force to the posterior, and vice versa. In the posterior limbs, long,
full propellers, low hip joint set well back, so as to afford room for
long femur and tibia, give great length of limb when extended,
enabling it to support the weight of the body and exert its propulsion for a long time; at the same time the power is more directly
applied when the head of the bone is lower down. So far as these
principles can be applied to the anterior limbs they hold true of
them as of the posterior extremities. All animals distinguished
for great speed have the angles of the bones most inclined to one
another; but while this mechanical arrangement gives great advantage for speed it is a source of weakness in bearing burdens or hauling. * * * The speed of the horse depends upon the length and
thickness of the locomotive muscles, the angles and lengths of the
bony levers on which they act, the freedom of their articular ligaments, the correlation of all the mechanical parts, and much also
on the nervous energy or will transmitted to the muscles, technically know as courage.—The Horse in Motion, J. D. B. Stillman.

Speedaway; Speedway. A straight trotting or running course.

Speed Cart. Road cart; combined speeding and road
cart; sulkyette. They are built much like a sulky, although
generally heavier, and are used for speeding and road purposes.
They have corduroy and cane seats, adjustable foot rests, seat
trays in which to carry small parcels; and are liked by gentlemen for ordinary road use. Breaking carts are built extra
strong, and have shafts three feet longer than those on a road
cart or sulky.

Speedy Cut. An injury to the inside of the fore leg, a
little below the knee, or carpus, at or near the point of contact
of that joint with the canon; inflicted by the foot of the opposite side during speed. The result of faulty conformation. If
the horse is sound at the time when sold, lameness resulting
from it, immediately afterwards, is not a breach of warranty
of soundness.

Speedy Cutters. Those horses of high action, which,
from interfering in consequence of faulty shape, cut the fore
leg from the knee down, are called "speedy cutters."

Spin. A spirited dash; a single effort at high speed; **to** "take a spin," is to give the horse a short exercise at a fast gait.

Splint. An inflammation of the shank-bone resulting in small bony swellings. When existing at the time of sale, and the cause of future lameness, a splint is a breach of warranty of soundness.

Splinter-bar. [Eng.] The cross-bar of a carriage to which the whipple-tree is attached.

Spoke. One of the standards of wood or steel which support the rim or felloe of a sulky wheel, from the hub or nave.

Sponge-out. The act of giving the horse's mouth a bath, or washing, by means of a sponge and cold water. The rules allow helpers to sponge out a horse not oftener than once in five times scoring.

Sport of Kings. Racing has been termed, by all the old writers on the history of the English turf, "the sport of kings"; and most of the sovereigns from the earliest times to the ascension of Queen Victoria, have been patrons of the turf. Edward II., (1307-1327), was particularly fond of horses. Edward III., (1327-1377), bought "running horses" at the price of £160 of the money of the present day. Henry VIII., (1509-1547), devoted a great deal of attention to improving the breed of horses, and obliged all orders of men to keep a certain number of horses in proportion to their rank and circumstances. Edward VI., (1547-1553), was the first sovereign to make the stealing of horses a capital offence. James I., (1603-1625), was a great lover of horses, was the originator of regulations relating to horse racing, and, indeed, has been called the "father of the English turf." During his reign the former crude methods of racing, without system, with no description of the horse being given, gave place to more scientific, accurate, and satisfactory trials. The horses were prepared for running by the discipline of food, physic, airing, sweating and clothing; the weights to be carried and the weights of riders were adjusted; the courses were measured, and flat racing was introduced. He built great stables at Newmarket, near the palace, which were afterwards rebuilt by Charles II., and in the middle of this century by the Rothschilds. Henry, Prince of Wales, son of James, cultivated horsemanship with great industry and satisfaction. Charles II., (1660-1685), at the restoration, honored the Newmarket races with his presence, and established there a mansion for his own use. He was an able and experienced rider, and a competitor at the races, entering

the horses in his own name. William III., (1689-1702), added
to the racing plates given in different places in the kingdom,
and established a riding school. Queen Anne, (1702-1714),
continued the bounty of her predecessors, and added several
plates. In 1712 her horses ran for the royal plates in her own
name, the last race by any of her horses having taken place July
30, 1714. Her consort, George, Prince of Denmark, took great
delight in racing. It was during Anne's reign that the Darley
Arabian was brought into England. About 1727, races were
held in one hundred and twelve towns and cities in England, ·
and five in Wales. George I., (1714-1727), and George II.,
(1727-1760), were great patrons of the turf; but the royal stud
was sold on the ascension of Queen Victoria, October 25, 1837,
for £16,476.

Spot the Favorite. To name the winner in a race.

Sprains. A forcible stretching of the muscles or fibrous
tissues beyond their natural length; in extreme cases accompanied by rupture of the parts. Slight sprains are generally
healed by rest; but until cured they are an unsoundness,
whether in slight or severe cases.

Spreaders. Devices for controlling or changing the gait;
widening the hind action; preventing striking or interfering;
forming a steady, open gait; stopping hitching and forging.
There are several patterns — some of which are attached to the
sulky shafts, others being in the simpler form of boots.

Spreaders; Expanders. Used for expanding the hoof,
in case of contractions, quarter crack and corns. They are
made in different forms.

I am not in favor of artificial spreaders of any kind. I believe the frog
    to be the best spreader in the world.—Artistic Horseshoeing,
    George E. Rich.

Spring a Curb, To. It is said of a horse which injures
or sprains the perforatus tendon which plays over the front of
the hock, that he has "sprung a curb." It is an unsoundness.

When a horse springs a curb with me, I first get the inflammation down
    in the usual way and then iodine it severely. I then let him up in
    his work, but jog him to keep him in as good condition as possible.
    I have generally found curbs to yield to this treatment. A curb is
    the least objectionable form of unsoundness.—Training the Trotting
    Horse, Charles Marvin.

Spring Bars. Those parts of the saddle which allow
the stirrup-leathers to be attached to, or detached from, the
saddle.

Sprint; Sprinter. A burst of high speed for a short
distance; a horse capable of only a short stay at great speed;
a quarter horse.

16

Spur. A pointed instrument worn on the heel by a horseman or rider, for the purpose of punishing the horse. The earliest medieval spurs were devoid of rowels, but had a single point; another form was that of a ball from which a short point projected called the ball and spike spur. The rowel was first introduced in the thirteenth century, although it was not common till the beginning of the fourteenth century. When a horse does not respond to the legs, or when he refuses to approach an object he does not like, it may be necessary to use the spur; but their use requires prudence, tact, good judgment and adaptability to the mental and physical character of the horse, for there is as much difference in the sensibility of the horse's flanks, as in that of the mouth. When the pressure of the legs becomes insufficient to completely collect the forces of the horse, the spur must be used — not violently, but with kindness, delicacy, and good management. The use of electrical spurs is prohibited by the rules of the Turf Congress.

> You may ride us
> With one soft kiss, a thousand furlongs, ere
> With spurs we beat an acre.
> —Hermione, in Shakespeare's Winter's Tale.

Spur. A small, metallic projection screwed to the toe of the hoof, to which a toe-weight is attached by means of a groove which fits the spur on the foot, holding it securely in place.

Spurs. Horny structures concealed in the tuft or lock of hair growing from the fetlock. See ERGOT.

Spurt. A forced pace in a race, generally made on the homestretch or at the finish in an effort to win; a dash of speed; a sprint.

Square Gaited. Pure gaited; a pure trotter. The pure, square-gaited trotter is perfectly balanced, and goes without jerking or hitching, every movement being smooth and true, like the revolution of a perfectly balanced wheel.

One can, with a little practice, judge whether a horse driven by another is trotting square by listening to the foot-falls. The sound of a fast, well balanced trotter's steps mark time as regularly as the swinging of a pendulum. Time is beaten, one, two, three, four; one, two, three, four—smoothly and accurately with the intervals strictly regular. Development ceases at that point where truly balanced and regular action is transformed into the jerky, hitching, irregular way of "getting there" that we so often see.—Training the Trotting Horse, Charles Marvin.

Stake. A race open to all complying with its published conditions, for which the prize is the total of the subscriptions, or entrance fees paid by the nominators, to which is generally added a specified sum by the association or track under whose auspices the stake is given; all of which belongs to the winner or winners, unless provided to the contrary in the conditions. Stakes are of different sums, for horses of different ages, and are usually named for prominent turf patrons, individuals, places, etc.

Stakeholder. A person chosen to hold the stakes, or amount of the match, in a match race, which must be deposited one day before the race is to come off, omitting Sunday, when the race becomes "play or pay."

Stakey Gait. A stiff, imperfect, constrained action of the fore legs; faulty knee action; such a horse is said to have a "stakey gait."

Stall. A room, or box; standing place for horses. The dimensions of stalls vary, but the generally recognized best sizes are: For a single stall, five feet wide, nine feet long; for a box, or room, fifteen feet by seventeen feet; or, better, if the size of the stable will allow it, eighteen feet by twenty feet.

Stall off a Rush. To head off, or prevent a spurt of speed from an opposing horse, at the finish, by which he attempts to win; to leave a contending horse behind; to shake him off.

It is a dangerous, and often a fatal mistake for a jockey to ease his horse, or to cease riding him, when leading and close to the winning-post; for by so doing he may make him stop, and may then be unable to get him into his stride again in time to "stall off a rush" from one of the others.—Riding, M. Horace Hayes, M. R. C. V. S.

Ormonde's last race was characterized by a great exhibition of gameness. The race was at Ascot, the distance over a mile, the finish up hill, and the company two of the best horses England has ever produced, Mr. Vyner's Minting, and Mr. Barclay's Bendigo. The pace was terrific, and the up hill finish particularly trying to Ormonde, yet he "stalled off" Minting's brilliant challenge, and won, after a desperate finish.—The London Sportsman.

Stallion. The male of the horse kind; an ungelded horse; one kept for breeding purposes.

Stallion. [Law.] Where a party does not come to an inn for entertainment as an ordinary wayfarer, but with a horse to be used, under a special arrangement in serving mares, the inn keeper is not bound to receive and treat the person as his guest, and is not liable for the destruction of the horse without his fault.

An inn keeper is not bound to permit his establishment to be made a depot for the propagation of horses.—American Reports, F. G. Thompson, San Francisco, 1877, 244-246.

Where the party came to an inn under a special arrangement previously made, whereby his stallion was to stand at the inn certain days each week for the purpose of serving mares, it has been held that the inn keeper was not subject to the common law liability for the preservation of the animal.—Cases decided in the Commission of Appeals of the State of New York. H. E. Sickles, Albany, 1876, 34-39.

Stand; Grand Stand. The principal stand, or pavilion, from which persons witness the contests of speed at race meetings.

Stand-house. An elevated court of great magnificence built by Charles II., of England, at Newmarket, about the year 1367, to enable him to see the races; and where the royal guests were received.

Standard. A horse is standard when his breeding meets the requirements of the rules controlling admission to standard rank. Down to and including volume third of the American Trotting Register, (1879), no standard of blood had been requisite to admission, the aim having been to ascertain and record the facts regarding a pedigree without reference to the trotting inheritance. But with volume four, (1882), the pedigrees commenced to be numbered consecutively; and appeared, based upon a standard, the rules of which had the sanction of the National Association of Trotting Horse Breeders. These rules were formulated in order to define what was meant by a standard bred trotting horse, and to establish a breed of trotters on a more intelligent basis than had then existed. This standard was fixed upon a trotting record of 2:30, or better; and the original rules were so framed as to embrace and admit all animals that were believed to have a sufficiently well-defined trotting inheritance to justify the expectation that they would transmit the ability to trot. Equality between the sexes was purposely ignored from the beginning. A mare was given admission by a performance of 2:30; but a stallion was obliged to have other qualifications besides performance. This greater stringency with stallions grew out of the purpose to discourage badly bred stallions from being kept for breeding purposes. The standard rules now in force, with the changes to go into effect January 1, 1895, follow:

First: Any trotting stallion that has a record of 2:30 or better; provided any of his get has a record of 2:35 trotting, or better; or provided his sire or dam is already a standard trotting animal.

Second: Any mare or gelding that has a trotting record of 2:30 or better, [whose sire or dam is already a standard animal]. The words in brackets will be added and in force after January 1, 1895.

Third: Any horse that is a sire of two trotters with records of 2:30 or better.

Fourth: Any horse that is the sire of one trotter with a record of 2:30 or better, provided he has either of the following additional qualifications: 1, A trotting record of 2:35 or better; 2, is the sire of two other animals with trotting records of 2:35; 3, has a sire or dam that is already a standard trotting animal.

Fifth: Any mare that has produced a trotter with a record of 2:30.

Sixth: The progeny of a standard trotting horse when out of a standard trotting mare.

Seventh: The female progeny of a standard trotting horse when out of a mare by a standard trotting horse.

[After January 1, 1895, rule seventh, as above, will be displaced by the following: *Seventh:* Any mare whose sire is standard and whose first and second dams are by standard horses.]

Eighth: The female progeny of a standard trotting horse out of a mare whose dam is a standard trotting mare.

Ninth: Any mare that has a trotting record of 2:35 or better whose sire or dam is a standard trotting animal.

[After January 1, 1895, rules eighth and ninth, as above, will be abolished.]

Standard Bred. A horse is standard bred when the produce of a standard trotting mare, by a standard trotting horse. The distinction of the terms "standard" and "standard bred" grows out of the manner in which animals become standard. Blue Bull became standard by the performance of his progeny, and not in virtue of his inheritance, hence he was not "standard bred." A mare comes into the standard by virtue of her performance in 2:30 or better, and nothing known of her pedigree, hence it cannot be said she was standard bred. But the progeny of Blue Bull out of this mare would be "standard bred" as soon as it was foaled, as both sire and dam were standard.

Standard by Inheritance. A term used in the same sense as standard bred; or a colt of a standard horse out of a mare that is standard.

Standard by Performance. A phrase denoting that the horse to which it applies has a trotting record of 2:30 or better, and is therefore entitled to standard registry by virtue of his own performance.

The best example of developed trotters is the case of such sons and daughters of non-standard parents that, by training development, become themselves standard by performance.—Wallace's Monthly.

Standing in the Stirrups. Standing in the saddle. At the start, in running races, the jockey sits down in the saddle, but as soon as the horse has got into his stride he should stand in the stirrups. This attitude is assumed in order to enable the rider to conform to the movements of the horse in the best possible manner. The body should be slightly bent forward, free from all stiffness, and the position such that the points of the shoulder, knee and toe should be in the same vertical line, the whole attitude characterized by grace and ease. But the jockey should always sit down at the finish.

Standing Jump. [Eq.] In a standing leap the horse steadily raises himself on his hind feet, more or less perpendicularly, according to the height and extent of the object to be passed over. Having balanced himself a moment, he commences his spring by very forcibly extending the previously contracted angles of his hind limbs, which action propels the body upward and forward, but more particularly to receive it in its descent, during which change of position the hinder limbs, which had been gathered up to keep them from interfering with the obstacle passed over, are now let down to receive the hind quarters.

Standing Martingale. When the standing martingale is attached to a properly fitted noseband, it restrains the horse from getting his head too high, makes the action of either snaffle or curb-bit more effective, and checks the inclination of a fresh horse to bounce or bolt. It should be so fitted as to hang loose until the moment that the horse attempts to take any improper liberty, when the pressure of the noseband over the sensitive junction of the bone and gristle will give him a hint to be quiet.

Staples. Metallic pieces somewhat similar in size and shape to Ds, which are firmly fixed to the tree of a saddle.

Star. A chief performer; a term applied to the champion of the turf for the year; as the saying of John Splan, "Guy was the star performer of the year."

Star-gazer. A term used to denote a horse that holds or keeps his head highly elevated, with the nose thrown out, when in motion.

A star-gazer with an ewe neck, or a borer that can only go with his nose close to the ground, is totally unfit for military purposes.—Seats and Saddles, Francis Dwyer.

Starring. Campaigning.

This starring system which has been so fashionable for a term of years has, without doubt, been a source of great injury to the trotting turf, not alone by making fast time the only attraction to draw people to the course, but inaugurating the hippodroming evil that has done far more injury. The large purses advertised meant only a division of the gate money; and people who had been induced to visit the arena, expecting to see a true struggle for the thousands of dollars said to be at stake, went away dissatisfied when the transparency of the humbug was made apparent.—Horse Portraiture, (1868), Joseph Cairn Simpson.

Starter; Starting Judge. The person who has control of the horses and drivers in a trotting race, (under the association rules and with the approval of the judges), from the first score in every heat until the word "go" is given; and in all cases the starting judge is the only person authorized to give the word. There are some advantages in having the starting judge occupy a stand by himself on the opposite side of the track from that of the timing judges; and where the plan has been tried, as it has in a few instances, it has given full satisfaction. In general it may be said in such cases that the attention of the starter is more completely given to the field, and that errors and mistakes in sending away, or giving the word, are not so liable to occur as where the mind of the starter is liable to be diverted from his business by the confusion or inadvertent remarks often made in the judges' stand at the moment of a send off. In all running races the starter has absolute control of horses and jockeys with power to fine or suspend jockeys, appoint assistants, and give such orders and take such measures as will secure to all a fair start. When the horses receive the word, or are sent off by drum or flag, there is no recall. In general, the use of the drum in starting running races has been abandoned, the flag being now chiefly used. The starter has a box of his own just against the inside fence, and although he often goes upon the course to give corrections or admonitions, he invariably starts from his box or near it. Running races are never started by word.

The starter should be honest and incapable of being swayed by fear, favor or prejudice; be cool in temperament; prompt in action; have a quick eye, and be a good judge of pace. He must be thoroughly conversant with the rules and their application, and "hew to the line" in their administration. His moral character and personal habits must be above reproach—the first in order to inspire confidence; the second to enable him to perform his arduous duties acceptably.

Starters. The horses starting in a race.

Station. The position of the horse when at rest, or in the attitude of standing almost motionless and touching the ground with his four feet, his head at ease, his whole body passive.

Stay; Stayer. The quality of endurance; bottom; possessed of courage; a horse that does not readily give in through weakness or lack of vitality and energy; one not discouraged. When two horses are equal in a race, the one that has the better position at the end of the race is the horse of greatest power. Hence a horse that has not won a heat cannot be equal to one that has won a heat. A horse that is second four times in a race is not as good as one that is first once, and third three times. If the race is concluded in four heats, and two horses have each second place in two heats, the one that is second in the last heat is the better of the two.

Stay a Distance. Ability of the horse to stay a distance, depends, (the horse being in good health and condition), upon, 1, The breathing power being good, or, in other words, the capacity of lung expansion being perfect; 2, the muscles working to advantage; 3, the entire conformation being of the required kind, and 4, the action of the limbs well balanced.

Steadiness in a trotting horse is as much a virtue to be cultivated as speed. The horse that sticks to his work, under any system, has the advantage over the flighty, headstrong performer.—Kentucky Stock Farm.

S. t. b. These letters given in a pedigree mean that the horse to which they refer is "said to be" by a given horse, or out of a given dam.

Steeplechasing. A contest over a given number of miles of "fair hunting country"—generally understood as meaning a section of country having pastures, plowed fields, hedges of different sorts, with and without ditches, posts and rails, open brooks and other obstacles, for the purpose of testing the best and speediest horse. Originated in Ireland in 1752. It is said the term arose from a party of fox-hunters on their return from an unsuccessful chase, who agreed to race to the village church, the steeple of which was in sight; he who first touched the church with his whip to be the winner. This account of its origin appears very probable. But the first steeplechase of which there is any accurate mention was in 1752, which was run over four and a half miles of country from the church of Buttevant to the spire of St. Leger church. It was not, however, till 1803 that the first regular steeplechase took place in Ireland, the "added money" to a race that year being "a hogshead of claret, a pipe of port and a quarter-cask of rum." This value was that they proved the excellence of the animal and tested the horsemanship of the rider. The old system was dangerous in the extreme and turf annals record many serious accidents resulting therefrom. In 1820 it was a favorite amusement with young fox-hunters, and men ventured large sums on the ability of their horses to cross a country. The meets in Ireland at that time were held for three days, during which the distance ran was four miles with six five-foot walls to take for the first day; on the second day the walls were reduced six inches, and on the third day six four-foot walls formed the course. In France in 1834, the start was "down the Rabit Mount, a short but steep declivity full of holes, after which several ugly places were crossed, including a river and swampy meadows." It is no wonder that such a race was not popular, as only the finish could be witnessed by spectators. In 1836 the Liverpool steeplechase was run near Aintree, "twice round a two mile course"; a great recommendation being that nearly the whole performance could be seen from the grand stand. In England, the Grand National Hunt Committee, which has been several times reorganized, and is now known as the "Huntsman's Grand National," was formed in 1866. Its rules now have the same authority over steeplechasing, that the Jockey Club rules, (which had refused to take any cognizance of disputes connected with steeplechasing and hurdle racing), does over the races on the running turf, and they are as rigidly enforced. In this country when steeplechases are run, they are, so far as may be, governed by the general rules of the American Turf Congress. In addition the special rules require that no steeplechase shall be of less distance than one mile; that no horse shall carry less than one hundred and twenty pounds; that horses running on the wrong side of a post or flag, (the limits of the course being flagged out or indicated by posts), and not turning back shall be disqualified; no rider can go over one hundred yards on any high road, lane or public thoroughfare, without being disqualified; riders going over any place where the ground is not flagged out, are not allowed to open any gate or wicket or go through any gateway or common passage from one enclosure to another, under penalty of being disqualified; no horse can be led over any fence by a bystander or any horseman not in the race, under penalty of disqualification. Steeplechasing was abolished by the American Jocky Club in 1888, but such races are run on courses of some of the members of the Turf Congress.

Steeplechaser. One who rides in steeplechases; a horse running, or trained to run in a cross-country chase.

Step. The forward or backward movement of one foot; often used synonymously with stride. It is understood to mean the distance spanned by two feet both resting on the ground. While this distance will vary with muscular energy, it is also limited by the anatomical proportions of the animal.

Stepper. A fast horse; one of fine action; as "that horse is a good stepper."

Stiff. This term means a horse that on public form, or in general estimation, should win the race; and that either the jockey, driver, or horse has been so fixed that he will not win. The term "bookmaker's stiff," has a similar meaning and is played at the expense of the public, and in the interest of the bookmakers.

Stiff 'un. [Eng.] A horse certain not to run.

Stifle. The joint of the hind leg of the horse, between the hip and the hock, and corresponding to the knee in man. It is on a line with the flank, near the abdomen. It is the office of the iliacus muscle to guard the abdomen from the injury to which it would be liable from the blows the stifle joint might give it, in its extreme and violent flexions; and when this muscle performs its work well it gives the fine "stifle action" so much admired.

Stifle Shoe. A special form of shoe exposing a curved surface to the ground, used in treating a stifled horse. It is placed upon the sound foot, with the effect of causing the horse to throw its weight on the weak joint, and thus strengthen it by use.

Stirrup. The support for the foot of a person mounted on horseback, attached to the saddle by means of an adjustable stirrup-strap; a metal loop with a corrugated foot-piece to prevent the foot from slipping. The stirrups of some western riding saddles, and also some of those used in the cavalry service have a strong front piece of leather or other material, which not only protects the front of the leg, but prevents the foot from pressing too far into the loop. Stirrups were unknown to the ancients. The Greeks rode bare back, or on a saddle consisting of a single pannel of sheepskin, or often of a piece of cloth folded several times and thus forming a pillion. Gracchus, a noble Roman, who was at the height of his fame about 126 B. C., fitted the highways with stones to enable the horsemen to mount. The methods of mounting must have been to vault; to step from a horse-block, or, as Xenophon said, "after the Persian manner," that is, to step from the back of a slave or captive who bent himself for the purpose. Warriors mounted with the aid of the spur. It had a hook upon the shaft, and, placed at the side of the horse, assisted the rider in mounting. Stirrups were used somewhat in the fifth century, but were not common even in the twelfth.

The saddle bow, pommel and cantle were invented in Constantinople toward the middle of the fourth century. Even later than this the stirrup came into use, appearing for the first time in the "Treatise on the Art of War," written by the Emperor Maurice at the end of the sixth century. These Byzantine innovations spread everywhere. It is beyond question that the Turks, for example, adopted with the saddle and spurs all the administrative forms of the Lower Empire, and many a usage which seems little in accord with their primitive genius.—A Phidian Horse: Art and Archæology on the Acropolis, From the French of Victor Cherbuliez, translated by Elizabeth Roberts.

Stirrup. A metallic loop for holding the foot of the driver, fastened on the inside of each thill of the sulky just in front of the cross-bar.

Stocking. White, reaching down to the coronet on the leg of a dark colored horse, and which comes up as high as the knee or hock, is termed a "stocking." When the white marking is shorter than this, it is called a sock.

Stone. [Eng.] The English imperial standard weight of fourteen pounds avoirdupois. The weight carried by horses in races is always reckoned as such a number of stone, and so many pounds; as, eight stone, twelve pounds.

Stonehenge. The *nom de plume* or pen name of John H. Walsh, F. R. C. S., known throughout England, Australia and America, as a writer on horsemanship and field sports. Born in 1810; died February 12, 1888. Edited the London *Field* from 1857 till his death; and was an industrious and voluminous writer. With a wide range of knowledge he combined thoroughness and accuracy, and his style is smooth and flowing. His treatise on "The Horse in Stable and Field," is one of the best books in the entire range of English and American horse literature.

Stop. To quit in a race.

Stops. On a bridle, used with reins which have buckles, to prevent the martingale rings catching on the buckles.

Stopping. Packing or filling for the horse's feet.

Before the horse is put away after work, the feet should be carefully cleaned and washed out, and stopped up with clay. We avoid, in all cases, the use of oils on the hoof, as oil will spoil any hoof, making it brittle. The cooling, cleansing, and moistening effect of washing is all that is necessary to keep a healthy hoof in good condition.—Training the Trotting Horse, Charles Marvin.

Straggling Start. A poor send off. "The field got the word with many of the horses straggling in the rear."

Straight-away. A straight course; the long, straight stretch of a course, like the three-fourths mile straight, or the 2,450 feet home stretch of Morris Park, N. Y. On this straight the famous horse El Rio Rey ran three-quarters of a mile in 1:11; and on the mile straight-away at Monmouth Park, N. J., the mighty Salvator ran the mile August 28, 1890, in 1:35¼.

Strangles, and bastard or false strangles, are, until cured, an unsoundness.

Stretch. One of the two straight sides of a course, as distinguished from the turns or ends.

Stride. The distance from the foot-print of any one leg to the foot-print of the same leg, when it comes next to the ground; or it may be described as the action of the limbs while that distance is being covered. The average stride of the fast gallop, or that of the race-horse at speed is about twenty-four feet; and that of the trotter about seventeen feet. **The stride** of Eclipse was twenty-five feet; Flying Dutchman and Volti- geur, in 1851, struggling head to head opposite York Strand, took a stride of twenty-four and a half feet. Martha Wilkes, in going a 2:09½ gait, made a stride of eighteen and a half feet. Actual measurement of strides shows that the stride is both extended and quickened, instead of quickened and shortened, when the speed is increased.

The trotting stride is made up of two supports and two flights. The time of both supports is alike, and the time of both flights corre- sponds. But the time of the supports is not the same as that of the flights. With different trotting movements their relative times materially change. The dwelling-gaited horse, for instance, unduly prolongs and supports. Just in proportion as the speed increases the time of the supports is lessened, and the length of the flights is increased. The time of the supports and the time of the flights of the two pairs of feet must necessarily correspond. But the length of the stride of the hind feet, with reference to that of the front feet, not only changes in the same horse at different rates of trotting speed, but also changes decidedly in different horses. * * * In the run the stride is divided into five parts instead of two, as in the trot, each limb taking its turn as supporter and propeller, with a scarcely appreciable interval between; and an interval between the last fore leg and the first hind one representing a fifth of the whole stride. Each limb, therefore, works one-fifth of each stride and rests the other four-fifths.—The Horse in Motion, J. D. B. Stillman.

String. A number of horses; as, the horses from one stable; "a great string"; the horses from a single stable shown at a fair by themselves.

Stringhalt; Chorea. The involuntary contractions of voluntary muscles, manifested by the sudden jerking up of one or both hind legs when the animal is walking. Stringhalt is not an unsoundness if the horse works well—it is only a defect; but if it results from an inflamed nerve, there is a question if it is not then an unsoundness, and in all cases it is best to have it excepted in warranty.

Stud. A collection of horses; as, the royal stud, the government breeding stud, a private stud.

Stud Book. A book containing the pedigrees and history of horses. The English Stud Book was established in 1791, and has been published annually ever since. The American Stud Book, (Wallace's,) was first published in 1867; and (Bruce's,) in 1873. See AMERICAN STUD BOOK, AMERI- CAN TROTTING REGISTER and RACING CALENDAR.

Stumbler. A horse which is habitually stumbling from faulty conformation, or in consequence of a weak, shuffling gait. Such a horse should never be used for saddle purposes.

A nag that puts his toe down first is almost sure to be a stumbler. —Training the Trotting Horse, Charles Marvin.

Stumbling. There are two kinds of stumblers. The one lifts his foot, at the walk, without throwing his weight too much forward at the same time, but he does not bend his knee sufficiently, or unduly depresses his toe, when putting the foot to the ground. If, at the conclusion of the step, there be an inquality on the ground, he will, in all probability, strike it and stumble, but generally he will not fall, for the mischance will not be sufficient to disturb the equilibrium of the body. The other and more dangerous kind of stumbler has generally straight shoulders, infirm fore legs, or cramped action. As he leans his weight too much forward, he is very liable to catch the ground with the toe of his advancing fore leg, a fall being the probable result, from the center of gravity of the body being well beyond the point of support of the fore legs. While a stumbling horse should never be ridden if any other can be had, yet if the rider knows a horse is inclined to stumble he should always ride him carefully and well up to the saddle so that he may get his hind legs well under him. A properly adjusted curb bit may be substituted for the snaffle; and in some instances peculiar shoeing may help to overcome the fault. Where stumbling is occasioned by inflammation of the feet arising from tightness of the shoes, or from unequal pressure from which cause he is liable to stumble, it is an unsoundness.

Subscription. A payment to a stake; an entrance fee.

Suburban Handicap. A great American race run annually at Coney Island, N. Y. Founded by James G. K. Lawrence of New York, and first run in 1884. The winners have been: 1884, Gen Monroe; 1885, Pontiac; 1886, Troubadour; 1887, Eurus; 1888, Elkwood; 1889, Raceland; 1890, Salvator; 1891, Loantaka; 1892, Montana; 1893, Lowlander; 1894, Ramapoo.

It holds the highest place in the affections and the enthusiasm of American turfmen.—New York Tribune.

Suffolk Park. A once famous race course established at Philadelphia in 1859, by James Kelly. It was opened September 8, of that year, with a race between Flora Temple and the California mare, Princess. Flora won the first heat in 2:43, and could have distanced her competitor; but distance was waived, and Flora won the third heat in 2:23. George M. Patchen, Dexter, May Queen, Goldsmith Maid, American Girl and other great ones have trotted over it. It was discontinued and cut up into building lots in 1890.

Sulk. Explained by the quotation:

You will find there is a grain of sulk in the make-up of many good race horses. It requires a good deal of tact and ingenuity to get out of such animals their full measure of speed.—T. J. Dunbar.

Sulky. The track vehicle used in a race with trotting horses; a light carriage fitted for but one person. In 1841, the Spirit of the Times, referring to the rules of the New York Trotting Club and the comparative tests of speed and weight in harness and under saddle, says: "The same weight has to be carried by the driver, exclusive of the weights of his sulky or match-cart, as by the same jockey in the saddle. These match-carts are of the neatest construction, and weigh generally ninety pounds, though they often weigh twenty pounds less, and there are one or two which weigh but fifty-three pounds!" From that date to 1892, a period of fifty-one years, there was little or no change in the general style of the track sulky. The main difference was in the use of better materials, a higher artistic finish and less weight. Yet fifty-three pounds was the exact weight of a Pray standard sulky, with wheels four feet seven inches high, weighed and measured by the author in September, 1893. But at the commencement of the season of 1892, a complete revolution in trotting was inaugurated by the use of the pneumatic wheel, the first experiments with which were made with a pair of bicycle wheels attached to an ordinary sulky. It was at the Detroit, Mich., meeting in July 1892, however, at which the new style sulky was first publicly recognized. The race won by Honest George took place there on July, 20 and 21, of that year, and this was the first race in which the pneumatic sulky was ever used at a prominent meeting in this country. Immediately manufacturers commenced to adapt their sulkies to the new requirements, and by the beginning of the season of 1893, pneumatic sulkies were in use upon all the leading tracks of the country. Builders not only made entirely new patterns but devised methods for changing over the high wheel to the bike wheel sulky, making stays of different kinds to fit the new wheel to the old axle. A great number of experiments took place before the pneumatic wheel was fully adjusted to its new uses, but these finally proved successful and in cases of entirely new or changed-over sulkys they have given the utmost satisfaction to owners, trainers and drivers. The high wheel sulky, like the stage coach, is a thing of history only. The two great advantages of the new sulky are the pneumatic tire and ball bearings. The height of the wheels is from twenty-six to twenty-eight inches. They are made of both wood and steel the tire being attached to the rim of the wheel. There are from twenty to twenty-four ball bearings in each wheel, (ten or twelve in each end of the hub), being held in the boxes by means of a cone-case or recess into which they are fitted. These bearings are of different sizes, the usual diameter being one-fourth or five-sixteenths of an inch. The weight of the pneumatic sulky is from thirty-eight to fifty-three pounds; the weight of a changed-over sulky from fifty-five to fifty-eight pounds. There is, however, another advantage in the less liability of accident on the track with the bike sulky. The air cushion absorbs the jar, and the driver's seat is so far above the wheel that he hears less of the vibration hence he can drive better having his mind more completely upon his work. There is also less risk of accidents occasioned by wheels locking, hub punching and spoke splitting. The low wheels are guarded upon the outside by the forks, thus reducing the possibility of accident to the minimum.

The exact influence of the bicycle sulky in bringing about the reduction of the pacing and trotting records has not yet been, and probably never will be, properly determined. That it has had some influence no one will deny; but that it has accelerated the speed of the record-breakers by four or five seconds is not within the bounds of reason. * * * If any large concession must be made to holders of records to the old-style sulky, Johnston must be considered the king-pin pacer of the annals of the American turf, and Maud S. the trotting queen. The bicycle sulky does its most perfect work on this, (Fleetwood), track of winding turns, sharp angles with ascending and descending grades and makes it take rank with the average regulation mile course.—The Horseman, December 7, 1893.

Sulky Case. A case made of canvas for the purpose of protecting a sulky when being transported on campaigns. A set consists of three pieces, one for each wheel, and one for the gear, each in the shape of sacks fitted to the parts they are to receive, buckled tightly, thus protecting them from dust and also from being marred.

Sulkyette. A close-hitch speeding cart; a combination road cart and jogging sulky, adapted for track work and runabout business.

Summary. A summary of a race should give the place and track upon which it took place; the date; the purse for which it was made; the conditions as to harness, wagon or saddle; the number of heats; the names, color and sex of the horses competing; the name of the sire of the horse, (and the dam if she is a winner of one or more heats); names of owners and drivers; positions of the horses, and time made. The names of pacers should be in *italics*. An entire horse should be entered as a horse, not as a stallion; and described in the summary as "b. h." The letters "b. s." should not be used.

Summary Against Time. Where a horse is started to beat his record it is called trotting against time. When the summary is published, if the horse lowers his record, his name and time are given first; if he does not beat his record they are given last. Thus:

SUMMARY.

Stockton, Cal., October 13, 1891. Palo Alto started to beat his record of 2:12¼.

| Time, | 1 |
| Palo Alto, | 2 |

Time: 2:12¾.

Supervisors. Officers appointed by the National Trotting Association to visit any meeting held on any track in its membership, to learn if the rules are properly observed, and take the time of horses in any heat or race, which facts may be received in evidence in any case pending.

Suppleness. [Eq.] The perfect harmony of all the forces of the horse when in obedience to the will of the rider.

Surcingle. A girth for a horse; a girth separate from a saddle or harness, passing around the body of the horse, retaining in place a blanket or saddle-cloth.

Suspension. Period of suspension; the time during which the horse is completely off the ground at any particular pace in motion, or when jumping.

Suspension. A penalty imposed. This penalty may be imposed upon a member, horse, owner or driver, having the force of disqualification during the time it is in operation, and making a conditional withholding of all their rights and privileges. It may be imposed for non-payment of dues, fines or entrance fees; giving a false pedigree or record of a horse; false statement of name or residence; refusing to give information; meddling with or disguising a horse; wrongfully entering in a class; for false protest; refusing to ride or drive; helping; any breach of decorum; foul driving, or other just cause. Suspension is usually limited to the season in which the order was issued, unless more explicitly stated in the order.

Suspensory Ligament. A very strong band or cord of nonelastic fibrous tissue, lying between the canon bone and the back tendon; "one of the most wonderful contrivances," says Prof. Stillman, "in the whole locomotive machinery of the horse." Its obvious mechanical use is to prevent over-extension of the fetlock-joint; and if this cord is ruptured or stretched the animal becomes what is termed "broken down," that is, the fetlock-joint sinks down, and the hoof has a tendency to tilt forwards and upwards.

Though a ligament only, with its action beyond the control of the will, it is no less an active organ whose function is indispensable to locomotion. The perfect equilibrium between the strength of the ligament and the force it is required to resist is of the utmost importance. If it yields too much, the fetlock is liable to strike the ground; if it is too rigid and it does not yield enough, there will be stiffness and a hobbling gait.—The Horse in Motion, J. D. B. Stillman.

Swallow the Bridle. A horse having too wide a mouth and too small a bit is said to "swallow the bridle."

Sweat Flaps. Pieces of leather which are placed under the girth straps of the saddle, on each side, to prevent the sweat of the horse from working through.

Sweat Out; Sweating Out. An exercise given a horse before a race for the purpose of sweating out his throat to put him in better condition. Such an exercise is usually about three miles at three-quarters speed.

Sweepstakes, is usually construed as meaning a race over all; a free-for-all. By the rules of the Turf Congress it means a race publicly declared open to all complying with its conditions, to be fulfilled, wholly or in part, subsequent to its closing or in handicaps subsequent to the acceptance of weight, and in which stakes are to be made for each horse.

Switched. A veterinary term meaning a glandered horse.

Switcher. A horse given to a habit of constantly switching the tail when in harness. It is a serious fault.

Symmetry. Beauty and harmony of exterior conformation in regard to size, shape and arrangement of the various parts of the body to some particular type of the useful horse. It possesses a different standard in that of the race or trotting horse from what it is in the Clyde or Hackney, but is present alike in each according to its own type.

T

Table. The free portion, crown or surface of the teeth which becomes worn by friction with the hard substances the horse takes as food, and by the constant contact with the teeth of the opposite jaw. There are five well defined periods in this dental table, as it changes from use in successive years: 1, The surface of the teeth forming the dental table is at first flattened from front to rear; 2, this table becomes oval; 3, it becomes rounded and its two diameters are nearly equal; 4, it becomes triangular with three borders, one anterior and two lateral; 5, the table is flattened from side to side and so remains to very old age.

Tags. The pendants, usually of copper, in the oval plate in the center of the bar of a mouthing bit. They lay upon the tongue, and by playing with them the attention of the horse is diverted, thus rendering him more easily subdued and managed.

Tail Male Line. A term used in a thoroughbred pedigree, by which is meant the horses tracing in direct male line to Herod on the side of the sire. For instance: Diomed, winner of the inauguration Derby in 1780, was by Florizel, son of Herod; young Eclipse winner of the second Derby by O'Kelly's Eclipse, etc.

Take Care of, To. A term expressive of a favor or advantage which a driver will give another if he can do so fairly; and also implying a choice for a horse that may be in the field. "If I can take care of you, I will," means that if the opportunity occurs as between the one spoken to and another, the driver will look out and give him the advantage. A judge in assigning positions to horses will say to a driver, "Mr. Blank, you have the pole"; and the answer may be given, "thank you for the favor," when, in fact, it was no favor of the judges, at all, the horse got the pole fairly in the drawing. The term is not to be taken as expressive of collusion or any understanding as between parties in a race.

The starter again took care of Manzanita in the sixth heat, and gave a start that can only be explained on the theory that he was so much interested in the great race that he failed to watch the field closely. —Training the Trotting Horse, Charles Marvin.

258

Take the Field. To stake one's money against the favorite, thus backing all the rest against a single horse.

Taking-off. The act of leaving the ground in making a leap or jump on horseback.

Talent, The. The ring; those who have inside information concerning the race, or a certain horse in the field; the knowing ones. The term originated in Australia.

The talent came down to Rigby to back Charlie B., but went home with lean pocket-books. The little gray horse from way-back surprised everybody by the way he won the race.—Portland Press.

And sinks from view forever, while the talent
Declare they never saw a sight so gallant.
—New South Wales paper.

Tan Gallop. A winter exercise ground for horses, built at Waterhall Farm, near Newmarket, Eng., in 1883. Said to be the finest ground of its kind in the world.

Tandem. A word meaning at length; one after another. Two or more horses harnessed and driven one before the other, instead of side by side, as in a span, or pair. A fashionable turn out.

Tap the Wire. To obtain surreptitious possession of the telegraph and extract the information with which it is charged, concerning a race, for fraudulent or unlawful purposes.

Tarpan. The wild horse of Tartary.

Tarsus. The hock joint.

Tattersall's. "The high-change of horse flesh." A mart for the sale of horses established by Richard Tattersall, near Hyde Park Corner, London, in 1766. The lease of the site having expired, the new premises at Brompton were erected and opened for business, April 10, 1865. The Tattersalls Companies in America was organized in 1892, for the sale of fine horses, with offices at New York; Cleveland, Ohio; Lexington, Ky., and Chicago, Ill.

Teaming a Race. Driving a race. The expression is very often heard among drivers, "I teamed a race," meaning that they drove a race; hence to team, is to drive.

Teeth. The horse has two sets of teeth: The milk teeth which appear at or soon after birth, known as those of the first dentition; and the permanent teeth, or those of the second dentition. The teeth are placed in each jaw in such a manner that they make the form of an arch—the convex part forward and the open part back toward the throat. The arch of each jaw is again classed by veterinarians into three sections —the anterior, or front; the intermediate, or middle, and the lateral, or back. In the first are located the incisors; in the second the tusks, and in the third the molars or grinders. The first are used to grasp and cut the food; the second to separate it, and the third to still finer reduce or crush it. On each side, directly behind the incisors, is a section of the jaw in which are no teeth, known in the lower jaw, as the bar of the jaw or mouth; while back of this are the molar teeth. In the adult animal there are in each jaw six incisors, two tush teeth and twelve molars, making a total of forty teeth for the horse. The tush teeth are generally absent in the mare, her total number being thirty-six. These tush teeth do not exist in the young animal, but in the place where they will appear when the horse becomes older, are sometimes found rudimentary teeth with no well-defined shape. Occasionally in both the young and adult animal, occur rudimentary premolar teeth called wolf teeth, which are four in number, two in each jaw, making the total number in such cases, forty-four. See AGE OF THE HORSE.

These little rudiments of teeth are, when properly understood, of great interest. Their diminutive size, irregular form and inconstant presence, combined with their history in the extinct horse-like animals, show them to be teeth which, for some reason to us at present unknown, have become superfluous, have been very gradually and slowly dispensed with, and are in the stage to which the horse has now arrived in its evolution, upon the point of disappearance. The presence of these so-called wolves' teeth alone is sufficient, if we had no other proof, to show that the horse is not an isolated creation, but one link in a great chain of organic beings.—The Horse, William Henry Flower, C. B.

The natural division of the two periods of age, as indicated by the temporary and the permanent teeth, is subdivided as follows: 1, The period of eruption of the incisors or the first dentition; 2, the leveling of these teeth and their progressive use; 3, the period of the falling out of the deciduous teeth and the appearance of the permanent ones; 4, the leveling of these latter; 5, the successive forms which their tables present as the teeth become worn away. * * * A thoroughbred with dense bones and hard teeth will wear the latter away much more slowly than a coarse-boned, lymphatic, common horse with softer substances in the teeth. The character of food to which a colt has been accustomed will stimulate or diminish the functional activity of the tooth, and, while hard substances would naturally wear a tooth faster than softer food, yet the animal which has been raised on the former will often have harder teeth than one which has not had to use them so severely.—Age of the Domestic Animals, Rush Shippen Huidekoper, M. D.

Temples. Those portions of the head, on each side of the forehead, between the ear and eye.

Ten Broeck. King of the running turf. Foaled on the farm of John Harper, Midway, Ky., in 1872. By imported Phaeton; dam, Fanny Hulton, by Lexington. He was a most unpromising colt, and at two years of age was a sickly looking animal one would hardly have taken as a gift. But at four years of age he had developed into a remarkable animal. In that year, September 16, 1876, carrying 104 pounds he lowered the record for two miles and five-eighths at **Lexington, Ky.**, to 4:58½, where it has remained ever since. Ten days after this, viz: On September 27, 1876, carrying the same weight, at Churchill Downs, Lexington, Ky., he ran the fastest four miles ever known and never equalled or surpassed since—7:15¾. As a five-year-old he was even speedier, and in a contest against time at Midway, Ky., May 24, 1877, lowered the record for one mile to 1:39¾, which stood as the record till 1890; and a week later, May 29, 1877, at Louisville, Ky., he ran two miles in 3:27½, carrying 110 pounds, which has never been beaten since. His last appearance on the course was at the Louisville, Ky., Jockey Club track, July 4, 1878, in a four mile heat race against the California mare, Mollie McCarthy, which up to that time had been unbeaten. The race was for $10,000 a side, and was witnessed by the largest crowd ever seen upon the Louisville course. The famous California mare was distanced. After this race he was retired from the turf, placed in the stud, and was the sire of some of the best runners on the turf. He was valued at $100,000. His death occurred at the stock farm of T. B. Harper, near Midway, Ky., June 28, 1887.

Terrets. Metallic eyes which screw into the saddle-tree of a harness through which the reins or driving-lines pass from the bit to the hands of the driver. A set embraces two terrets and one water-hook, the latter holding the check or bearing rein in place. These trimmings for a harness are made in a great variety of style and finish.

The Braid. A whip, or whip-lash. To apply the braid is to flog or punish a horse; to use the whip.

The Rest Nowhere. A distanced field. A term in popular use at race tracks the world over, to denote the unplaced horses. Originated from the expression made by the famous Colonel O'Kelly, at Epsom, Eng., May 3, 1769, when called upon to place the horses on occasion of the first race run by the celebrated horse, Eclipse. "Eclipse first, the rest nowhere," was Colonel O'Kelly's vigorous description of this remarkable race, hence the term now used.

Thick Wind. One of the several forms of disease affecting the breathing organs of the horse, allied to that of roaring, whistling and heaves. In many cases it is the forerunner of broken wind, or heaves, and when it proceeds from inflammation it is an unsoundness.

Thigh. The thigh of the horse is bordered by the stifle, flank, croup, buttock and gaskin, from which it is separated by a horizontal line drawn from the upper end of the straight line made by the hamstring, which proceeds towards the thigh from the point of the hock.

Thoroughbred. The natural aristocrat of the equine race. It means that a horse's pedigree can be traced for generations from sires and dams of English pure blood, or from Arabs, Barbs, (Barbary States), or Persians, recorded in the stud-book. While this is the former well understood definition, its meaning has become somewhat modified in recent years. It now generally means a horse whose pedigree contains the requisite number of crosses to insure freedom from any considerable contamination of cold blood. One possessing five crosses to animals of pure blood, untainted with mongrel strains, is regarded a thoroughbred. The difference between thoroughbred and standard bred, is that the former is bred to run and the latter to trot,—hence the terms running bred and trotting bred, frequently used in referring to the two classes. Strictly speaking, however, no horse is thoroughbred that does not trace, without contaminating blood, to Oriental origin. In other words, the horses of the first blood, or such as are nearest possible to the Eastern stock, are: Those immediately produced from an Arabian or Barb; any stallion crossed with an English mare, which has already been crossed with a Barb or Arabian stallion, in the first degree; or that which has sprung from two crosses in the same degree.

The term thoroughbred was originally used exclusively as the name by which the English race-horse was designated. The thoroughbred horse is peculiarly a British production. * * * The term thoroughbred, as applied to horses, is used to designate the running horse. * * * A recent cross with an imported Arab or Barb, while it does not vitiate the blood nor render an animal ineligible as a thoroughbred, is not usually regarded as desirable, from the fact that the course of selection which has been practiced by the breeders of thoroughbred horses in England and America for the last one hundred years, has given us a race that is generally considered to be far superior to the Oriental horse of to-day for speed, size and stoutness.—Horse Breeding, J. H. Sanders.

The race-horse, or, rather, the thoroughbred horse, from his symmetry, power, graceful action, light, elastic form, speed and stamina, is, beyond question, the highest type of the equine family. He possesses more of the beauties of formation than any animal which approximates to him in size and shape; he excels all others in the intelligent expression of his countenance and shape of his head; and in the simplicity, compactness and completeness of his digestive organs, the great leverage of his hocks and hind quarters, and the wonderful mechanism displayed in the construction of his legs and feet.—The Thoroughbred Horse, S. D. Bruce.

The advantages of thoroughbred blood, as they seem to me, are that it gives higher finish, better quality of bone, better joints and superior wind and lung power. I do not base my claims for thoroughbred blood on gameness. My belief is that gameness comes, in great part, from pure, frictionless action. It is practically a truth that speed makes gameness. Some thoroughbreds have more trotting action than others. In selecting a thoroughbred mare to breed to a trotting stallion, we pay great attention to form, action and head. Some thoroughbreds are more brainy and level headed than others, and from one of these of the right conformation bred to a stallion of great brain and action-controlling power, the chances of getting a high class trotter are good. I do not claim that you can get trotters as uniformly this way as by breeding from trotting mares, but you can, with the properly mated sire and dam, get horses of high class by this line of breeding horses, of great finish and hard, fine quality.—Training the Trotting Horse, Charles Marvin.

Thorough-pin. A sprain of the tendons above the knee and behind the bone of the forearm; or of the tendon which plays over the back of the hock, to the inner side of the bony process which forms its point. When so large as to render it likely that lameness will follow, it has been proven an unsoundness.

Three in Five. A race, or purse, the conditions of which are that three out of five heats must be won by one horse, in order to entitle him to the race and purse, or stake.

Three-quarter Shoe. A shoe, one side of which is shorter than the other; so that when on the foot, the wall of the short side, measuring from the heel, is uncovered for a distance of two inches, or a little more. It is used for relieving from pressure the parts of the foot near a corn.

Three-quarter Speed. A gait used by many of the best trainers in working the trotting horse previous to a race; the principle being never to work a horse at high speed, or, rather, full speed, that being kept in reserve for the actual test of the race.

Budd Doble taught me that a horse could be put in condition with a great deal less fast work than I had at that time supposed possible. His idea was to give them plenty of what we call three-quarter speed, with longer work from a mile to a mile-and-a-half, and then two mile heats.—Life with the Trotters. John Splan.

Three-ride Business. [Eng.] The crack way of running over hurdles, in which just three strides are taken mechanically between each hurdle.

Three Straight-aways. A term applied to a race won in three straight heats.

Throat-latch. That part of the crownpiece of the bridle which serves to prevent it from slipping over the horse's head by passing under his throat.

Throw a Heat. A term used to express that act of a driver or rider, by which a heat is lost at the finish—evidently by design; to pull up and let an opponent dash by one at the close of a heat; to give the heat away when it might have been won; to drop anchor.

Thrush. An inflammation of the secreting membrane of the frog, with fœtid discharge from the cleft. Where it is the result of contraction, as is often the case, it is an unsoundness.

Tilting Table. An operating table used by veterinary surgeons in casting a horse. The animal is placed close to the table, as to a wall. His head, body and legs are securely strapped to it, and, by means of adjustable levers operated by a crank and cogs, the table is brought down to a horizontal position, and the horse is lying on his side upon it ready to be operated upon.

Time. This word, as applied to races, is used to indicate the duration of time which it takes a horse to go a given distance, in order to ascertain the greatest speed attainable, or the greatest distance which can be passed over in a given time. All races in this country are timed by official timers, or judges, the time is recorded, and set against the horse making the fastest time in a heat or race, the time always being taken from the horse first to pass under the wire at the finish. On the English turf there is no official record of time made at races. To what a degree breeding and training have improved the trotting time in this country in seventy years, is shown by the following outline table: In 1820, the best mile in harness was about 3:00; in 1830, the best mile in harness was 2:40; in 1840, the best time under saddle was by Dutchman, 2:28; in 1850, the best time under saddle was by Lady Suffolk, 2:26½; in 1860, the best time in harness was by Flora Temple, 2:19¾; in 1870, the best time in harness was by Dexter, 2:17¼; in 1880, the best time in harness was by Jay-Eye-See, 2:10; in 1890, the best time in harness was by Sunol, 2:08¼; in 1893, the best time in harness was by Directum, 2:05¼.

There commonly has to be a conjunction of favorable circumstances, in order to enable a horse to make extraordinary time. Therefore, when it is found that one which has not made such time, can beat those which have, race after race, all of them being apparently in good condition, a reasonable presumption is raised that the trotter in question will, at no distant day, beat the time at the head of the record, as well as the horses which made it.—The Trotting Horse of America, Hiram Woodruff.

Timer. A chronograph; a split-second watch used in taking the time made by horses in a race.

Timer. A person appointed as timing judge, to take the time made by the horses in each heat. The National rules require that two official timers shall take the time of the horses in races; the American rules require three, and the rules of the Turf Congress say there shall be "one or more, not to exceed three." These officials are appointed by the president of the track or association, or they may be appointed by the judges. In announcing the time made, it is usual, where there is a disagreement in watches, to give the average time taken by all of them.

Time Board. The score board upon which the time of the heat and rank of the horses, at the close of each heat, is hung out in front of the judges' stand.

Time Between Heats. The time allowed drivers and horses by the trotting rules, between heats, is: Mile heats, twenty minutes; mile heats in a three in five race, twenty-five minutes; two mile heats, thirty minutes; three mile heats, thirty-five minutes; and if there should be a four mile race, forty minutes. The racing rules are: In heats of three-fourths of a mile, and of one mile, twenty minutes; in heats of two miles, twenty-five minutes; in heats of three miles, thirty-five minutes, and in heats of four miles, forty minutes.

Time Not a Bar. By the trotting rules time made under the saddle, or on snow or ice, as well as time made when two or more horses are harnessed together, shall constitute a bar for races of the same character, but shall not be a bar for races of a different character; but time to wagon is a record or a bar, as the case may be, in races of every character.

Time Performance. A measure of speed against time. The trotting rules and rules of the Trotting Register Association require that a performance against time must be made at a regular meeting of a track or society in National or American membership; strictly in accordance with the trotting rules; not to interfere with, or take place pending the close of another race; in the presence of three judges and three timers; the meeting must be duly advertised; the entries properly made, and it must not take place earlier than ten o'clock of the day set for the performance. Match races are regarded as performances against time.

Time Record. In all public races, and in all performances against time, the time made in each heat must be accurately taken and placed in a record which must be signed by the judges at the close of the heat, as well as by the timers and the clerk of the course. If it should be made to appear to the boards of review or appeals, upon investigation, that any record had been fraudulently obtained, such time shall be regarded a bar, not a record.

Time, Suppression of. The act of withholding from the public the actual time made by a horse in a heat. The suppression of time at a public race is regarded and treated as a fraud by all the associations; and such acts are punishable by heavy fines and expulsions from the courses within the membership of the trotting and racing congresses.

Tin Cup; Tin-Cupper; Tin Cup Record. A term of derision; a record against time as distinguished from one made in a race; a horse having a record gained at a private trial against the watch. About 1885 trials of young horses against time, or for some private prize, usually a silver cup or piece of plate, became very popular. Such horses were being put into the 2:30 by the hundred, starting for no real consideration, and with little or no guaranty that such time had been made by them as was claimed. The matter became an abuse, and was the occasion of so much wrong that great reproach came to be attached to such records. The American Sportsman said: "A horse with a tin cup record cuts no figure and is a drug on the market; and the men who turn out any more of them require a guardian." Wallace's Monthly said: "If regulations cannot be devised that will secure some slight test of a colt's racing qualities in winning his record, then we are in favor of wiping out tin cup records, standard stakes records, private matches and all that, and of putting every youngster on an equality." After long discussion the matter was taken in hand by the American, and later by the National Trotting Association, whereby judicious regulations were adopted governing all time performances, which are now in force by all societies and tracks in membership with either association, and which are recognized by the American Trotting Register Association. See AGAINST TIME, and TIME PERFORMANCES.

Time performance according to rule is just as potent as one made in a race—both are measures of speed, properly designated. The rules now in force by the national associations throw around time performances the proper restriction desired by all prominent breeders. —Turf, Field and Farm.

Tip. Private information or advice on the chances of a horse winning. "A straight tip" is information which comes direct from an owner or trainer, and which is supposed to be trustworthy.

No matter what paper or tout proclaims,
Take only the tip from Truthful James;
He is up to all the dodges and games,
And money's not wasted by Truthful James.
—The Sporting Times.

Tip. A racing tip for the front of a horse's foot; a half-shoe; a plate extending around the toe from quarter to quarter. Youatt, the English authority, in his work on the horse published in 1831 said: "Tips are short shoes, reaching only half round the foot, and worn while the horse is at grass, in order to prevent the crust being torn by the occasional hardness of the ground, or the pawing of the animal." As re-invented by Mr. Joseph Cairn Simpson of California, the tip was placed on the foot like a shoe, and tapered or feathered to a point to keep the hoof as level as possible. Subsequently the tip was made of nearly a uniform thickness, having a quarter of an inch of metal filed square. A shoulder was cut in the wall, and so much of the sole as the width of the web required, and all back of the shoulder was left full and rounded with a file to protect the edge.

I have given tips a very fair trial, and have found that at least on our gravelly soil they fail to sufficiently protect the feet of horses in training. On a soft soil for jogging, for a horse not in hard training or for a horse with contracted heels, they are excellent, but are inadequate protection as a rule, in the wear and tear of constant track-work.—Training the Trotting Horse, Charles Marvin.

As a rule a horse that is short in the pasterns wears away the toes very quickly, and such a horse can wear tips successfully. On the other hand a horse long in the pasterns wears the heels rapidly and on such a horse tips will not prove of service.—Scientific Horseshoeing, William Russell.

I believe if our trotting tracks were not quite so hard there are a great many horses that would go better if shod in tips. I have watched this matter at every opportunity which presented itself to me, have tried tips on a number of horses, and am satisfied that for a horse to go well in them the track must be especially prepared.— Life with the Trotters, John Splan.

Tipster. An informer on a race; a tout.

Tipsters are almost all swindlers.—The Badminton Library: Racing, The Earl of Suffolk and Berkshire, and W. G. Craven.

Tire. The hoop or rim of iron used to bind or hold the felloe or fellies of wheels to secure them from wearing or breaking—referring particularly to the old style high-wheel sulky, or carriage wheel. Sulky tires, formerly invariably of iron, are now almost invariably of rubber, hence the tire is not used to hold the felloe together, as the felloe is made of steel or wood in one continuous section. These rubber tires are made in various patterns, all on the pneumatic principle differing much in details of construction. Some are formed in a single compound tube; others are made in two parts, having an outer and an inner tube, the latter being the air receptacle. Some tires are laced; some are ribbed or corrugated, lengthwise, on the outer surface; some formed entirely whole; some are cemented to the felloe, others are attached without cement, so as to be easily removed. By a laced tire is meant that the outer tube or cover is laced in one or more places, very similarly to the way a shoe is laced; the cause for this being that it leaves an opening by which the inner tube may be removed in case of necessity for repairing or replacing the tube. When a pneumatic tire has been some time used and has become flat or soft, it is said to be "deflated." See RUBBER TIRE; PNEUMATIC TIRE.

To Break the Record. When a horse makes faster or lower time in a class than that which has been made; or reduces the record for a certain age, or way of going, below where it has stood, is to break or cut the record.

To Draw Rein.   To stop; to pull up.

To Give Rein.   To let a horse have his head; to let him out at speed.

To Harness.   A race announced to be trotted to harness, means that it is to take place to a sulky.

To Horse.   A term meaning that one is mounted; that the person is on horseback.

To Lay Over.   To surpass; to excel; to have more speed; to lay over him in a race, means that one has a faster horse than his opponent.

To Make the Running.   To make the pace at the beginning of a race by causing a second-class horse to set off at high speed, with a view of giving a better chance to a staying horse.

To Rein Up.   To bring the horse to a halt; to stop.

To Ride the Great Horse.   An historic phrase used in old times in England, signifying to practice horsemanship in the fashion of the day.

To Ride to Hounds.   To take part in a fox-hunt; to follow the chase.

To Take Up the Running, is to go off at full speed from a slower pace; to take the lead in a race.

To Wagon.   A race announced to be trotted to wagon, means to a four-wheeled track skeleton.

Toe.   The front part of the foot, or shoe.

Toe-out; Toe-in.   Horses that are pigeon toed or splay-footed generally toe-out or toe-in.   Such are structural defects and in most cases are beyond the scope of farriery to remedy.

Toe-weights.   Small metal knobs screwed or otherwise attached to the hoofs of the horse's feet.   There are various patterns, among them: Miles' adjustable stick-fast, toe and side; Fenton's security; Chicago welded spur weight, resting on a spur welded to the front of the shoe and projecting up in front of the toe of the hoof; side weights; Mitchell weight; Dot side weight, leather, lead filled; Duplex side weight; Pocket weight, made of leather and filled with sheet lead admitting of changes in weight; Clark's eclipse, toe and side; Boss toe and side, 2, 3, 4 and 6 ounces, attached to the boot or scalper; Boston, 2, 3, 4, 6 and 8 ounces.

The necessity for toe-weights or heavy shoes lies in some defect of conformation or of gait, and when a trotter is obliged to carry a heavy load in this manner his feet and legs suffer.—Road, Track and Stable, H. C. Merwin.

Continued soundness with toe-weights at a high rate of speed, is a natural impossibility. The fastest trotter, for a spurt, that the world has produced, has been compelled to wear toe-weights, and after a few wonderful dashes, she is a cripple. They may have added many to the list of fast trotters, but have added just as many to the list of hopeless cripples. In due course of time the toe-weight will be remembered only as a cruel appliance to overcome antagonistic instincts in the trotter.—Wallace's Monthly, 1881.

Tongs-Across-a-Wall. [Eq.] A phrase descriptive of a seat in riding which depends for its balance upon the stirrup, renouncing all contact of the legs with the horse's body.

Topping the Wall. [Eng.] An act by which the horse strikes the wall with his hind feet to send him with renewed effort or spring beyond some object on the opposite side that he did not see till partially over; and to do which he had not used sufficient power in his spring when he rose. It is an act which is considered evidence of very superior training.

Toppy. Stylish; showy. A term used to describe the general appearance and carriage of a horse, as in the expressions, "a toppy bay;" "a pair of toppy grays."

Tout. A horse watcher; an agent on the lookout for any information or circumstance as to a horse's capabilities or condition, or anything pertaining to the race. Various training quarters are regularly "touted" by men well versed in their business, and the information obtained is given to tipsters who give it to the public either through the columns of the sporting press, or by means of letters and telegrams.

Touts, when known, shall be debarred the privileges of the race courses and grounds.—Rules of the American Turf Congress.

Touts are thieves who steal stable secrets, either by spying on horses in their gallops and trials, or by bribing servants to betray their masters, and to betray any important information on horses however acquired.—The Badminton Library: Racing, The Earl of Suffolk and Berkshire, and W. G. Craven.

Trace. One of the two straps belonging to a harness, by which a sulky or buggy is drawn by the horse harnessed to it; a tug.

Track. A race course. Tracks are made straight, oval and kite-shaped; and also in some cases, of other and peculiar shape according to the condition of the land upon which they are built. The lengths are generally one-half mile, and one mile respectively. The land required for a half mile track is fourteen acres; for a mile track forty-nine acres, where the homestretch is sixty-five feet, and the backstretch forty feet wide; and no track should be narrower than this, many are wider. A better width is seventy feet for the homestretch and fifty feet for the backstretch; while some modern built tracks are seventy-six feet for the former, and sixty for the latter. A half mile track should be as wide as a mile track. The area given above does not include land upon which to set buildings outside the track circle, but simply that required for the track surface. A natural rather than an artificial soil is the best for a track, provided it is of the right kind; but a soil that is naturally sandy is not favorable, as it is light and cuppy. If such is to be used as the foundation, it must be covered with a dressing of seven to nine inches of clay loam, in order to make a good surface. The best soil for a track is a strong, fertile, deep loam; indeed the richer and tougher the soil the better, and if there is some peat or crude vegetable matter in its composition it is better still. A good surface for a track is made of blocks of strong loam, twelve inches square, set like paving blocks, then thoroughly impacted and dressed. Such a track has a springy quality and will retain its elasticity for years. If kept in proper condition it will not sore up a horse. It is as necessary that the soil of a track be rich, as it is that of a field; then it has life, will not become dead, and will last. It needs an occasional dressing of manure plowed into the surface and finished off. Next it must have an abundance of water—in fact all the soil will retain and not become too soft; this renders it always moist, makes it easy and yielding. It is not a difficult matter to lay out a half-mile or mile track—any ordinary surveyor can do it by following the rules given below; but to lay out a kite track is a more complicated matter, on account of the angles and details involved, and such a work requires the services of a competent engineer.

To Lay Out a Half-mile Track. Draw two parallel lines six hundred feet long and four hundred and fifty-two feet, five inches apart. Half-way between the extreme ends of the two parallel lines drive a stake, then loop a wire around the stake long enough to reach to either side. Then make a true curve with the wire, putting down a stake as often as a fence-post is needed. When this operation is finished at both ends of the six hundred foot parallel lines the track is laid out. The inside fence will rest exactly on the line drawn, but the track must measure a half-mile three feet from the fence. The track should rise one-fourth inch to the foot from the pole to the outside on straight work. The turns should be thrown up one foot and three inches in every ten feet of width, or five feet on a forty foot turn. The stretches may be from forty-five to sixty feet long, and the throwing up of the turns should be commenced on both stretches for both turns, and worked toward the apex of each.

To Lay Out a Mile Track. Draw a line through an oblong center four hundred and forty yards in length, setting a stake at each end. Then draw a line on either side of the first line, exactly parallel with and four hundred and seventeen feet and two inches from it, setting stakes at either end of them. This will give an oblong square four hundred and forty yards long, and eight hundred and thirty-four feet and four inches wide. At each end of these three lines set stakes. Next fasten a cord or wire four hundred and seventeen feet and two inches long, to the center stake of this parallelogram, and then describe a half-circle, driving stakes as often as it is necessary to set a fence post. When the circle is made at both ends of this parallelogram there will be two straight sides and two circles which, measured three feet from the fence, will be exactly one mile. The turns should be thrown up one foot in ten feet of width, from the pole to the outside, so that a turn forty feet wide would, at its highest point, be four feet higher at the outside than at the pole. Tracks should always be built with reference to attaining the highest degree of speed. What is termed a regulation track, strictly speaking, is one on which the stretches and turns are each eighty rods long, (for a mile track); and forty rods long, (for a half-mile track). These, however, vary—as on some mile tracks the turns are ninety rods long, and the stretches seventy rods long; and on some half-mile tracks the turns are forty-five, and the stretches thirty-five rods long. The judges' stand should be placed back one hundred and fifty feet from the commencement of the first turn. A track is fast or slow according to its condition. "To the texture of the surface and the thoroughness of its manipulation, much more than to the shape and grades is attributable the wonderful speed records that have been made at Terre Haute." When the track becomes loose, first use a planer, following with a dressing harrow, finishing with a float; all the time keeping the work back of the teams. To be in the best condition tracks must have a true, hard face, finishing off with a beautiful, elastic cushion. Other conditions being equal half-mile courses are rated from three to five seconds slower than mile courses. The half-mile course is altogether the most popular for spectators as they are enabled to keep the horses in sight with comparative ease during the entire race. In 1893 the National Trotting Association had a membership of 558; and the American Trotting Association of 806, making a total of 1364 tracks in the membership of these associations. The national associations have never adopted any special shape for a regulation track—all that is necessary is that it must be exactly one thousand seven hundred and sixty yards in length; whether straight away, kite, oval or ring-shaped.

The great point in track building is to get a perfect cushion—one that is smooth, springy and clean, where there is a certain amount of yielding when the foot strikes, but yet no softness of surface. The aim is to have the track smooth yet springy, to have it clean without being hard, and elastic without being clinging.—Training the Trotting Horse, Charles Marvin.

The kite track is considered to be about two seconds faster than the ordinary or regulation track, because it consists almost entirely of two long stretches; but it is of course very unsatisfactory to the spectator, who is able to see in any real sense, only the beginning and the finish of the race. It seems unlikely that these tracks will long be tolerated.—Road, Track and Stable, H. C. Merwin.

Track, Covered. The only covered mile track in the world is that at the breeding farm of Henry C. Jewett, Jewettville, (near Buffalo), N. Y. It is completely covered, shingled and painted, forming an enclosure 5286 feet long. The building is lighted by twenty thousand panes of glass, has a grand stand that will seat twenty-five persons, and has electric bells at each quarter post. The surface of the track is made in a series of small grades the highest of which is thirteen feet in one hundred, so that the muscles of the horse are changed six times in going one mile.

Track Decorum. By the trotting rules, improper language to officers or judges, or to drivers, owners, trainers, riders or attendants; loud shouting; making improper use of the whip, or other improper conduct is strictly forbidden during the pendency of a heat, and is punishable by fine, suspension or expulsion.

Track Rules. The special rules relating more particularly to tracks are: That the track shall be measured by a competent civil engineer, and its exact length obtained three feet from the pole, that is, from the inside fence or ditch, and his certificate of measurement, made under oath, shall be deposited with the secretary of that national association of which the track is a member; that horses called for a race have the exclusive right of the course, all other horses being obliged to leave the track; that horses meeting on a track shall pass to the left, and that the track must be level. Upon this last point the rule of the American Trotting Register Association is, that "the registrar is instructed not to accept for purposes of registration the record of any animal not made on a track where the start and finish are not on the same level." If a track is not in membership with the national associations, a person winning a premium or purse has no redress for non-payment of the same; but if it is an association track the management can be suspended for non-payment of premiums.

Track-sick. A term used to denote that almost indescribable unwillingness of a horse to respond to his driver when in training. It does not always result from being out of condition, but is more often due to overwork and injudicious training, being especially common with young colts. As a rule it is advisable to give but very little driving on a circular track before the age of three years.

There can be nothing but harm come of working a jaded, failing, track-sick and spiritless colt.—Training the Trotting Horse, Charles Marvin.

Track-work. Fitting for races.

Trailing. When a driver is known to be following around the course during a heat, close to the leading horse, he is said to be "trailing."

In the third heat I trailed until we turned into the homestretch, at which point I swung the Chief well to the outside, and when I gave him his head the white-faced fellow made short work of the others. —Life with the Trotters, John Splan.

Trainer; Training. One whose profession it is to train and fit horses for track purposes; the art of fitting a horse for races. The trainer was formerly a person who trained grooms privately for gentlemen who kept horses, and the jockeys and drivers grew up from lads who lived with them. With the vast increase and importance of the turf business within the past twenty-five years, the demand has been great for a class of persons of peculiar ability and having characteristics specially fitting them for the care, training and driving of trotting and race horses. This demand has developed in America some of the most famous drivers the world has ever seen; and in the greatest races horses have been driven by men of consummate genius and ability. While in many cases trainers have come up from stable boys having a natural love for horses and driving, it is true that the most successful trainers are those who are well educated, know something of the anatomy of the horse, understand the veterinary art, have a special fondness for horses, and are good judges of human nature. The art of training a horse for the turf is one of the highest in the whole animal economy. No specific rules can be given for it, so much depends upon the breeding, age, constitution and peculiar characteristics of the different animals which the trainer handles. The general care, feed, shoeing, amount of work, rubbing, bandaging, conditioning—all vary with the individual, and must become a special study with the trainer in each case. Little upon these points can come from books— most must be based on repeated experience.

There is as much difference between training a 2:10 and a 2:20 horse, as there is between sharpening a razor and an ordinary jack-knife;

18

any boy can sharpen a jack-knife, but it takes a barber to keep a razor in order.—Life with the Trotters, John Splan.

In all that pertains to his craft the trainer must be an expert, studying and knowing the constitutions, tempers, defects and capabilities of his horses as though they were his children. He must be sober and vigilant, implicitly trusting no man but himself, yet appearing to repose the frankest confidence in his grooms, while he exercises the keenest supervision over them.—The Badminton Library: Racing, The Earl of Suffolk and Berkshire, and W. G. Craven.

Train-on. Clever at training in the line or habit desired. To "train on well," is to act kindly under training; to improve in speed by training and working.

Trammel. An ancient as well as modern instrument for changing the gait of horses. Gervase Markham, who published his "Cheape and Good Hvsbandry," in 1616, in that chapter devoted to the "ordering of the great horse," describes trammels as "leathers so fixed that the horse cannot put forward his fore legge, but he must perforce hale his hinder legge after it." Modern trammels are of leather, fitted to the horse's legs to regulate his motions, and are often used in teaching a horse to amble.

Trapezium. The real definition of this word is, a quadrilateral—no two sides of which are equal; but in the description of the exterior parts of the horse it refers to the prominence on the posterior surface, or back part of the knee.

It is true that many horses are cut away under the knee to that extent that the leg is weakened, and will not stand constant hard work; but we must distinguish between the horse with an unusually well developed trapezium bone which forms the prominence, and the one which is illy formed by being too much cut away under the joint.—E. A. A. Grange, V. S., Michigan State College Experiment Station.

Traps; Trappings. An outfit for a track horse; boots, bandages, clothing and necessary stable equipments.

Trappy. A short, rapid, snappy, high-stepping gait is said to be a "trappy" gait.

Trappiness. [Eng.] A term applied to any hedge, fence or obstacle which is dangerous to take or pass, from a part of it being concealed, like a brook or ditch on the opposite side of a fence or hedge, not seen in approaching it. "It was not the size of this fence," says Mr. Coventry, in Badminton, "but its *trappiness* to which trainers and riders objected."

Travelling-gear. A track term denoting the legs, muscles and locomotory organs of the horse. Mr. Marvin, in describing one of the colts which he trained, says: "Her travelling-gear was good from the ground up."

Traversing. [Eq.] The motion by which a saddle horse passes to the right and left, alternately, by the bearing of the reins or the legs of the rider.

Tray. An adjustable box, fitted to slip into place under the seat of a road cart or sulkyette, for carrying packages, removable when not wanted.

Tread. The face or surface of a pneumatic tire.

Tread. A tread is said to have taken place, when the inside of the coronet of one hind foot is struck by the calk of the shoe on the other foot, inflicting a bruised or contused wound.

Tree. The wood and iron framework of the saddle.

Trey-team. A team of three horses harnessed abreast. The world's record for best speed with a trey-team, to the close of 1893. is that made by Belle Hamlin, Globe and Justina, at Cleveland, Ohio, July 31, 1891, 2:14.

Trial Record. A term meaning the time made by a horse in a private trial. It is one, however, having no significance as to the value of a horse, as no trial time is recognized by any competent authority. The race record is the only test of speed that has any value.

Trio, The Wonderful. The three horses that have exercised the greatest influence upon the race of English thoroughbreds, viz: The Byerly Turk; the Darley Arabian, and the Godolphin Arabian.

Tripping. A habit, generally the result of bad conformation, and in such cases cannot be called a vice. If due to tenderness of the foot, old lameness, a groggy gait, or habitual carelessness and idleness, it must in such cases accompany a horse hardly worth attempting to correct of the fault.

Trot. A natural gait; the medium pace. The order of movement in the trot is left fore foot, right hind foot, right fore foot, left hind foot. Thus the left fore and right hind foot move in unison, striking the ground together; then in turn the right fore foot and left hind foot complete the revolution. Hence the trot is most properly termed the diagonal gait. In this gait there are two feet as bases of support instead of one—the complete step, therefore, emits two beats. The imprints left upon the ground by a horse at trotting speed show these characteristics: Sometimes the print of the hind foot remains behind that of the fore foot; sometimes they are both made in the exact place; sometimes the hind one goes in advance of that of the front one. Hence these have been termed the ordinary, the short and the long trotting step. When the velocity of the trot is carried to its extreme limit, the hind foot going far beyond the step of the fore foot, the stride reaches its highest limit, and this gait is termed the broken trot, and the flying trot.

The beauties of the trot consist in its regularity, gracefulness, height and speed—but it is extremely rare to find all these combined in the same horse. Its regularity is indicated by the synchronism of the beats and the uniformity of the step. Its gracefulness consists in its lightness, ease and suppleness, as well as in the parallelism of the planes of oscillation of the members in their relation to the medium plane. Its height is associated with the energy of propulsion and the length of the projection. The speed depends upon the length of the projection. The speed depends upon the length of the steps and the frequency of their repetition in a given time. * * * All horses do not trot in the same manner. There are some in which the extension of the whole anterior is carried to such an extreme that the contact of the foot with the ground, after a short time of arrest, seems almost to be effected upon the heels. The movements of the posterior members are equally very extended, whence an energetic effort of propulsion, much more *action*, as we are in the habit of saying. Again there are some light trotters which emit but faint beats when trotted upon a hard road or pavement; others on the contrary emit heavy sounds under these circumstances. Some rock themselves from the fact of very great corpulence or a vicious axis of the members. Some raise their legs insufficiently from the ground, scrape the floor; others elevate them excessively, trot from the knees which is so much loss of force. Others again lack harmony between the movements of the fore, and those of the hind limbs, or have some anatomical defect of certain regions which detracts from the grace and ease of the gait, and even exposes them to many accidents. Some, in fact, even *show their shoes* from excessive flexion of the pastern upon the fetlock.—The Exterior of the Horse, Armand Goubaux and Gustave Barrier.

Trotter. A horse kept for speed; a trotting bred horse; a fast horse; the noblest equine product of the modern, highly developed American civilization. The American trotter of to-day usually traces to one or more of the following ancestors; Messenger, True Briton and Diomed, all thoroughbreds; Bellfounder, a Norfolk trotter; Grand Bashaw, a Barb; Pilot, a Canadian pacer; Blue Bull, an Ohio pacer. In his conformation he should be without blemish, harmonious and well constructed in body and limb. If the loins are slightly weak and the withers rather low these are not grave defects and may be overlooked; but he must have a powerful croup, thighs, buttocks, legs and hocks; also, long neck, shoulders and forearms; he must not be too horizontal in the croup; the inclination of the superior segments of the legs must be normal; he must have width, height and depth of chest; wide, thick, neat and clean joints; in a word he must possess all the characteristics of a beautiful conformation. It is when in motion that a trotter can be best judged. By the action, lengthened, hugging the ground and regular; by the extent and complete projection of the fore legs, and by the energetic action of the hind legs, he will show to the best advantage his spirit and characteristics as a trotter.

The American trotter is now practically a thoroughbred.—Prof. Robert Wallace, University of Edinburgh, Scotland.
The truth seems to be that great trotters, like great men, inherit from their mothers what has aptly been termed the subtle ambition to succeed.—Road, Track and Stable, H. C. Merwin,

The uniformity with which the trotting-bred trotter trots, and trots fast, shows how completely the intelligent and scientific breeding of the past ten or twenty years has tended to eliminate elements of uncertainty and to establish a breed which is attracting purchasers from every country of the known world for our trotters.—The Horseman.

Trotters. There were in the United States, to the close of the year 1893, about ten thousand trotters in the 2:30 list; one thousand and eight in the 2:20 class; one hundred and eighty with records of 2:15 or better; six with records of 2:08 or better, and one with a record of 2:04.

Trotting-bred. A term meaning that the horse so bred has a trotting inheritance, not a running inheritance. It is a specific, definite term, easily understood, legitimate, expressive and appropriate.

Trotting Equilibrium. A perfectly balanced action; the smooth, even gait of the horse when in rapid motion.

Trotting Families. There are six well defined, representative families of American trotters, viz: 1, Hambletonian; 2, Mambrino; 3, Clay; 4, Morgan; 5, Bashaw; 6, Pilot. Hambletonian was by Abdallah by Mambrino by imported Messenger. Mambrino, the greatest son of Messenger, was the founder of two of the noblest trotting families in all history, Mambrino Chief and Hambletonian, the latter standing at the head as the greatest of all trotting prgenitors. Henry Clay was by Andrew Jackson, by a son of an imported Barb. Justin Morgan was said to have been a son of True Briton, by a thoroughbred, Traveller. The Bashaw family is closely related to the Clays, having had a common ancestry in Young Bashaw, the sire of Andrew Jackson. The originator of the Pilot family was a famous black pacing horse, Pilot, from Canada, of unknown blood, a horse having great power to produce trotters out of running mares. From these sources have come a large number of sub-families—some of which are very famous and almost entitled to the distinction of being called families—which have become widely dispersed, each embracing many celebrated individuals. From the first we have the Volunteers, Abdallahs, Almonts, Messenger Durocs, Happy Hediums, Electioneers, Wilkeses and Dictators. From the second have came the Woodford Mambrinos, Clark Chiefs and Mambrino Patchens. From the third we have the George M. Patchens, Moors, Sultans and Cassius M. Clays. From the fourth we have the Lamberts, Morrills, Fearnaughts, Ethan Allens, Knoxes and Golddusts. From the fifth have descended the Long Island Black Hawks, Andrew Jacksons, Mohawks, and Greens Bashaws. From the last we have the well known families of pacing origin—the Copperbottoms, Royal Georges,

Hiatogas, Blue Bulls, Columbuses and Young Bashaws—which cannot be omitted from any list of the original trotting families of America. It is the province of the trotting and pacing registers and year books to record the pedigrees and performances of the progeny of these famous sires.

Trotting for Blood. When a horse is trotting hard and square, often against odds, he is said to be "trotting for blood;" to trot on merit.

The ringer has, in a few instances, by giving up blood money, apparently escaped, for a time, the vigilance of the legal authorities.— Wallace's Monthly.

Trotting Instinct. By animal instinct is understood the propensity of producing effects which appear to be those of reason and knowledge, because they apparently transcend the general intelligence or experience of the creature. Hence the term trotting instinct is held to mean the instinctive propensity of the colt to trot; the sum of all inherited qualities; the trotting bred colt trots because he represents the accumulated trotting instinct of many former generations of trotters. The term was first used in American turf literature in 1872.

The sedate brute on the road does not care whether another horse passes him or not; he hears a carriage behind him—it does not disturb him; he sees it pass him—it does not annoy him. Not so with the racer, or the roadster which may share his blood. He hears another wagon behind him—he is immediately interested: he sees it turn out to go by—he is more interested—he objects, and says, as plainly as horse can say, "No, you don't!" His ancestors have been bred for so many generations to get ahead and keep ahead, that it is with him an instinct, an innate passion born with him, an inherited part of his constitution, to not only go fast, but to go faster than his competitor.—Prof. W. H. Brewer, Yale University.

Trueing the Gait. The art of training the trotter in order to overcome any erratic gait or unbalanced action; to teach a horse to trot true and square.

Trustee. The first horse in America to trot twenty miles inside of one hour. "The incomparable Trustee," says Henry William Herbert in his "Horse of America." By imported Trustee, (imported into the United States in 1835), by Catton; dam, Fanny Pullen, foaled about 1835, bred by Sullivan Pullen, Augusta, Maine; by Winthrop Messenger, by imported Messenger. His celebrated race took place over the famous old Union Course, L. I., N. Y., Friday, October 20, 1848. In this race he hauled a driver weighing 145 pounds in a sulky weighing 150 pounds. Time: 59:35½.

The odds at starting were 100 to 40. The word "go" was given so vehemently that the horse broke, but he caught his step and never broke again throughout the whole performance. In trotting the ninth and tenth miles, the horse fell off a few seconds, and many persons thought that he was tiring; but judges remarked, as he passed the stand, that he was going perfectly at ease with ears playing. On the fifteenth mile the odds on time declined a little. On the seventeenth a horse was galloped by his side to encourage him; on the eighteenth it was even betting; on the nineteenth fifty to forty was offered on the horse. On commencing the twentieth mile his driver let the horse out, and he came in, apparently as fresh as when he started, doing his twentieth mile the fastest of the match in 2:51¼. In his stable an hour after the match he exhibited no distress, and on the following day was as fine as silk.—Horse and Horsemanship of the United States, Henry William Herbert.

Truss. A frame composed of two pieces, the top and bottom cords of which are connected by means of braces and stays, so that it shall be incapable of change by any turning of the bars or joints. Hence truss-axle, truss-shaft and truss-wheels are certain forms of these parts of the sulky in the construction of which the principle of the truss is applied.

Tug; Trace. The leather straps attached to the breastplate, which, connecting with the whippletree, are used for drawing the sulky or buggy.

Turf. This word came into use when horse racing in England, in the early days of the sport, literally took place on the turf; that is, on grass fields, sod or turf. But as racing became more and more technical they began to have definite tracks, or courses, and the word has remained, while the thing for which it stood has become obsolete. Hence, in England, as in this country, the word turf means racing, although it applies more especially to the running races, while the distinctive terms—running turf and trotting turf—are now generally used.

Turfite. An attendant upon races; one who is an authority on turf matters; a person familiar with horses, tracks, racing, records made, and all sports of the turf.

Turf Circle. The in-field, or ground within the circle of the course; persons who engage in racing—hence, the "turf circle" has the same meaning, applied to horsemen, as the term "court circle" or "legal circle" would, applied to the members of the legal profession.

Turf Law. A term which includes the enforcement of the rules of the trotting and running congresses, and the consideration of all cases of fine, suspension or expulsion of members, horses or individuals, which may come before the boards of appeals or review, for adjudication.

Turf law, in its best sense, should be rigidly enforced, by dispensing equal and exact justice to all, without fear, favor or affection.—Kentucky Stock Farm.

Turning a Horse. Every horse is said to have a strong and a weak side. In turning a horse, restive under the saddle, turn him on his weak side.

Turn-up. A sudden piece of luck. Bookmakers are said to have a "turn-up" when an unbacked horse wins.

Turrets. Circular metallic stays placed on each side of the saddle, through which the reins pass. See TERRETS.

Tushes; Tusks. The four canine teeth of the adult horse, corresponding exactly with the tusks of the boar, and the great corner teeth of the lion and dog; but in all the Equidæ they perform a very subordinate office, not being required either as a means of defence, or for the purpose of seizing prey. There are no temporary tushes in the horse, and in the mare they are either entirely absent or in a very rudimentary form.

Twenty-milers. Horses that have trotted twenty miles within one hour. Only six horses in the United States have ever performed this feat, viz: 1. Trustee, ch. g. by imported Trustee; dam, Fanny Pullen, Union Course, Long Island, N. Y., October 20, 1848, 59:35½. 2. Lady Fulton, b. m., breeding unknown, Centreville, Long Island, N. Y., July 12, 1855, 59:55. 3. Captain McGowan, ro. h., breeding unknown, Boston, Mass., October 31, 1865, 58:25. 4. John Stewart, b. g. by Tom Wonder, pacer; dam, by Hambletonian, (Harris'), Oakland, California, April 4, 1868, 59:23. 5. Mattie Howard, ch. m., breeding unknown, San Francisco, California, December 7, 1871, 59:30½. 6. Controller, b. g., by Gen. Taylor, by the Morse Horse, San Francisco, California, April 20, 1878, (to wagon), 58:57.

Two-forty-eight, and one-half. The first recorded time of a mile made in less than three minutes, in this country, was by the Boston horse, at Philadelphia, Pa., in August, 1870, in 2:48½.

Two-in-three. A race of heats best two in three, in which a horse winning two heats, or distancing the field, wins the race.

Two-pluck-one. A term used to describe a jockey's or driver's trick, by which one horse may be sent ahead to set the pace and tire a contending horse with which he may be quite evenly matched, when, at the right time, a third horse which has been trailing and is comparatively fresh, is sent along to measure strides and take the lead. Thus, in nearly every instance, two horses can tire and vanquish a third, even though he may have several seconds the advantage in speed and endurance.

Two-ten, (2:10). Twenty-three trotters have trotted in 2:10 or better, since Maud S. was first to enter the list in

1884, when she got a record of 2:09¼; and since 1883, when Johnston was the first to enter the pacing 2:10 list, it has a total of thirty-four pacers in 2:10, or better. This is to the close of 1893.

Two Thousand Guineas. An important fixed event of the English turf, inaugurated in 1809, and run annually since that date. It is the opening three-year-old event of the year, and is open to both colts and fillies. Run over the Rowley mile at Newmarket, a distance of one mile and eleven yards.

Two-thirty, (2:30). All performances carrying an animal into the 2:30 list for the first time, must be made at a regular meeting, under control of the executive officers of tracks which are members of the National or American trotting associations, where stakes, purses or premiums have been duly opened and advertised. "Regular meeting" is a term used as opposite to that of a special meeting, called only for the purpose of giving a horse a record. These regulations apply to matches, as well as to all other trotting performances. To the close of 1893 ten thousand trotters and two thousand pacers held records of 2:30, or better.

Two-twenty, (2:20). To the close of 1893 the two-twenty list contained a total of one thousand and eight animals.

T. Y. C. [Eng.] Letters meaning the two-year-old course. It is a short course, not shorter than five-eighths, nor longer than three-fourths of a mile.

As chasers many of them that have been looked on as T. Y. C. animals stay with ease for three miles or more, with a turn of speed for the home run.—The Badminton Library: Racing, The Earl of Suffolk and Berkshire, and W. G. Craven.

Tympany. Acute gastric indigestion, or intestinal colic.

U

Under Saddle. A term used to denote a running race; a race in which jockeys ride on horseback.

Ungual Phalanx. The single terminal bone of the horse's foot; the last joint of his toe; the hoof.

Union Course. A famous race course on Long Island, New York, formed in 1821, and discontinued in 1888. Here, in 1823, the celebrated race took place between the great Henry, the "pride of the South," and American Eclipse, in the presence of fifty thousand people. Henry won the first, and Eclipse the second and third heats. In 1842 the New Jersey mare, Fashion, beat the Virginia horse, Boston, on this course. Dexter's first race was over this course. Many of Flora Temple's triumphs were achieved here, and here she twice defeated George M. Patchen. Here Ethan Allen ran for stallion honors; here George Wilkes' first victory was achieved, and here he defeated Lady Thorne and American Girl.

Unit. The action of each limb of the horse when in motion or in propulsion, is said to be a "unit."

Unknown. A term used in a pedigree signifying that the particular sire or dam to which it refers was of unknown breeding; an element of uncertain quality in a horse's pedigree. Each animal has two parents, four grandparents, and, in theory, at least, eight, sixteen, thirty-two ancestors, each generation of ancestors doubling. Now, in plotting a pedigree, especially of any of the older thoroughbred horses, many of the diverging branches of ancestry will end in "unknown"— oftener in regard to a dam than a sire. As an instance, it may be mentioned that in the pedigree of old Eclipse foaled in 1764, and who lived till near the end of the century, (doubtless the most celebrated horse of his day), if one traces it back he will soon come upon twelve unknown dams. It is claimed by many expert authorities that these unknown dams are a source of great strength and vitality to a pedigree.

Unplaced. Having no position; a horse not winning any part of a purse is said to be "unplaced."

Pathfinder ran unplaced for the Derby of 1840.—The Badminton Library: Racing, The Earl of Suffolk and Berkshire, and W. G. Craven.

Unsoundness. Any deviation from nature. That horse is unsound which labors under disease, or that has some alteration of structure which does interfere, or is likely to interfere, with his natural usefulness. Unsoundness is classed under three heads: 1. Absolute unsoundness—those cases wherein there can be no question either from a veterinary or legal standpoint. 2. Relative unsoundness, or defects which may not be unsoundness, according to circumstances, such as their nature and position, the age of the animal and the nature of the work demanded of it. 3. Hereditary unsoundness, or those cases of well-defined transmission to offspring. A list of diseases and other alterations of structure causing unsoundness, is given: Asthma; blindness; bog spavin; bone spavin; broken wind; catarrh, (nasal gleet); capped hock; capped knee; cough; curb; corns; canker; contracted feet; cribbing; cutting; eczema, (mange); farcy; false quarter; founder; glanders; grease; groggy gait; heaves, (broken wind); knees bent forward; knuckling with the pastern joint, or joints; laminitis, (founder); navicular disease; ophthalmia; paralysis; poll evil; pumice sole; quidding; quittor; rheumatism; ringbone, (if near the heels so as to alter the flexibility of the cartilage); roaring; sand crack; stringhalt, (when due to diseased nerve); splint; swollen knees; shying, (if from diseased eyes); strangles; stumbling, (occasioned by inflammation of the foot); thorough pin; thick wind; thrush; wind galls; wind sucking, (in later stages when it affects the digestive organs); whistling; weakness of sinews; wounds, (till cured). In addition to this list the following notes are given: When the use of a bar or round shoe is constantly required for corns, sand crack or thrush, its use is an evidence of unsoundness; long pasterns, which indicate an unnatural elongation of the tendons, are evidence of unsoundness; a wen upon the windpipe, or upon a main vein or artery, is an unsoundness; if the frog is so altered in structure as to be perpetually tender, it is an unsoundness; soft enlargements upon the limbs, during formation, and until their result is known, are an unsoundness; a distended, bulky, unnaturally large stomach, or barrel, is often an indication of dropsy, and in such cases is an unsoundness; in case medicine is required, until the effects of the medicine are removed it constitutes an unsoundness; every species of lameness and tenderness is an unsoundness, until removed; a horse may be serviceable without being absolutely sound.

[Law.] The question of unsoundness is a mixed question of law and fact.—Massachusetts Reports, 8 Gray, 1861, p. 432.

The rule of unsoundness is, that if, at the time of the sale, the horse has any disease which actually does diminish the natural usefulness of the animal, so as to make him less capable of work of any description, or which, in its ordinary progress, will diminish the natural usefulness of the animal; or if the horse has, either from disease or accident, undergone any alteration of structure, that either does at the time, or in its ordinary effects will diminish the natural usefulness of the horse, such horse is unsound.

Unsteady. Said of a horse that is good and solid against time, but behaves bad in company.

Untried. By the early racing rules an untried stallion or mare was one whose get or produce had never run in public. The Turf Congress rules now say: "An untried horse is one that has not produced a winner before and up to any certain specified time."

Up. A horse is said to be "up" in a heat when he breaks; the word is also used to denote a horse that is beaten, as, "it is all up with him; he's up," that is, he is done.

Up in Your Arms. An expression used by drivers meaning that the horse of which it is said is prompt; alert; always responsive; "up and dressed;" ready; "right up in your arms."

Up to Weight, means that a driver is just the weight required by the rules of the trotting turf, viz: One hundred and fifty pounds.

Used. A term synonymous with aged, and indicates the time when the horse has become prematurely old.

V

Valve-stem. A small metal tube inserted through the felloe of a bicycle sulky wheel through which to pump air into the pneumatic tire by means of an air pump.

Van. A large covered, or enclosed wagon. The first recorded instance, in the history of the English turf, of a race horse being transported to the course, was in 1836, when Elis, owned by Lord Lichfield, was safely conveyed from Danebury to Doncaster in a large van which had been constructed for the purpose of carrying show cattle, the wheels of which were about eighteen inches high. It was drawn by four fast horses. The horse won the St. Leger the odds being ten thousand to one. In 1837 Crucifix and San-volatile were vanned from Danebury to Newmarket. About 1840 horses first began to be conveyed by rail in England.

Vanner. [Eng.] A term used to describe the van, or express horse of London and other large English cities. A horse weighing 1,300 to 1,400 pounds, and standing 15.3 to 16 hands high, strong built, with good flat bones and sound feet, having bold, free action. A near approach to the standard van horse would be a cross between a Cleveland Bay, or Coach stallion, and a cross bred, or grade draft mare. The vans used in London, Liverpool and Glasgow are two-wheeled spring wagons, used where the dray is regarded as too slow or cumbersome. Van horses take a load of a ton to a ton and a half, trotting with it at a fair trot most of the time, unless the grade is very heavy.

Vault. To vault into the saddle is a feat often performed by skillful riders who have long practiced it. Standing on the ground facing the near or left side of the horse, the left hand is placed on the pommel of the saddle, and with a single leap or bound the rider gains his seat in an instant. See STIRRUP.

Vehicle. Any carriage moving on land by means of horses, either on wheels or runners.

V. S. These letters, after the name of a person, mean that the man whose name is given is a veterinary surgeon.

entitled, from having taken a diploma at a veterinary college, to so use them.

Vet. A term, for short, given to an unlearned country horse doctor.

Veterinary; Veterinarian. The surgical or medical treatment of domestic animals, especially the horse; one who practices the science of veterinary medicine and surgery.

Veterinary Schools. The first veterinary school in the world was established at La Guillatière, near Lyons, France, by Claude Bourgelot, in 1762; and by a royal order dated June 30, 1764, King Louis XV. gave to this institution the title of the "Royal Veterinary School." The second school in France was established at Alfort in 1765. The veterinary institute at Vienna, Austria, was opened in 1767. The Royal Veterinary School at Brussels, Belgium, was established in 1832. Russia has three veterinary institutes, one each at Kharkov, Dorpot and Kazan, all maintained and regulated by the government. The Royal Danish Veterinary School at Copenhagen was founded in 1773. The first veterinary school in Sweden was founded at Skara, in 1726. The Royal Veterinary School at Stuttgart, Germany, was established in 1796; and there are also veterinary schools at Hanover and Munich. The Veterinary Institute at Berlin was founded in 1786. The Royal Veterinary College, London, England, was founded by St. Bell, a Frenchman, in 1792. The Ontario Veterinary College was established in 1862; and the Montreal Veterinary College in 1866. In this country veterinary colleges have been established as follows: American, New York, 1875; Harvard University, Cambridge, Mass., 1882; Chicago, Illinois, 1883; University of Pennsylvania, 1885; Cincinnati, Ohio; Des Moines, Iowa; Kansas City, Missouri, 1892; United States, Washington, D. C.; McKillop, Chicago, Ill.; Cornell University, Ithaca, N. Y., 1894.

Vice. An imperfection in a horse; something more than a fault or blemish; a bad trick. A horse free from vice is one having no bad habits that make him dangerous, or that are injurious to his health, or that in any way diminish his natural usefulness.

The longer I live the more fully I am convinced that vice in a horse signifies cruelty on the part of man. Vice forms no part of a horse's normal condition.—Horse and Man, Rev. J. G. Wood.

A vice is a bad habit, and a habit to constitute a vice must either be shown by the temper of the horse so as to make him dangerous or diminish his natural usefulness, or it must be a habit decidedly injurious to his health.—American and English Law Encyclopædia.

List of vices in the horse: Aversion to special objects; backing when harnessed in a carriage; balking, (when so fixed as to become a bad habit); bolting, (when caused by defective sight it is an unsoundness); biting; boring; buck-jumping; cribbing, crib-biting, (where it has not yet resulted in a fixed disease, or caused a change of structure, in which case it is an unsoundness); chucking up the head; disagreeable to approach; disagreeable to groom; difficult to harness; difficult to mount; difficult to shoe; eating the bedding, (leading to impaired health); gibbing; getting loose from the headstall; hanging back in the halter; halter-casting; hard mouth; inveterate rolling: kicking; leaping into the manger; mischievous or decidedly capricious temper; pawing in the stable; propping; rearing; restiveness, (uneasiness); running when in harness; shying from nervousness, (if from disease in the eyes it is an unsoundness); skittishness; striking with the fore feet; stopping suddenly; starting or jumping when harnessed before the driver is ready; weaving; wind-sucking.

Vulcanized Rubber. The substance of which the pneumatic tire of a bicycle sulky is made. The caoutchouc is incorporated with sulphur and subjected to a strong heat whereby it combines chemically with the sulphur and assumes, on cooling, a hard consistency much resembling that of horn.

W

W. This letter, in connection with the names of horses in summaries of races, and in the trotting and pacing registers, indicates that the race was to wagon.

Wagon, in turf language, always refers to what is known as a skeleton.

Wagon Trotting. World's record to the close of 1893. One mile: Guy, bl. g. by Kentucky Prince, dam, Flora Gardner by American Star, (14), 1893, against time, 2.13. Two miles: Dexter, br. g. by Hambletonian, dam, Clara, by American Star, 1865, against time, 4:56¼. Three miles: Longfellow, (pacer), ch. g. by Red Bill, dam unknown, 1868, (in a race), 7:53. Five miles: Longfellow, (pacer), ch. g. by Red Bill, dam unknown, (in a race), 1870, 14:15. Ten miles: Julia Aldrich, ch. m., breeding unknown, (in a race), 1858, 29:04¼.

Waist. The narrowest part of the seat of a saddle—about midway between the pommel and cantle.

Waiting. A waiting race; not forcing the race at the start; the practice of running slowly at the start of a race allowing the horses to lead, to see how the other horses are going. It is sometimes a good rule to wait. The rider can see how the horses are going and then can remain for the present where he is, or go in front. Again most horses go better and settle down in their gallop sooner with a lead than without one.

Waiting in Front. A term used in running races where the driver is obliged to wait in the front lead, on account of having a horse that cannot be kept behind without more being taken out of him than the extra speed would do were he allowed to go freely. This is to be understood as saying that the rider should merely keep in front without forcing the running on his own account, and should simply conform to the pace of those immediately behind him, until the moment arrives for him to make his effort. But he should never keep back at the risk of fighting for the finish.

The art of waiting in front is a great one to learn; for if occasion should arise, it may often be practiced with the utmost advantage.—The Badminton Library: Racing, The Earl of Suffolk and Berkshire, and W. G. Craven.

I have often seen men in running and trotting races both make a very serious mistake, particularly in riding or driving what we call a waiting race. Always remember that some other man may have the tools to do just as well with, as you can.—Life with the Trotters, John Splan.

Waive Weight and Distance. To waive weight and distance in a race is to mutually disregard the rules; to go at catch weight. It is often said that a race is under National rules "waiving weight and distance." But no race under the rules can be so made. A race either conforms to the rules or it does not; if any particular rule is waived no one can be enforced.

Walk. The slowest pace of the horse; an elementary act of progression is a step, a series of steps is the walk; that pace in which one foot is not raised until its fellow is upon the ground, and in which the horse always has two feet upon the ground at the same time, (whereas in the trot there is always a space of time, of greater or less duration, in which all the feet are off the ground), while the diagonal ones are being advanced. A fast walk is the most valuable gait a horse can acquire for general business purposes, and it has a great part to perform in fitting a horse for rapid locomotion. Youatt relates, in his work on the horse, that in 1793 a Hackney mare named Sloven, travelled at a walk the distance of twenty-two miles in three hours and fifty-two seconds.

When the horse quickens his walk he does not at once change his pace but extends his strides and makes them more uniform, until further extension becomes difficult when he will break into a trot in which there are never more than two feet upon the ground at a time.— The Horse in Motion, J. D. B. Stillman.

Walk-over. A walk-over is a race in which all the contestants but one fail to appear. In order for him to win the race it is necessary for him to go the whole distance prescribed; but as there is nothing to compete against him he may walk the entire distance if he chooses. By the racing rules a walk-over by any horse entitles him to only one half of the added money in stakes. The trotting rules award no purse or added money for a walk-over; but in a stake race a walk-over is entitled to all the stake money and forfeit, unless the conditions provide otherwise.

Wall-eye. A horse is said to have a wall-eye when the iris, (that part of the eye by which the light admitted to the retina is regulated), is of a light or white color.

Wall of the Foot. That portion of the front and sides of the horse's foot extending from the coronet, (the border-line where the skin joins the hoof), in an oblique direction, to the ground; the crust; the natural bearing part of the

19

foot. **It is upon the wall** that the shoe rests, and through it the nails confining it are driven. The wall is deepest in front, and diminishes toward the quarters and heels, becoming thinner; while at its angles of inflection, (the points of the heels), it is strong. The wall is fibrous, the fibres passing directly parallel to each other from the coronet to the ground, each fibre being moulded on, as fast as secreted, by one of the minute tufts of blood vessels lodged in the cavity at the coronet.

Warming-up Heat. An exercise previous to a race; a jogging heat between a real heat; a test of speed to bring a horse to his best edge.

Warranty. [Law.] A general or express warrant is an unconditional undertaking that the horse is really what the warrantor professes it to be. In the United States, says the American and English Encyclopædia of Law, there is always an implied contract that the vendor, (seller), has a right to dispose of the article which he sells. A general warrant is an unconditional undertaking, therefore, that a horse really is what the warrantor professes it to be. There is no particular form of words necessary to constitute a warranty. A warrant may be qualified—as if the vendor says, "I never warrant, but he is sound as far as I know." In this case an action for breach can be maintained if it can be proved that the seller *knew* the horse was unsound. A warranty may be limited as to time, as, for instance, "after twenty-four hours I do not warrant." The seller of a horse in making warranty may except some defect of which he knows, or he may expressly state in what particulars only, he warrants the animal. A general warranty does not cover obvious defects in a horse; being such they are plain to the buyer and require no skill to detect. But if the purchaser suspects a defect and wishes to examine and try the horse, but the seller objects and says, "I will warrant him," he is liable for the defect. Where, however, there is no opportunity of inspecting, *caveat emptor* does not apply. If a man not knowing the age of a horse, but having a written pedigree which he received with him, sell a horse of the age stated in the pedigree, at the same time stating he knows nothing of him but what he learned from the pedigree, he is not liable to an action when it is shown that the pedigree is false.

Warrant; Warranty. To make good a statement or bargain; a certificate that a horse is as represented. It is not requisite that a warranty should be in writing, even though a written receipt is given for the money. In Allen vs. Pink—a celebrated English case—the receipt did not include any terms of sale, and the buyer proved a verbal warranty. The warranty of a horse does not go forward, but back from the time of its date. The following is a good form of warranty:

Hammond's Grove, Me., April 30, 1894. Received this day of George Cony, five hundred dollars for a bay mare called Lida, by Cushnoc, dam by Glenarm, warranted six years old and under seven, sound in wind and limb, free from vice, and quiet to drive. Eugene H. Smith.

Wartles. Sitfasts resulting from saddle galls on the back of a horse.

Wash-ball Seat. [Eq.] A seat in riding disregarding all balance.

Washer. An iron or leather collar fitted to the end of an axle-tree against which the wheel wears to prevent friction and retain the oil.

Washy. A horse that perspires over-freely after slight exertion or little exercise, is said to be "washy," a "washy horse." In some cases the question has been raised that a horse habitually washy was unsound, but it has not been so held.

I have often heard people say that Rarus was a weak and washy horse. I don't think that needs any denial, as his performances are the strongest arguments against it.—Life with the Trotters, John Splan.

Water-hook. A metallic hook placed in the center of the saddle of a harness, between the terrets, for the purpose of holding the check-rein in place.

Water-jump. [Eng.] A jump over a brook or ditch in the steeplechase course. A jump very safe and easy if the taking-off and landing are firm and sound; but difficult and dangerous if level, marshy, soft and cut up by cattle drinking at its sides. With firm turf to take-off from and land upon a horse has repeatedly cleared thirty feet; but twelve feet of a brimming brook will stop the best part of a large field.

Weak Foot. Any weakness of the foot, the result of disease causing a change of structure, is an unsoundness.

Weak Sinews. When sinews at the back of the fore legs become thickened, between the knee and the pastern joint, producing weakness or irritation, it is an unsoundness.

Weaving. A continuous motion of the head, neck and body, from side to side, like the shuttle of a weaver passing through the web—hence the name given to this peculiar, incessant and unpleasant action of the horse. It indicates an impatient, irritable temper, and a dislike to the confinement of the stall. A horse that is a weaver will seldom carry flesh well, and is unpleasant to ride or drive. The habit is a serious vice.

Web of a Shoe. The main bar or body of the horse-shoe; the entire rim; that part which rests upon, or is fitted to the wall of the foot.

Weeding-out Sale. A sale in which the breeder, wishing to dispose of a part of his stud, weeds out animals that are good and sound, but which, for one reason or another he does not wish to breed from, and places them at a public sale.

Weights. By the rules of the New York Trotting Club, in 1841, every trotting horse that started in a race, whether match, purse or stake, was obliged to carry 145 pounds, the weight of the vehicle not to be considered. In 1844 the rules of the New York Jockey Club were: Two years old, a feather; three years old, 90 pounds; four years old, 104 pounds; five years old, 114 pounds; six years old, 121 pounds; seven years and upwards, 126 pounds. An allowance of three pounds was made to mares, fillies and geldings. By the present rules of the Turf Congress, a feather weight is 75 pounds; and in all races, except steeplechases, the limit may be said to be 130 pounds. But in all races exclusively for two-year olds, the weight is 118 pounds; and in races exclusively for three-year olds, the weight is 122 pounds. In trotting races—National and American rules—to wagon or in harness, the weight is 150 pounds; and under saddle, (the saddle and whip only, to be weighed with the rider), 145 pounds.

Weights. Extra attachments to the shoe or foot of the horse to correct the action, balance the gait, or overcome structural defects of motion. Weights are fastened to the toe and also to the sides of the hoof; while more frequently the extra weight required is wrought into the web of the shoe in the particular place where it is needed, so that the shoe becomes the extra weight. These weights vary from two to eight ounces, and frequently are as heavy as twelve ounces.

Weight-bearers. The fore legs of the horse as distinguished from the propellers, or hind legs. Dr. William Fearnley, a celebrated English veterinarian, was the first to class the fore legs as the weight bearers, and the hind legs as the propellers. He fixed the coffin-joint as the focus of weight in the foot, and decided that if the foot be either too high or too low at the heel, or if the proper angle of the ground surface with the line of the coronet be changed, the focus of weight will be disturbed, (or in other words will be thrown too far backward or forward), hence the importance of keeping the foot properly leveled was apparent. Mr. Marvin says he is not entirely sure whether in the trotting horse the fore leg has strictly no other function than weight-bearing; but Prof. Stillman says that in both actions, that of weight bearer and also of propeller, the fore leg does more than its share. M. Baucher, the eminent French savant, is also authority for the statement that the weight borne by the anterior and posterior extremities, as determined by placing them upon different weighing machines, was as 210 for the former to 174 for the latter, the total weight of the horse being 850 pounds.

Weight-carrier; Weight-puller. A term meaning, generally, a horse capable of carrying more than the required weight for his age or class, and yet maintaining the extreme of his speed; one pulling, in a race, a driver who is overweight; a horse that is handicapped, as, "Nelson was handicapped by the twenty pounds overweight of his owner, who drove him." Mr. Marvin utters a self-evident truth when he says: "Other things being equal, the horse that carries the least weight will stay better, go faster and remain sounder than the weight-carriers." The weight-carrying power of the race horse depends upon these particular points of conformation: 1. Length and obliquity of shoulder blade; 2, strong loin muscles; 3, good substance and fine quality of bone; 4, pasterns not too sloping; 5, absence of undue weight of body beyond that which would be necessary for the movements of the limbs, and for the performance of the various vital functions.

Weight-cloths. Loaded saddle cloths used in racing. They are fitted with pockets, and made to carry different weights, with the amount of each marked on the inside, from four to twenty-five pounds. It is said that Lord George Bentinck, the great English turfman, had a large number of saddle cloths exactly alike excepting in weight, by means of which weights from four to sixty pounds could be carried. The sheet lead forming the weights should be covered with wash leather; and the weight-cloths should be put on well forward, the leads being equally distributed on each side.

Weight for Age. The standard weight apportioned to horses according to their ages; a standard used only in races where the different ages can start, special weights being fixed for races in which only horses of the same age may start. Weight is not only based upon age, but on the distance to be run, and as the year passes away the horses grow older and the weight is increased. Thus, as an example, a three-year-old which carries, at a half mile, 104 pounds in January, would be weighted 106 in February; 107 in March; 109 in April; 110 in May; 111 in June; 113 in July; 115 in August; 116 in September, and 117 in October, November and December.

Weight-pocket. A receptacle in a horse's boot for receiving weight for the purpose of balancing the action. Used instead of toe or side weights upon the foot, or a weighted shoe. The material used for weight is usually sheet lead, or shot. A boot so fitted is called a weighted or leaded boot.

Weighing in, and Weighing Out, is required of all jockeys and drivers; weighing out at the start, weighing in at the finish of the heat or race. The Turf Congress rules require that horses must bring in within two pounds of the weight taken out. It is said that drivers will very often shrink from two to two and a half or three pounds in driving a hard, hotly contested race.

Well-bred. A term often used in describing a horse, but one having no real significance or value; nor does it increase the worth of the animal. An attested pedigree is the only recognized evidence of merit in the breeding of a horse that possesses added value.

Welcher. A race-course swindler who makes bets, takes the money if he wins and absconds if he loses. Originated from the nursery rhyme:

"Taffy was a Welshman, Taffy was a thief."

Welter; Welter Weight. To lap over. A welter weight is 28 pounds added to weight for age; and a " heavy welter " is 40 pounds added to weight for age. It is understood that this weight took its name from a place in Ireland, much frequented during the earlier history of the English turf.

In welters we impose penalties on professional jocks, because we know that they have been trained in a certain school; whereas we have no standard of comparison for gentleman riders.—Seats and Saddles, Francis Dwyer.

Wen. A wen on the upper part of the windpipe, or upon a main artery or vein, is an unsoundness; but on other parts as on the top of the hock, (capped hock), elbow, or place of little consequence, it is a blemish.

Went to Pieces. Said of a horse that breaks, is unsteady and unmanageable in a race; as, " in the third heat Hector, driven by Vet Witham, went to pieces in bad shape."

Wheels. With the use of the pneumatic tire for sulkys a specialty at once came into track vehicle manufacture—that of the making of wheels to be attached to the high sulky, to convert it into a "bike." These wheels are constructed of both steel and wood, are from 26 to 28 inches in height, weigh from 14 to 16 pounds per pair, and are made in a variety of patterns. The rims are of steel, cold rolled, or of wood; the hubs are of steel; the spokes are of both wood and steel; the ball or roller bearings are inclosed in recesses or cones in each end of the hub, and adjusted by means of a spanner wrench, these cones being dust and water proof; the pneumatic tire being fitted securely to the rim.

Whims of the horse are bad or vicious habits; faults. They are: Lolling the tongue, doubling it up, or constantly protruding it from the mouth; striking the lower lip against the upper one; rubbing the lower extremity of the head against the manger; rubbing the tail against surrounding objects; shaking the head up and down, or jerking the reins, when being driven; grasping the branches of the bit with the lower lip; tearing the blanket with the teeth; resting one hind foot upon the other; lying down cow-fashion; stripping the halter; pawing in the stable.

Whip. A name applied to a noted driver or reinsman; as " Mr. Thayer was a great whip in his day."

Whip. A light hand implement used in driving, riding, correcting or educating horses. The trotting rules prescribe the following lengths to be used in races: For saddle horses, 2 ft. 10 in.; sulkies, 4 ft. 8 in.; wagons, 5 ft. 10 in.; double teams, 8 ft. 6 in.; tandems and four-in-hands, unlimited. A snapper not longer than three inches is allowed in addition to the above mentioned lengths. The running rules limit the weight of a whip at one pound, but do not regulate its length.

The whip and spur, injudiciously used, have lost many races.—How to Train the Race-horse, Lieut. Col. Warburton.

The whip is to be kept very much in the background while you are cultivating confidence in your horse. It is more likely to prove an obstacle than an aid.—The Trotting Horse of America, Hiram Woodruff.

The whip should never be picked up before the last thirty or forty yards, nor should more than two or three cuts be given. When a jockey begins to flog two or three hundred yards from home, we need not be surprised at seeing his horse, after answering the call for ten or a dozen strides, go slower and slower as he nears the judge's box. During a race, hold the whip with the lash down, and the jockey should strike his horse nowhere except just behind the girth.

Whip-hand. [Eq.] The right hand.

Whip-spur. A spur attached to the thumb-button on the stock of a sulky whip, to be used in urging the horse, if necessary, at the finish of a race. It is adjustable and may be removed should the driver desire.

Whip Training. The method of some horse trainers of driving a horse without bit, line or reins, simply by the motions of the whip. It illustrates the beauty and simplicity of man's power over this magnificent animal, and the high degree of intelligence which he possesses. The method is acquired by the horse in from four to six weeks' practice.

Whipping his Boot. A trick of the jockey for the purpose of deluding his opponent. It is tried by the rider of the speedier horse in the hope of inducing the rider of a stayer to slacken speed from the idea that he has the race in hand, and that there is no use in hurrying.

Whippletree. The bar to which the traces, or tugs of a harness are fastened, and by which the sulky or buggy is drawn.

Whirlbone; round-bone; trochanter. The hip joint. Relied upon by all experts as a standard point for measurement of the exterior conformation of the horse.

Whisperer, The. The name by which Con Sullivan, of County Cork, Ireland, was known all over Great Britain. He was a most extraordinary person, who possessed great power over vicious horses, subduing them by whispering in their ear. He tamed the vicious horse, Rainbow, owned by Col. Westenra, and Mr. Wholey's horse, King Pippin, in 1804, the latter a terribly savage beast. With the latter horse The Whisperer was shut up in his stable all night, but in the morning the horse would follow him like a dog, obeying every word instantly, allowing persons to put their hand in his mouth, and standing as gentle as a lamb. How he obtained this wonderful command over the horse has never been known.

Whistler. A horse that breathes hard. Whistling is one of the variations of sound emitted by a horse known as a roarer. It is legal unsoundness.

He therefore excited plenty of bidding when put up for sale afterwards, and although a "whistler," is worth the five hundred and twenty guineas at which he was knocked down.—London Field.

White, as a color in horses, is popularly indicative of weakness, and horses of this color are also believed to be slow, lymphatic, and deficient in energy and vital courage. They are easily soiled, difficult to keep clean, and are said to be more liable to pink-eye and similar diseases than horses of solid color.

White-boned. A family of pure, milk white horses in Germany. They are foaled pure white, and most of them are wall-eyed, or glass eyed. They are of good size, uniform in color, and have been in-bred for a long series of years.

White Horse of Berkshire, Scouring of the. The "vale of the white horse" is located between Abingdon and Uffington, in the county of Berks, England. It takes its name from a massive figure of a galloping horse rudely chiseled on the side of a steep chalk hill, 893 feet high. The figure is about 374 feet in length, and can be seen at a distance of ten or twelve miles in a fair day when the sun is shining upon it. Tradition attributes its cutting to King Alfred, and regards it as a monument of the victory won by him over the Danes in the great battle of Ashdown in 871. He is said to have carved a horse, rather than any other object, because that was the device borne on the Saxon standard. As, in the course of time, the trench which forms the figure of the horse would naturally become grown over, the people living in the vicinity have a custom of meeting, each year, on a certain day, for the purpose of "scouring," or cleaning it This day is made the occasion of a festival, at which manly games and sports are indulged in for prizes. Hence the term, "scouring of the white horse," which has become classic through the story of Mr. Thomas Hughes, the English novelist.

Whoa. A word which is the only safeguard in many cases of accident. It should never be used in the education or handling of horses, excepting when the horse is in motion, and you wish him to stop. Do not use it generally, and on every occasion—as on entering the horse's stall and you wish him to stand over, or when harnessing him and he is restive. For all these instances have other and significant words; but have the horse so educated that when you are driving, in case the rein, or bit, or breeching strap should break, or anything else be out of place, he would instantly stop at the word "whoa." It is not difficult to so teach him, and when under complete discipline in this respect his value is increased tenfold for all road, driving or speed purposes. In the old days of racing some drivers taught their horses to increase their speed at the loud shouting of the words "whoa, whoa!" (for the purpose of breaking up other horses on the back stretch), but the days of such methods in driving have, happily, passed away forever.

Win in a Canter. An easy finish in a running race. To "win in a canter" is to so far distance the other horses in the field, that urging at the end of the race is needless, and one can come home at an easy jog.

Winners' Handicap. Weights for a race of winning horses. Thus, the winning horses of previous races being pitted together in a race royal, are first handicapped according to their respective merits; the horse that has won three races has to carry a greater weight than the horse that has won only two; and this latter more than its competitor, who is winner of a single race only.

Winning a Heat. In heats of one, two, three or four miles, a horse not winning one heat in three cannot start for a fourth, unless he has made a dead heat. In heats best three in five, a horse not winning a heat in the first five is not entitled to start for a sixth, unless he has made a dead heat— but these horses thus ruled out have a right to a share of the premium, or purse, according to their rank at the close of their last heat.

Winning Horse. A horse must win a majority of the heats which are required by the conditions of a race, to be entitled to the stake or purse; but if he distances all competitors in one heat, the race is terminated and he receives the entire purse or stakes contended for, unless the special conditions of the race provide otherwise.

Winning Sires. Stallions, the producers of horses that have been great winners in the races of the year; or which have put the largest number of sons and daughters within the low-record lists.

Winnings. The sums of money in stakes, purses and premiums won by a horse in races during a year or a series of years. Thus: The winnings of Eclipse during his life-time are said to have amounted to $125,000; King Herod is said to have won a total of over £200,000; Ormonde won for his owner, the Duke of Westminster, nearly $145,000; Domino won as a two-year-old, in a single year, $176,730.

Winchester. The famous war-horse of Gen. P. H. Sheridan. He was foaled in 1858 near Grand Rapids, Michigan. He came into Gen. Sheridan's possession in 1862, and went through the Mississippi campaign, and was afterwards transferred to the Army of the Potomac, going through numerous engagements. In 1863 he carried his master in the celebrated ride from Winchester to Cedar Creek, Va., a distance of twenty miles, keeping in advance of the General's staff and escort the whole distance. Winchester went through between eighty-five and ninety battles, and was wounded three times. He died at Chicago, Ill., October 2, 1878.

Wind. The breath of a horse. "Sound of wind," in a warranty, means that the horse warranted has no disease or imperfection in his windpipe, larynx or bronchi, (air passages), like grunting, high-blowing, thick wind or whistling.

Windage. The resistance to the air of any body passing through it at a rapid rate. A term much used in connection with the description and testing of different kinds of sulky wheels.

Wind-galls; Wind-puffs. The name given to soft, puffy bunches the size of a hickory nut, which frequently occur on the fore leg at the upper part of the fetlock joint, between the tendon and the shin bone. They occasionally develop on the hind leg. The joints and tendons at these parts are furnished with sacs filled with a lubricating substance known as synovia, and when these sacs become over-distended with this fluid it produces wind-puffs, or wind-galls. Hunters, hurdle racers and trotters with excessive knee action, are all predisposed to this form of injury. Complete rest will generally effect a cure.

Wind-split. Broken wind.

Wind-sucker. A term applied to a horse having the heaves. Wind-sucking renders the horse unsound.

Wings. The projecting ends at the heel of a shoe, bent forward and inward, to rest on the bars of the foot.

Winkers. The side pieces of a blind bridle.

Wire-edge. When a horse is in high fettle, is rank for a race and in the highest condition to do his best at speed, he is said to be " wire-edged."

If your horse is particularly rank, work him alone until you get the wire-edge off him, then take your prompter and show him that he is not going to be hurt.—Life with the Trotters, John Splan.

Wire, The. Home; the score; a goal in a trotting race; to " come under the wire first," is to win the heat.

Wire Snaffle. Explained by the quotation:

A fancy bit, worthy of only a junk-shop.—The Bridle Bits, Col. J. C. Battersby.

Wiring-in. A peculiar form of contraction affecting the fore feet, and occasionally the hind feet of horses. In most cases it is the inside heel which contracts, and when this occurs the horse is said to " wire in."

Withers. The bony ridge which is the forward continuation of the back. Its posterior limit runs into that of the back in a gradual manner; its anterior termination ends abruptly at the crest; at its sides the shoulders meet.

W. O. Following the name of a horse in the trotting and pacing records, means a walk-over.

Wobble. An unsteady gait; the warning of a break. Mr. Splan, in describing one of his races with Rarus, says: " He went steadily true all the way to the head of the stretch, and there he made a wobble, as though he was going to break." Mr. Marvin describes a race between Rarus and Goldsmith Maid, in which Budd Doble had said that the mare was " wobbling throughout the entire heat," and Mr. Splan replied, " Well, she has wobbled as good a mile as ever she did in her life." This instance is believed to be the only one in trotting annals in which a horse "wobbled" during the entire heat.

Woodruff, Hiram Washington. Born at Birmingham, N. J., February 22, 1817; died at Jamaica Plains, Long Island, N. Y., March 15, 1867. He trained and drove Flora Temple, Dutchman, Topgallant, Paul Pry, Lady Suffolk, Ajax, Hector and Dexter. Author of a treatise on training and driving, entitled "The Trotting Horse of America." "He carried the American trotting horse triumphantly over the gap which lies between 2:40 and 2:18."

Word, The. The magic word "go," given to the field by the starter. Drivers "get the word;" the starting judge "gives the word."

Work; Work-out. Training; the art of putting a horse in condition for a race; more or less exercise for the purpose of fitting the horse to go to the extreme point of his speed capacity. The amount of work must invariably be regulated by the age, condition and peculiar characteristics of the horse, and for this no fixed rules can be given; individual experience must be the only guide.

In training, the trouble you will find it very hard to fight against will be the tendency to give too much work. You will like to see your colt go another brush, and when he is going fast and true you will hate to stop him. Development ceases when you get out the last link. The brush should never extend beyond the point where you do not believe he can be improved with the next step. When a horse tires he loses control of his legs and feet, in a great measure, and if weighted the trouble is aggravated. He breaks, he falters in his gait, strikes himself, goes to hitching, hobbling—anything to rest himself—and, as a natural consequence of this work, goes back in his speed, and loses precision in action.—Training the Trotting Horse, Charles Marvin.

I worked my horse out about three days before the race, and then and there decided to back him and try to beat Goldsmith Maid. * * * The first thing to do, in working a horse, is to teach him to score. * * * Instead of driving him one mile in 2:30, drive him a two mile heat in 5:20; that would be each mile in 2:40, which would condition his body and help to strengthen his weak legs. I think a day's work like this given him once a week, with moderate jogging the balance of the time and a little opening-out the day before you want to work him again, will be all that will be necessary for him to have. The nearer you get to your race, the shorter work the horse should have; that is, instead of giving him four or five heats, give him two or three, with occasional brushes at nearly the top of his speed.—Life with the Trotters, John Splan.

Working Gait. Half speed. "The tendency, in most training, is to overwork," says Mr. Splan, "but if trainers confine themselves to a working gait it will be almost impossible to overwork a horse." What would be a working gait for one horse, however, would not for another; as a 2:10 horse could be worked at a much faster gait than a 2:30 horse. It is entirely a matter of individuality on the part of the horse, and one in which the driver must be governed largely by experience.

Working Track. A private track in connection with breeding establishments, usually of one-half or three-fourths of a mile; not a public track.

Wounds of every description, however slight they may be, since there is no certainty as to how they may terminate, stamp a horse as unsound.

Wry Tail, or an oblique tail, is caused by the contraction of the muscles of the tail on one side. It is a serious blemish.

Y

Yankee. The first horse to trot a mile inside of three minutes, in America, so far as the records show, was "the horse, Yankee, from New Haven, Conn.," which trotted a mile on the Harlem, N. Y., course, in June, 1806, in 2:59.

Year Books. The recognized authoritative publication for all trotting and pacing records of the American turf, is Wallace's Year Book, issued annually, of which nine volumes have been published up to 1894. For the racing turf the authority is Goodwin's [formerly Kirke's] Official Turf Guide, published annually.

Yeomanry Races. [Eng.] In the yeomanry races those who enter are obliged to deliver despatches to an officer known to be posted at a certain spot a given number of miles away, across country. Each man carries his despatch, and the first to place it in the hands of the officer, wins the race.

Yielding. Responding. The act by which the horse gives up resistance to the bit and reins, when the latter are brought into tension to place the horse under control.

Yoke. A metal attachment connected to the shaft of a sulky by means of a clip and a forged beveled bolt, milled and threaded to receive a nut, for the purpose of holding the upper ends of the braces used to support the pneumatic wheel, when attached to the high sulky.

Z

Zone. A slender, intermediate band of soft, light-colored horn, situated between the horny sole of the foot and the inner face of the lower margin of the wall, which unites the two in a solid and perfect manner. This is often called by farriers, (horseshoers), the "white line."

STANDARD BOOKS

PUBLISHED BY

ORANGE JUDD COMPANY

NEW YORK
935-441 Lafayette Street

CHICAGO
Marquette Building

BOOKS sent to all parts of the world for catalog price. Discounts for large quantities on application. Correspondence invited. Brief descriptive catalog free. Large illustrated catalog, six cents.

Soils

By CHARLES WILLIAM BURKETT, Director Kansas Agricultural Experiment Station. The most complete and popular work of the kind ever published. As a rule, a book of this sort is dry and uninteresting, but in this case it reads like a novel. The author has put into it his individuality. The story of the properties of the soils, their improvement and management, as well as a discussion of the problems of crop growing and crop feeding, make this book equally valuable to the farmer, student and teacher.

There are many illustrations of a practical character, each one suggesting some fundamental principle in soil management. 303 pages. 5½ x 8 inches. Cloth $1.25

Insects Injurious to Vegetables

By Dr. F. H. CHITTENDEN, of the United States Department of Agriculture. A complete, practical work giving descriptions of the more important insects attacking vegetables of all kinds with simple and inexpensive remedies to check and destroy them, together with timely suggestions to prevent their recurrence. A ready reference book for truckers, market-gardeners, farmers as well as others who grow vegetables in a small way for home use; a valuable guide for college and experiment station workers, school-teachers and others interested in entomology of nature study. Profusely illustrated. 5½ x 8 inches. 300 pages. Cloth $1.50

The Cereals in America

By THOMAS F. HUNT, M.S., D.Agri., Professor of Agronomy, Cornell University. If you raise five acres of any kind of grain you cannot afford to be without this book. It is in every way the best book on the subject that has ever been written. It treats of the cultivation and improvement of every grain crop raised in America in a thoroughly practical and accurate manner. The subject-matter includes a comprehensive and succinct treatise of wheat, maize, oats, barley, rye, rice, sorghum (kafir corn) and buckwheat, as related particularly to American conditions. First-hand knowledge has been the policy of the author in his work, and every crop treated is presented in the light of individual study of the plant. If you have this book you have the latest and best that has been written upon the subject. Illustrated. 450 pages. 5½ x 8 inches. Cloth. $1.75

The Forage and Fiber Crops in America

By THOMAS F. HUNT. This book is exactly what its title indicates. It is indispensable to the farmer, student and teacher who wishes all the latest and most important information on the subject of forage and fiber crops. Like its famous companion, "The Cereals in America," by the same author, it treats of the cultivation and improvement of every one of the forage and fiber crops. With this book in hand, you have the latest and most up-to-date information available. Illustrated. 428 pages. 5½ x 8 inches. Cloth. $1.75

The Book of Alfalfa

History, Cultivation and Merits. Its Uses as a Forage and Fertilizer. The appearance of the Hon. F. D. COBURN'S little book on Alfalfa a few years ago has been a profit revelation to thousands of farmers throughout the country, and the increasing demand for still more information on the subject has induced the author to prepare the present volume, which is by far the most authoritative, complete and valuable work on this forage crop published anywhere. It is printed on fine paper and illustrated with many full-page photographs that were taken with the especial view of their relation to the text. 336 pages. 6½ x 9 inches. Bound in cloth, with gold stamping. It is unquestionably the handsomest agricultural reference book that has ever been issued. Price, postpaid . . . $2.00

Clean Milk

By S. D. BELCHER, M.D. In this book the author sets forth practical methods for the exclusion of bacteria from milk, and how to prevent contamination of milk from the stable to the consumer. Illustrated. 5 x 7 inches. 146 pages. Cloth. $1.00

Bean Culture

By GLENN C. SEVEY, B.S. A practical treatise on the production and marketing of beans. It includes the manner of growth, soils and fertilizers adapted, best varieties, seed selection and breeding, planting, harvesting, insects and fungous pests, composition and feeding value; with a special chapter on markets by Albert W. Fulton. A practical book for the grower and student alike. Illustrated. 144 pages. 5 x 7 inches. Cloth. $0.50

Celery Culture

By W. R. BEATTIE. A practical guide for beginners and a standard reference of great interest to persons already engaged in celery growing. It contains many illustrations giving a clear conception of the practical side of celery culture. The work is complete in every detail, from sowing a few seeds in a window-box in the house for early plants, to the handling and marketing of celery in carload lots. Fully illustrated. 150 pages. 5 x 7 inches. Cloth. $0.50

Tomato Culture

By WILL W. TRACY. The author has rounded up in this book the most complete account of tomato culture in all its phases that has ever been gotten together. It is no second-hand work of reference, but a complete story of the practical experiences of the best posted expert on tomatoes in the world. No gardener or farmer can afford to be without the book. Whether grown for home use or commercial purposes, the reader has here suggestions and information nowhere else available. Illustrated. 150 pages. 5 x 7 inches. Cloth. $0.50

The Potato

By SAMUEL FRASER. This book is destined to rank as a standard work upon Potato Culture. While the practical side has been emphasized, the scientific part has not been neglected, and the information given is of value, both to the grower and the student. Taken all in all, it is the most complete, reliable and authoritative book on the potato ever published in America. Illustrated. 200 pages. 5 x 7 inches. Cloth. $0.75

Dwarf Fruit Trees

By F. A. WAUGH. This interesting book describes in detail the several varieties of dwarf fruit trees, their propagation, planting, pruning, care and general management. Where there is a limited amount of ground to be devoted to orchard purposes, and where quick results are desired, this book will meet with a warm welcome. Illustrated. 112 pages. 5 x 7 inches. Cloth. $0.50

Cabbage, Cauliflower and Allied Vegetables

By C. L. ALLEN. A practical treatise on the various types and varieties of cabbage, cauliflower, broccoli, Brussels sprouts, kale, collards and kohl-rabi. An explanation is given of the requirements, conditions, cultivation and general management pertaining to the entire cabbage group. After this each class is treated separately and in detail. The chapter on seed raising is probably the most authoritative treatise on this subject ever published. Insects and fungi attacking this class of vegetables are given due attention. Illustrated. 126 pages. 5 x 7 inches. Cloth. $0.50

Asparagus

By F. M. HEXAMER. This is the first book published in America which is exclusively devoted to the raising of asparagus for home use as well as for market. It is a practical and reliable treatise on the saving of the seed, raising of the plants, selection and preparation of the soil, planting, cultivation, manuring, cutting, bunching, packing, marketing, canning and drying insect enemies, fungous diseases and every requirement to successful asparagus culture, special emphasis being given to the importance of asparagus as a farm and money crop. Illustrated. 174 pages. 5 x 7 inches. Cloth. . $0.50

The New Onion Culture

By T. GREINER. Rewritten, greatly enlarged and brought up to date. A new method of growing onions of largest size and yield, on less land, than can be raised by the old plan. Thousands of farmers and gardeners and many experiment stations have given it practical trials which have proved a success. A complete guide in growing onions with the greatest profit, explaining the whys and wherefores. Illustrated. 5 x 7 inches. 140 pages. Cloth. $0.50

The New Rhubarb Culture

A complete guide to dark forcing and field culture. Part I—By J. E. MORSE, the well-known Michigan trucker and originator of the now famous and extremely profitable new methods of dark forcing and field culture. Part II—Compiled by G. B. FISKE. Other methods practiced by the most experienced market gardeners, greenhouse men and experimenters in all parts of America. Illustrated. 130 pages. 5 x 7 inches. Cloth. $0.50

Alfalfa

By F. D. Coburn. Its growth, uses and feeding value. The fact that alfalfa thrives in almost any soil; that without reseeding it goes on yielding two, three, four and sometimes five cuttings annually for five, ten or perhaps 100 years; and that either green or cured it is one of the most nutritious forage plants known, makes reliable information upon its production and uses of unusual interest. Such information is given in this volume for every part of America, by the highest authority. Illustrated. 164 pages. 5 x 7 inches. Cloth. $0.50

Ginseng, Its Cultivation, Harvesting, Marketing and Market Value

By Maurice G. Kains, with a short account of its history and botany. It discusses in a practical way how to begin with either seed or roots, soil, climate and location, preparation, planting and maintenance of the beds, artificial propagation, manures, enemies, selection for market and for improvement, preparation for sale, and the profits that may be expected. This booklet is concisely written, well and profusely illustrated, and should be in the hands of all who expect to grow this drug to supply the export trade, and to add a new and profitable industry to their farms and gardens without interfering with the regular work. New edition. Revised and enlarged. Illustrated. 5 x 7 inches. Cloth. . . . $0.50

Landscape Gardening

By F. A. Waugh, professor of horticulture, University of Vermont. A treatise on the general principles governing outdoor art; with sundry suggestions for their application in the commoner problems of gardening. Every paragraph is short, terse and to the point, giving perfect clearness to the discussions at all points. In spite of the natural difficulty of presenting abstract principles the whole matter is made entirely plain even to the inexperienced reader. Illustrated. 152 pages. 5 x 7 inches. Cloth. $0.50

Hedges, Windbreaks, Shelters and Live Fences

By E. P. Powell. A treatise on the planting, growth and management of hedge plants for country and suburban homes. It gives accurate directions concerning hedges; how to plant and how to treat them; and especially concerning windbreaks and shelters. It includes the whole art of making a delightful home, giving directions for nooks and balconies, for bird culture and for human comfort. Illustrated. 140 pages. 5 x 7 inches. Cloth. $0.50

Farm Grasses of the United States of America

By WILLIAM JASPER SPILLMAN. A practical treatise on the grass crop, seeding and management of meadows and pastures, description of the best varieties, the seed and its impurities, grasses for special conditions, lawns and lawn grasses, etc., etc. In preparing this volume the author's object has been to present, in connected form, the main facts concerning the grasses grown on American farms. Every phase of the subject is viewed from the farmer's standpoint. Illustrated. 248 pages. 5 x 7 inches. Cloth. . . **$1.00**

The Book of Corn

By HERBERT MYRICK, assisted by A. D. SHAMEL, E. A. BURNETT, ALBERT W. FULTON, B. W. SNOW and other most capable specialists. A complete treatise on the culture, marketing and uses of maize in America and elsewhere, for farmers, dealers and others. Illustrated. 372 pages. 5 x 7 inches. Cloth. **$1.50**

The Hop—It's Culture and Care, Marketing and Manufacture

By HERBERT MYRICK. A practical handbook on the most approved methods in growing, harvesting, curing and selling hops, and on the use and manufacture of hops. The result of years of research and observation, it is a volume destined to be an authority on this crop for many years to come. It takes up every detail from preparing the soil and laying out the yard to curing and selling the crop. Every line represents the ripest judgment and experience of experts. Size, 5 x 8; pages, 300; illustrations, nearly 150; bound in cloth and gold; price, postpaid, ... **$1.50**

Tobacco Leaf

By J. B. KILLEBREW and HERBERT MYRICK. Its Culture and Cure, Marketing and Manufacture. A practical handbook on the most approved methods in growing, harvesting, curing, packing and selling tobacco, with an account of the operations in every department of tobacco manufacture. The contents of this book are based on actual experiments in field, curing barn, packing house, factory and laboratory. It is the only work of the kind in existence, and is destined to be the standard practical and scientific authority on the whole subject of tobacco for many years. 506 pages and 150 original engravings. 5 x 7 inches. Cloth. **$2.00**

Bulbs and Tuberous-Rooted Plants

By C. L. ALLEN. A complete treatise on the history, description, methods of propagation and full directions for the successful culture of bulbs in the garden, dwelling and greenhouse. The author of this book has for many years made bulb growing a specialty, and is a recognized authority on their cultivation and management. The cultural directions are plainly stated, practical and to the point. The illustrations which embellish this work have been drawn from nature and have been engraved especially for this book. 312 pages. 5 x 7 inches. Cloth. . . . $1.50

Fumigation Methods

By WILLIS G. JOHNSON. A timely up-to-date book on the practical application of the new methods for destroying insects with hydrocyanic acid gas and carbon bisulphid, the most powerful insecticides ever discovered. It is an indispensable book for farmers, fruit growers, nurserymen, gardeners, florists, millers, grain dealers, transportation companies, college and experiment station workers, etc. Illustrated. 313 pages. 5 x 7 inches. Cloth. $1.00

Diseases of Swine

By Dr. R. A. CRAIG, Professor of Veterinary Medicine at the Purdue University. A concise, practical and popular guide to the prevention and treatment of the diseases of swine. With the discussions on each disease are given its causes, symptoms, treatment and means of prevention. Every part of the book impresses the reader with the fact that its writer is thoroughly and practically familiar with all the details upon which he treats. All technical and strictly scientific terms are avoided, so far as feasible, thus making the work at once available to the practical stock raiser as well as to the teacher and student. Illustrated. 5 x 7 inches. 190 pages. Cloth. $0.75

Spraying Crops—Why, When and How

By CLARENCE M. WEED, D. Sc. The present fourth edition has been rewritten and reset throughout to bring it thoroughly up to date, so that it embodies the latest practical information gleaned by fruit growers and experiment station workers. So much new information has come to light since the third edition was published that this is practically a new book, needed by those who have utilized the earlier editions, as well as by fruit growers and farmers generally. Illustrated. 136 pages. 5 x 7 inches. Cloth. $0.50

Successful Fruit Culture

By SAMUEL T. MAYNARD. A practical guide to the cultivation and propagation of Fruits, written from the standpoint of the practical fruit grower who is striving to make his business profitable by growing the best fruit possible and at the least cost. It is up-to-date in every particular, and covers the entire practice of fruit culture, harvesting, storing, marketing, forcing, best varieties, etc., etc. It deals with principles first and with the practice afterwards, as the foundation, principles of plant growth and nourishment must always remain the same, while practice will vary according to the fruit grower's immediate conditions and environments. Illustrated. 265 pages. 5 x 7 inches. Cloth. $1.00

Plums and Plum Culture

By F. A. WAUGH. A complete manual for fruit growers, nurserymen, farmers and gardeners, on all known varieties of plums and their successful management. This book marks an epoch in the horticultural literature of America. It is a complete monograph of the plums cultivated in and indigenous to North America. It will be found indispensable to the scientist seeking the most recent and authoritative information concerning this group, to the nurseryman who wishes to handle his varieties accurately and intelligently, and to the cultivator who would like to grow plums successfully. Illustrated. 391 pages. 5 x 7 inches. Cloth. . . . $1.50

Fruit Harvesting, Storing, Marketing

By F. A. WAUGH. A practical guide to the picking, storing, shipping and marketing of fruit. The principal subjects covered are the fruit market, fruit picking, sorting and packing, the fruit storage, evaporating, canning, statistics of the fruit trade, fruit package laws, commission dealers and dealing, cold storage, etc., etc. No progressive fruit grower can afford to be without this most valuable book. Illustrated. 232 pages. 5 x 7 inches. Cloth. $1.00

Systematic Pomology

By F. A. WAUGH, professor of horticulture and landscape gardening in the Massachusetts agricultural college, formerly of the university of Vermont. This is the first book in the English language which has ever made the attempt at a complete and comprehensive treatment of systematic pomology. It presents clearly and in detail the whole method by which fruits are studied. The book is suitably illustrated. 288 pages. 5 x 7 inches. Cloth. $1.00

Feeding Farm Animals

By Professor THOMAS SHAW. This book is intended alike for the student and the farmer. The author has succeeded in giving in regular and orderly sequence, and in language so simple that a child can understand it, the principles that govern the science and practice of feeding farm animals. Professor Shaw is certainly to be congratulated on the successful manner in which he has accomplished a most difficult task. His book is unquestionably the most practical work which has appeared on the subject of feeding farm animals. Illustrated. 5½ x 8 inches. Upward of 500 pages. Cloth. $2.00

Profitable Dairying

By C. L. Peck. A practical guide to successful dairy management. The treatment of the entire subject is thoroughly practical, being principally a description of the methods practiced by the author. A specially valuable part of this book consists of a minute description of the far-famed model dairy farm of Rev. J. D. Detrich, near Philadelphia, Pa. On this farm of fifteen acres, which twenty years ago could not maintain one horse and two cows, there are now kept twenty-seven dairy cattle, in addition to two horses. All the roughage, litter, bedding, etc., necessary for these animals are grown on these fifteen acres, more than most farmers could accomplish on one hundred acres. Illustrated. 5 x 7 inches. 200 pages. Cloth. $0.75

Practical Dairy Bacteriology

By Dr. H. W. CONN, of Wesleyan University. A complete exposition of important facts concerning the relation of bacteria to various problems related to milk. A book for the classroom, laboratory, factory and farm. Equally useful to the teacher, student, factory man and practical dairyman. Fully illustrated with 83 original pictures. 340 pages. Cloth. 5½ x 8 inches. $1.25

Modern Methods of Testing Milk and Milk Products

By L. L. VANSLYKE. This is a clear and concise discussion of the approved methods of testing milk and milk products. All the questions involved in the various methods of testing milk and cream are handled with rare skill and yet in so plain a manner that they can be fully understood by all. The book should be in the hands of every dairyman, teacher or student. Illustrated. 214 pages. 5 x 7 inches. $0.75

Animal Breeding

By THOMAS SHAW. This book is the most complete and comprehensive work ever published on the subject of which it treats. It is the first book which has systematized the subject of animal breeding. The leading laws which govern this most intricate question the author has boldly defined and authoritatively arranged. The chapters which he has written on the more involved features of the subject, as sex and the relative influence of parents, should go far toward setting at rest the wildly speculative views cherished with reference to these questions. The striking originality in the treatment of the subject is no less conspicuous than the superb order and regular sequence of thought from the beginning to the end of the book. The book is intended to meet the needs of all persons interested in the breeding and rearing of live stock. Illustrated. 405 pages. 5 x 7 inches. Cloth. . . $1.50

Forage Crops Other than Grasses

By THOMAS SHAW. How to cultivate, harvest and use them. Indian corn, sorghum, clover, leguminous plants, crops of the brassica genus, the cereals, millet, field roots, etc. Intensely practical and reliable. Illustrated. 287 pages. 5 x 7 inches. Cloth. $1.00

Soiling Crops and the Silo

By THOMAS SHAW. The growing and feeding of all kinds of soiling crops, conditions to which they are adapted, their plan in the rotation, etc. Not a line is repeated from the Forage Crops book. Best methods of building the silo, filling it and feeding ensilage. Illustrated. 364 pages. 5 x 7 inches. Cloth. $1.50

The Study of Breeds

By THOMAS SHAW. Origin, history, distribution, characteristics, adaptability, uses and standards of excellence of all pedigreed breeds of cattle, sheep and swine in America. The accepted text book in colleges, and the authority for farmers and breeders. Illustrated. 371 pages. 5 x 7 inches. Cloth. $1.50

Clovers and How to Grow Them

By THOMAS SHAW. This is the first book published which treats on the growth, cultivation and treatment of clovers as applicable to all parts of the United States and Canada, and which takes up the entire subject in a systematic way and consecutive sequence. The importance of clover in the economy of the farm is so great that an exhaustive work on this subject will no doubt be welcomed by students in agriculture, as well as by all who are interested in the tilling of the soil. Illustrated. 5 x 7 inches. 337 pages. Cloth. Net . . . $1.00

Land Draining

A handbook for farmers on the principles and practice of draining, by MANLY MILES, giving the results of his extended experience in laying tile drains. The directions for the laying out and the construction of tile drains will enable the farmer to avoid the errors of imperfect construction, and the disappointment that must necessarily follow. This manual for practical farmers will also be found convenient for reference in regard to many questions that may arise in crop growing, aside from the special subjects of drainage of which it treats. Illustrated. 200 pages. 5 x 7 inches. Cloth. . . $1.00

Barn Plans and Outbuildings

Two hundred and fifty-seven illustrations. A most valuable work, full of ideas, hints, suggestions, plans, etc., for the construction of barns and outbuildings, by practical writers. Chapters are devoted to the economic erection and use of barns, grain barns, horse barns, cattle barns, sheep barns, cornhouses, smokehouses, icehouses, pig pens, granaries, etc. There are likewise chapters on birdhouses, doghouses, tool sheds, ventilators, roofs and roofing, doors and fastenings, workshops, poultry houses, manure sheds, barnyards, root pits, etc. 235 pages. 5 x 7 inches. Cloth. . . . $1.00

Irrigation Farming

By LUTE WILCOX. A handbook for the practical application of water in the production of crops. A complete treatise on water supply, canal construction, reservoir and ponds, pipes for irrigation purposes, flumes and their structure, methods of applying water, irrigation of field crops, the garden, the orchard and vineyard, windmills and pumps, appliances and contrivances. New edition, revised, enlarged and rewritten. Profusely illustrated. Over 500 pages. 5 x 7 inches. Cloth. $2.00

Forest Planting

By H. NICHOLAS JARCHOW, LL.D. A treatise on the care of woodlands and the restoration of the denuded timberlands on plains and mountains. The author has fully described those European methods which have proved to be most useful in maintaining the superb forests of the old world. This experience has been adapted to the different climates and trees of America, full instructions being given for forest planting of our various kinds of soil and subsoil, whether on mountain or valley. Illustrated. 250 pages. 5 x 7 inches. Cloth. $1.50

The Nut Culturist

By ANDREW S. FULLER. A treatise on the propagation, planting and cultivation of nut-bearing trees and shrubs adapted to the climate of the United States, with the scientific and common names of the fruits known in commerce as edible or otherwise useful nuts. Intended to aid the farmer to increase his income without adding to his expenses or labor. Cloth. 12mo. $1.50

Cranberry Culture

By JOSEPH J. WHITE. Contents: Natural history, history of cultivation, choice of location, preparing the ground, planting the vines, management of meadows, flooding, enemies and difficulties overcome, picking, keeping, profit and loss. Illustrated. 132 pages. 5 x 7 inches. Cloth. . . $1.00

Ornamental Gardening for Americans

By ELIAS A. LONG, landscape architect. A treatise on beautifying homes, rural districts and cemeteries. A plain and practical work with numerous illustrations and instructions so plain that they may be readily followed. Illustrated. 390 pages. 5 x 7 inches. Cloth. $1.50

Grape Culturist

By A. S. FULLER. This is one ot the very best of works on the culture of the hardy grapes, with full directions for all departments of propagation, culture, etc., with 150 excellent engravings, illustrating planting, training, grafting, etc. 282 pages. 5 x 7 inches. Cloth. $1.50

Gardening for Young and Old

By JOSEPH HARRIS. A work intended to interest farmers' boys in farm gardening, which means a better and more profitable form of agriculture. The teachings are given in the familiar manner so well known in the author's "Walks and Talks on the Farm." Illustrated. 191 pages. 5 x 7 inches. Cloth. $1.00

Money in the Garden

By P T. QUINN. The author gives in a plain, practical style instructions on three distinct, although closely connected, branches of gardening—the kitchen garden, market garden and field culture, from successful practical experience for a term of years. Illustrated. 268 pages. 5 x 7 inches. Cloth. $1.00

Greenhouse Construction

By Prof. L. R. Taft. A complete treatise on greenhouse structures and arrangements of the various forms and styles of plant houses for professional florists as well as amateurs. All the best and most approved structures are so fully and clearly described that any one who desires to build a greenhouse will have no difficulty in determining the kind best suited to his purpose. The modern and most successful methods of heating and ventilating are fully treated upon. Special chapters are devoted to houses used for the growing of one kind of plants exclusively. The construction of hotbeds and frames receives appropriate attention. Over 100 excellent illustrations, especially engraved for this work, make every point clear to the reader and add considerably to the artistic appearance of the book. 210 pages. 5 x 7 inches. Cloth, $1.50

Greenhouse Management

By L. R. Taft. This book forms an almost indispensable companion volume to Greenhouse Construction. In it the author gives the results of his many years' experience, together with that of the most successful florists and gardeners, in the management of growing plants under glass. So minute and practical are the various systems and methods of growing and forcing roses, violets, carnations, and all the most important florists' plants, as well as fruits and vegetables described, that by a careful study of this work and the following of its teachings, failure is almost impossible. Illustrated. 382 pages. 5 x 7 inches. Cloth. $1.50

Fungi and Fungicides

By Prof. Clarence M. Weed. A practical manual concerning the fungous diseases of cultivated plants and the means of preventing their ravages. The author has endeavored to give such a concise account of the most important facts relating to these as will enable the cultivator to combat them intelligently. 90 illustrations. 222 pages. 5 x 7 inches. Paper, 50 cents; cloth. $1.00

Mushrooms. How to Grow Them

By William Falconer. This is the most practical work on the subject ever written, and the only book on growing mushrooms published in America. The author describes how he grows mushrooms, and how they are grown for profit by the leading market gardeners, and for home use by the most successful private growers. Engravings drawn from nature expressly for this work. 170 pages. 5 x 7 inches. Cloth. $1.00

Rural School Agriculture

By Charles W. Davis. A book intended for the use of both teachers and pupils. Its aim is to enlist the interest of the boys of the farm and awaken in their minds the fact that the problems of the farm are great enough to command all the brain power they can summon. The book is a manual of exercises covering many phases of agriculture, and it may be used with any text-book of agriculture, or without a text-book. The exercises will enable the student to think, and to work out the scientific principles underlying some of the most important agricultural operations. The author feels that in the teaching of agriculture in the rural schools, the laboratory phase is almost entirely neglected. If an experiment helps the pupil to think, or makes his conceptions clearer, it fills a useful purpose, and eventually prepares for successful work upon the farm. The successful farmer of the future must be an experimenter in a small way. Following many of the exercises are a number of questions which prepare the way for further research work. The material needed for performing the experiments is simple, and can be devised by the teacher and pupils, or brought from the homes. Illustrated. 300 pages. Cloth. 5 x 7 inches. $1.00

Agriculture Through the Laboratory and School Garden

By C. R. Jackson and Mrs. L. S. Daugherty. As its name implies, this book gives explicit directions for actual work in the laboratory and the school garden, through which agricultural principles may be taught. The author's aim has been to present actual experimental work in every phase of the subject possible, and to state the directions for such work so that the student can perform it independently of the teacher, and to state them in such a way that the results will not be suggested by these directions. One must perform the experiment to ascertain the result. It embodies in the text a comprehensive, practical, scientific, yet simple discussion of such facts as are necessary to the understanding of many of the agricultural principles involved in every-day life. The book, although primarily intended for use in schools, is equally valuable to any one desiring to obtain in an easy and pleasing manner a general knowledge of elementary agriculture. Fully illustrated. 5½ x 8 inches. 462 pages. Cloth. Net . $1.50

Soil Physics Laboratory Guide

By W. G. Stevenson and I. O. Schaub. A carefully outlined series of experiments in soil physics. A portion of the experiments outlined in this guide have been used quite generally in recent years. The exercises (of which there are 40) are listed in a logical order with reference to their relation to each other and the skill required on the part of the student. Illustrated. About 100 pages. 5 x 7 inches. Cloth. , $0.50

The New Egg Farm

By H. H. STODDARD. A practical, reliable manual on producing eggs and poultry for market as a profitable business enterprise, either by itself or connected with other branches of agriculture. It tells all about how to feed and manage, how to breed and select, incubators and brooders, its labor-saving devices, etc., etc. Illustrated. 331 pages. 5 x 7 inches. Cloth. $1.00

Poultry Feeding and Fattening

Compiled by G. B. FISKE. A handbook for poultry keepers on the standard and improved methods of feeding and marketing all kinds of poultry. The subject of feeding and fattening poultry is prepared largely from the side of the best practice and experience here and abroad, although the underlying science of feeding is explained as fully as needful. The subject covers all branches, including chickens, broilers, capons, turkeys and waterfowl; how to feed under various conditions and for different purposes. The whole subject of capons and caponizing is treated in detail. A great mass of practical information and experience not readily obtainable elsewhere is given with full and explicit directions for fattening and preparing for market. This book will meet the needs of amateurs as well as commercial poultry raisers. Profusely illustrated. 160 pages. 5 x 7 1-2 inches. Cloth. . $0.50

Poultry Architecture

Compiled by G. B. FISKE. A treatise on poultry buildings of all grades, styles and classes, and their proper location, coops, additions and special construction; all practical in design, and reasonable in cost. Over 100 illustrations. 125 pages. 5 x 7 inches. Cloth. $0.50

Poultry Appliances and Handicraft

Compiled by G. B. FISKE. Illustrated descriptions of a great variety and styles of the best homemade nests, roosts, windows, ventilators, incubators and brooders, feeding and watering appliances, etc., etc. Over 100 illustrations. Over 125 pages. 5 x 7 inches. Cloth. $0.50

Turkeys and How to Grow Them

Edited by HERBERT MYRICK. A treatise on the natural history and origin of the name of turkeys; the various breeds, the best methods to insure success in the business of turkey growing. With essays from practical turkey growers in different parts of the United States and Canada. Copiously illustrated. 154 pages. 5 x 7 inches. Cloth. . . $1.00

Farmer's Cyclopedia
of Agriculture ✿ ✿

*A Compendium of Agricultural Science and Practice
on Farm, Orchard and Garden Crops, and the
Feeding and Diseases of Farm Animals*

By EARLEY VERNON WILCOX, Ph. D.
and CLARENCE BEAMAN SMITH, M. S.

*Associate Editors in the Office of Experiment Stations, United States
Department of Agriculture.*

THIS is a new, practical and complete presentation of the whole subject of agriculture in its broadest sense. It is designed for the use of agriculturists who desire up-to-date, reliable information on all matters pertaining to crops and stock, but more particularly for the actual farmer. The volume contains

Detailed directions for the culture of every

important field, orchard, and garden crop

grown in America, together with descriptions of their chief insect pests and fungous diseases, and remedies for their control. It contains an account of modern methods in feeding and handling all farm stock, including poultry. The diseases which affect different farm animals and poultry are described, and the most recent remedies suggested for controlling them.

Every bit of this vast mass of new and useful information is authoritative, practical, and easily found, and no effort has been spared to include all desirable details. There are between 6.000 and 7,000 topics covered in these references, and it contains 700 royal 8vo pages and nearly 500 superb halftone and other original illustrations, making the most perfect Cyclopedia of Agriculture ever attempted.

*Handsomely bound in cloth, $3.50; half morocco
(very sumptuous), $4.50, postpaid*

ORANGE JUDD COMPANY, 439-441 Lafayette Street, New York, N. Y.
Marquette Building, Chicago, Ill.

CPSIA information can be obtained
at www.ICGtesting.com
Printed in the USA
LVHW111035311221
707526LV00012B/234

9 781729 868249